SATURDAY AM

PRESENTS...

CLOCK STRIKER

VOLUME 1

"I'M GONNA BE A SMITH!"

BY **ISSAKA GALADIMA**
WITH **FREDERICK L. JONES**

ROCKPORT

CONTENTS

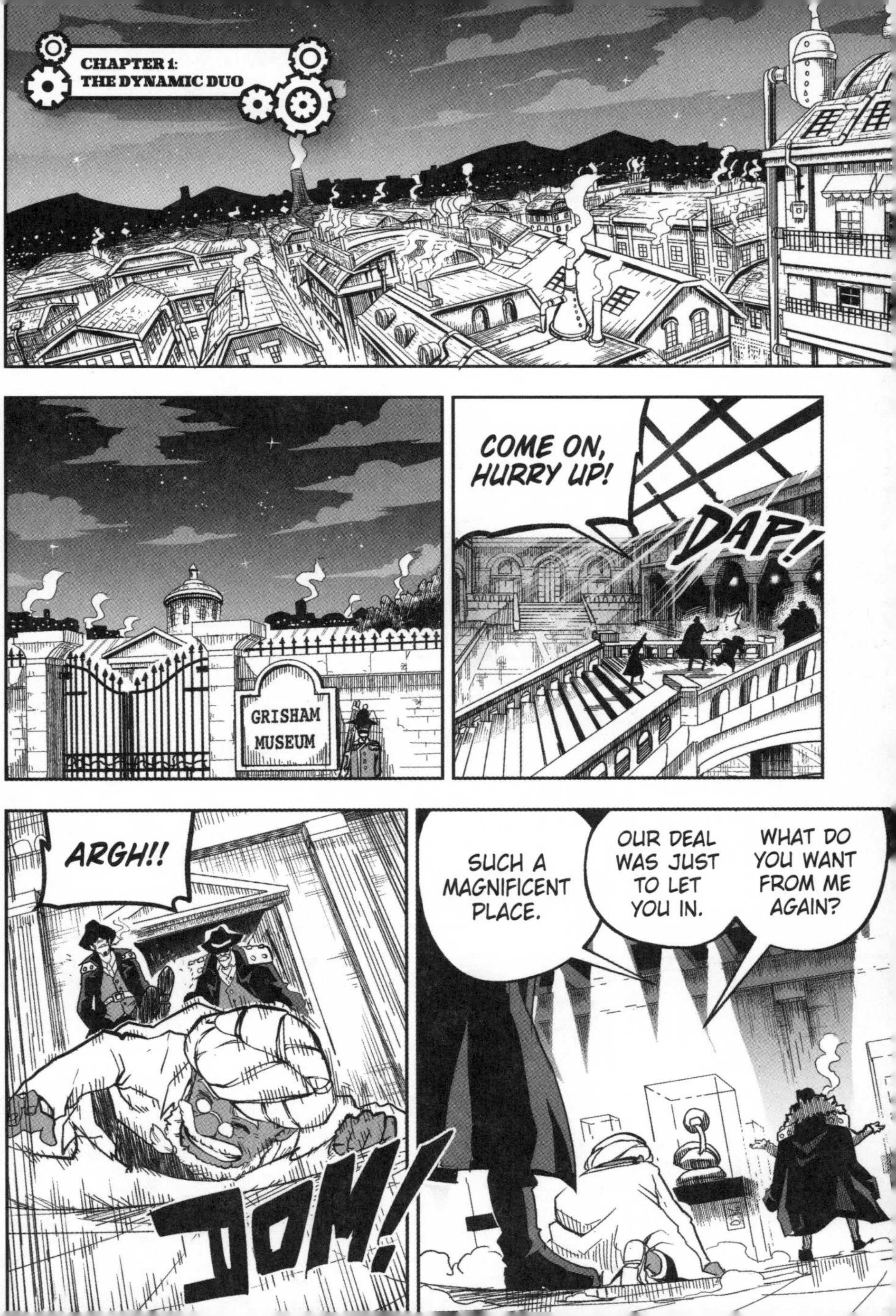
CHAPTER 1:
THE DYNAMIC DUO
GRISHAM MUSEUM
COME ON, HURRY UP!
DAP!
ARGH!!
DOM!
SUCH A MAGNIFICENT PLACE.
OUR DEAL WAS JUST TO LET YOU IN.
WHAT DO YOU WANT FROM ME AGAIN?

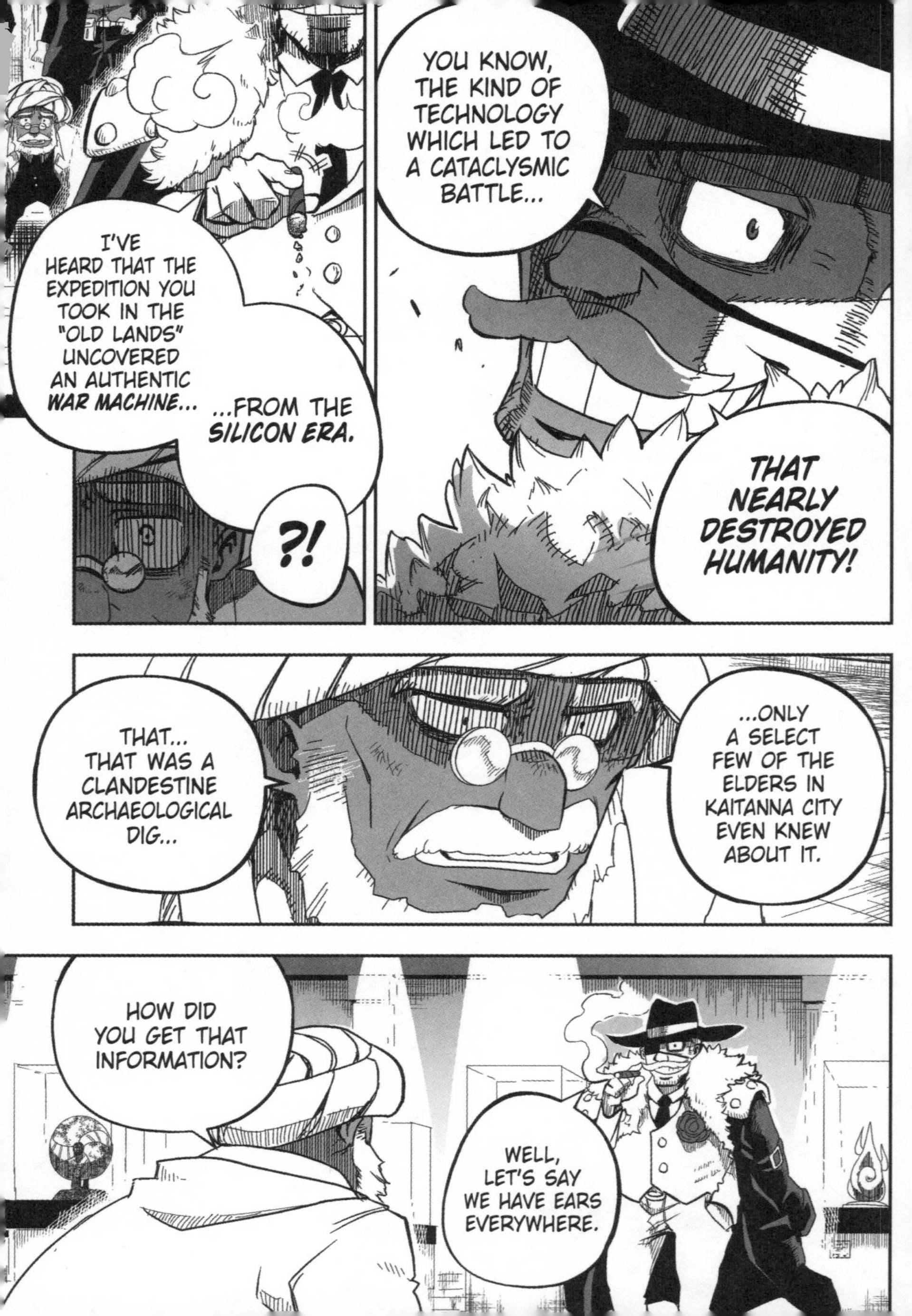
I'VE HEARD THAT THE EXPEDITION YOU TOOK IN THE "OLD LANDS" UNCOVERED AN AUTHENTIC WAR MACHINE...
...FROM THE SILICON ERA.
?!
YOU KNOW, THE KIND OF TECHNOLOGY WHICH LED TO A CATACLYSMIC BATTLE...
THAT NEARLY DESTROYED HUMANITY!
THAT... THAT WAS A CLANDESTINE ARCHAEOLOGICAL DIG...
...ONLY A SELECT FEW OF THE ELDERS IN KAITANNA CITY EVEN KNEW ABOUT IT.
HOW DID YOU GET THAT INFORMATION?
WELL, LET'S SAY WE HAVE EARS EVERYWHERE.

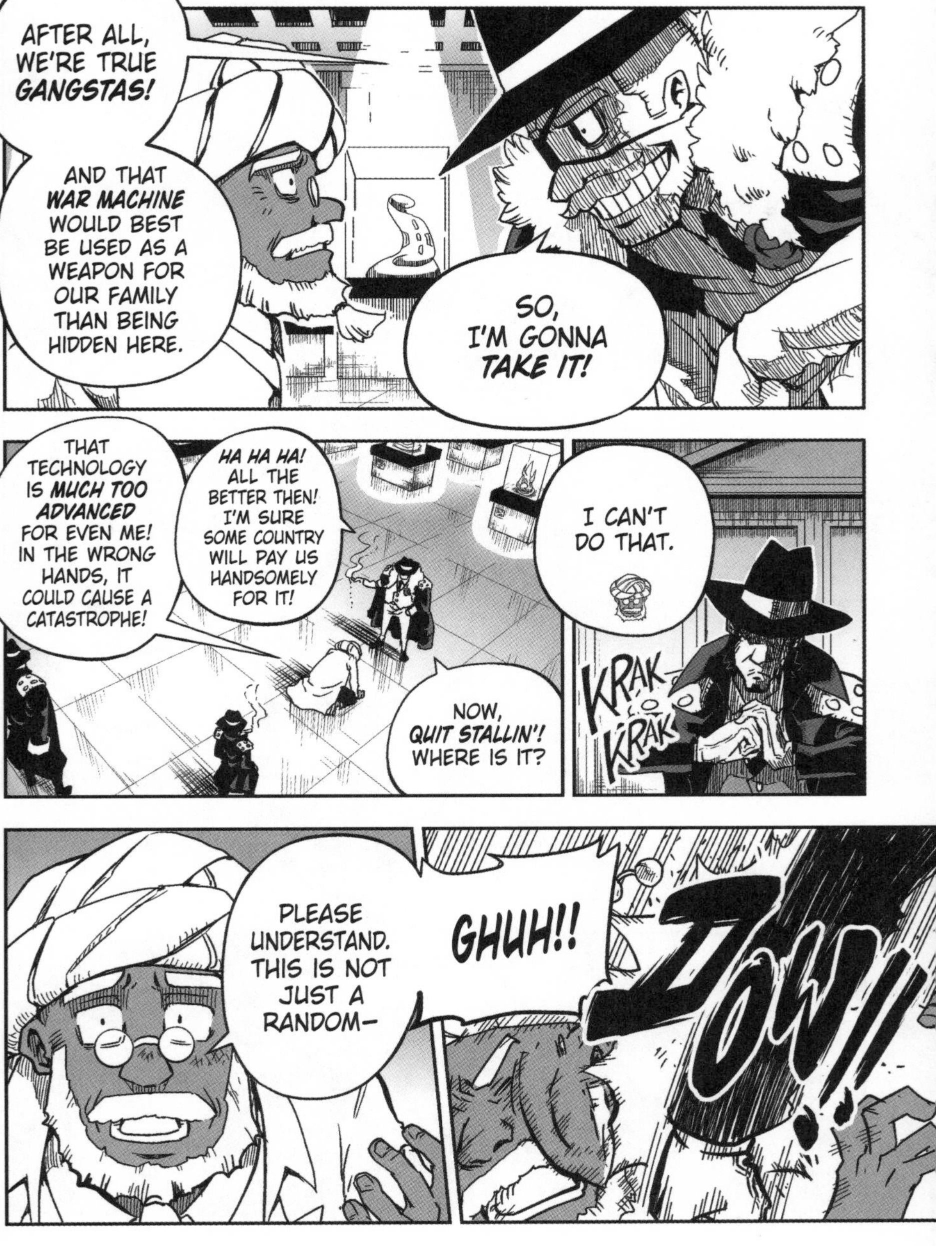
AFTER ALL, WE'RE TRUE GANGSTAS!
AND THAT WAR MACHINE WOULD BEST BE USED AS A WEAPON FOR OUR FAMILY THAN BEING HIDDEN HERE.
SO, I'M GONNA TAKE IT!
THAT TECHNOLOGY IS MUCH TOO ADVANCED FOR EVEN ME! IN THE WRONG HANDS, IT COULD CAUSE A CATASTROPHE!
HA HA HA! ALL THE BETTER THEN! I'M SURE SOME COUNTRY WILL PAY US HANDSOMELY FOR IT!
NOW, QUIT STALLIN'! WHERE IS IT?
I CAN'T DO THAT.
KRAK KRAK
PLEASE UNDERSTAND. THIS IS NOT JUST A RANDOM–
GHUH!!
ZOW!!

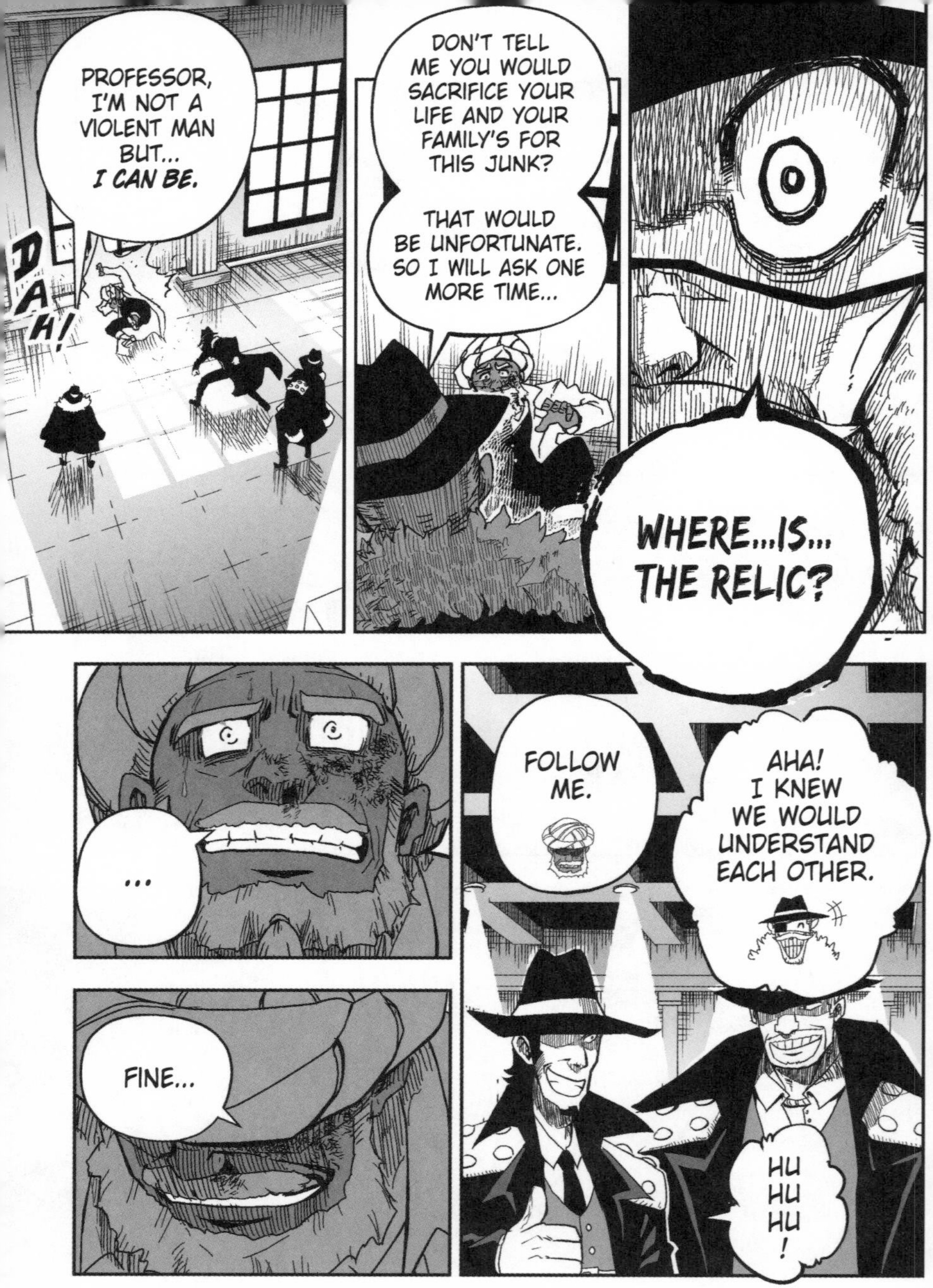
PROFESSOR, I'M NOT A VIOLENT MAN BUT... I CAN BE.
DAAH!
DON'T TELL ME YOU WOULD SACRIFICE YOUR LIFE AND YOUR FAMILY'S FOR THIS JUNK?
THAT WOULD BE UNFORTUNATE. SO I WILL ASK ONE MORE TIME...
WHERE...IS... THE RELIC?
...
FINE...
FOLLOW ME.
AHA! I KNEW WE WOULD UNDERSTAND EACH OTHER.
HU HU HU!

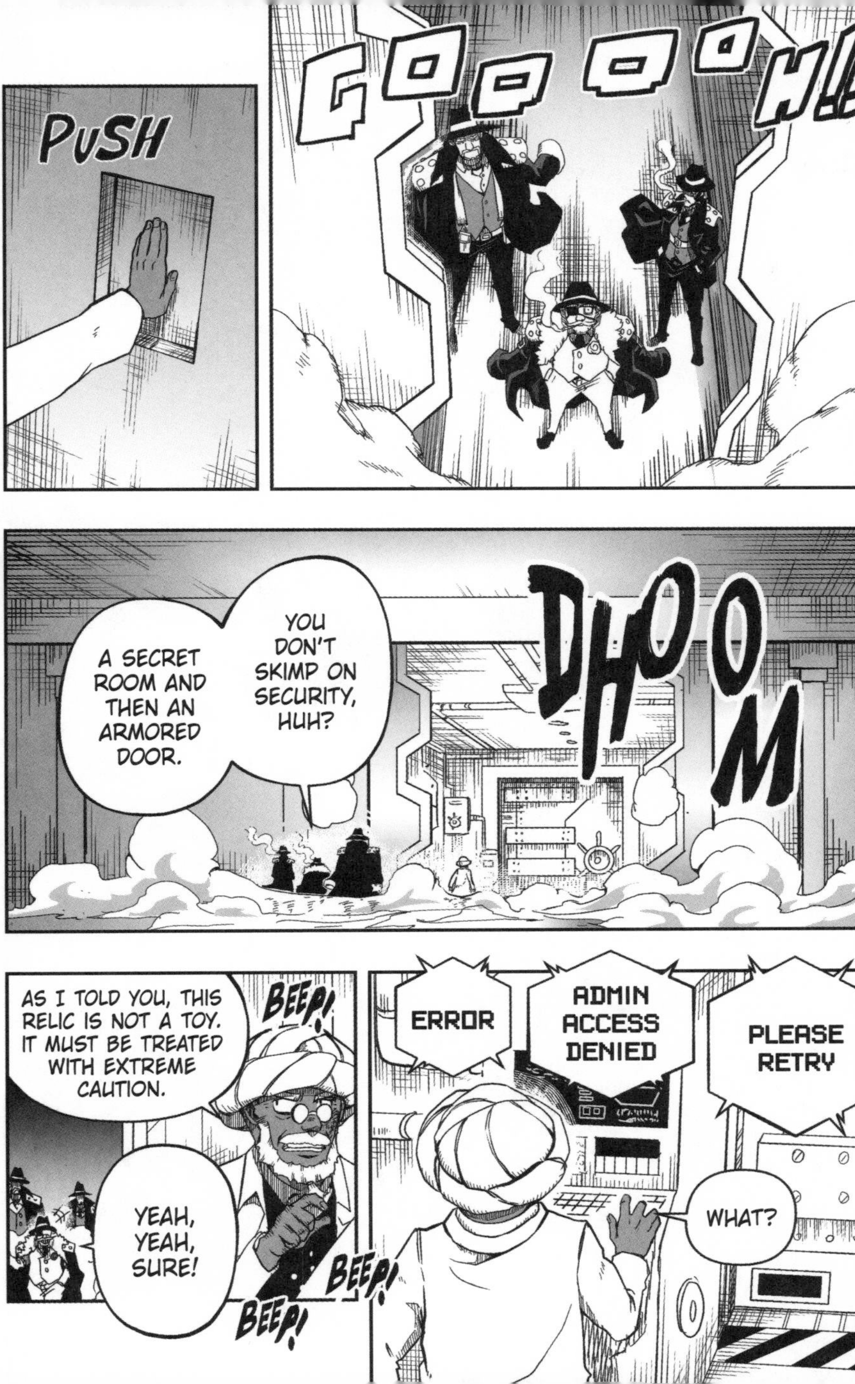
PUSH
GOOOOOH!!
A SECRET ROOM AND THEN AN ARMORED DOOR.
YOU DON'T SKIMP ON SECURITY, HUH?
DHOOM
AS I TOLD YOU, THIS RELIC IS NOT A TOY. IT MUST BE TREATED WITH EXTREME CAUTION.
BEEP!
YEAH, YEAH, SURE!
BEEP!
BEEP!
ERROR
ADMIN ACCESS DENIED
PLEASE RETRY
WHAT?

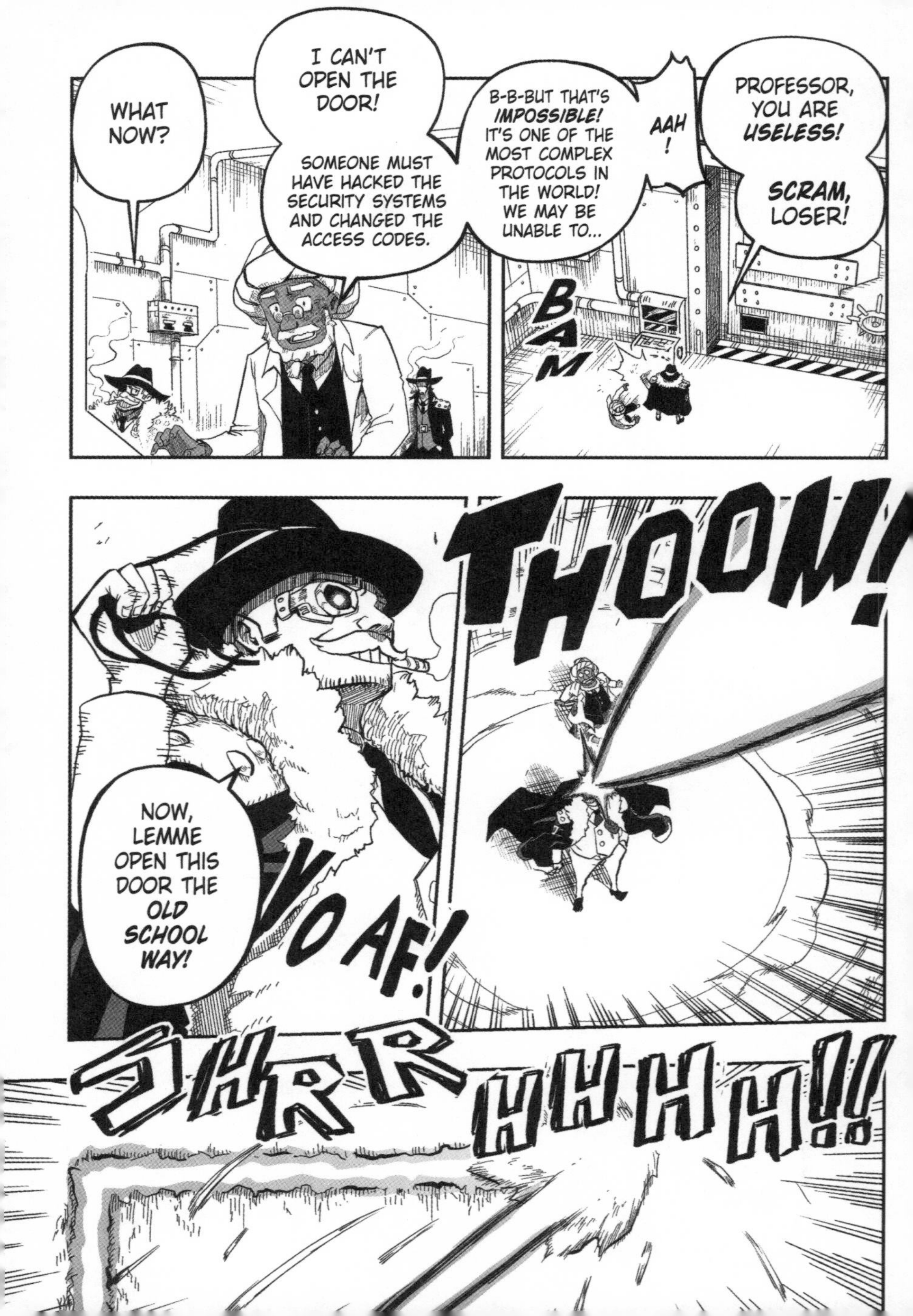
WHAT NOW?
I CAN'T OPEN THE DOOR!
SOMEONE MUST HAVE HACKED THE SECURITY SYSTEMS AND CHANGED THE ACCESS CODES.
B-B-BUT THAT'S *IMPOSSIBLE!* IT'S ONE OF THE MOST COMPLEX PROTOCOLS IN THE WORLD! WE MAY BE UNABLE TO...
AAH!
PROFESSOR, YOU ARE *USELESS!*
SCRAM, LOSER!
BAM
NOW, LEMME OPEN THIS DOOR THE **OLD SCHOOL WAY!**
VOAF!
THOOM!
SHRRHHHHH!!

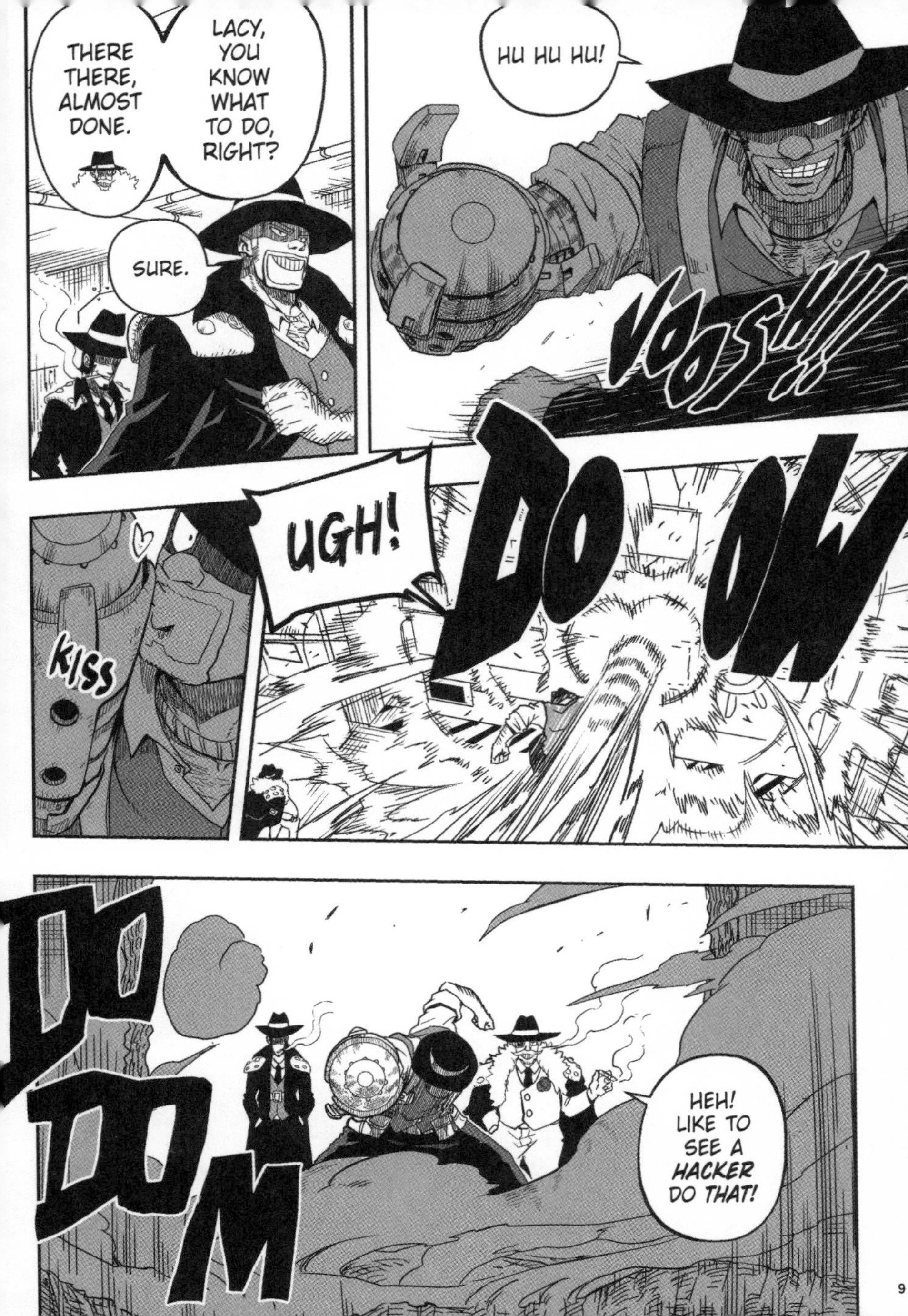
THERE THERE, ALMOST DONE.
LACY, YOU KNOW WHAT TO DO, RIGHT?
SURE.
HU HU HU!
VOOSH!!
KISS
UGH!
DOOW
DODOM
HEH! LIKE TO SEE A ***HACKER*** DO ***THAT***!

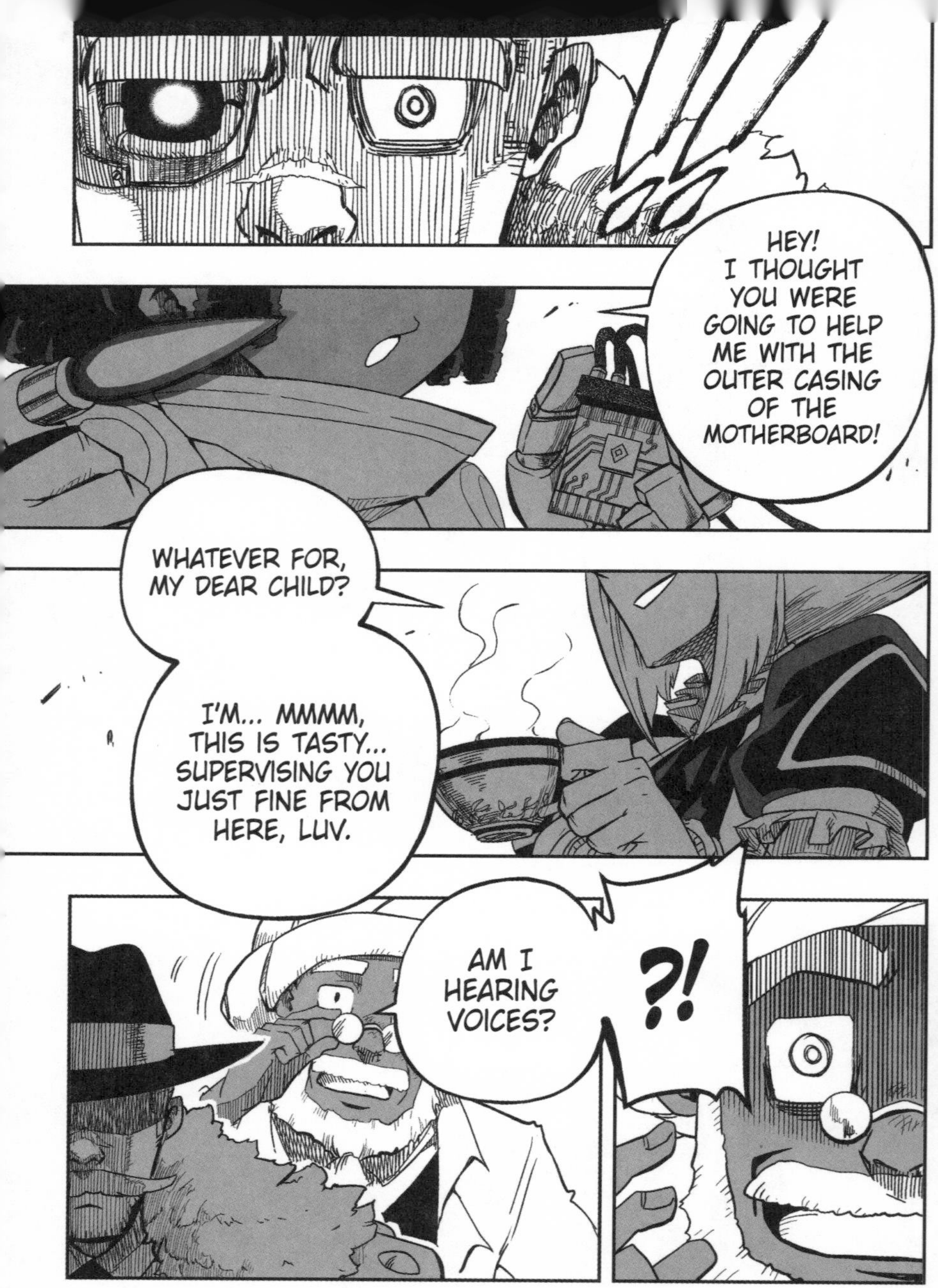
HEY! I THOUGHT YOU WERE GOING TO HELP ME WITH THE OUTER CASING OF THE MOTHERBOARD!
WHATEVER FOR, MY DEAR CHILD?
I'M... MMMM, THIS IS TASTY... SUPERVISING YOU JUST FINE FROM HERE, LUV.
AM I HEARING VOICES?
?!

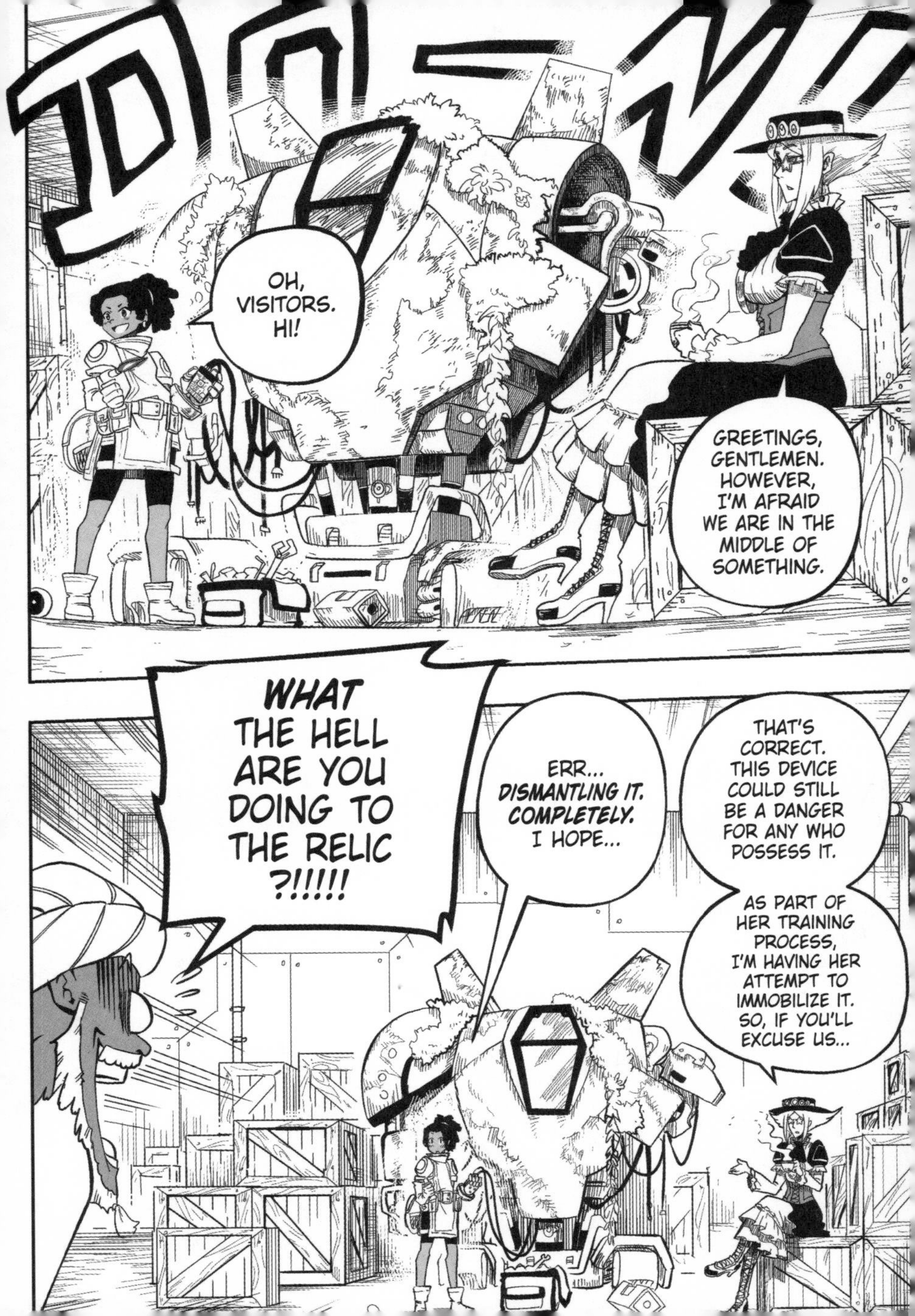
OH, VISITORS. HI!
GREETINGS, GENTLEMEN. HOWEVER, I'M AFRAID WE ARE IN THE MIDDLE OF SOMETHING.
WHAT THE HELL ARE YOU DOING TO THE RELIC ?!!!!!
ERR... *DISMANTLING IT. COMPLETELY.* I HOPE...
THAT'S CORRECT. THIS DEVICE COULD STILL BE A DANGER FOR ANY WHO POSSESS IT.
AS PART OF HER TRAINING PROCESS, I'M HAVING HER ATTEMPT TO IMMOBILIZE IT. SO, IF YOU'LL EXCUSE US...

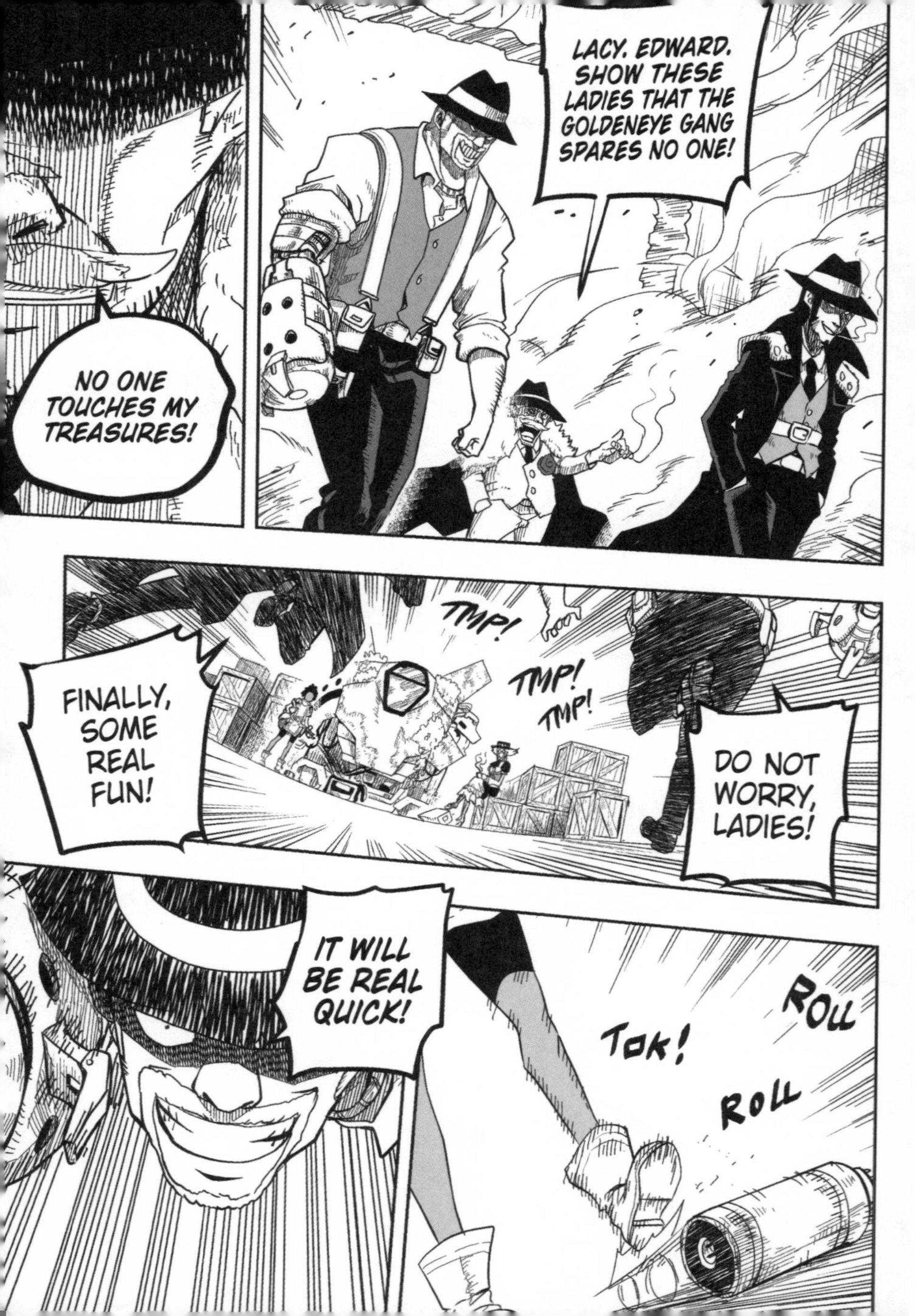
NO ONE TOUCHES MY TREASURES!
LACY. EDWARD. SHOW THESE LADIES THAT THE GOLDENEYE GANG SPARES NO ONE!
FINALLY, SOME REAL FUN!
TMP!
TMP!
TMP!
DO NOT WORRY, LADIES!
IT WILL BE REAL QUICK!
ROLL
TOK!
ROLL

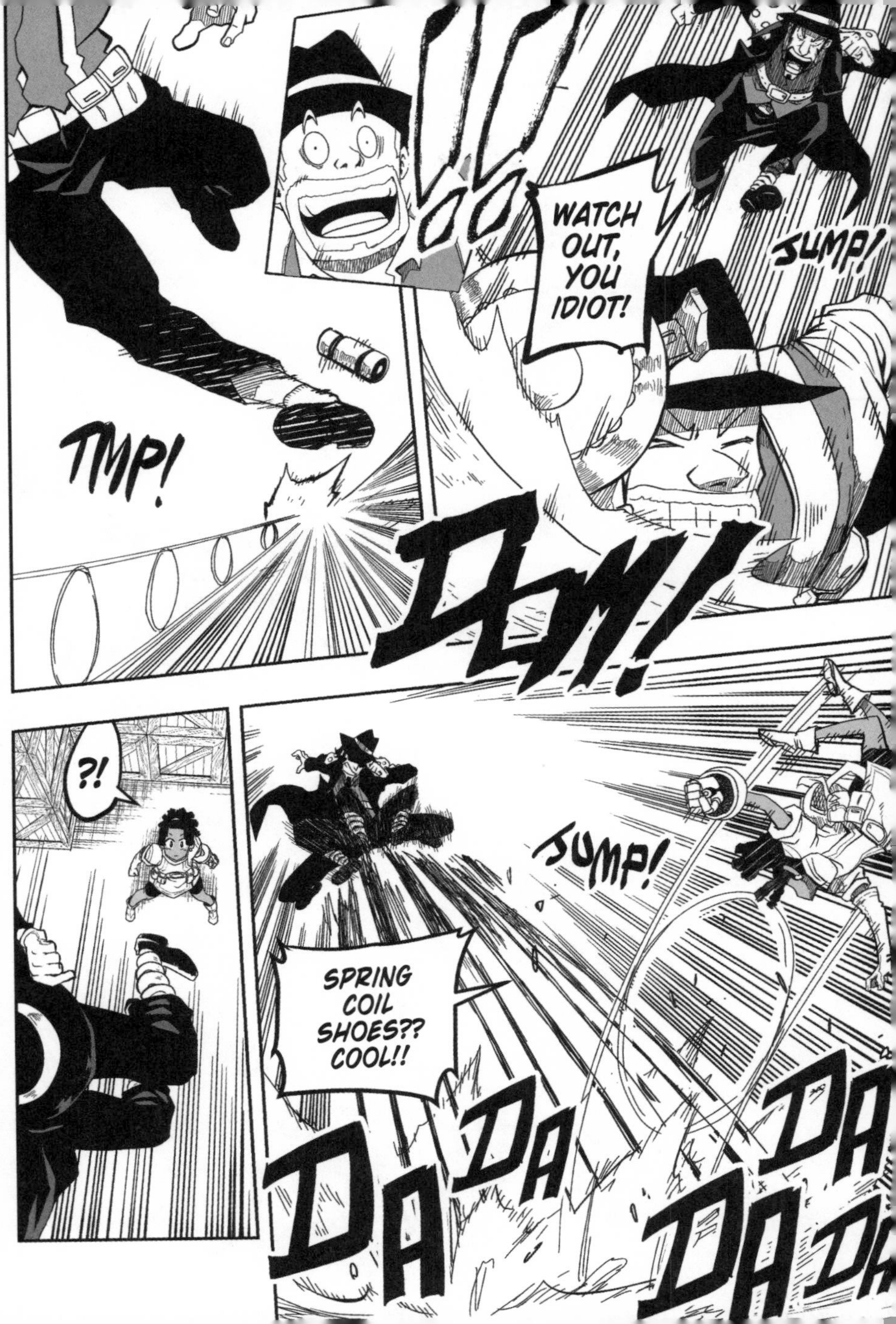
TMP!
WATCH OUT, YOU IDIOT!
JUMP!
ZAM!
?!
JUMP!
SPRING COIL SHOES?? COOL!!
DA DA DA DA DA

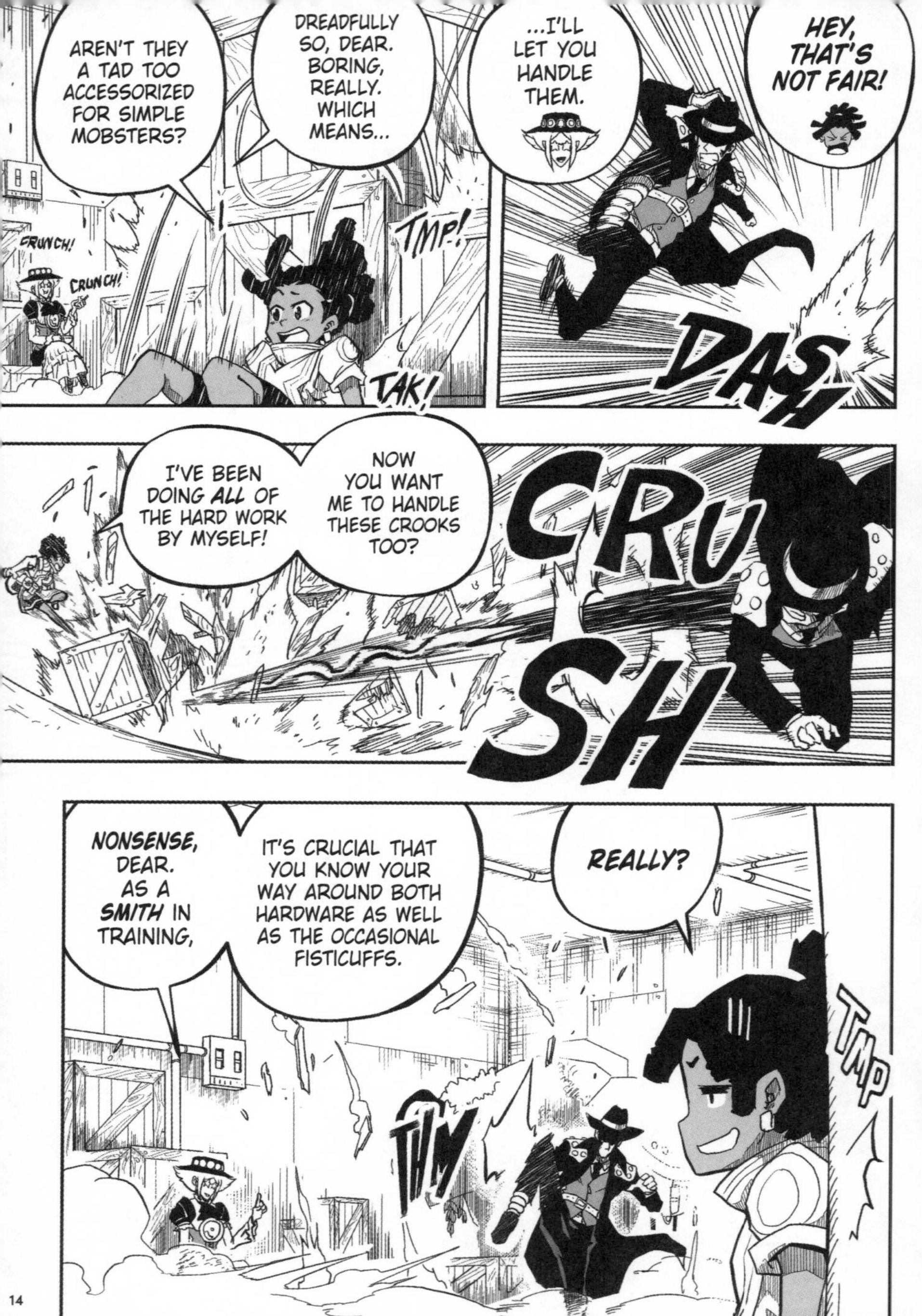
AREN'T THEY A TAD TOO ACCESSORIZED FOR SIMPLE MOBSTERS?
DREADFULLY SO, DEAR. BORING, REALLY. WHICH MEANS...
CRUNCH!
CRUNCH!
TMP!
TAK!
...I'LL LET YOU HANDLE THEM.
HEY, THAT'S NOT FAIR!
DASH
I'VE BEEN DOING ALL OF THE HARD WORK BY MYSELF!
NOW YOU WANT ME TO HANDLE THESE CROOKS TOO?
CRUSH
NONSENSE, DEAR. AS A SMITH IN TRAINING,
IT'S CRUCIAL THAT YOU KNOW YOUR WAY AROUND BOTH HARDWARE AS WELL AS THE OCCASIONAL FISTICUFFS.
REALLY?
THM
TMP

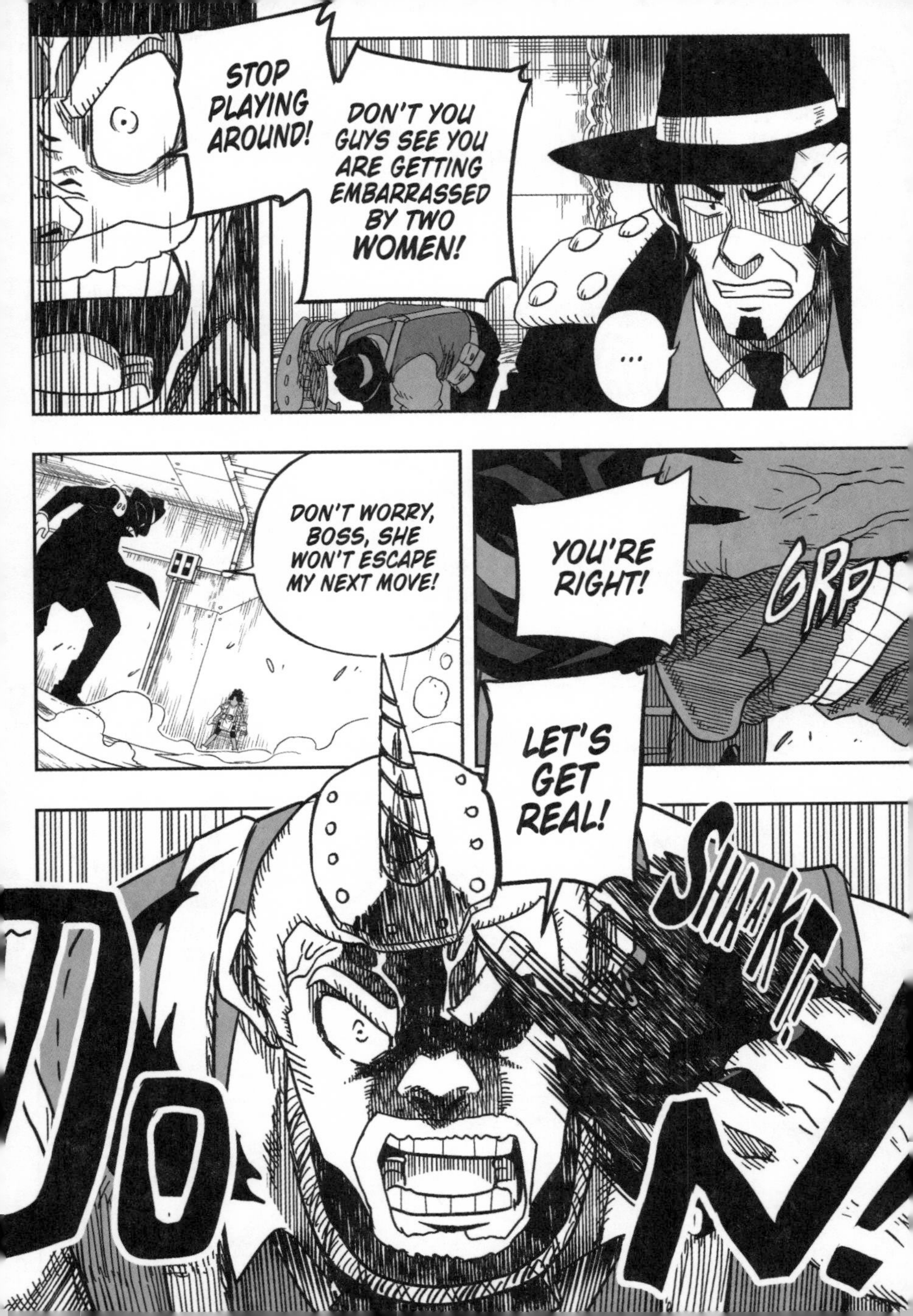
STOP PLAYING AROUND!
DON'T YOU GUYS SEE YOU ARE GETTING EMBARRASSED BY TWO WOMEN!
...
DON'T WORRY, BOSS, SHE WON'T ESCAPE MY NEXT MOVE!
YOU'RE RIGHT!
GRP
LET'S GET REAL!
SHAAKT!
DON!

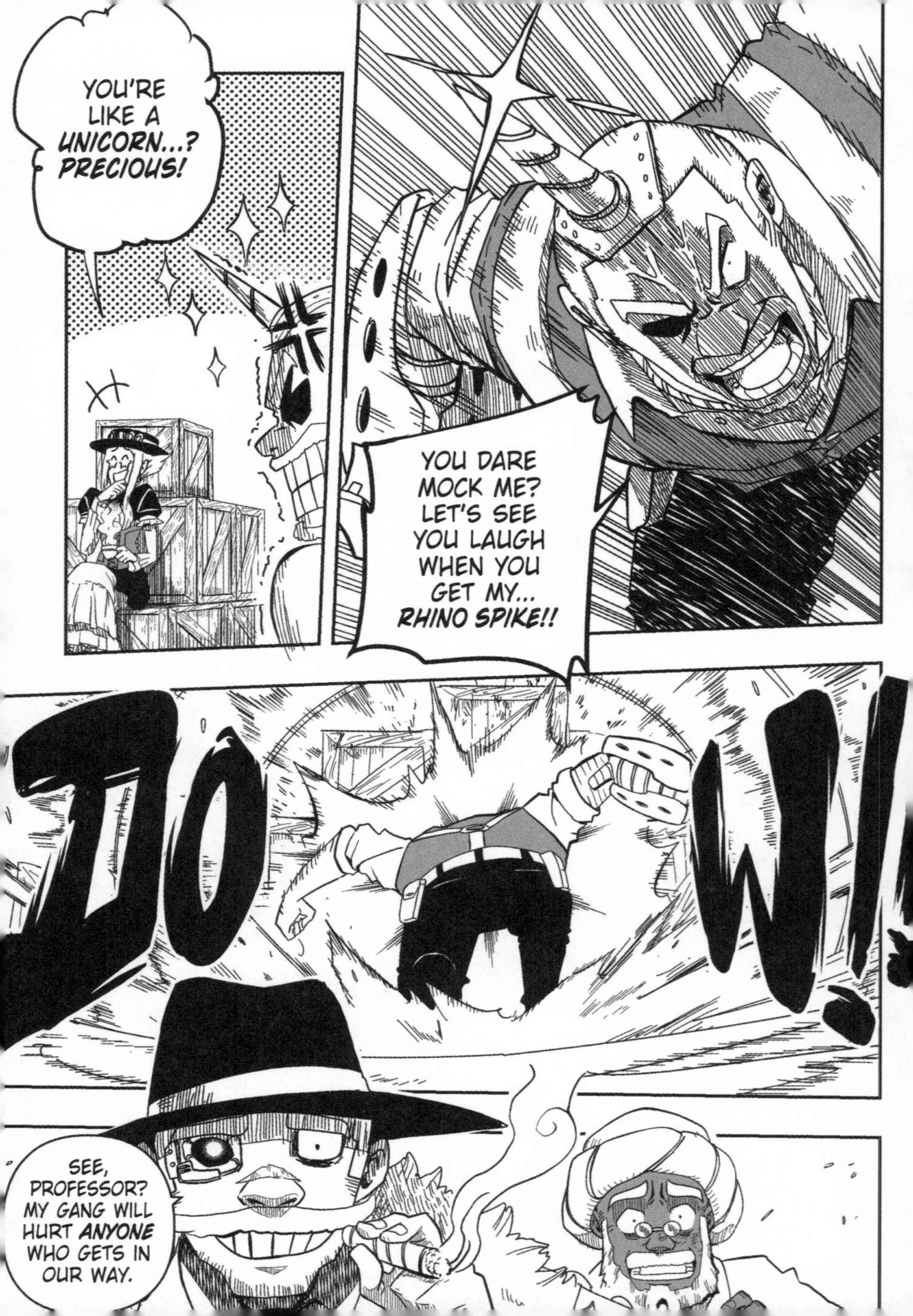
YOU'RE LIKE A *UNICORN...? PRECIOUS!*
YOU DARE MOCK ME? LET'S SEE YOU LAUGH WHEN YOU GET MY... *RHINO SPIKE!!*
DO W!!
SEE, PROFESSOR? MY GANG WILL HURT ***ANYONE*** WHO GETS IN OUR WAY.

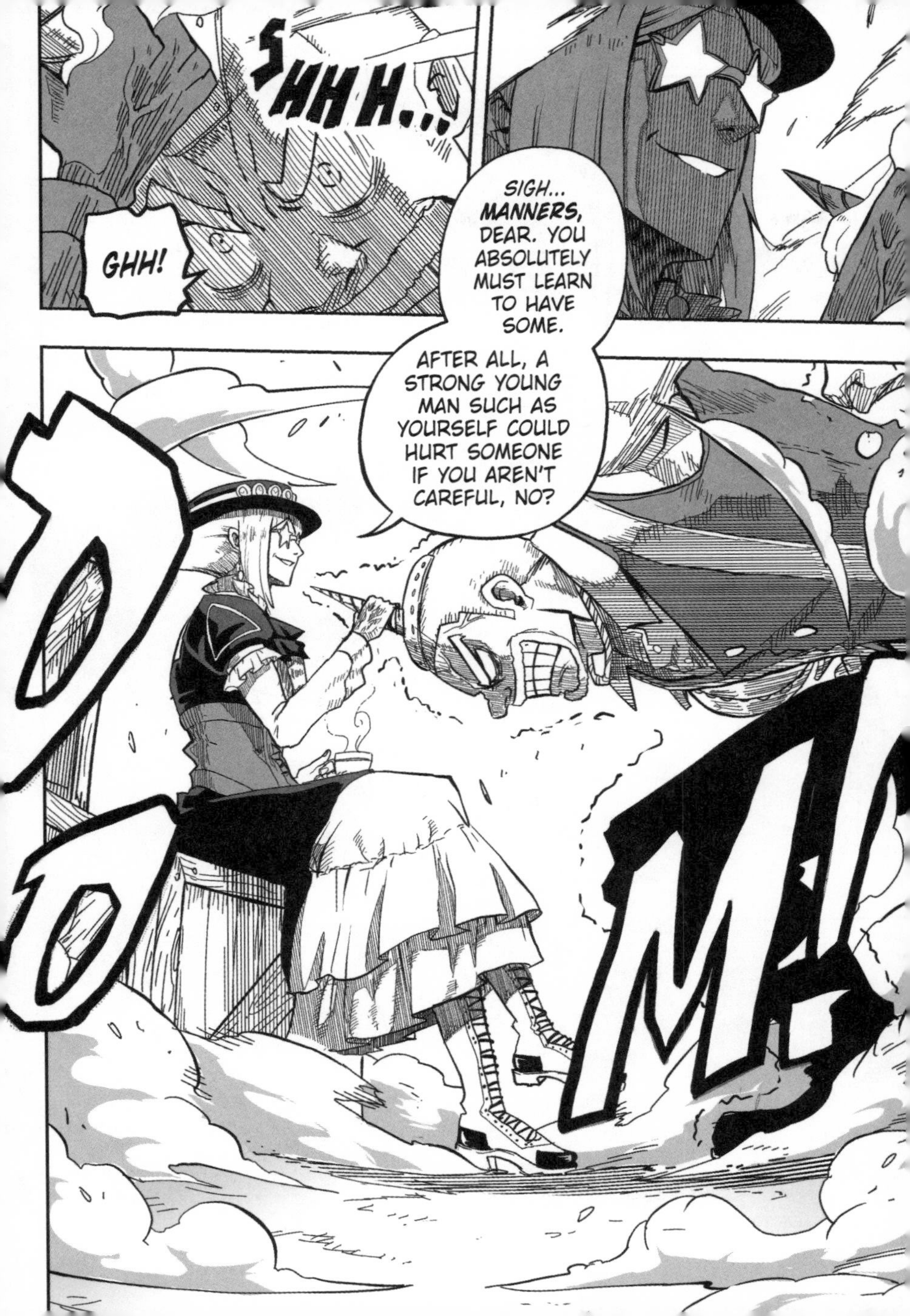
SHHH...!
GHH!
SIGH... MANNERS, DEAR. YOU ABSOLUTELY MUST LEARN TO HAVE SOME.
AFTER ALL, A STRONG YOUNG MAN SUCH AS YOURSELF COULD HURT SOMEONE IF YOU AREN'T CAREFUL, NO?

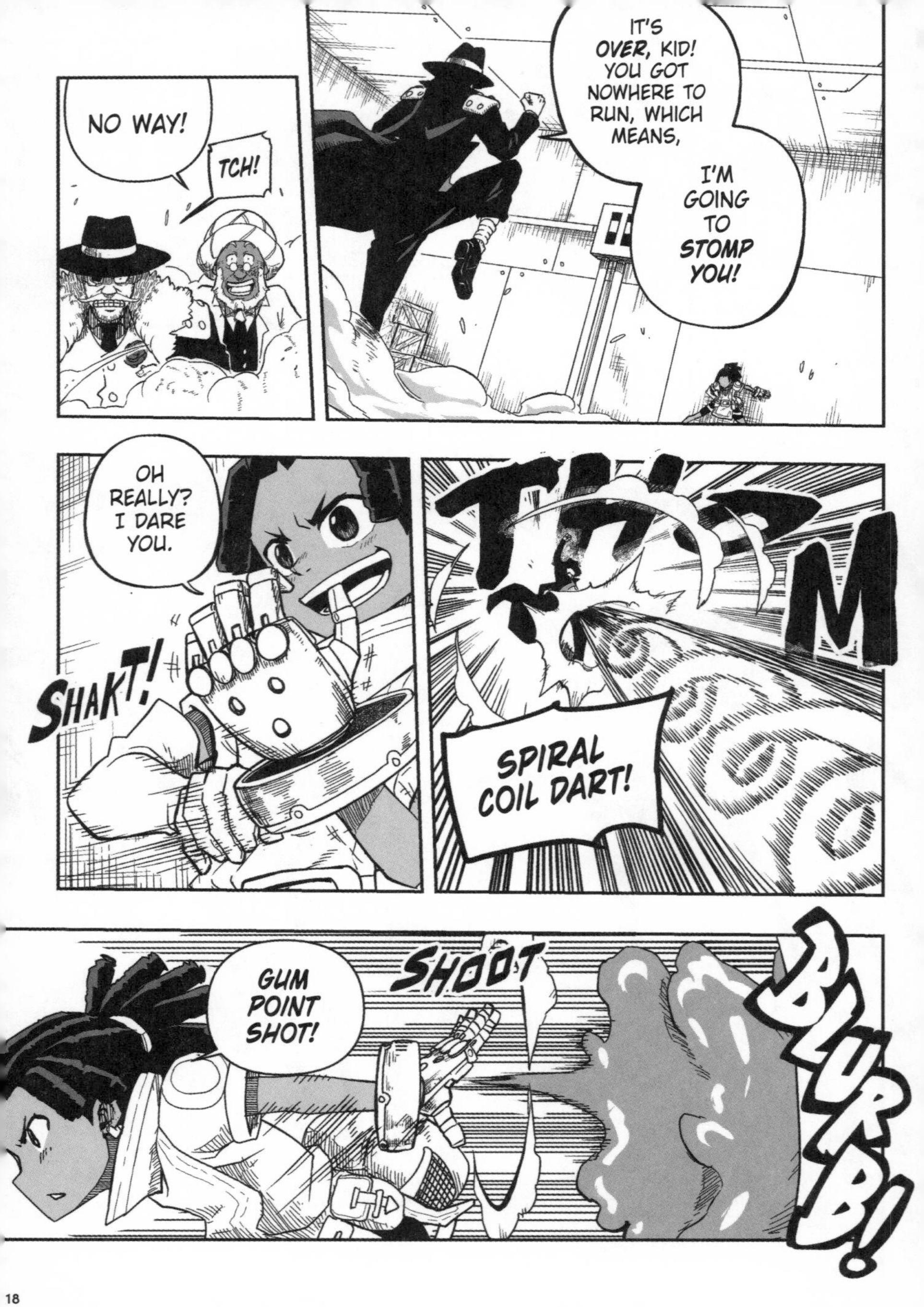
NO WAY!
TCH!
IT'S OVER, KID! YOU GOT NOWHERE TO RUN, WHICH MEANS,
I'M GOING TO STOMP YOU!
OH REALLY? I DARE YOU.
SHAKT!
THOOM
SPIRAL COIL DART!
GUM POINT SHOT!
SHOOT
BLURB!

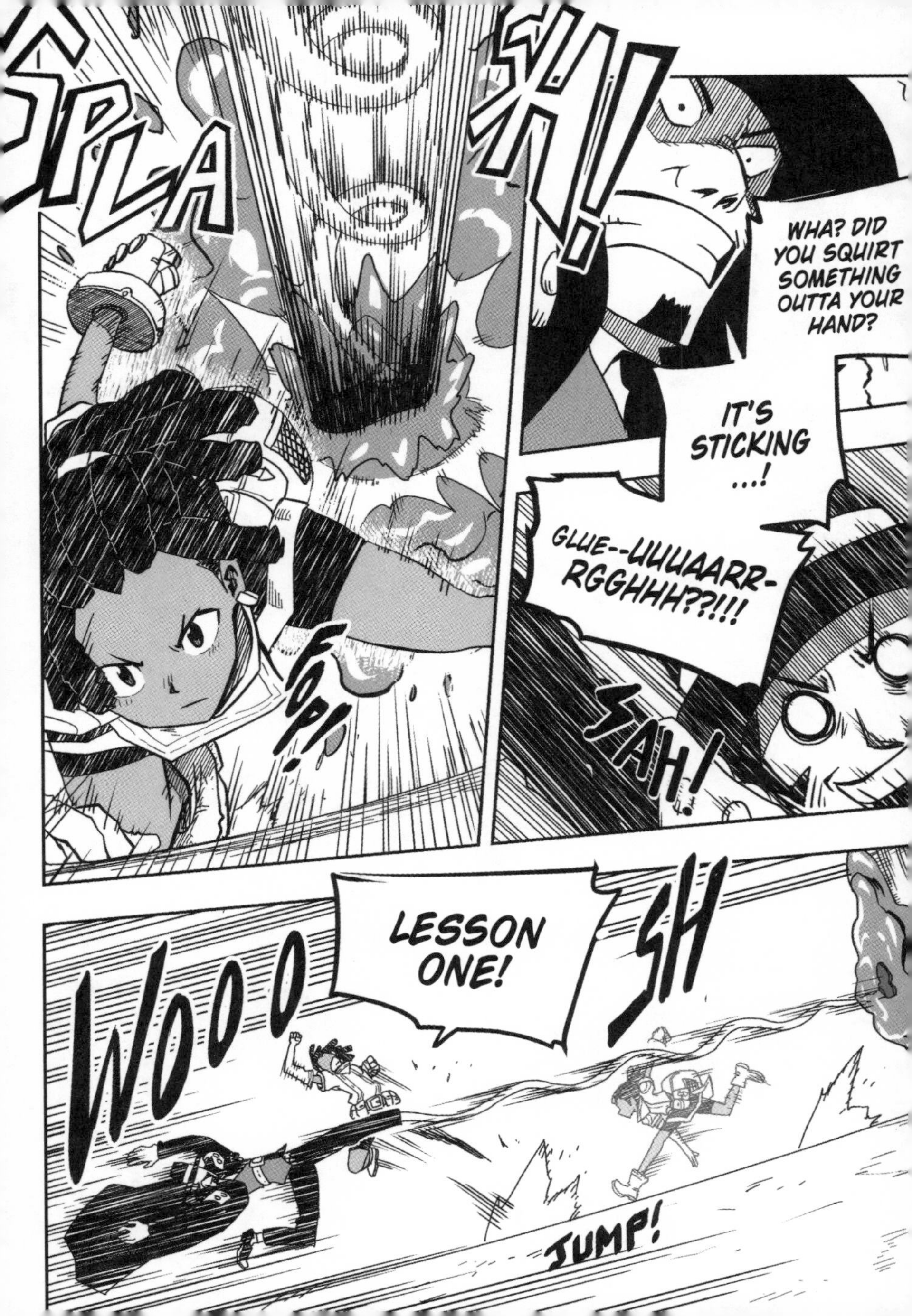
SPLASH!
FOOP!
WHA? DID YOU SQUIRT SOMETHING OUTTA YOUR HAND?
IT'S STICKING ...!
GLUE--UUUAARR-RGGHHH??!!!
SAH!
WOOOSH
LESSON ONE!
JUMP!

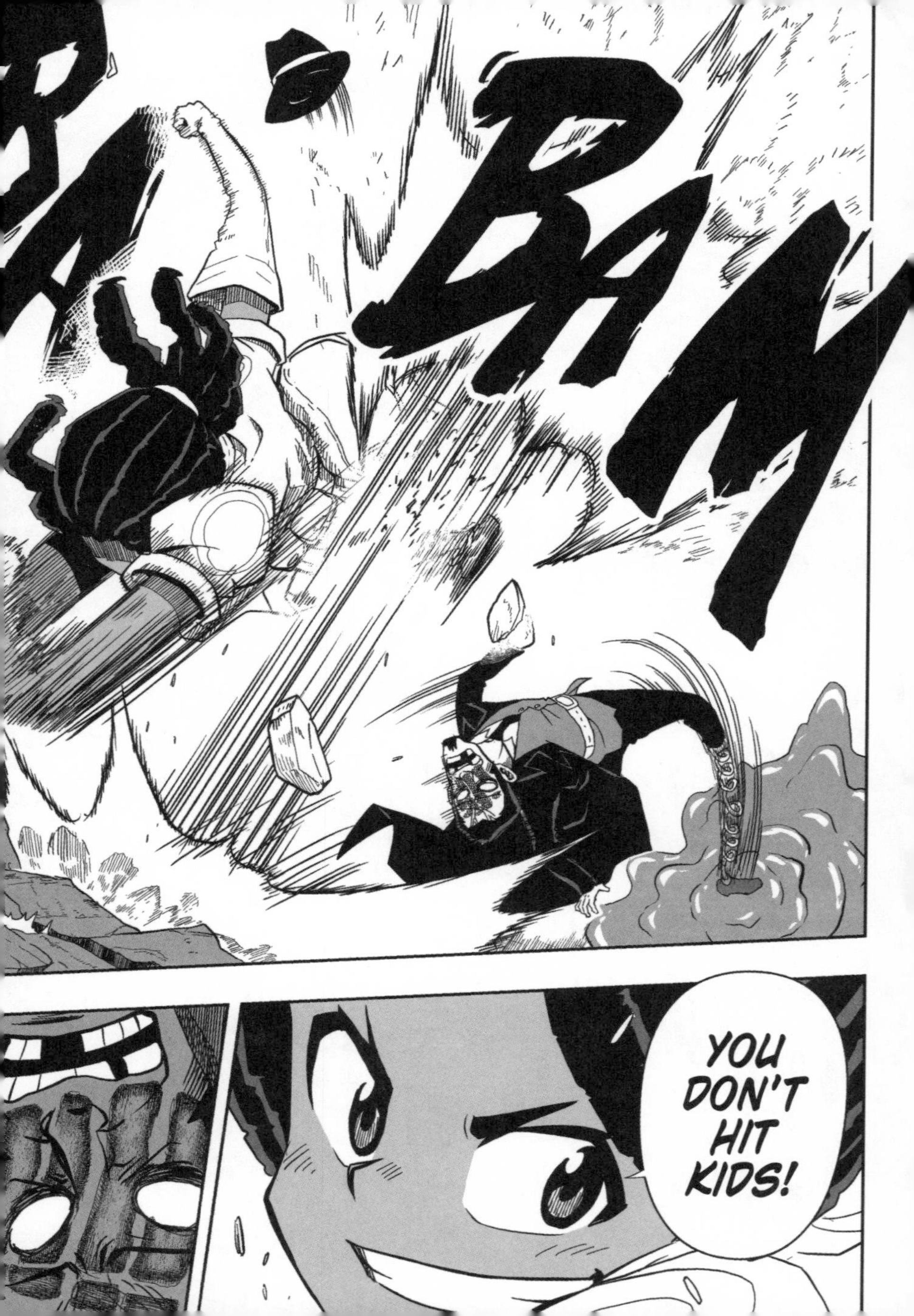
BA
BAM
YOU DON'T HIT KIDS!

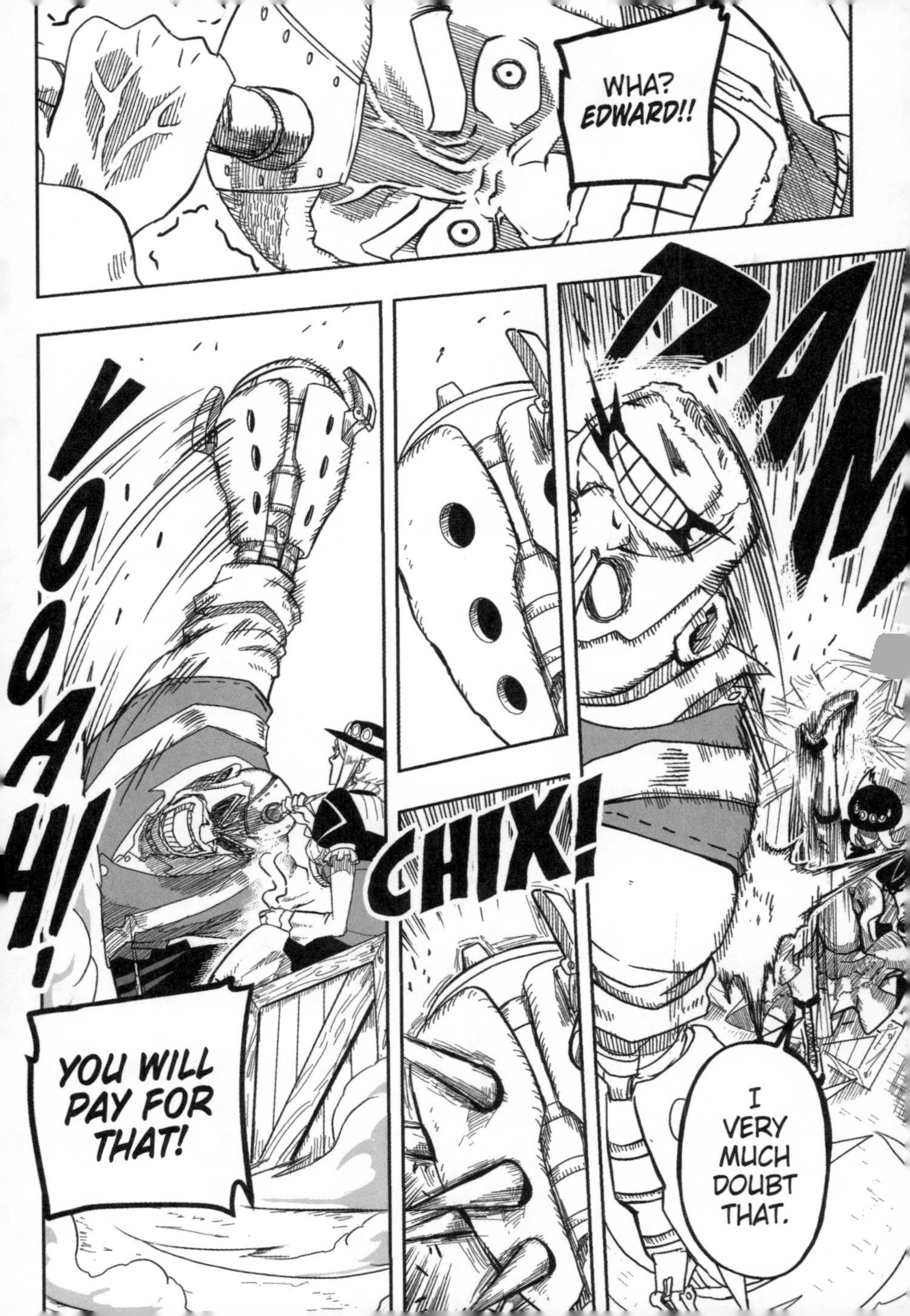
WHA? EDWARD!!
VOOAH!!
YOU WILL PAY FOR THAT!
CHIK!
DAM
I VERY MUCH DOUBT THAT.

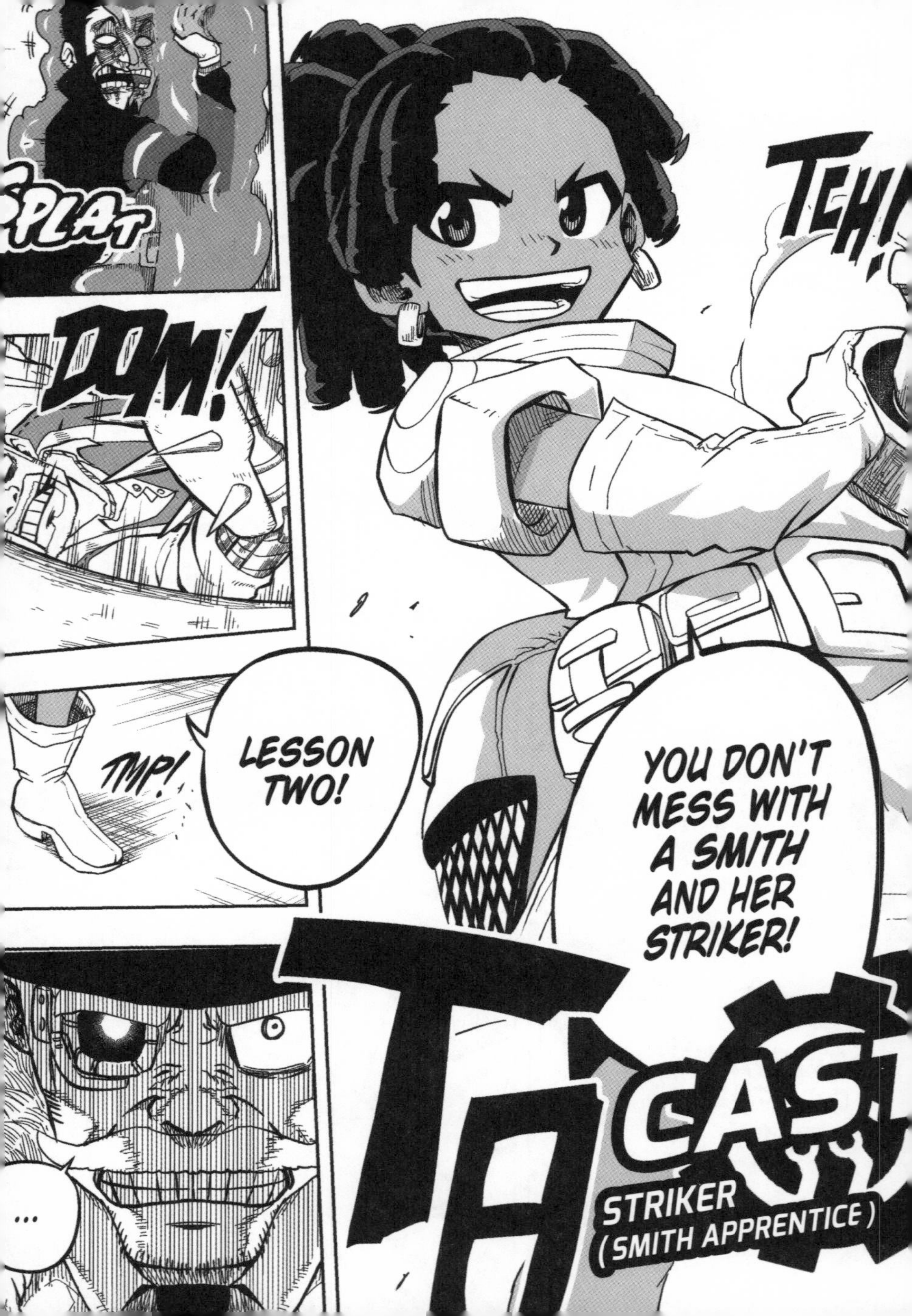
SPLAT
DOM!
TMP!
LESSON TWO!
...
TCH!
YOU DON'T MESS WITH A SMITH AND HER STRIKER!
TA
CAST
STRIKER
(SMITH APPRENTICE)

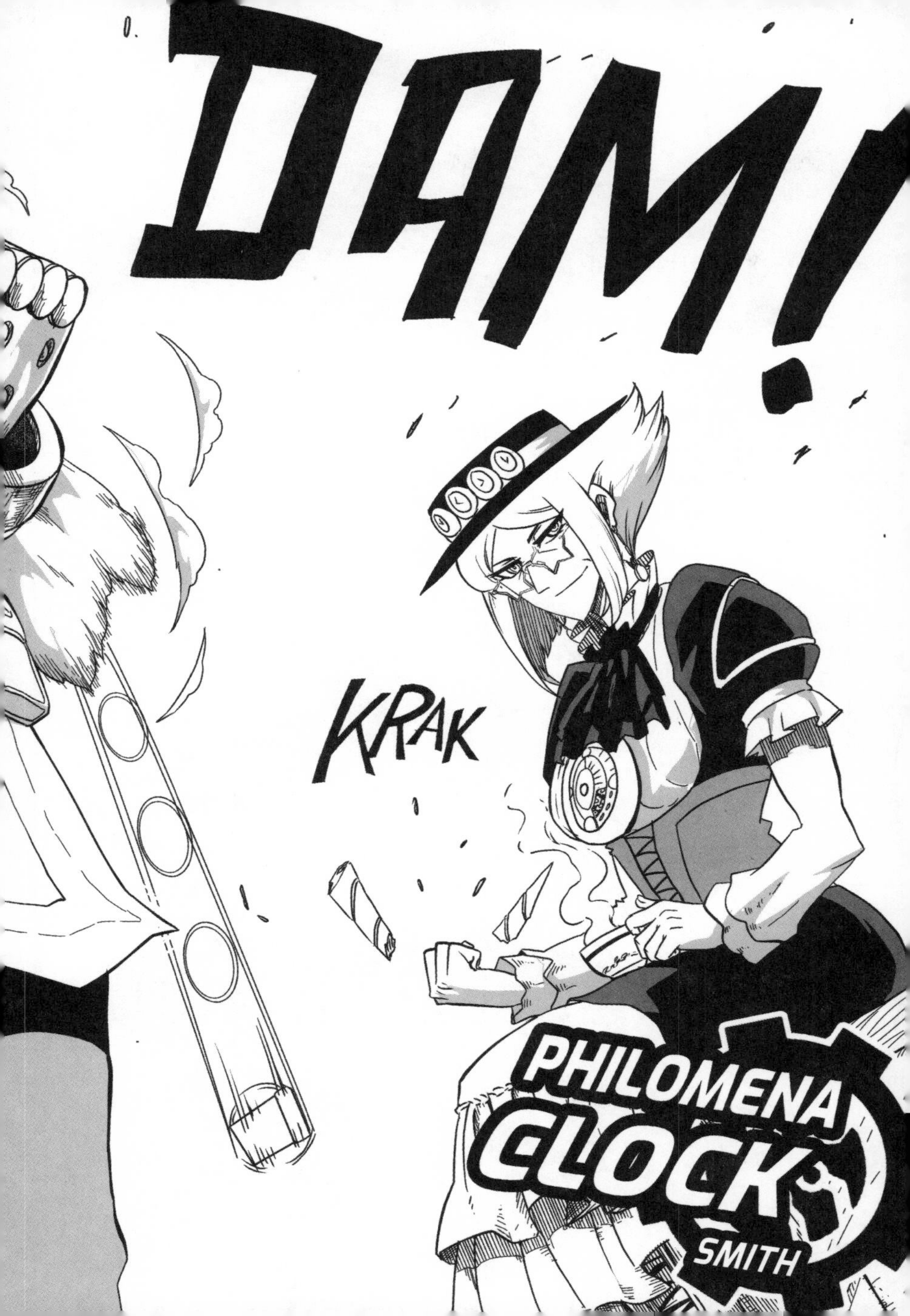
DAM!
KRAK
PHILOMENA
CLOCK
SMITH

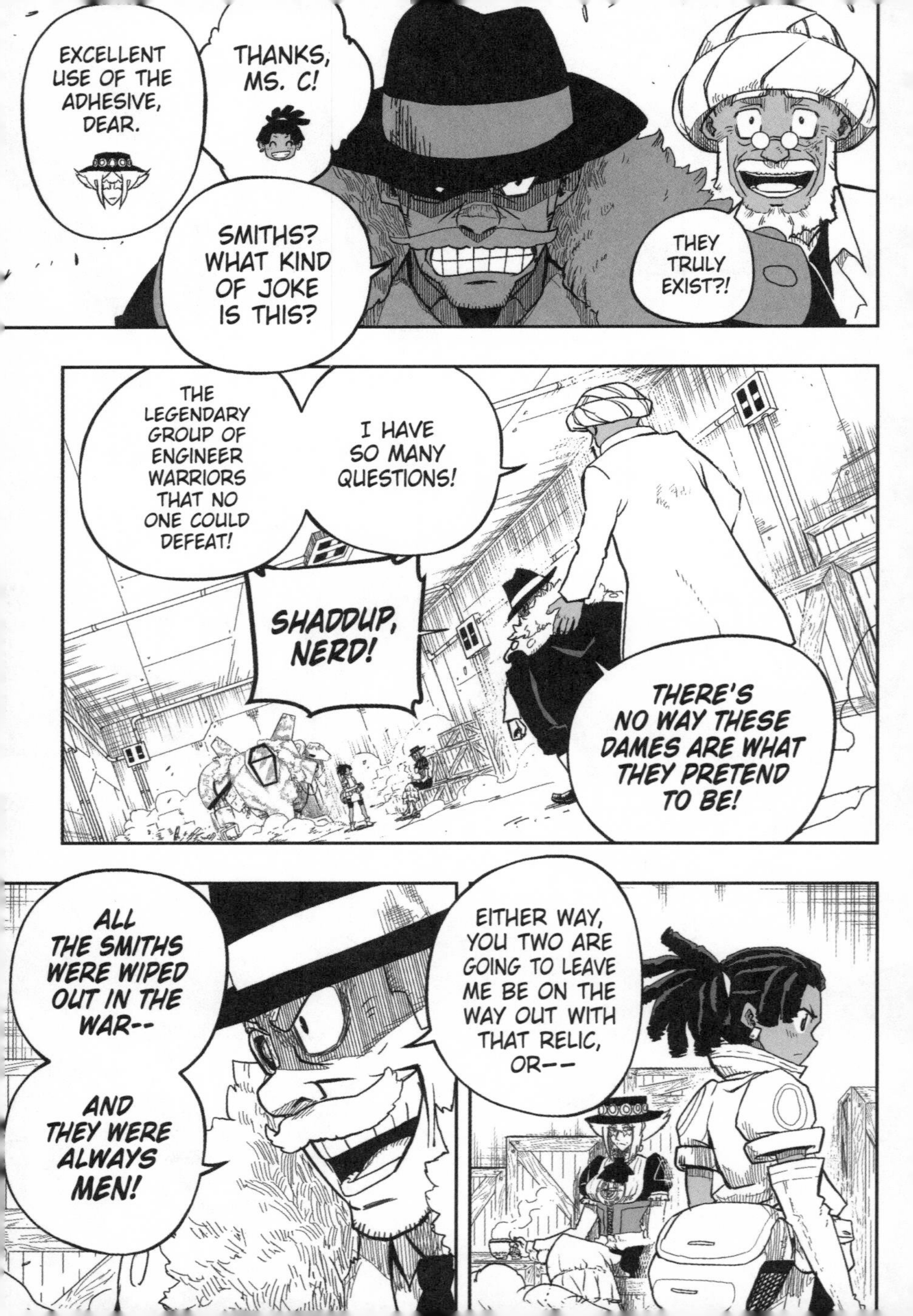

EXCELLENT USE OF THE ADHESIVE, DEAR.
THANKS, MS. C!
SMITHS? WHAT KIND OF JOKE IS THIS?
THEY TRULY EXIST?!
THE LEGENDARY GROUP OF ENGINEER WARRIORS THAT NO ONE COULD DEFEAT!
I HAVE SO MANY QUESTIONS!
SHADDUP, NERD!
THERE'S NO WAY THESE DAMES ARE WHAT THEY PRETEND TO BE!
ALL THE SMITHS WERE WIPED OUT IN THE WAR--
AND THEY WERE ALWAYS MEN!
EITHER WAY, YOU TWO ARE GOING TO LEAVE ME BE ON THE WAY OUT WITH THAT RELIC, OR--

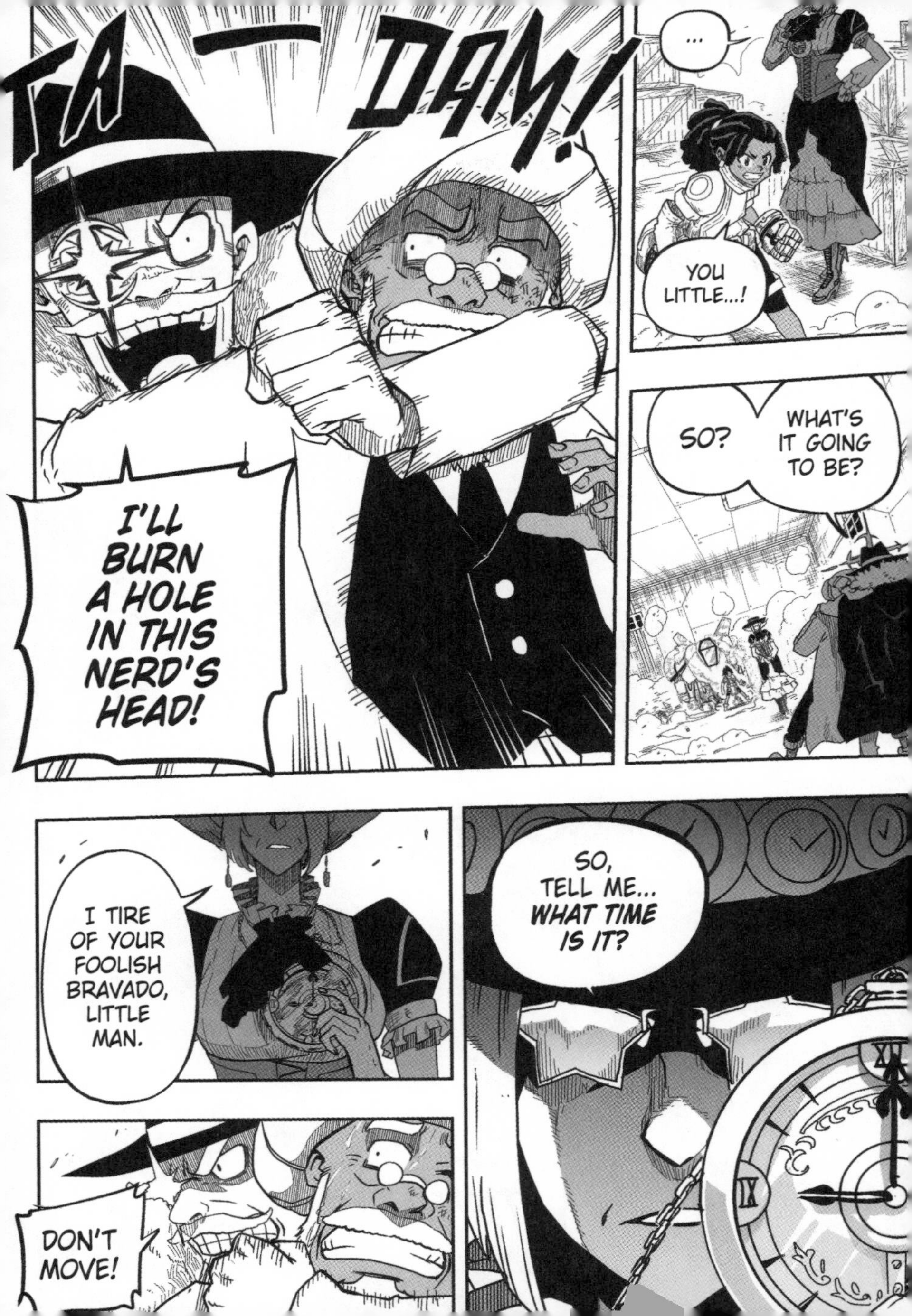
TA — DAM!
I'LL BURN A HOLE IN THIS NERD'S HEAD!
...
YOU LITTLE...!
SO?
WHAT'S IT GOING TO BE?
I TIRE OF YOUR FOOLISH BRAVADO, LITTLE MAN.
DON'T MOVE!
SO, TELL ME... WHAT TIME IS IT?

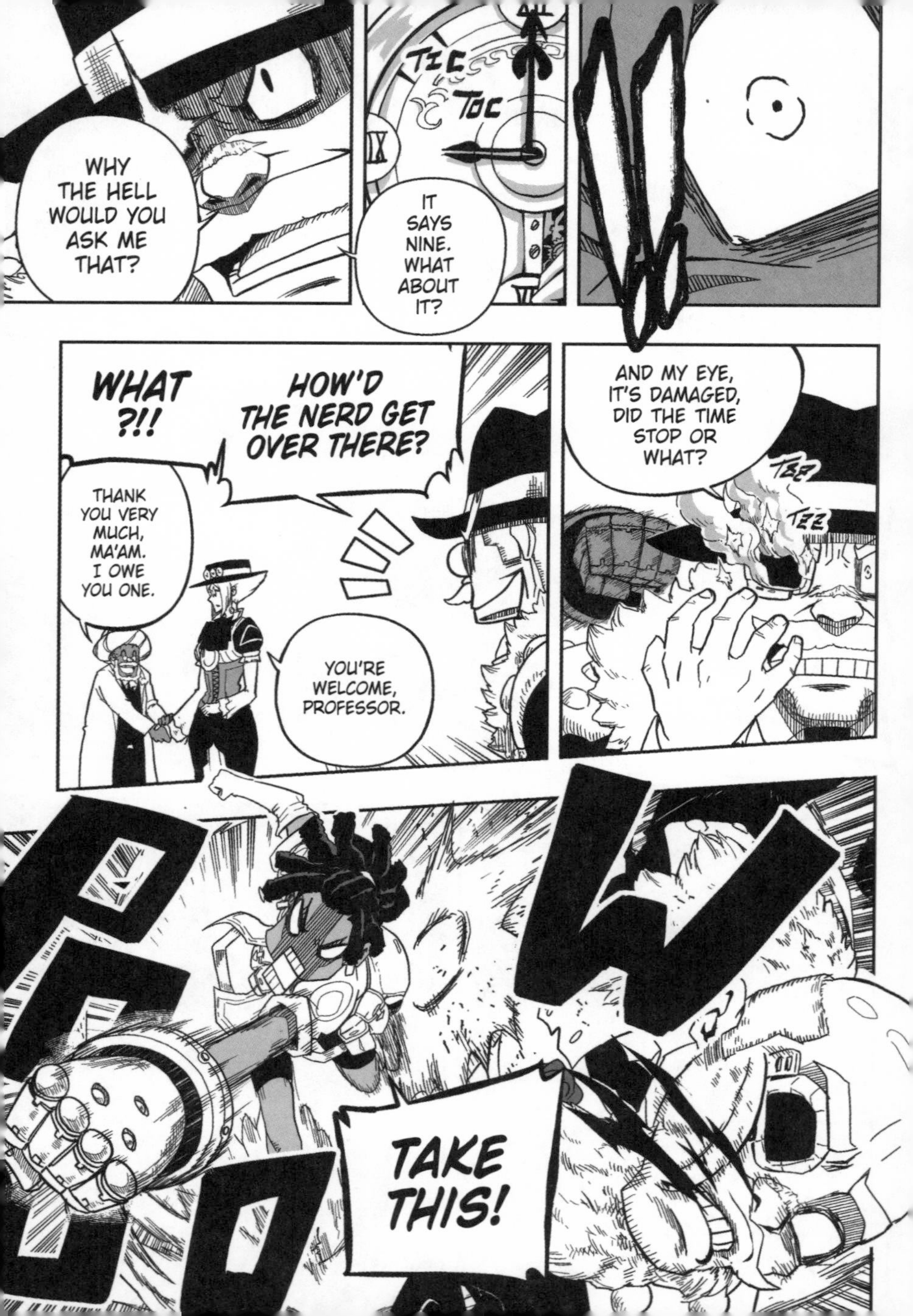
WHY THE HELL WOULD YOU ASK ME THAT?
TIC
TOC
IT SAYS NINE. WHAT ABOUT IT?
WHAT ?!!
HOW'D THE NERD GET OVER THERE?
THANK YOU VERY MUCH, MA'AM. I OWE YOU ONE.
YOU'RE WELCOME, PROFESSOR.
AND MY EYE, IT'S DAMAGED, DID THE TIME STOP OR WHAT?
TZZ
TZZ
TAKE THIS!

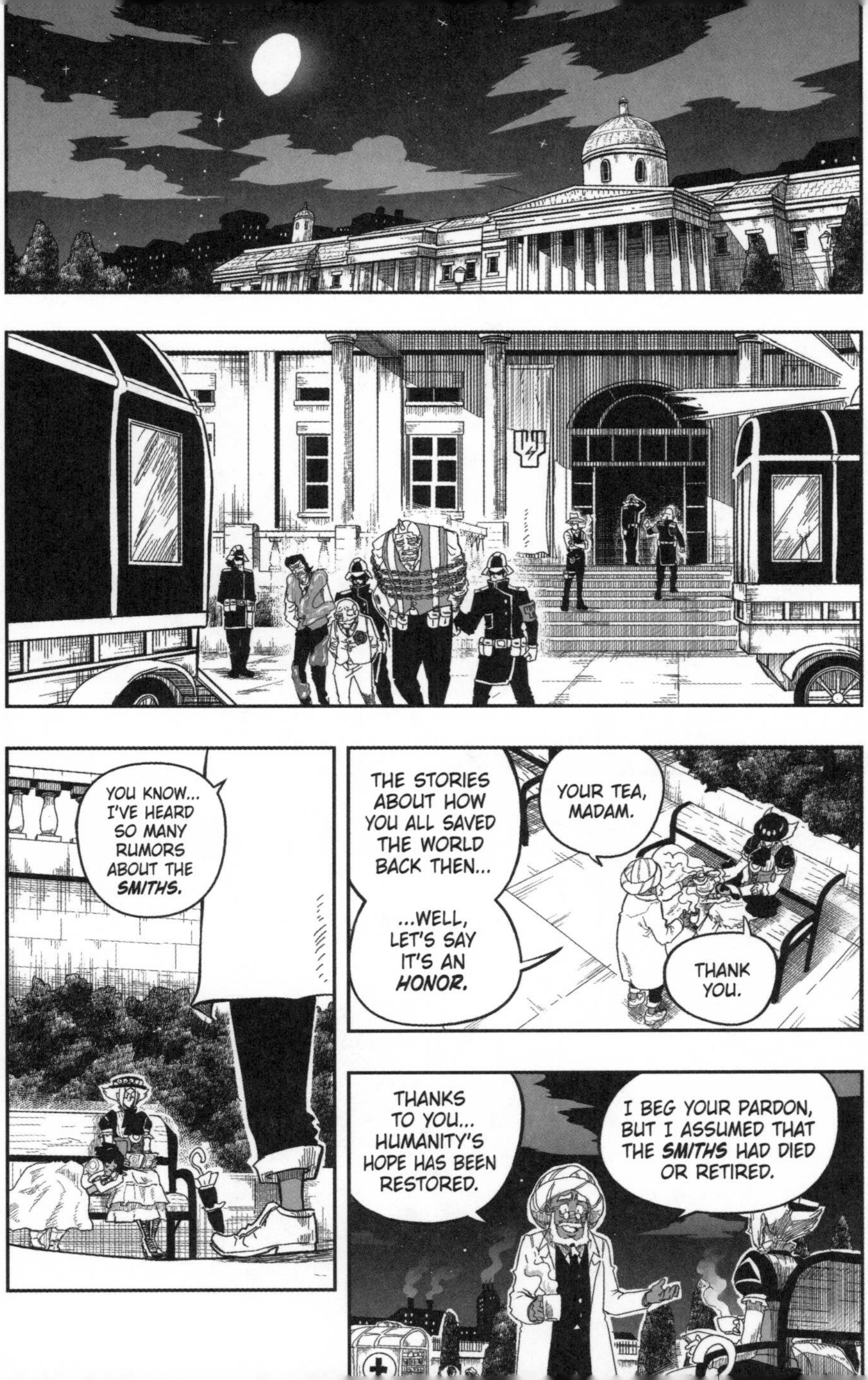

YOU KNOW... I'VE HEARD SO MANY RUMORS ABOUT THE SMITHS.
THE STORIES ABOUT HOW YOU ALL SAVED THE WORLD BACK THEN...
...WELL, LET'S SAY IT'S AN HONOR.
YOUR TEA, MADAM.
THANK YOU.
THANKS TO YOU... HUMANITY'S HOPE HAS BEEN RESTORED.
I BEG YOUR PARDON, BUT I ASSUMED THAT THE SMITHS HAD DIED OR RETIRED.

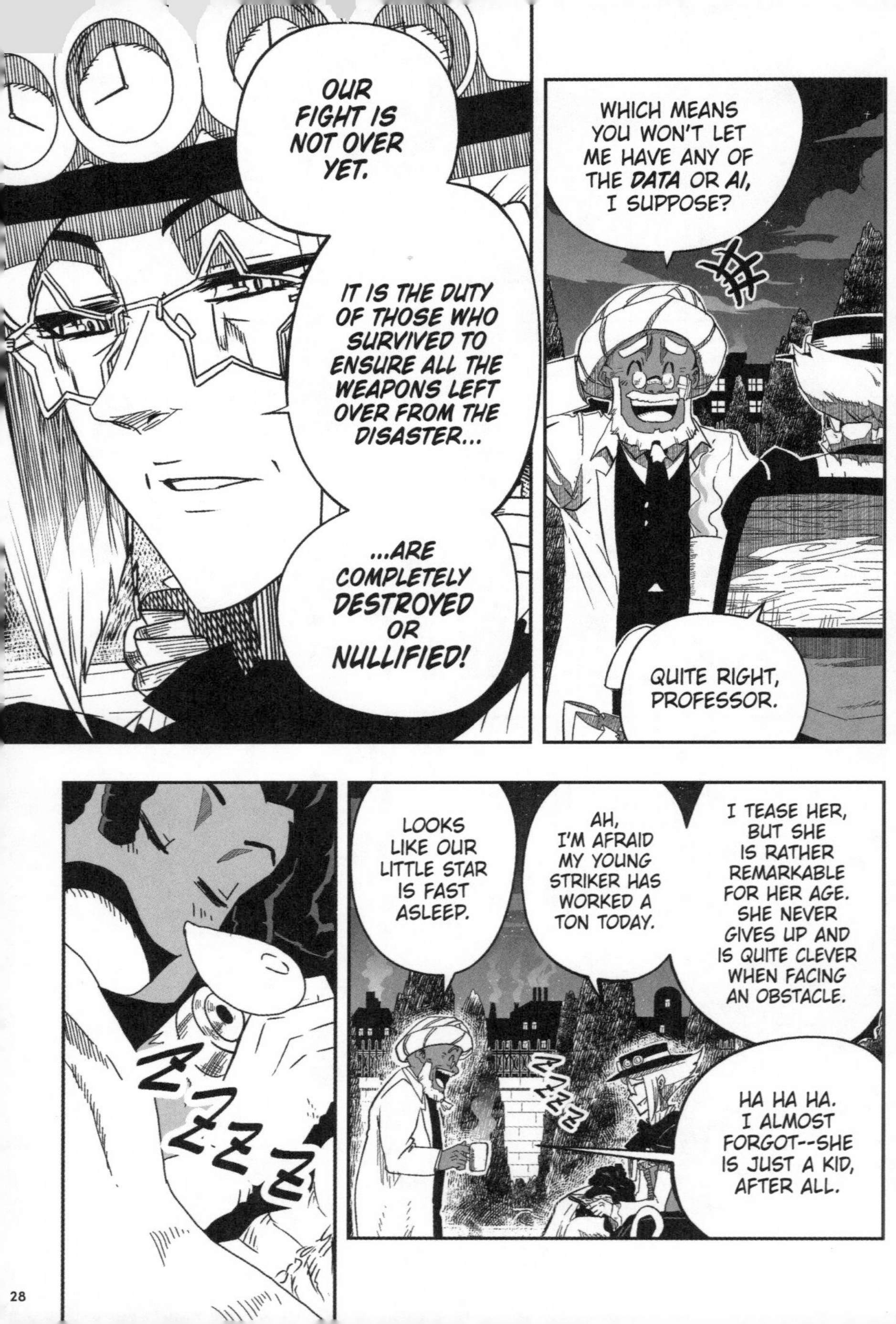
OUR FIGHT IS NOT OVER YET.
IT IS THE DUTY OF THOSE WHO SURVIVED TO ENSURE ALL THE WEAPONS LEFT OVER FROM THE DISASTER...
...ARE COMPLETELY DESTROYED OR NULLIFIED!
WHICH MEANS YOU WON'T LET ME HAVE ANY OF THE *DATA* OR *AI*, I SUPPOSE?
QUITE RIGHT, PROFESSOR.
LOOKS LIKE OUR LITTLE STAR IS FAST ASLEEP.
AH, I'M AFRAID MY YOUNG STRIKER HAS WORKED A TON TODAY.
I TEASE HER, BUT SHE IS RATHER REMARKABLE FOR HER AGE. SHE NEVER GIVES UP AND IS QUITE CLEVER WHEN FACING AN OBSTACLE.
HA HA HA. I ALMOST FORGOT--SHE IS JUST A KID, AFTER ALL.

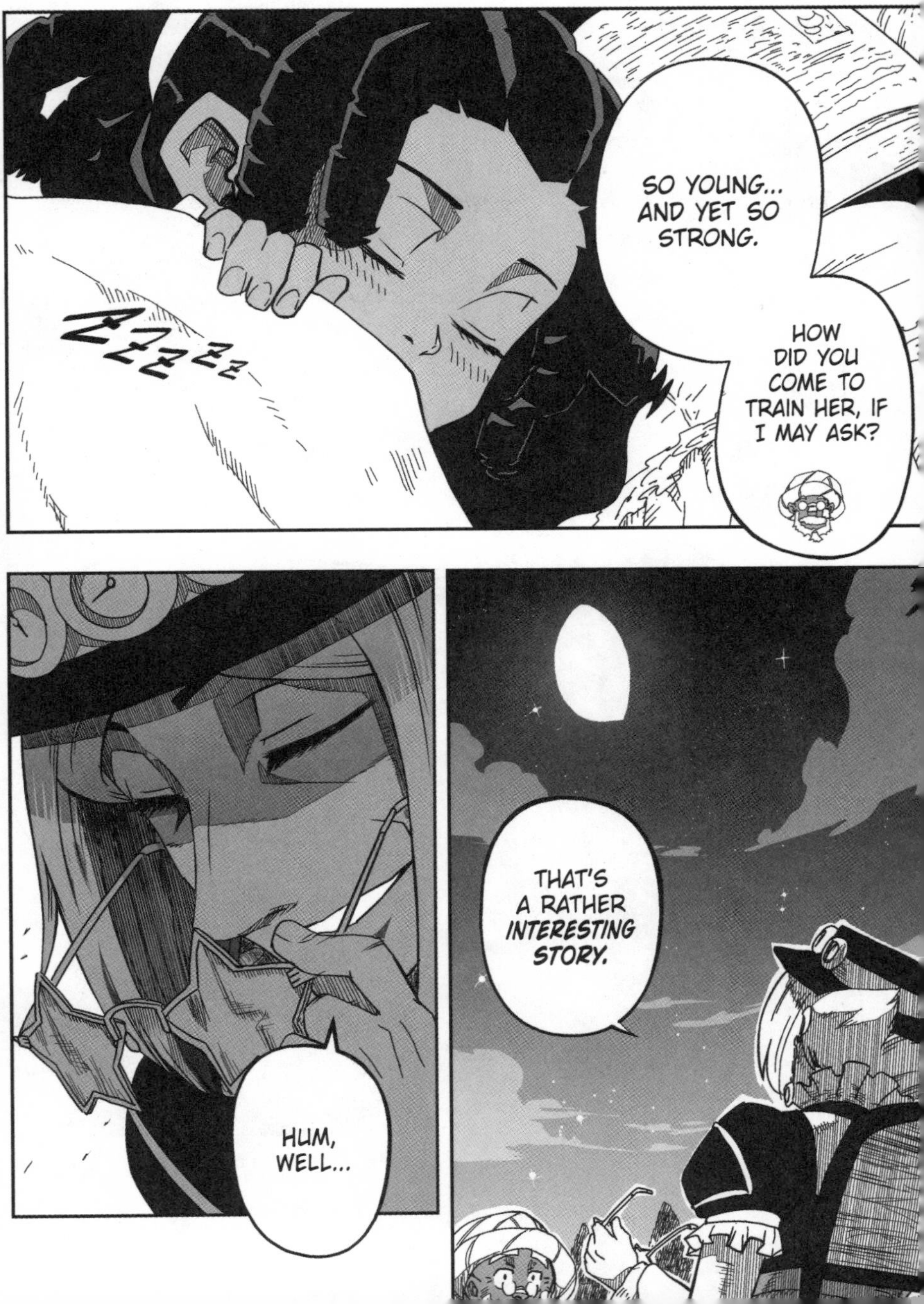
ZZZZzz
SO YOUNG... AND YET SO STRONG.
HOW DID YOU COME TO TRAIN HER, IF I MAY ASK?
HUM, WELL...
THAT'S A RATHER *INTERESTING* STORY.

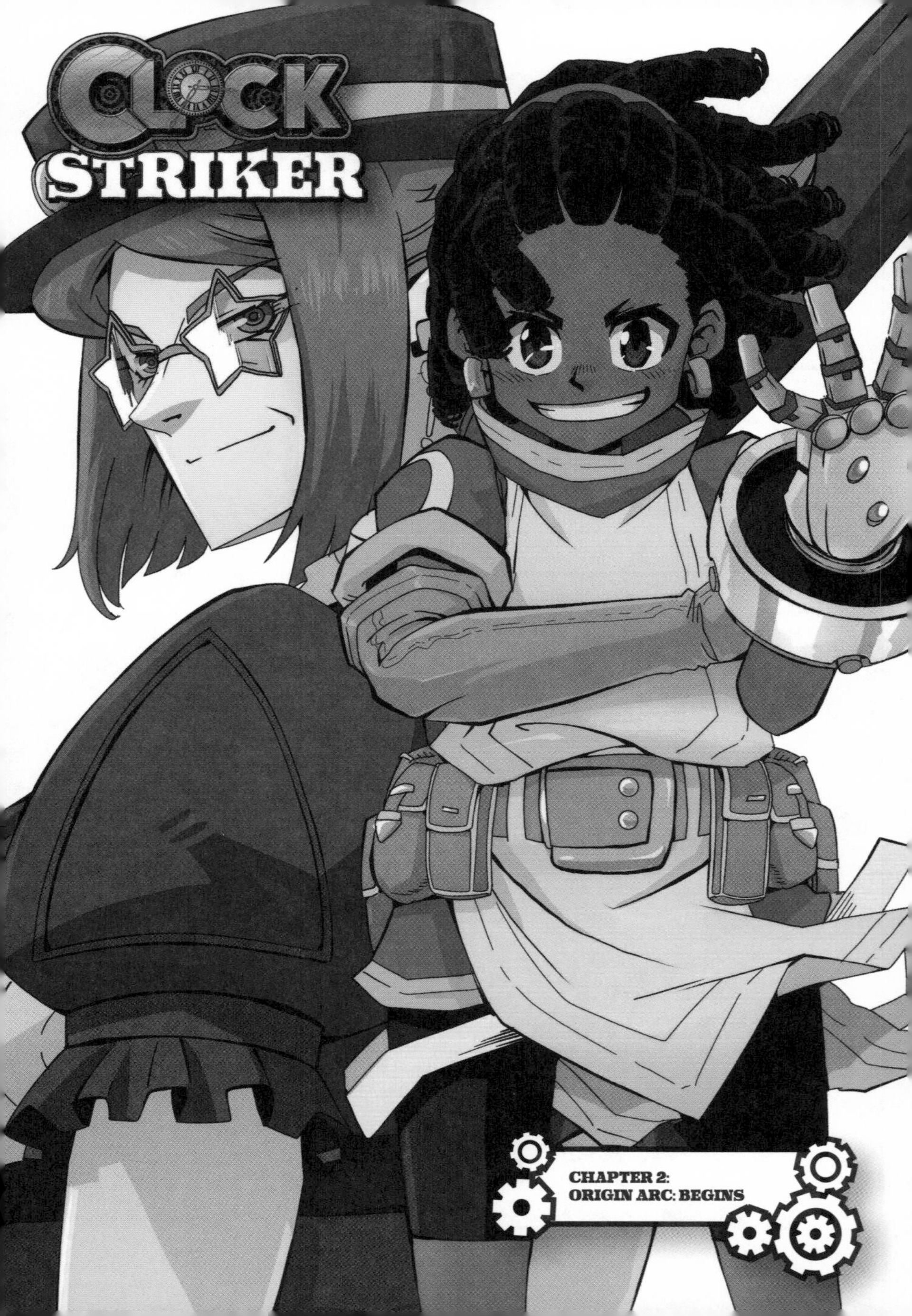
CLOCK
STRIKER
CHAPTER 2:
ORIGIN ARC: BEGINS

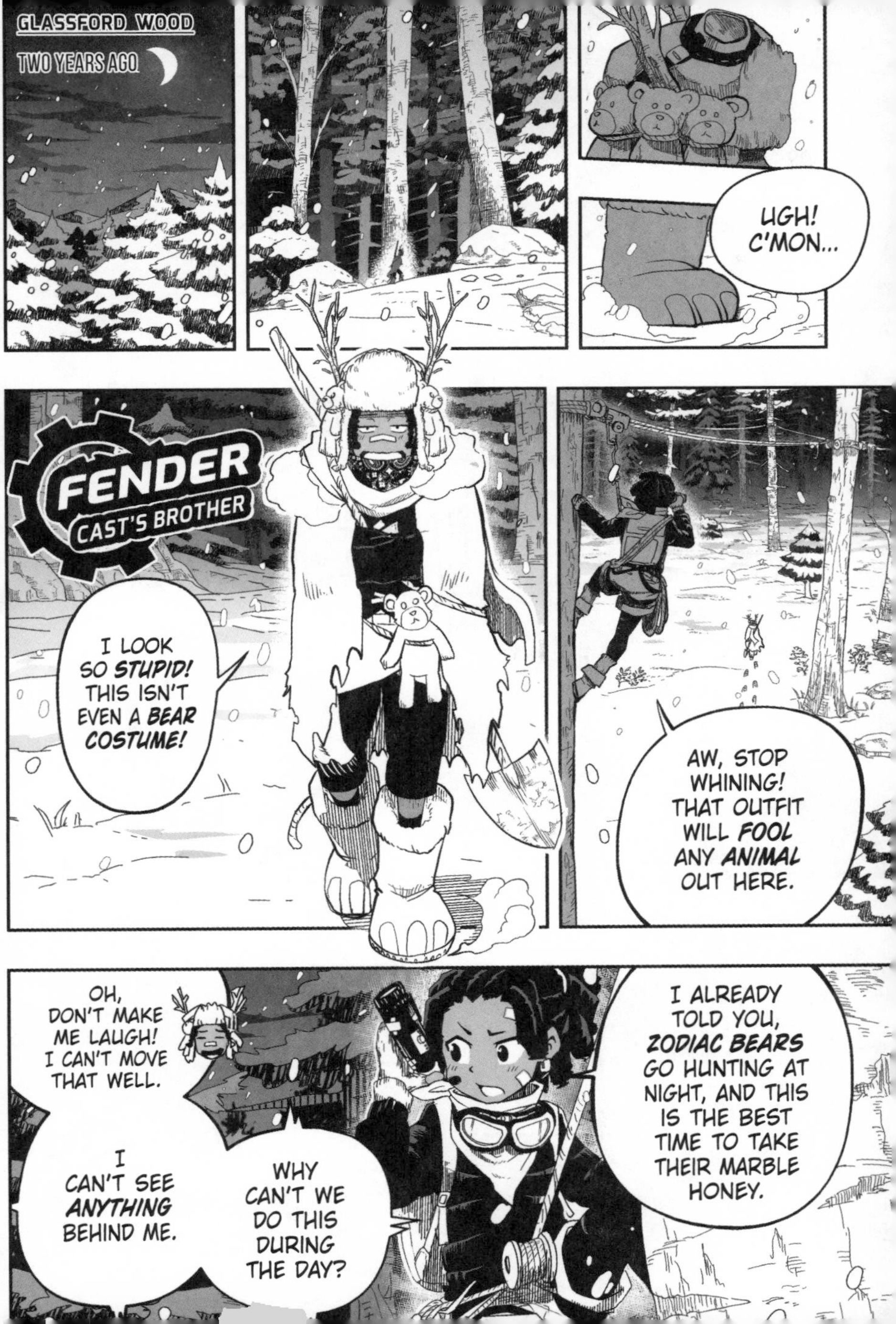
GLASSFORD WOOD
TWO YEARS AGO
UGH! C'MON...
FENDER
CAST'S BROTHER
I LOOK SO STUPID! THIS ISN'T EVEN A BEAR COSTUME!
AW, STOP WHINING! THAT OUTFIT WILL FOOL ANY ANIMAL OUT HERE.
OH, DON'T MAKE ME LAUGH! I CAN'T MOVE THAT WELL.
I CAN'T SEE ANYTHING BEHIND ME.
WHY CAN'T WE DO THIS DURING THE DAY?
I ALREADY TOLD YOU, ZODIAC BEARS GO HUNTING AT NIGHT, AND THIS IS THE BEST TIME TO TAKE THEIR MARBLE HONEY.

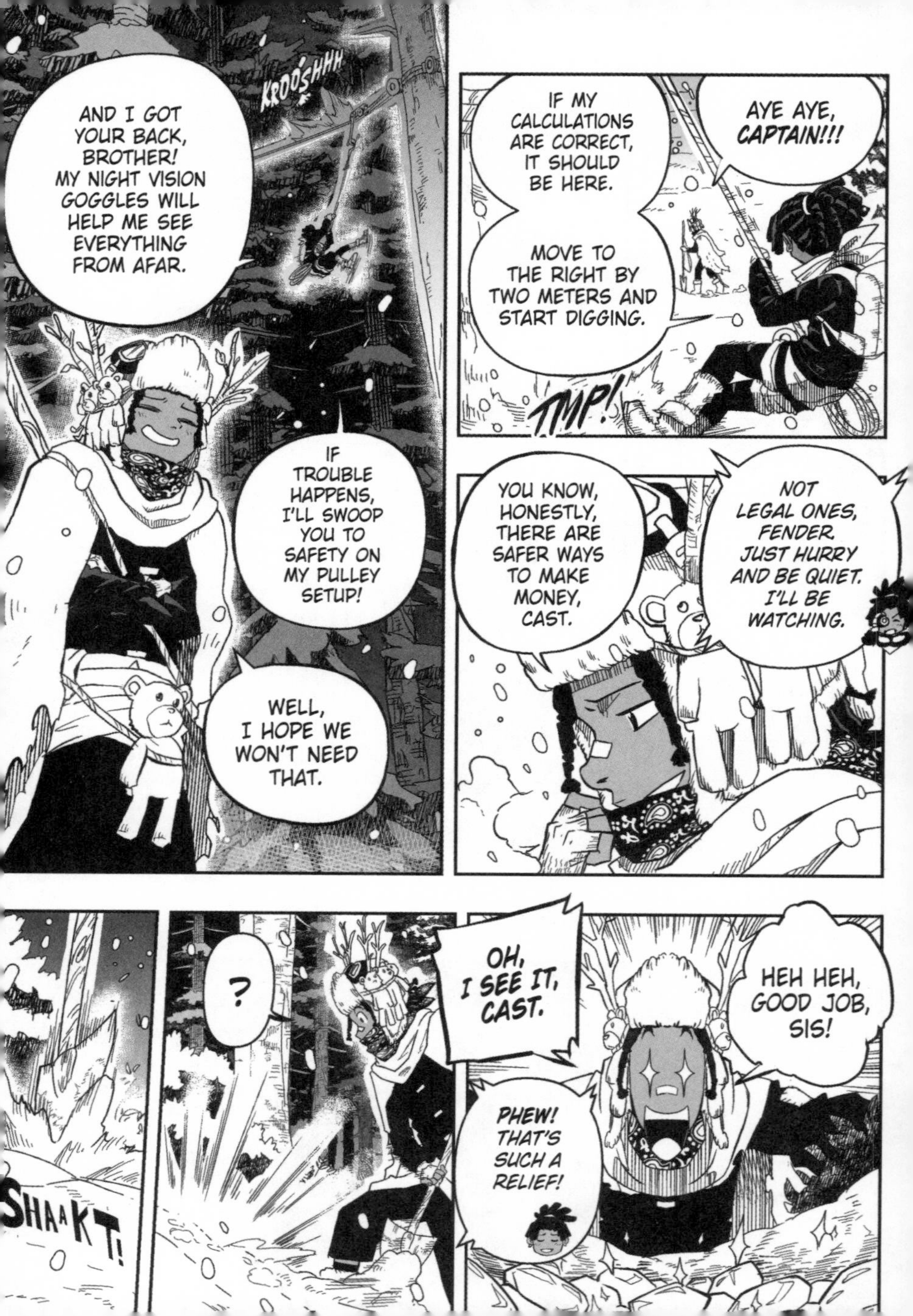
KROOSHHH
AND I GOT YOUR BACK, BROTHER! MY NIGHT VISION GOGGLES WILL HELP ME SEE EVERYTHING FROM AFAR.
IF TROUBLE HAPPENS, I'LL SWOOP YOU TO SAFETY ON MY PULLEY SETUP!
WELL, I HOPE WE WON'T NEED THAT.
IF MY CALCULATIONS ARE CORRECT, IT SHOULD BE HERE.
MOVE TO THE RIGHT BY TWO METERS AND START DIGGING.
AYE AYE, CAPTAIN!!!
TMP!
YOU KNOW, HONESTLY, THERE ARE SAFER WAYS TO MAKE MONEY, CAST.
NOT LEGAL ONES, FENDER. JUST HURRY AND BE QUIET. I'LL BE WATCHING.
SHAAKT!
?
OH, I SEE IT, CAST.
HEH HEH, GOOD JOB, SIS!
PHEW! THAT'S SUCH A RELIEF!

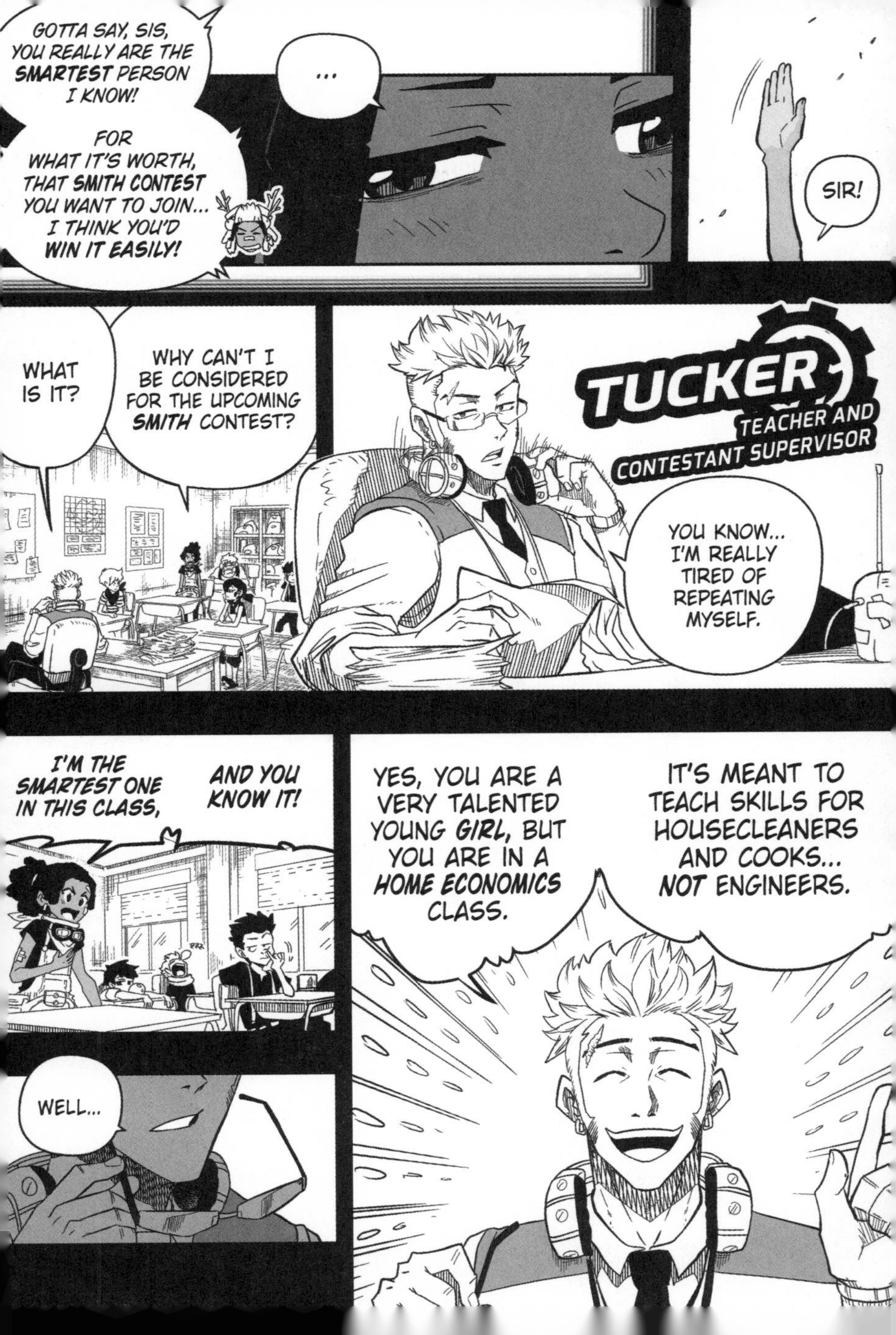
GOTTA SAY, SIS, YOU REALLY ARE THE SMARTEST PERSON I KNOW!
FOR WHAT IT'S WORTH, THAT SMITH CONTEST YOU WANT TO JOIN... I THINK YOU'D WIN IT EASILY!
...
SIR!
WHAT IS IT?
WHY CAN'T I BE CONSIDERED FOR THE UPCOMING SMITH CONTEST?
TUCKER
TEACHER AND CONTESTANT SUPERVISOR
YOU KNOW... I'M REALLY TIRED OF REPEATING MYSELF.
I'M THE SMARTEST ONE IN THIS CLASS,
AND YOU KNOW IT!
WELL...
YES, YOU ARE A VERY TALENTED YOUNG GIRL, BUT YOU ARE IN A HOME ECONOMICS CLASS.
IT'S MEANT TO TEACH SKILLS FOR HOUSECLEANERS AND COOKS... NOT ENGINEERS.

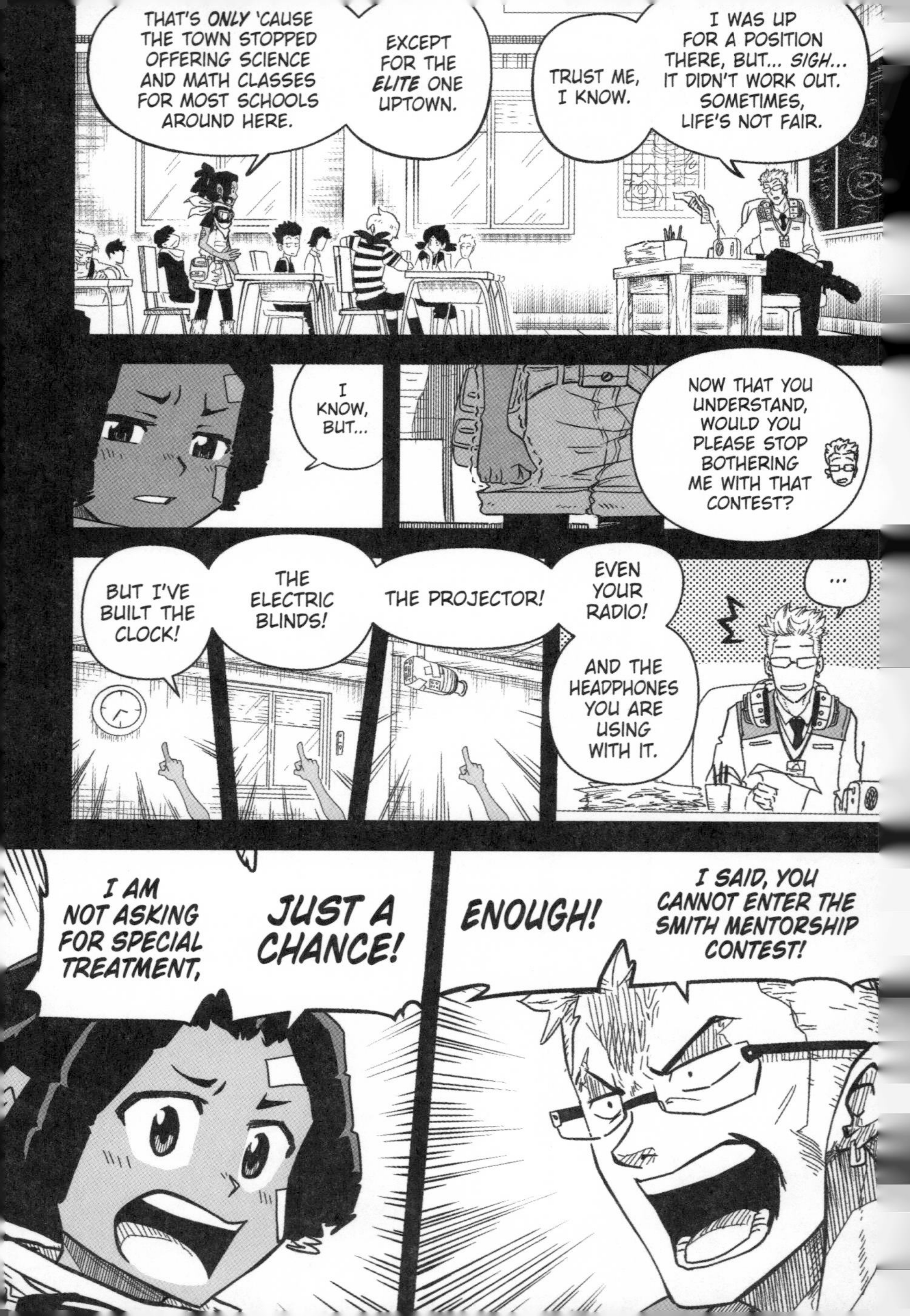
THAT'S *ONLY* 'CAUSE THE TOWN STOPPED OFFERING SCIENCE AND MATH CLASSES FOR MOST SCHOOLS AROUND HERE.
EXCEPT FOR THE *ELITE* ONE UPTOWN.
TRUST ME, I KNOW.
I WAS UP FOR A POSITION THERE, BUT... *SIGH*... IT DIDN'T WORK OUT. SOMETIMES, LIFE'S NOT FAIR.
I KNOW, BUT...
NOW THAT YOU UNDERSTAND, WOULD YOU PLEASE STOP BOTHERING ME WITH THAT CONTEST?
BUT I'VE BUILT THE CLOCK!
THE ELECTRIC BLINDS!
THE PROJECTOR!
EVEN YOUR RADIO!
AND THE HEADPHONES YOU ARE USING WITH IT.
...
I AM NOT ASKING FOR SPECIAL TREATMENT,
JUST A CHANCE!
ENOUGH!
I SAID, YOU CANNOT ENTER THE SMITH MENTORSHIP CONTEST!

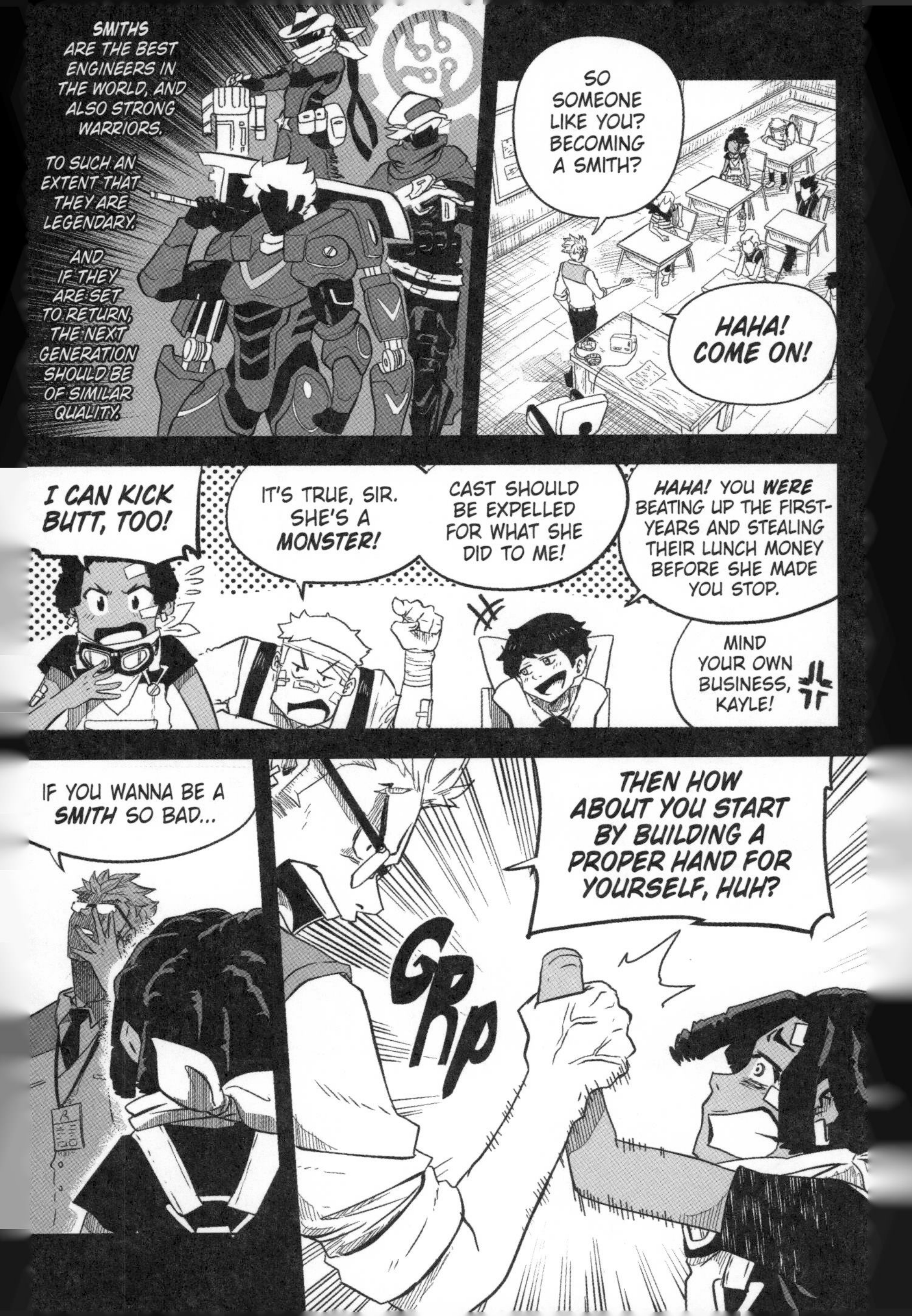
SMITHS ARE THE BEST ENGINEERS IN THE WORLD, AND ALSO STRONG WARRIORS.
TO SUCH AN EXTENT THAT THEY ARE LEGENDARY.
AND IF THEY ARE SET TO RETURN, THE NEXT GENERATION SHOULD BE OF SIMILAR QUALITY.
SO SOMEONE LIKE YOU? BECOMING A SMITH?
HAHA! COME ON!
I CAN KICK BUTT, TOO!
IT'S TRUE, SIR. SHE'S A MONSTER!
CAST SHOULD BE EXPELLED FOR WHAT SHE DID TO ME!
HAHA! YOU WERE BEATING UP THE FIRST-YEARS AND STEALING THEIR LUNCH MONEY BEFORE SHE MADE YOU STOP.
MIND YOUR OWN BUSINESS, KAYLE!
IF YOU WANNA BE A SMITH SO BAD...
THEN HOW ABOUT YOU START BY BUILDING A PROPER HAND FOR YOURSELF, HUH?
GRIP

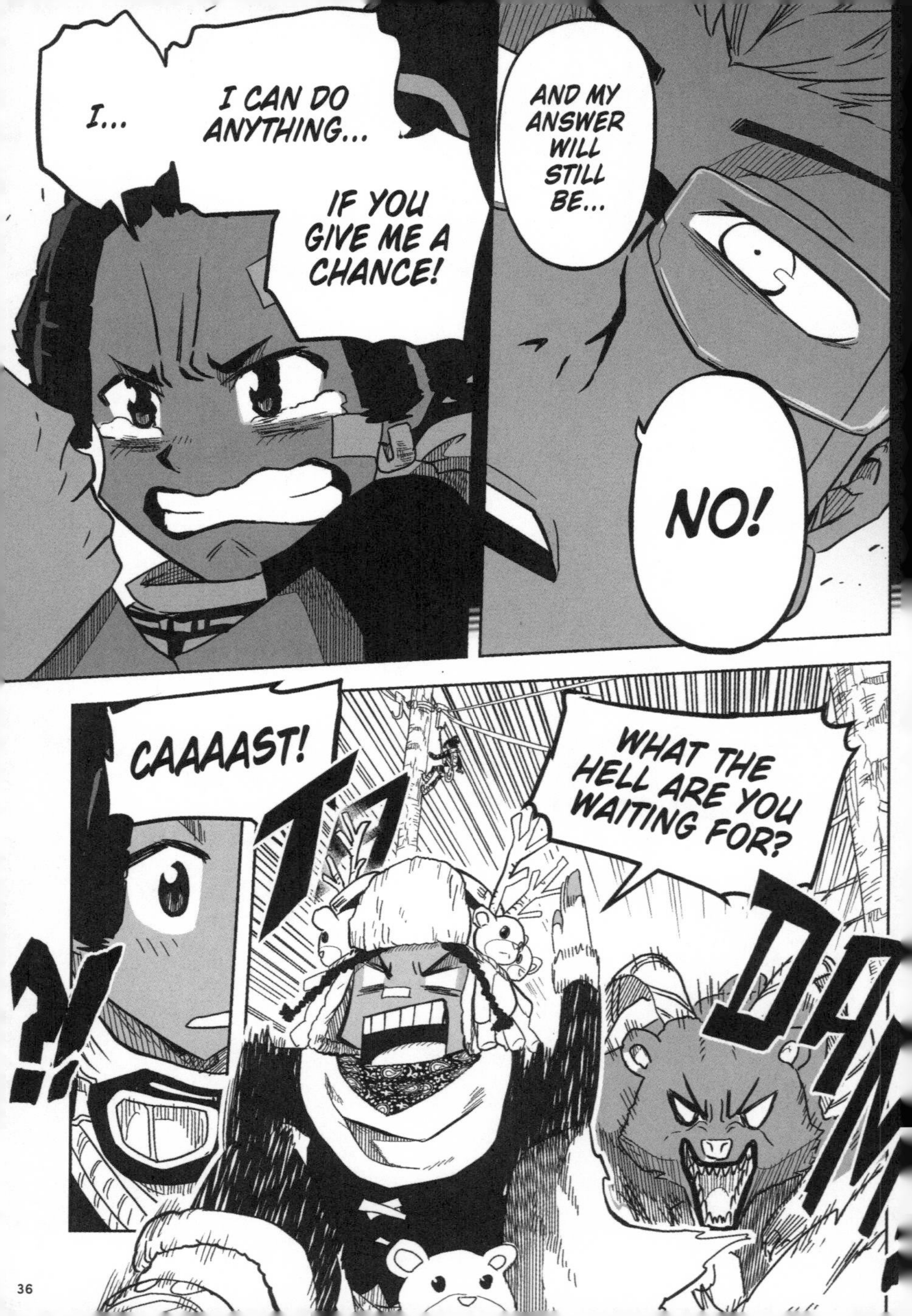
I...
I CAN DO ANYTHING...
IF YOU GIVE ME A CHANCE!
AND MY ANSWER WILL STILL BE...
NO!
CAAAAST!
?!
WHAT THE HELL ARE YOU WAITING FOR?

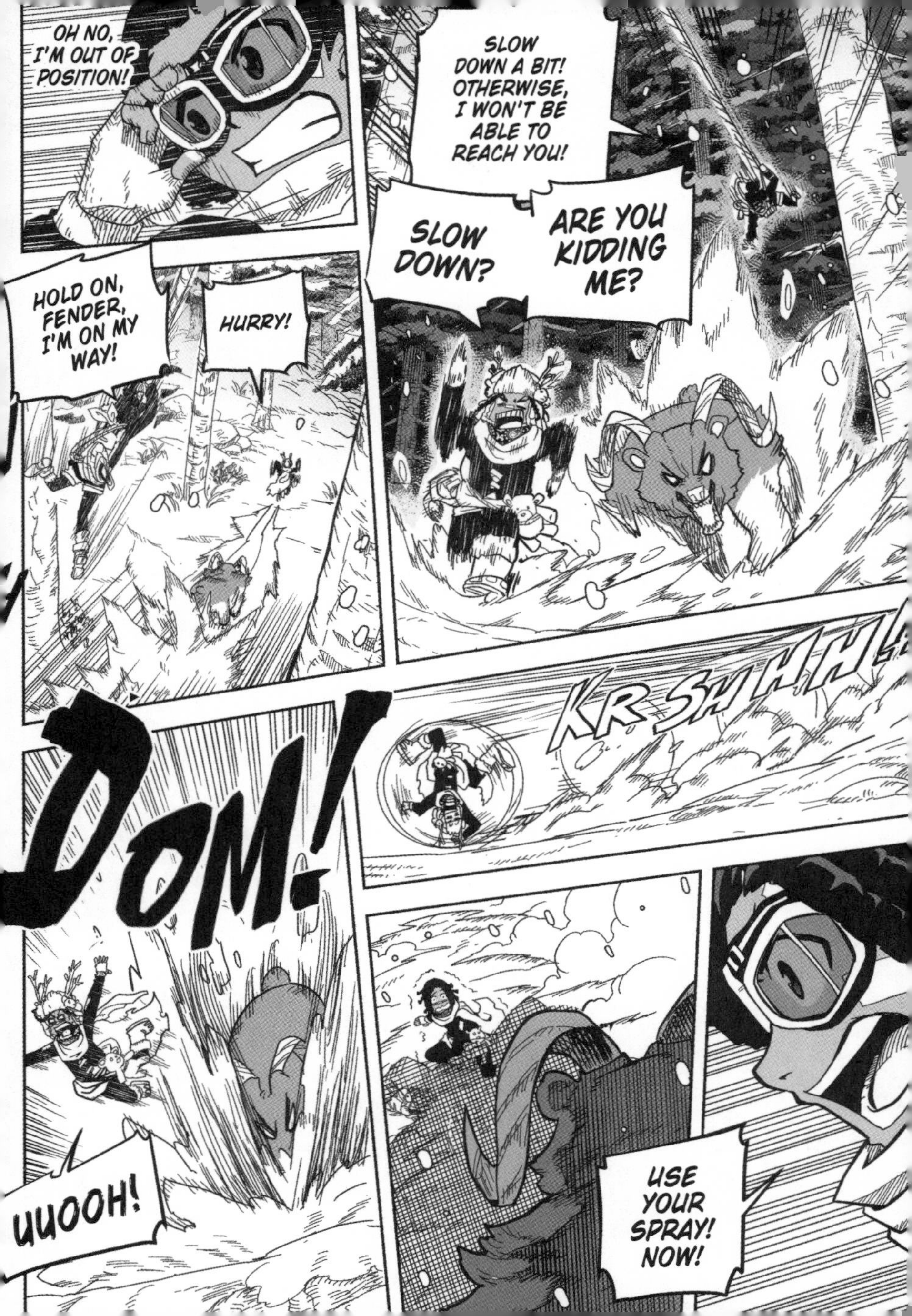
OH NO, I'M OUT OF POSITION!
SLOW DOWN A BIT! OTHERWISE, I WON'T BE ABLE TO REACH YOU!
HOLD ON, FENDER, I'M ON MY WAY!
HURRY!
SLOW DOWN?
ARE YOU KIDDING ME?
DOM!
KRSHHH
UUOOH!
USE YOUR SPRAY! NOW!

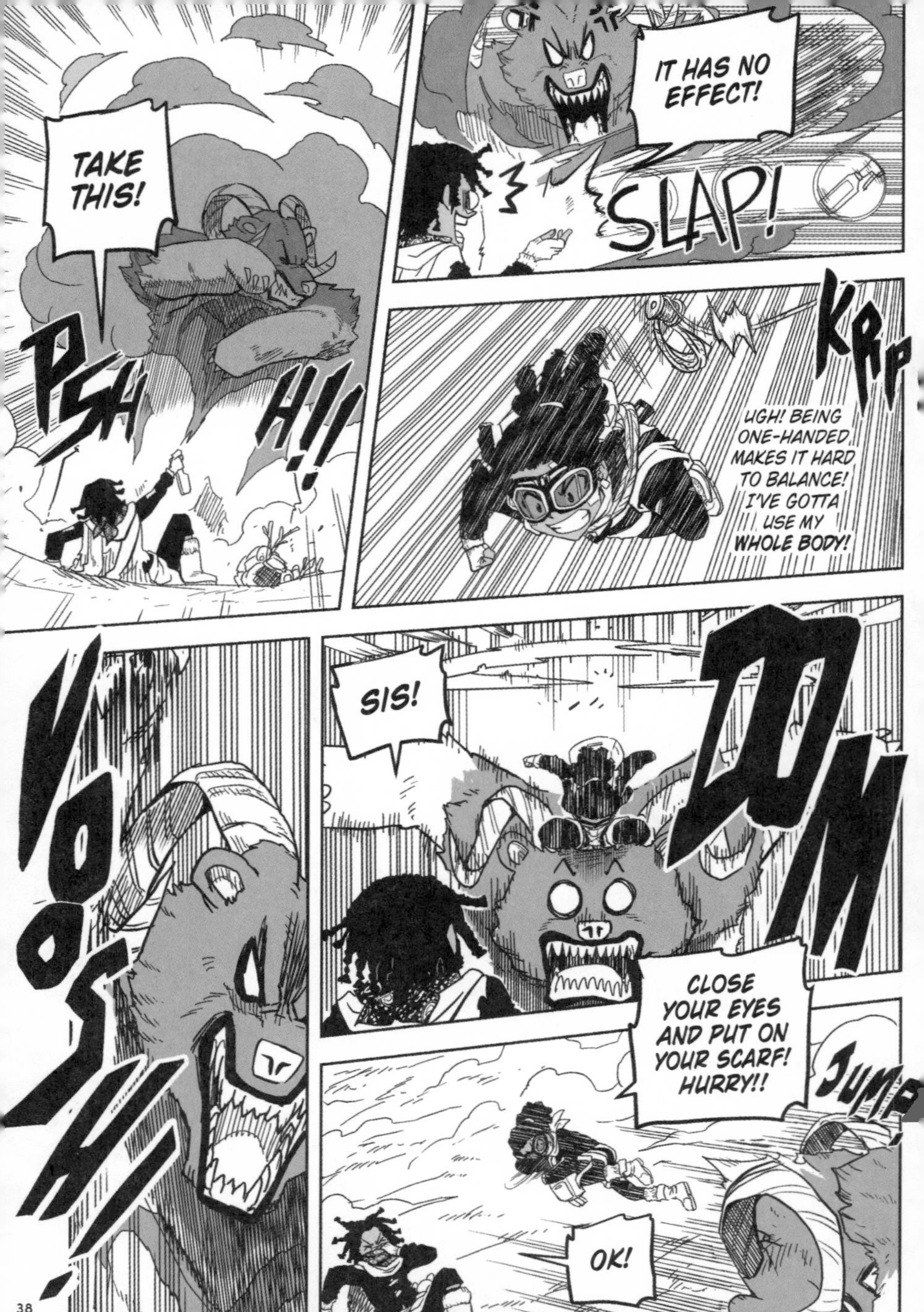
TAKE THIS!
PSHH!!
IT HAS NO EFFECT!
SLAP!
KRP
UGH! BEING ONE-HANDED MAKES IT HARD TO BALANCE! I'VE GOTTA USE MY WHOLE BODY!
VOOSH!
SIS!
DOM
CLOSE YOUR EYES AND PUT ON YOUR SCARF! HURRY!!
JUMP
OK!

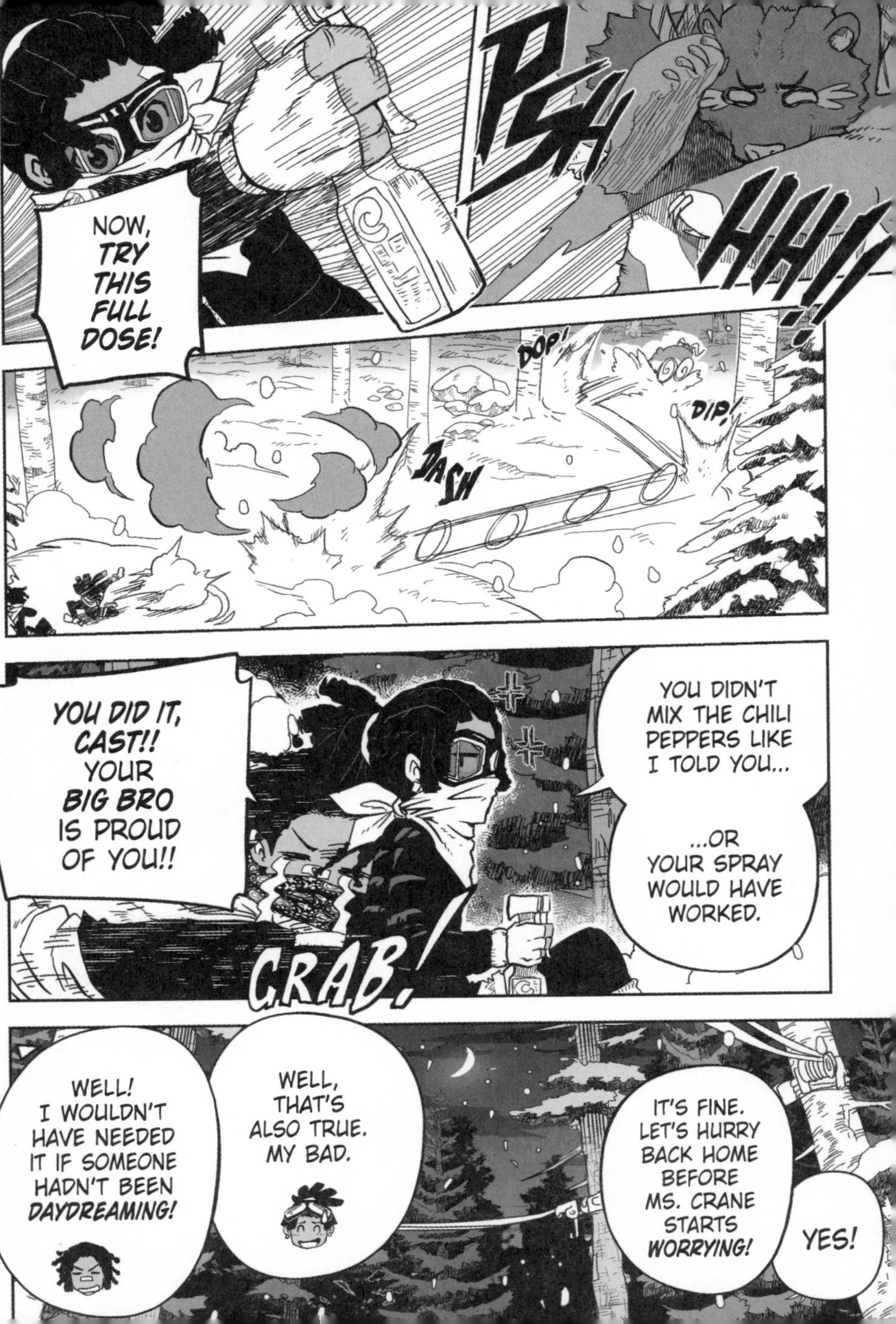

NOW, TRY THIS FULL DOSE!
PSSH
AHH!!
DOP!
DIP!
DASH
YOU DID IT, CAST!! YOUR BIG BRO IS PROUD OF YOU!!
YOU DIDN'T MIX THE CHILI PEPPERS LIKE I TOLD YOU...
...OR YOUR SPRAY WOULD HAVE WORKED.
GRAB!
WELL! I WOULDN'T HAVE NEEDED IT IF SOMEONE HADN'T BEEN DAYDREAMING!
WELL, THAT'S ALSO TRUE. MY BAD.
IT'S FINE. LET'S HURRY BACK HOME BEFORE MS. CRANE STARTS WORRYING!
YES!

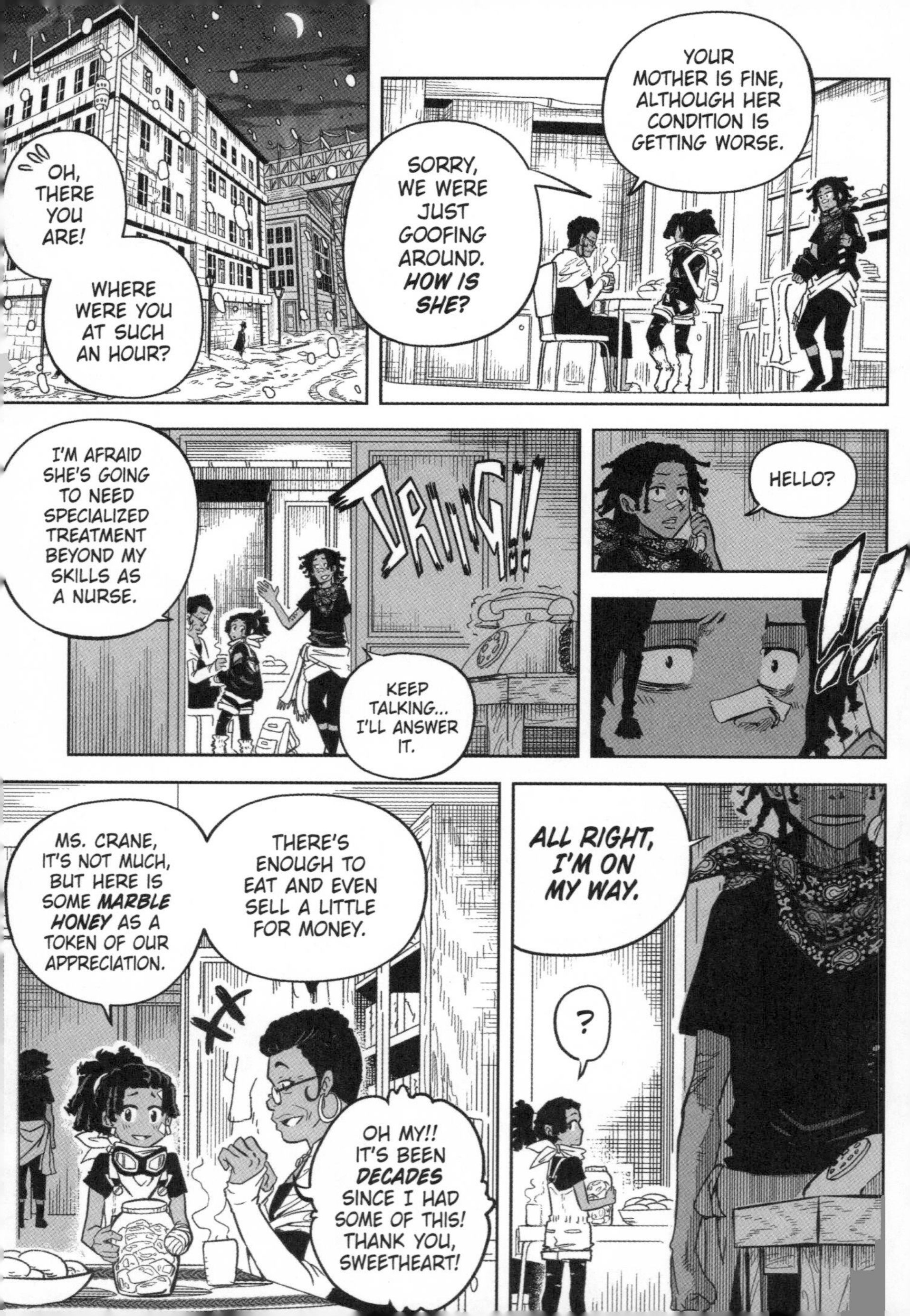
OH, THERE YOU ARE!
WHERE WERE YOU AT SUCH AN HOUR?
SORRY, WE WERE JUST GOOFING AROUND. *HOW IS SHE?*
YOUR MOTHER IS FINE, ALTHOUGH HER CONDITION IS GETTING WORSE.
I'M AFRAID SHE'S GOING TO NEED SPECIALIZED TREATMENT BEYOND MY SKILLS AS A NURSE.
DRIIIG!!
KEEP TALKING... I'LL ANSWER IT.
HELLO?
MS. CRANE, IT'S NOT MUCH, BUT HERE IS SOME *MARBLE HONEY* AS A TOKEN OF OUR APPRECIATION.
THERE'S ENOUGH TO EAT AND EVEN SELL A LITTLE FOR MONEY.
OH MY!! IT'S BEEN *DECADES* SINCE I HAD SOME OF THIS! THANK YOU, SWEETHEART!
ALL RIGHT, I'M ON MY WAY.
?

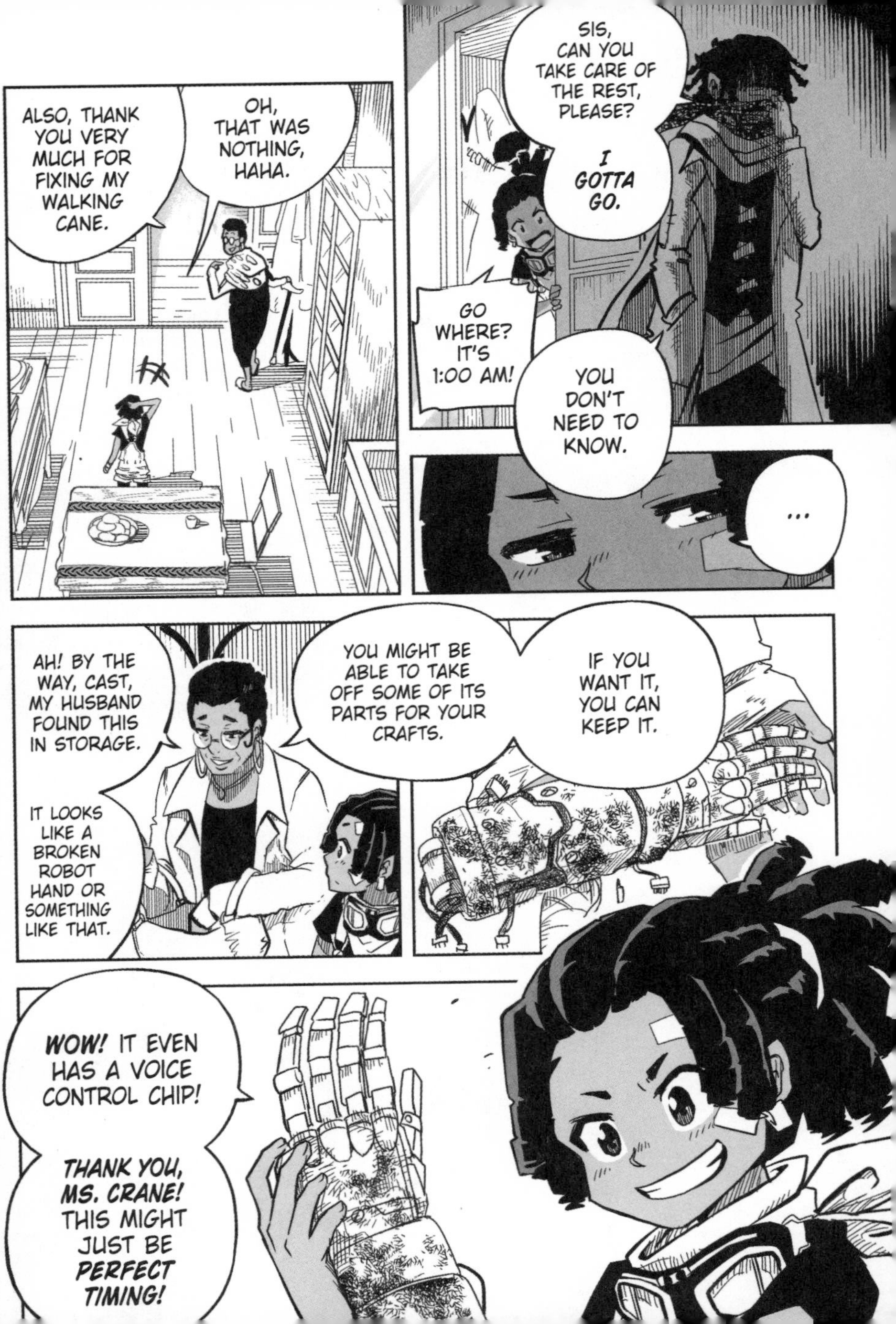
ALSO, THANK YOU VERY MUCH FOR FIXING MY WALKING CANE.
OH, THAT WAS NOTHING, HAHA.
SIS, CAN YOU TAKE CARE OF THE REST, PLEASE?
I GOTTA GO.
GO WHERE? IT'S 1:00 AM!
YOU DON'T NEED TO KNOW.
...
AH! BY THE WAY, CAST, MY HUSBAND FOUND THIS IN STORAGE.
IT LOOKS LIKE A BROKEN ROBOT HAND OR SOMETHING LIKE THAT.
YOU MIGHT BE ABLE TO TAKE OFF SOME OF ITS PARTS FOR YOUR CRAFTS.
IF YOU WANT IT, YOU CAN KEEP IT.
WOW! IT EVEN HAS A VOICE CONTROL CHIP!
THANK YOU, MS. CRANE! THIS MIGHT JUST BE PERFECT TIMING!

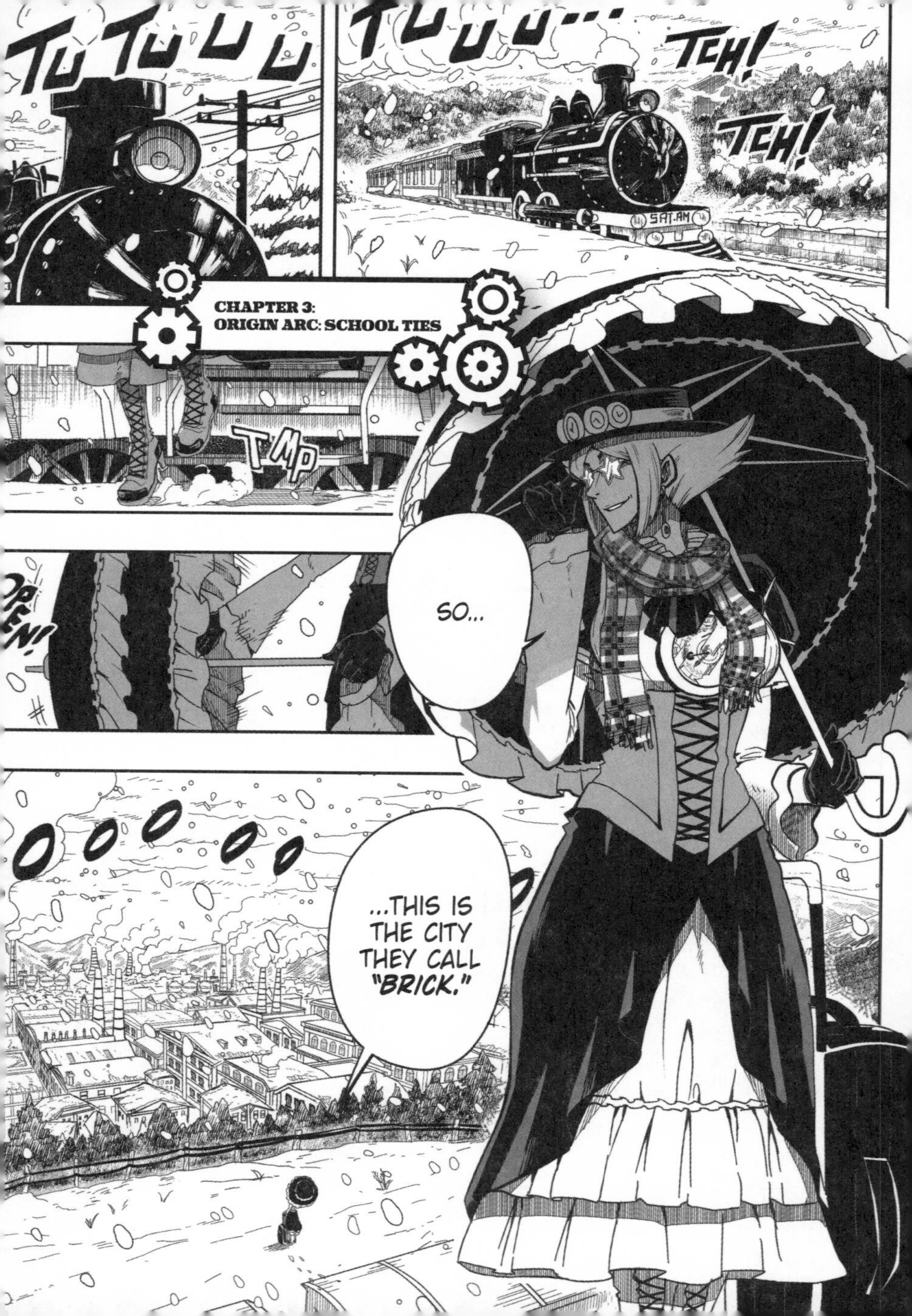
TU TU U U
TU U U...
TCH!
SAT.AM
TCH!
CHAPTER 3:
ORIGIN ARC: SCHOOL TIES
TMP
OPEN!
SO...
OOOOOO
...THIS IS THE CITY THEY CALL "BRICK."

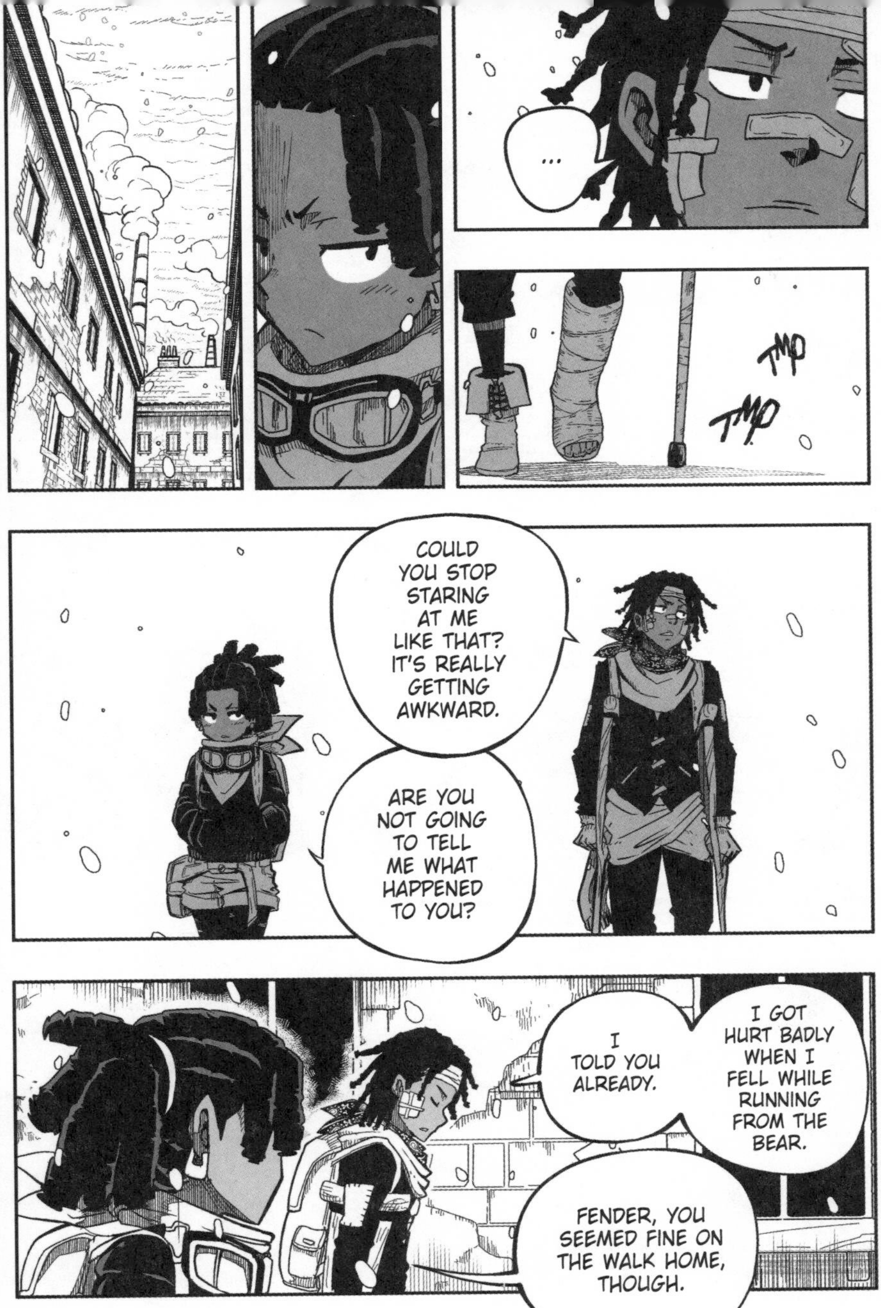
...
TMP
TMP
COULD YOU STOP STARING AT ME LIKE THAT? IT'S REALLY GETTING AWKWARD.
ARE YOU NOT GOING TO TELL ME WHAT HAPPENED TO YOU?
I TOLD YOU ALREADY.
I GOT HURT BADLY WHEN I FELL WHILE RUNNING FROM THE BEAR.
FENDER, YOU SEEMED FINE ON THE WALK HOME, THOUGH.

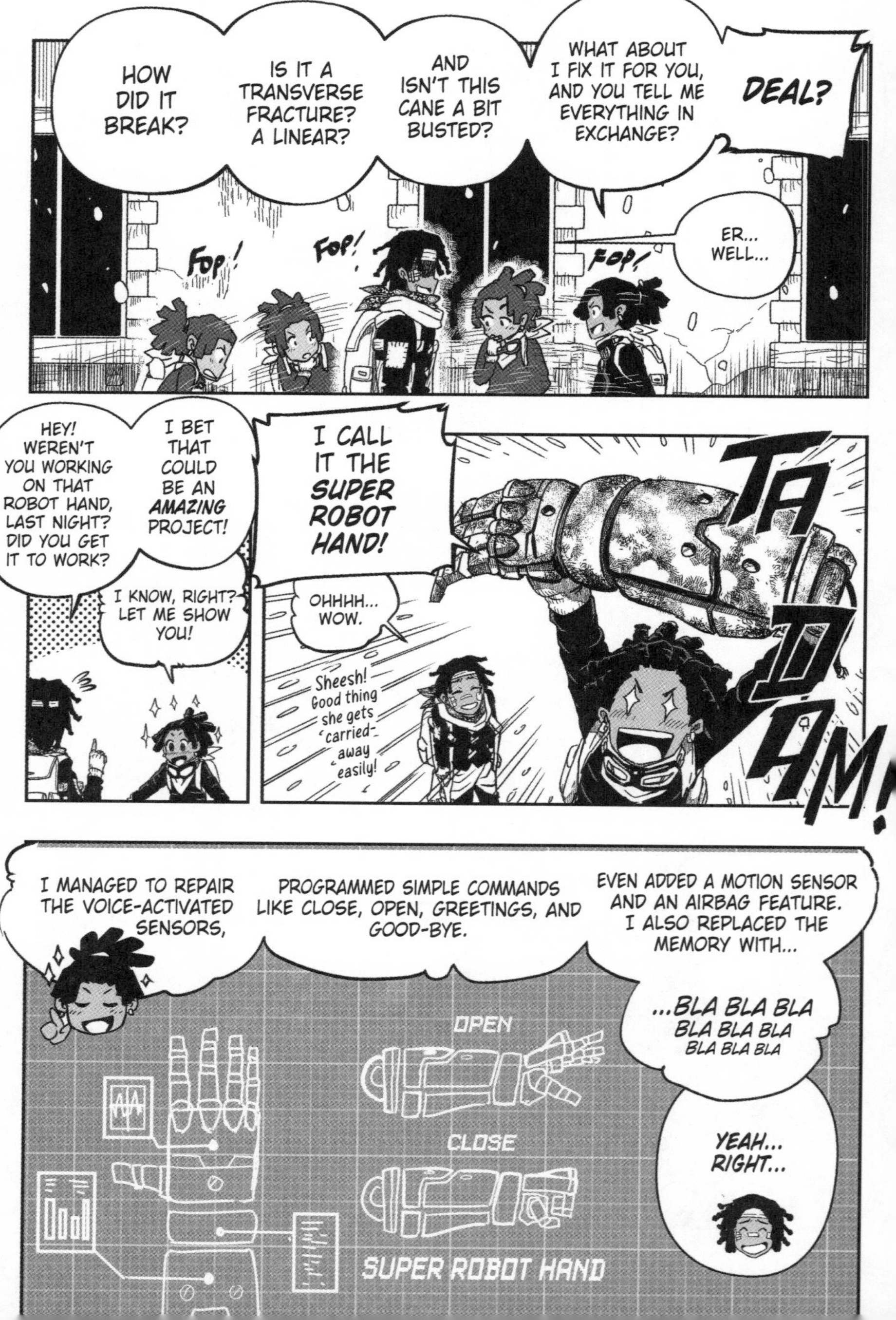
HOW DID IT BREAK?
IS IT A TRANSVERSE FRACTURE? A LINEAR?
AND ISN'T THIS CANE A BIT BUSTED?
WHAT ABOUT I FIX IT FOR YOU, AND YOU TELL ME EVERYTHING IN EXCHANGE?
DEAL?
FOP!
FOP!
FOP!
ER... WELL...
HEY! WEREN'T YOU WORKING ON THAT ROBOT HAND, LAST NIGHT? DID YOU GET IT TO WORK?
I BET THAT COULD BE AN AMAZING PROJECT!
I KNOW, RIGHT? LET ME SHOW YOU!
I CALL IT THE SUPER ROBOT HAND!
OHHHH... WOW.
Sheesh! Good thing she gets carried away easily!
TA DAM!
I MANAGED TO REPAIR THE VOICE-ACTIVATED SENSORS,
PROGRAMMED SIMPLE COMMANDS LIKE CLOSE, OPEN, GREETINGS, AND GOOD-BYE.
EVEN ADDED A MOTION SENSOR AND AN AIRBAG FEATURE. I ALSO REPLACED THE MEMORY WITH...
...BLA BLA BLA BLA BLA BLA BLA BLA BLA
OPEN
CLOSE
SUPER ROBOT HAND
YEAH... RIGHT...

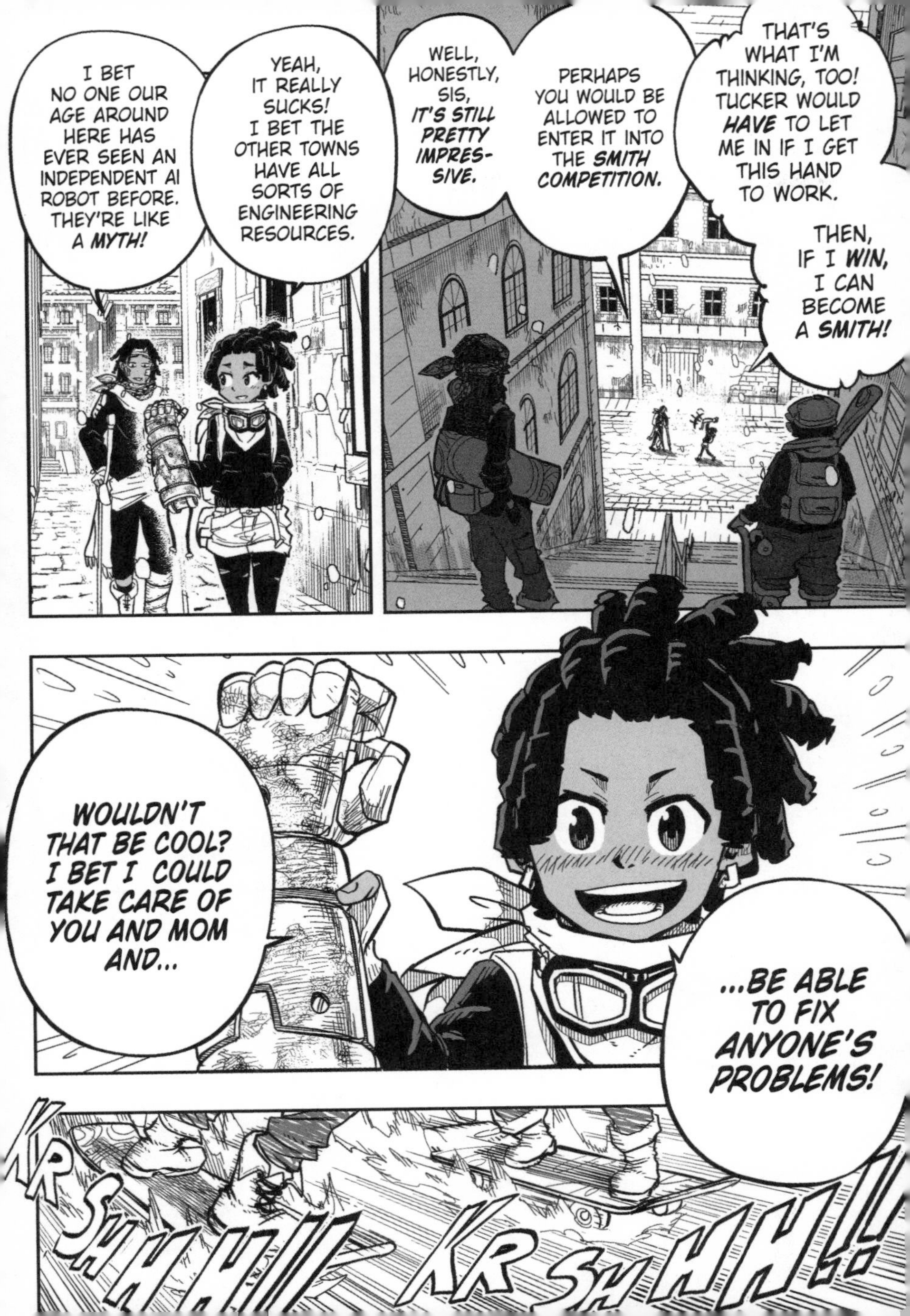
I BET NO ONE OUR AGE AROUND HERE HAS EVER SEEN AN INDEPENDENT AI ROBOT BEFORE. THEY'RE LIKE A *MYTH!*
YEAH, IT REALLY SUCKS! I BET THE OTHER TOWNS HAVE ALL SORTS OF ENGINEERING RESOURCES.
WELL, HONESTLY, SIS, *IT'S STILL PRETTY IMPRES-SIVE.*
PERHAPS YOU WOULD BE ALLOWED TO ENTER IT INTO THE ***SMITH COMPETITION.***
THAT'S WHAT I'M THINKING, TOO! TUCKER WOULD ***HAVE*** TO LET ME IN IF I GET THIS HAND TO WORK.
THEN, IF I ***WIN,*** I CAN BECOME A ***SMITH!***
WOULDN'T THAT BE COOL? I BET I COULD TAKE CARE OF YOU AND MOM AND...
...BE ABLE TO FIX ANYONE'S PROBLEMS!
KRSHHH!!
KRSHHH!!

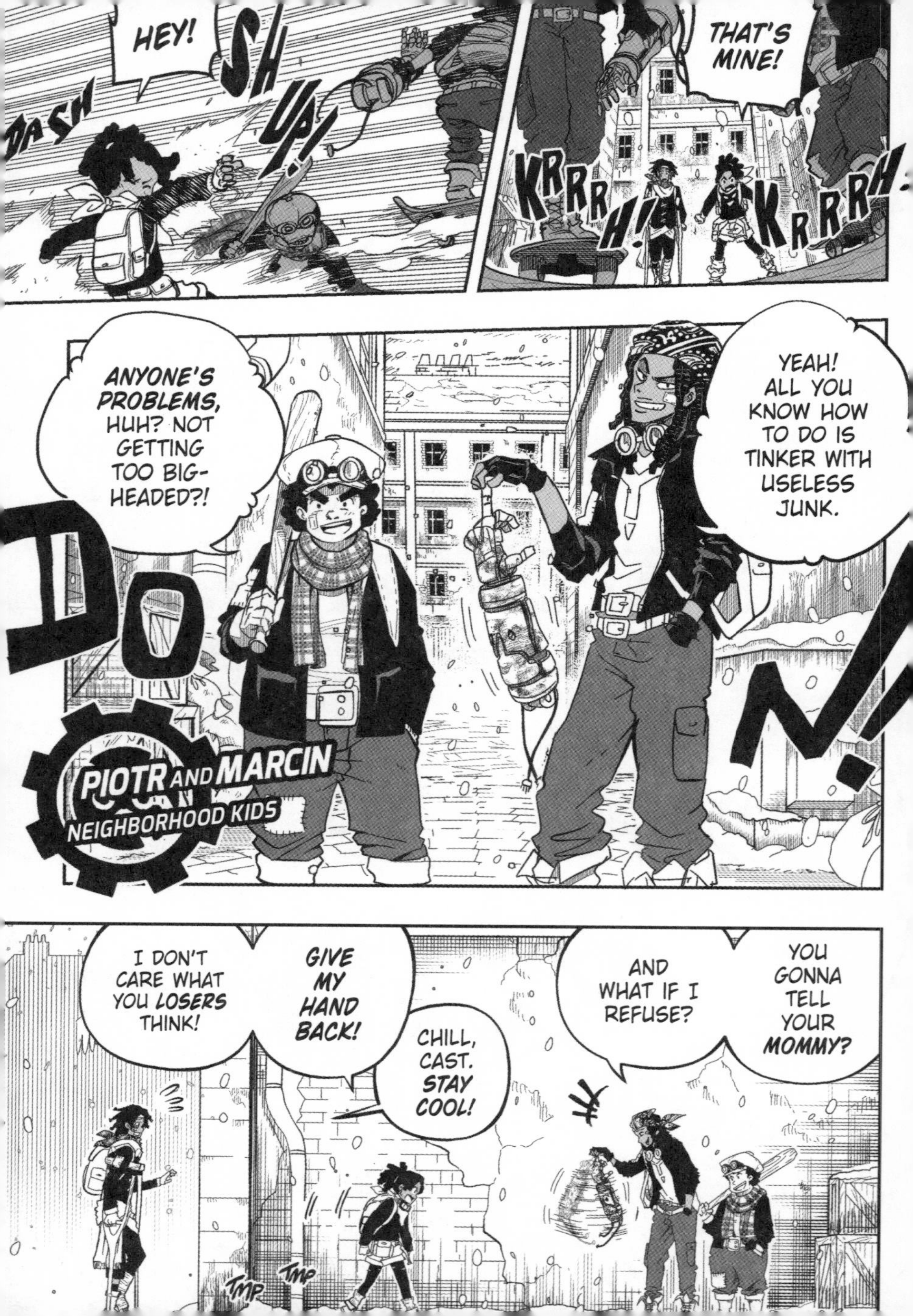
HEY!
DASH
SHUP!
THAT'S MINE!
KRRRH!
KRRRRH
ANYONE'S PROBLEMS, HUH? NOT GETTING TOO BIG-HEADED?!
YEAH! ALL YOU KNOW HOW TO DO IS TINKER WITH USELESS JUNK.
DOM!!
PIOTR AND MARCIN
NEIGHBORHOOD KIDS
I DON'T CARE WHAT YOU LOSERS THINK!
GIVE MY HAND BACK!
CHILL, CAST. STAY COOL!
AND WHAT IF I REFUSE?
YOU GONNA TELL YOUR MOMMY?
TMP
TMP

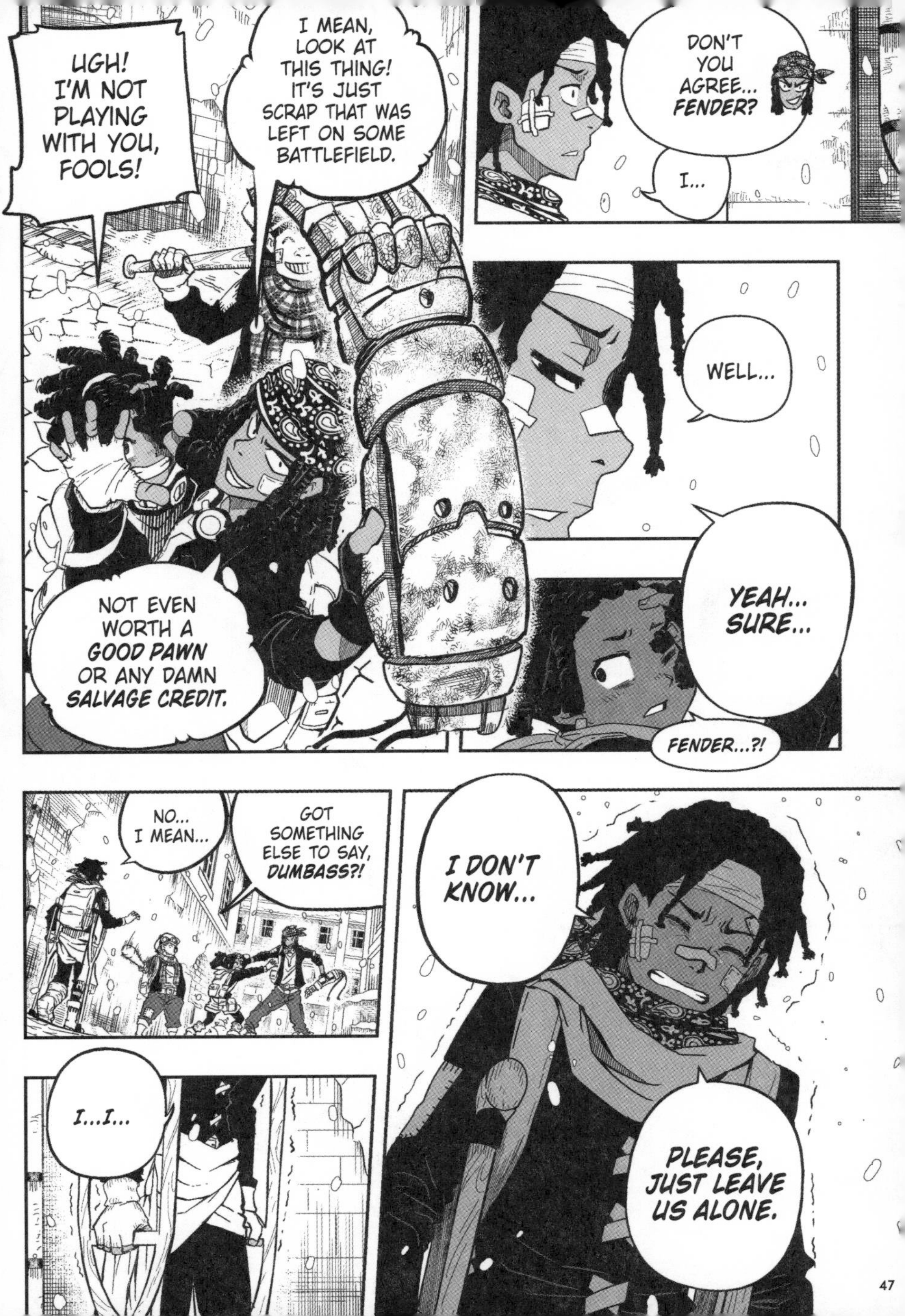
UGH! I'M NOT PLAYING WITH YOU, FOOLS!
I MEAN, LOOK AT THIS THING! IT'S JUST SCRAP THAT WAS LEFT ON SOME BATTLEFIELD.
NOT EVEN WORTH A GOOD PAWN OR ANY DAMN SALVAGE CREDIT.
DON'T YOU AGREE... FENDER?
I...
WELL...
YEAH... SURE...
FENDER...?!
NO... I MEAN...
GOT SOMETHING ELSE TO SAY, DUMBASS?!
I...I...
I DON'T KNOW...
PLEASE, JUST LEAVE US ALONE.

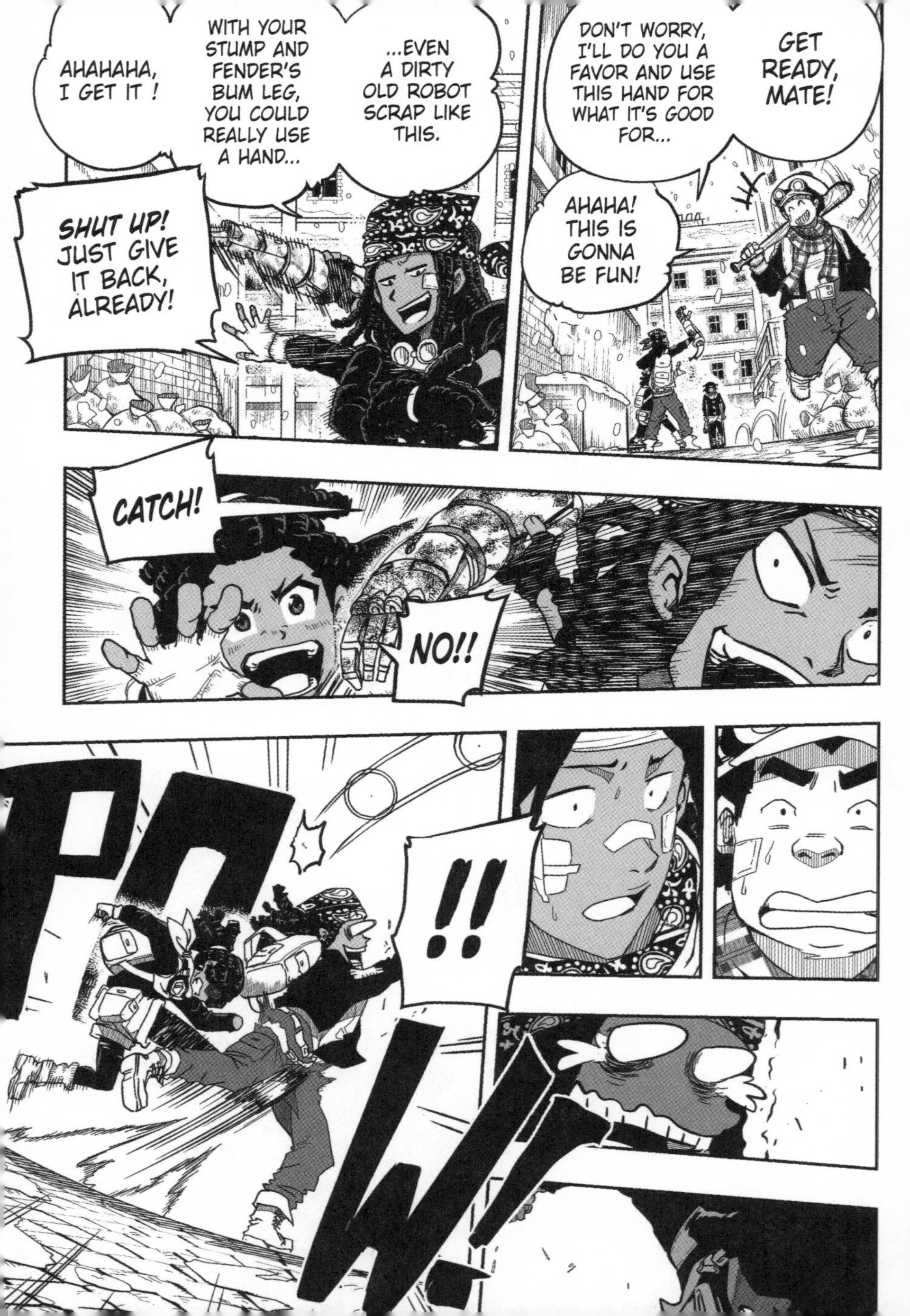
AHAHAHA, I GET IT !
WITH YOUR STUMP AND FENDER'S BUM LEG, YOU COULD REALLY USE A HAND...
...EVEN A DIRTY OLD ROBOT SCRAP LIKE THIS.
SHUT UP! JUST GIVE IT BACK, ALREADY!
DON'T WORRY, I'LL DO YOU A FAVOR AND USE THIS HAND FOR WHAT IT'S GOOD FOR...
GET READY, MATE!
AHAHA! THIS IS GONNA BE FUN!
CATCH!
NO!!
!!

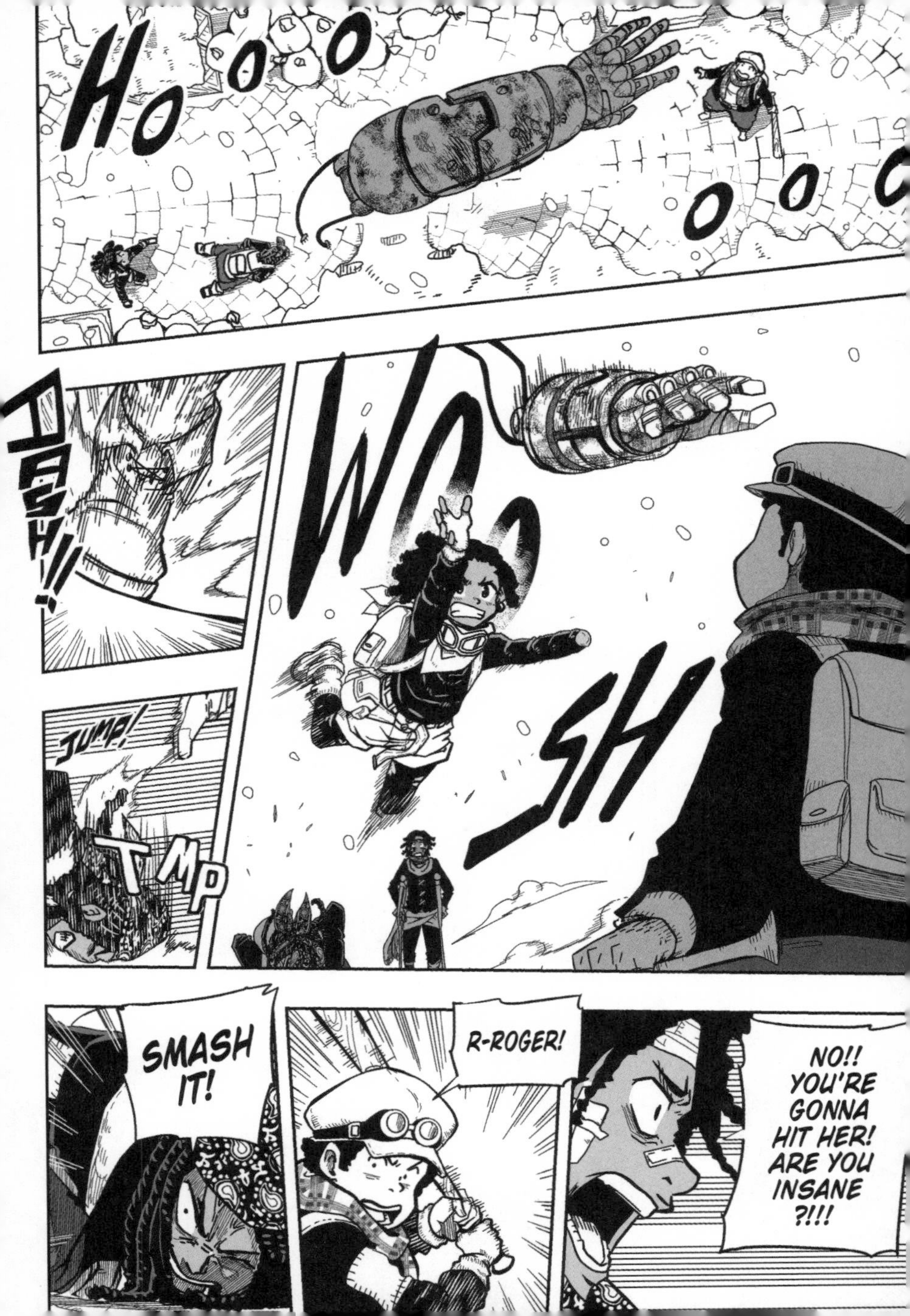
HOOOOOOOO
BASH!!
JUMP!
TMP
WOOSH
SMASH IT!
R-ROGER!
NO!! YOU'RE GONNA HIT HER! ARE YOU INSANE ?!!!

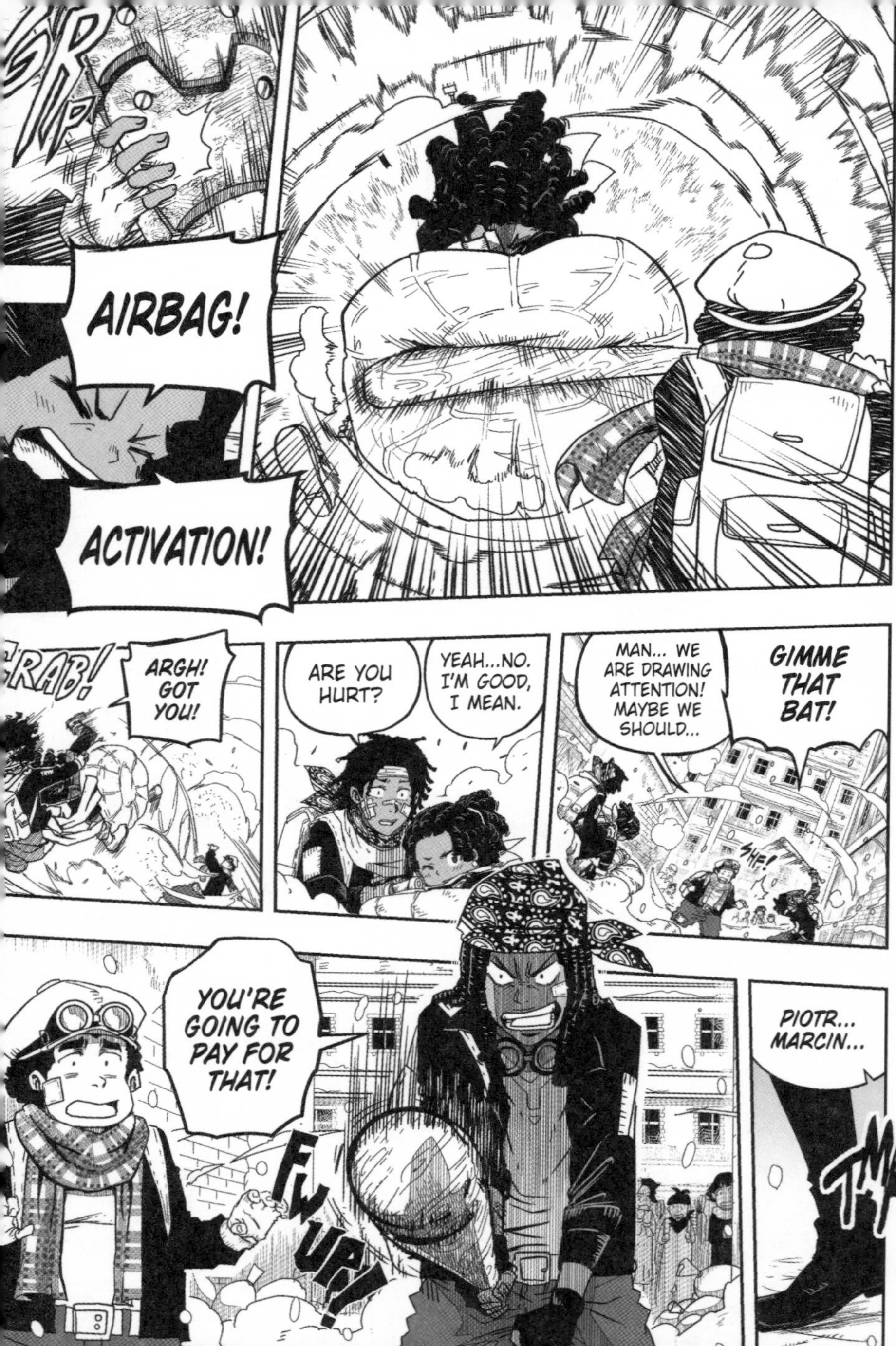
SRIP
AIRBAG!
ACTIVATION!
GRAB!
ARGH! GOT YOU!
ARE YOU HURT?
YEAH...NO. I'M GOOD, I MEAN.
MAN... WE ARE DRAWING ATTENTION! MAYBE WE SHOULD...
GIMME THAT BAT!
SHF!
YOU'RE GOING TO PAY FOR THAT!
FWUP!
PIOTR... MARCIN...
TMP

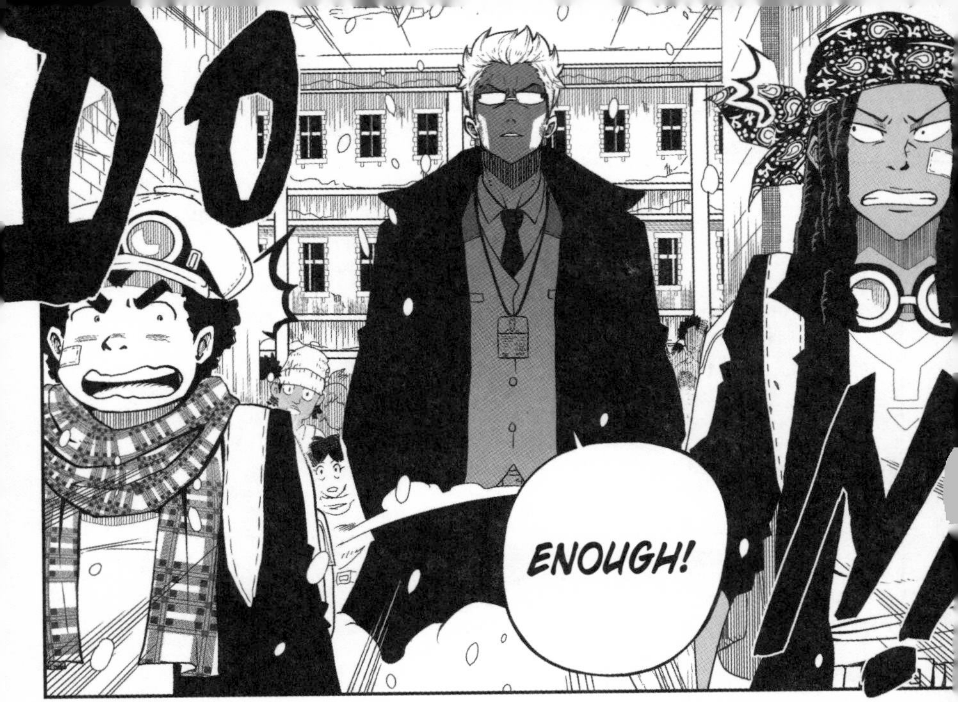
ENOUGH!

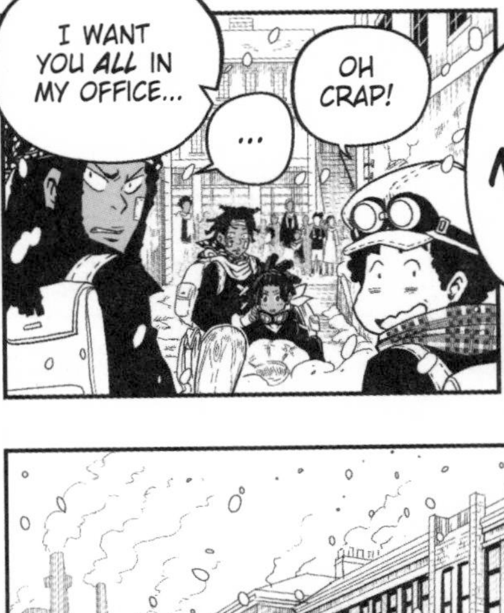
I WANT YOU ALL IN MY OFFICE...
...
OH CRAP!

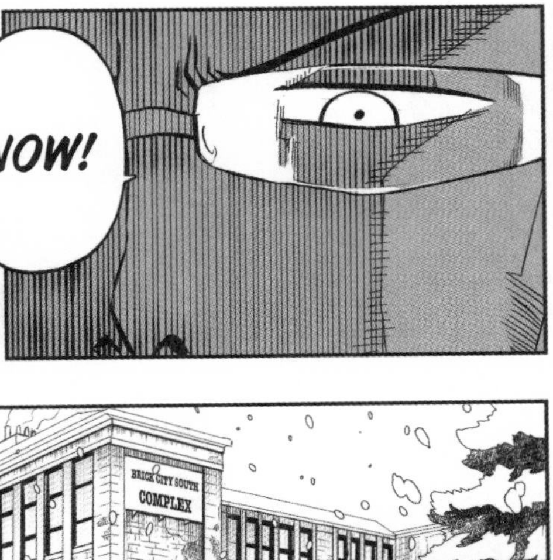
NOW!

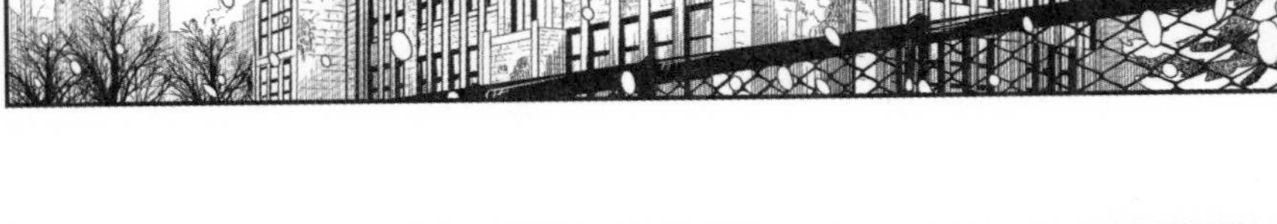
BRICK CITY SOUTH
COMPLEX

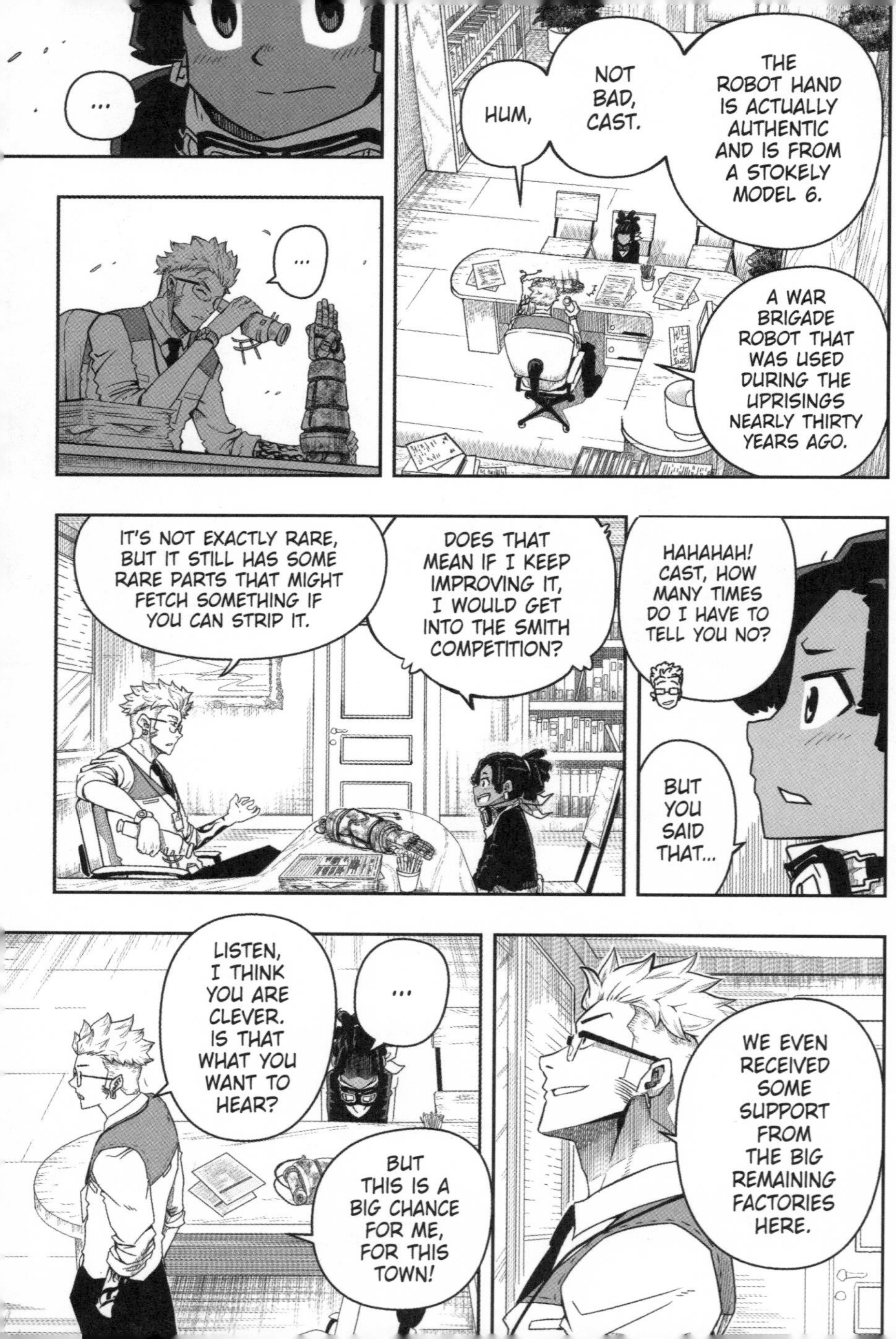
...
...
HUM,
NOT BAD, CAST.
THE ROBOT HAND IS ACTUALLY AUTHENTIC AND IS FROM A STOKELY MODEL 6.
A WAR BRIGADE ROBOT THAT WAS USED DURING THE UPRISINGS NEARLY THIRTY YEARS AGO.
IT'S NOT EXACTLY RARE, BUT IT STILL HAS SOME RARE PARTS THAT MIGHT FETCH SOMETHING IF YOU CAN STRIP IT.
DOES THAT MEAN IF I KEEP IMPROVING IT, I WOULD GET INTO THE SMITH COMPETITION?
HAHAHAH! CAST, HOW MANY TIMES DO I HAVE TO TELL YOU NO?
BUT YOU SAID THAT...
LISTEN, I THINK YOU ARE CLEVER. IS THAT WHAT YOU WANT TO HEAR?
...
BUT THIS IS A BIG CHANCE FOR ME, FOR THIS TOWN!
WE EVEN RECEIVED SOME SUPPORT FROM THE BIG REMAINING FACTORIES HERE.

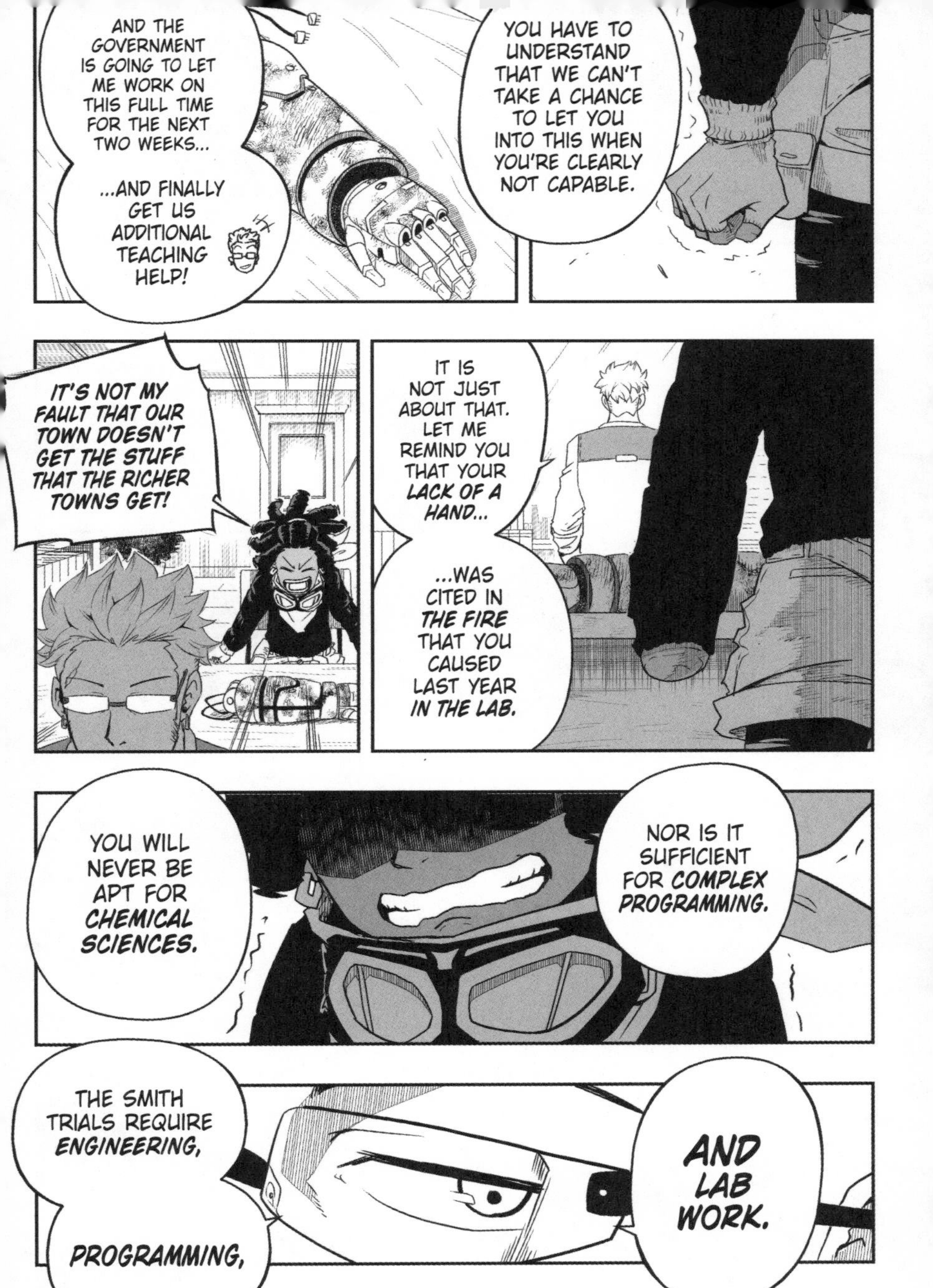
AND THE GOVERNMENT IS GOING TO LET ME WORK ON THIS FULL TIME FOR THE NEXT TWO WEEKS...
...AND FINALLY GET US ADDITIONAL TEACHING HELP!
YOU HAVE TO UNDERSTAND THAT WE CAN'T TAKE A CHANCE TO LET YOU INTO THIS WHEN YOU'RE CLEARLY NOT CAPABLE.
IT'S NOT MY FAULT THAT OUR TOWN DOESN'T GET THE STUFF THAT THE RICHER TOWNS GET!
IT IS NOT JUST ABOUT THAT. LET ME REMIND YOU THAT YOUR LACK OF A HAND...
...WAS CITED IN THE FIRE THAT YOU CAUSED LAST YEAR IN THE LAB.
YOU WILL NEVER BE APT FOR CHEMICAL SCIENCES.
NOR IS IT SUFFICIENT FOR COMPLEX PROGRAMMING.
THE SMITH TRIALS REQUIRE ENGINEERING,
PROGRAMMING,
AND LAB WORK.

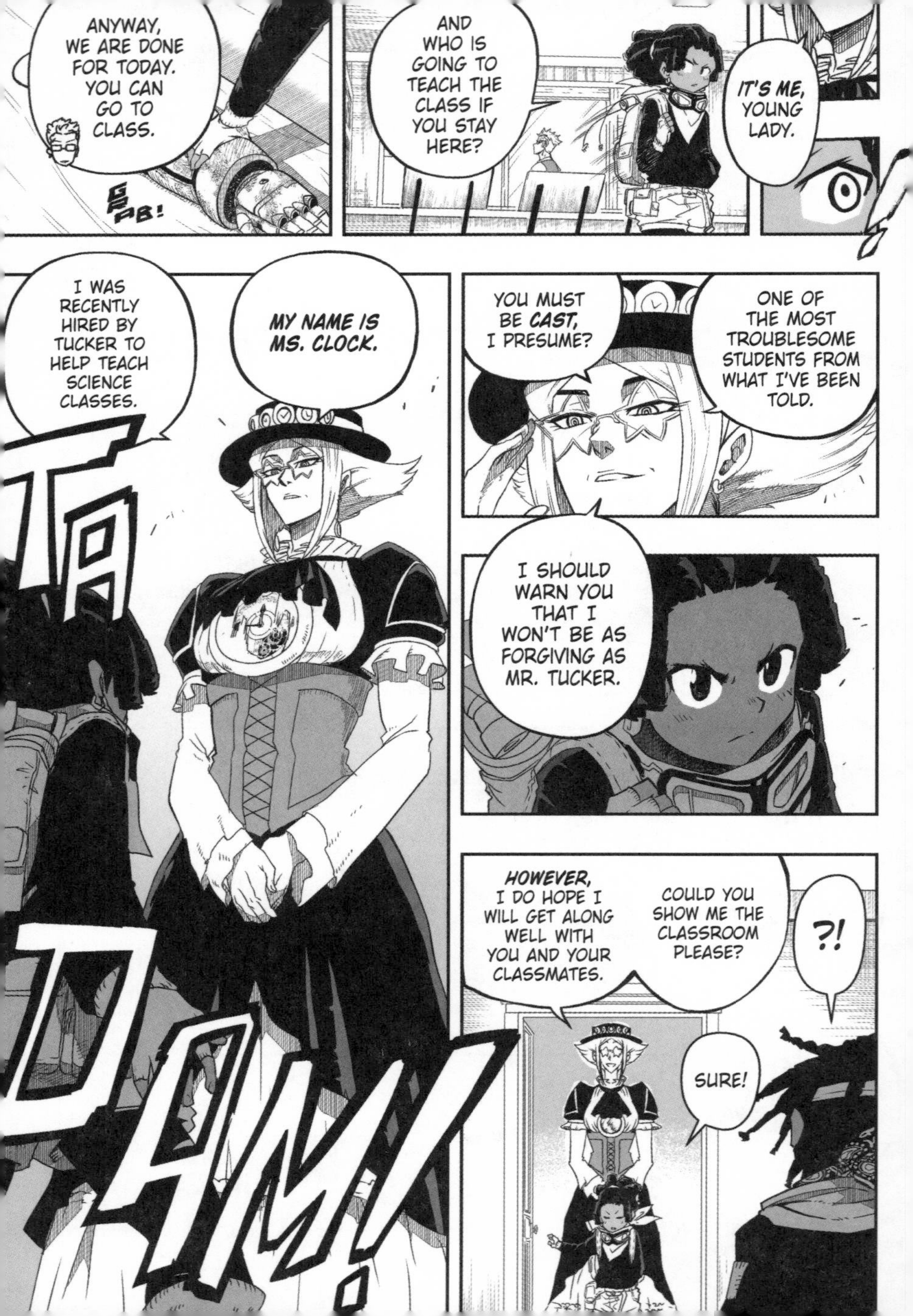
ANYWAY, WE ARE DONE FOR TODAY. YOU CAN GO TO CLASS.
GRPB!
AND WHO IS GOING TO TEACH THE CLASS IF YOU STAY HERE?
IT'S ME, YOUNG LADY.
I WAS RECENTLY HIRED BY TUCKER TO HELP TEACH SCIENCE CLASSES.
MY NAME IS MS. CLOCK.
TADAM!
YOU MUST BE CAST, I PRESUME?
ONE OF THE MOST TROUBLESOME STUDENTS FROM WHAT I'VE BEEN TOLD.
I SHOULD WARN YOU THAT I WON'T BE AS FORGIVING AS MR. TUCKER.
HOWEVER, I DO HOPE I WILL GET ALONG WELL WITH YOU AND YOUR CLASSMATES.
COULD YOU SHOW ME THE CLASSROOM PLEASE?
?!
SURE!

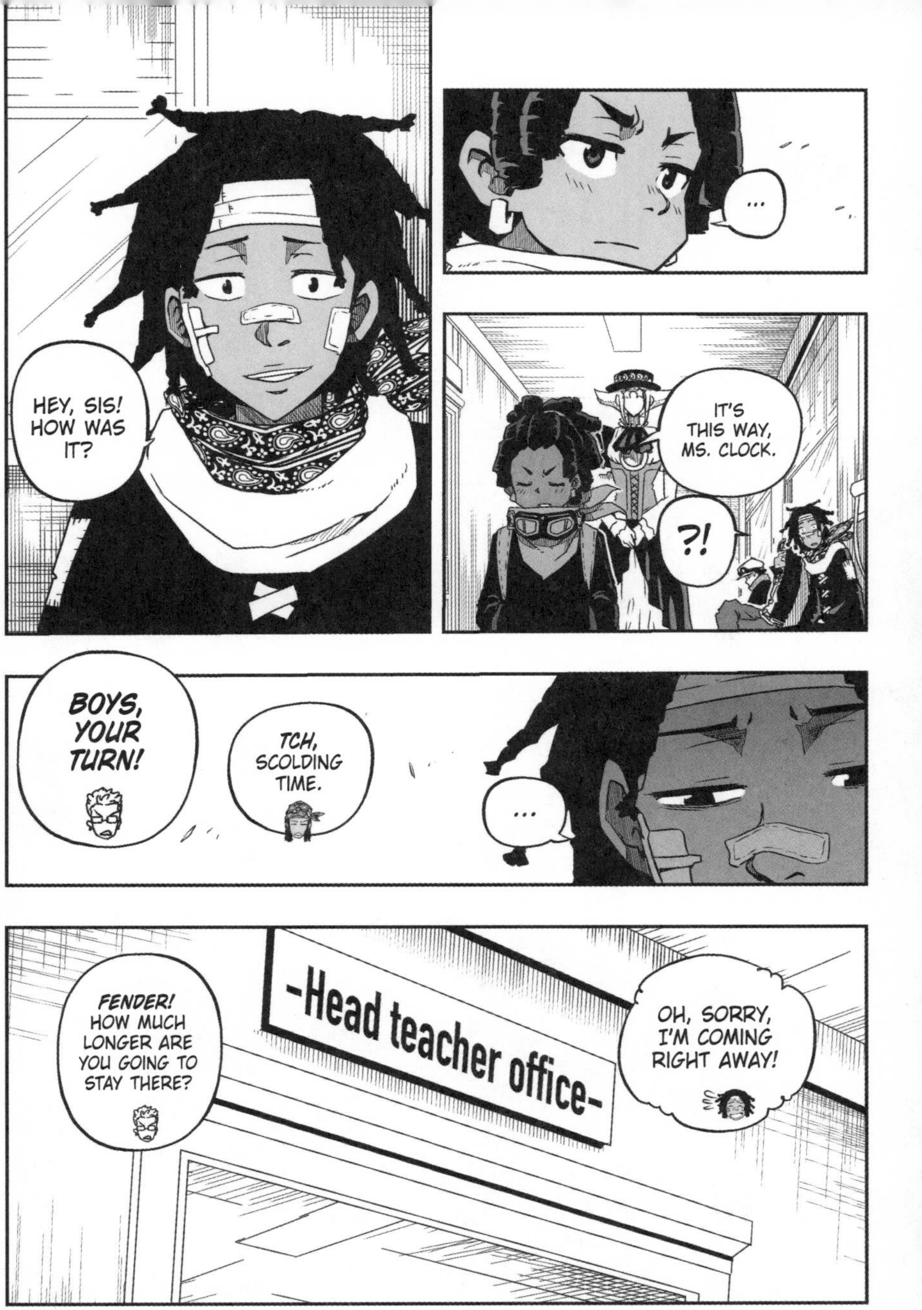
HEY, SIS! HOW WAS IT?
...
IT'S THIS WAY, MS. CLOCK.
?!
BOYS, YOUR TURN!
TCH, SCOLDING TIME.
...
FENDER! HOW MUCH LONGER ARE YOU GOING TO STAY THERE?
-Head teacher office-
OH, SORRY, I'M COMING RIGHT AWAY!

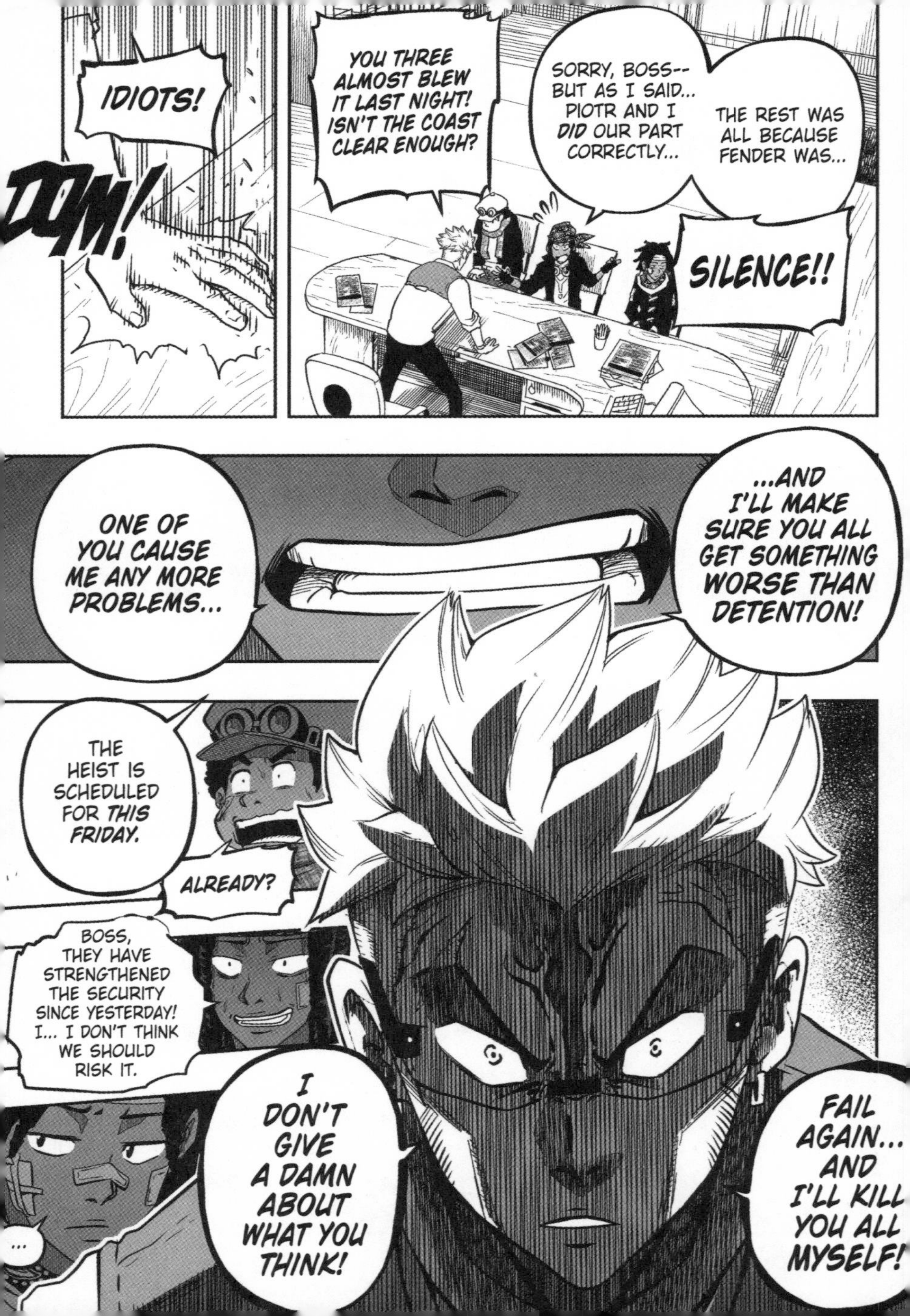
IDIOTS!
DOM!
YOU THREE ALMOST BLEW IT LAST NIGHT! ISN'T THE COAST CLEAR ENOUGH?
SORRY, BOSS-- BUT AS I SAID... PIOTR AND I DID OUR PART CORRECTLY...
THE REST WAS ALL BECAUSE FENDER WAS...
SILENCE!!
ONE OF YOU CAUSE ME ANY MORE PROBLEMS...
...AND I'LL MAKE SURE YOU ALL GET SOMETHING WORSE THAN DETENTION!
THE HEIST IS SCHEDULED FOR THIS FRIDAY.
ALREADY?
BOSS, THEY HAVE STRENGTHENED THE SECURITY SINCE YESTERDAY! I... I DON'T THINK WE SHOULD RISK IT.
...
I DON'T GIVE A DAMN ABOUT WHAT YOU THINK!
FAIL AGAIN... AND I'LL KILL YOU ALL MYSELF!

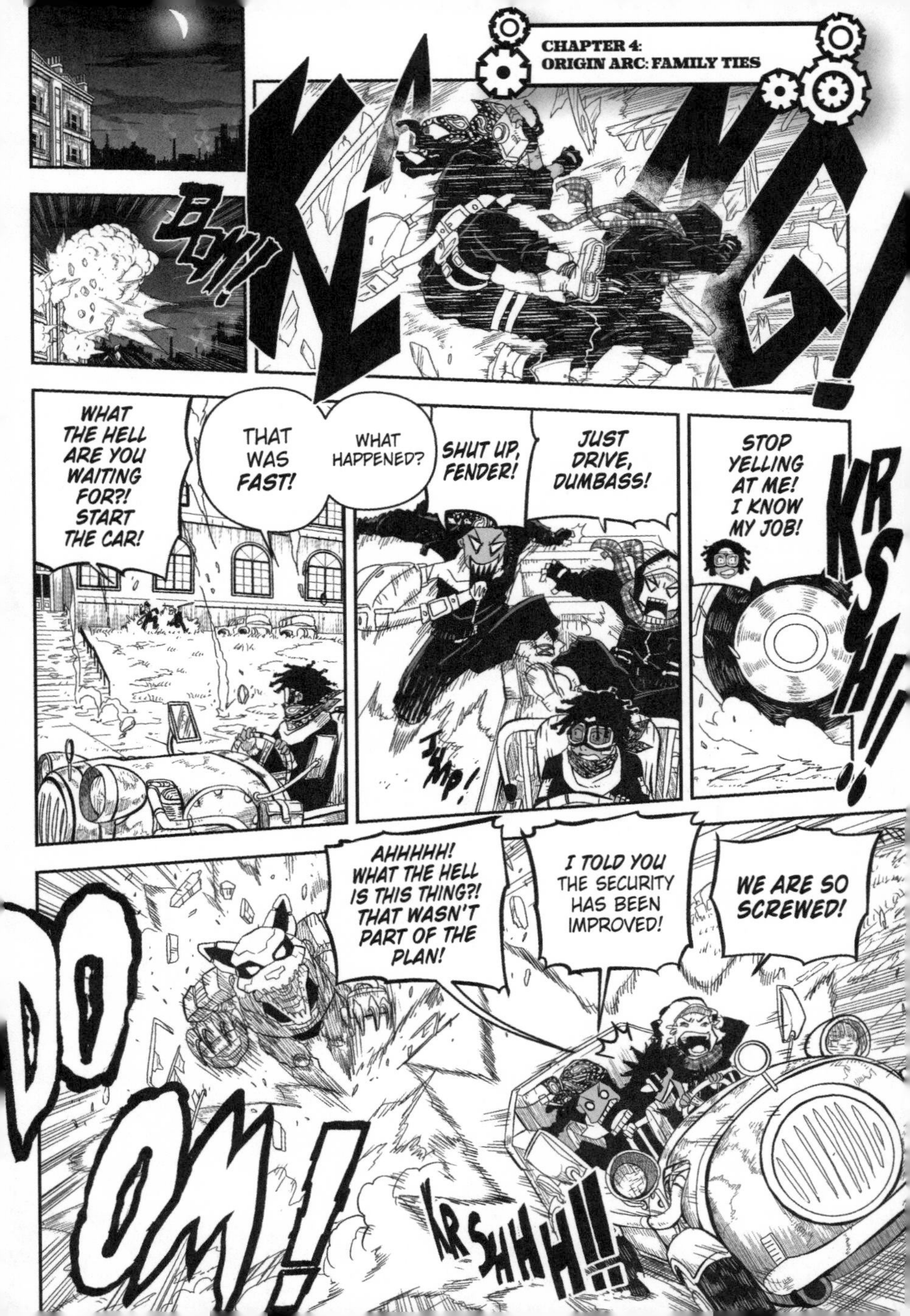
CHAPTER 4:
ORIGIN ARC: FAMILY TIES
BOOM!!
KLANG!
WHAT THE HELL ARE YOU WAITING FOR?! START THE CAR!
THAT WAS FAST!
WHAT HAPPENED?
SHUT UP, FENDER!
JUST DRIVE, DUMBASS!
JUMP!
STOP YELLING AT ME! I KNOW MY JOB!
KRSH!!!
DOOM!
AHHHHH! WHAT THE HELL IS THIS THING?! THAT WASN'T PART OF THE PLAN!
I TOLD YOU THE SECURITY HAS BEEN IMPROVED!
WE ARE SO SCREWED!
KRSHHHH!!!

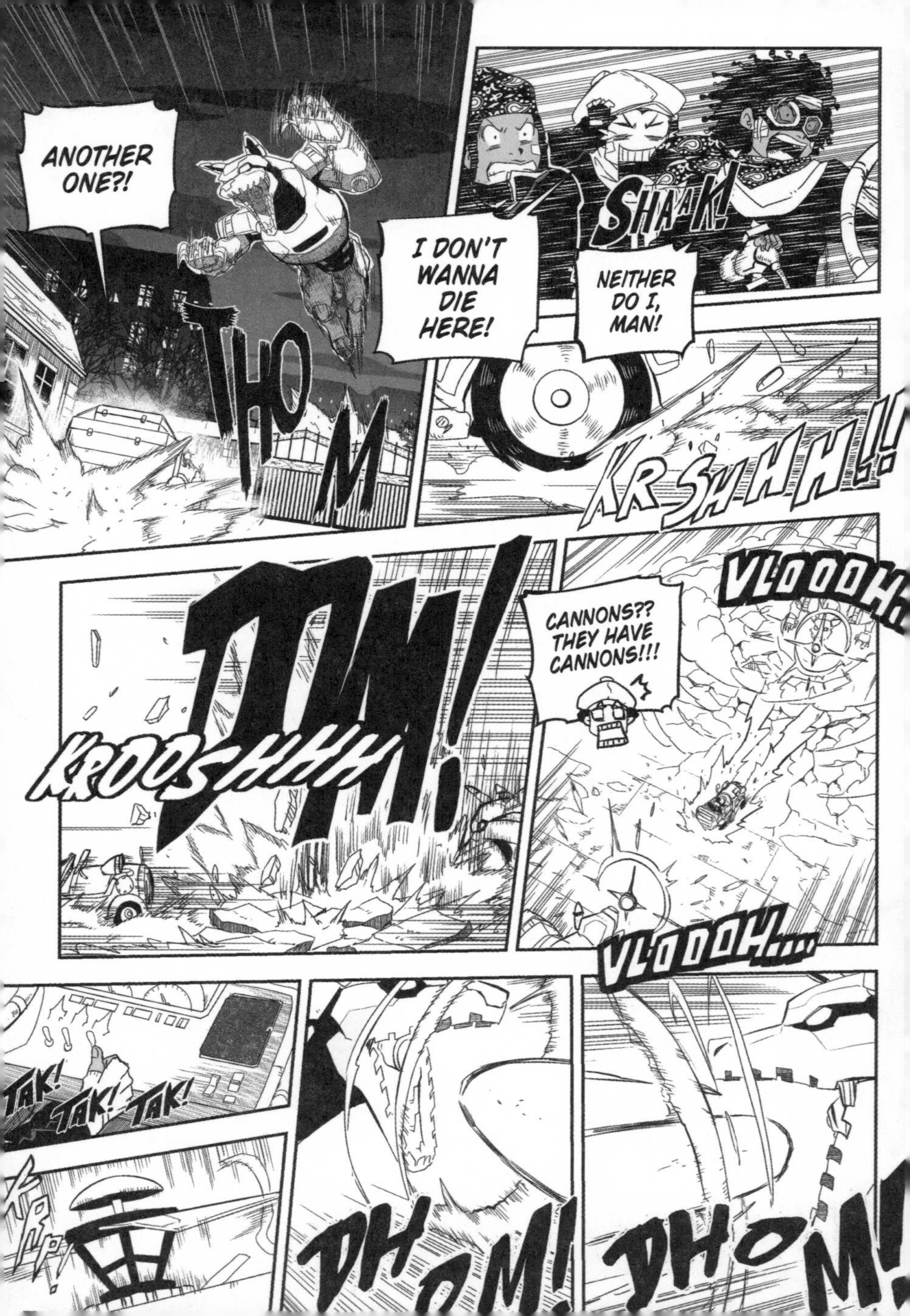
ANOTHER ONE?!
THOOM
SHAAK!
I DON'T WANNA DIE HERE!
NEITHER DO I, MAN!
KRSHHHH!!
DOM!
KROOSHHHH
VLOOOH...
CANNONS?? THEY HAVE CANNONS!!!
VLOOOH....
TAK! TAK! TAK!
KRP!
DHOM!
DHOM!

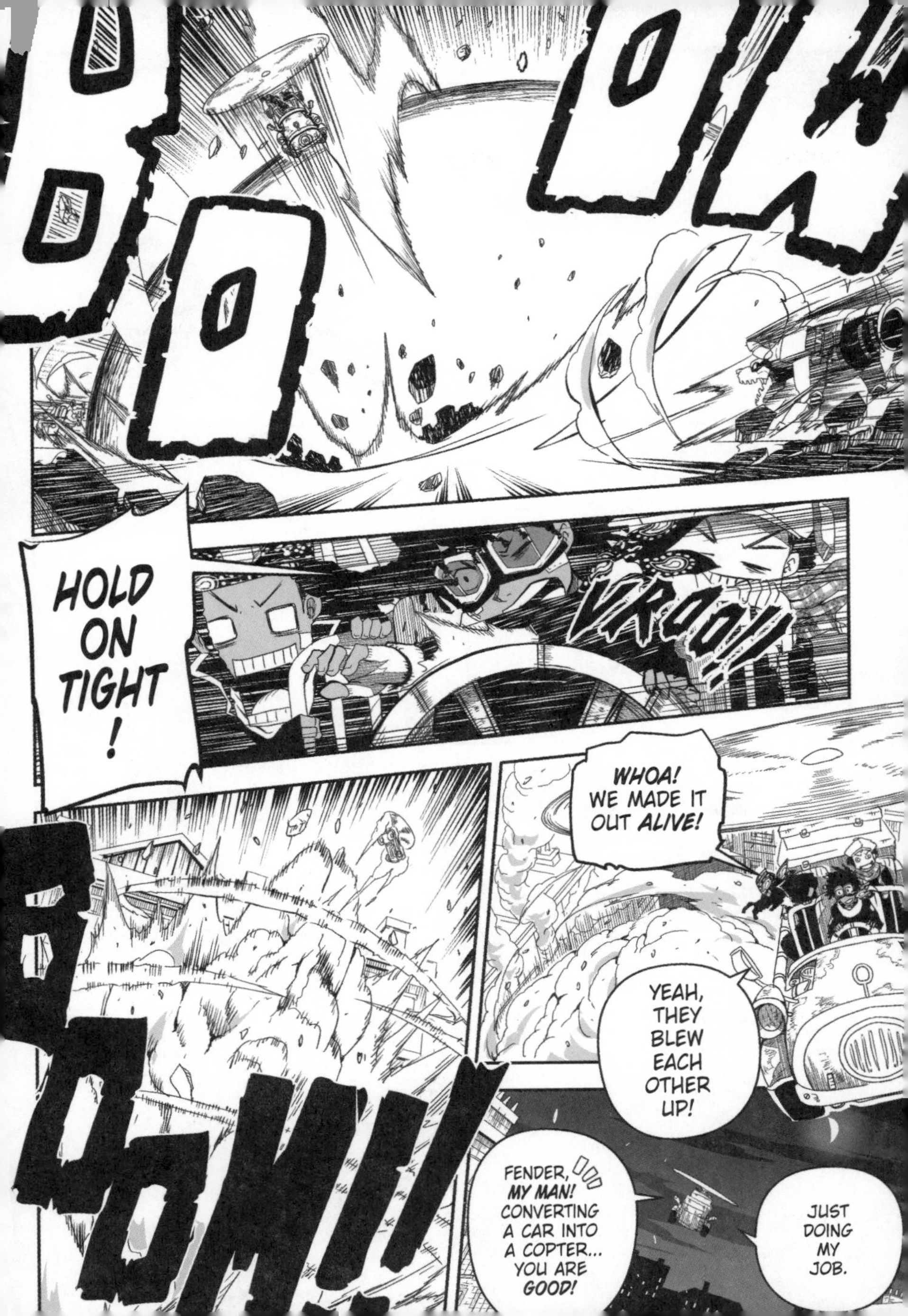
HOLD ON TIGHT!
VROOM!!
WHOA! WE MADE IT OUT *ALIVE!*
YEAH, THEY BLEW EACH OTHER UP!
FENDER, *MY MAN!* CONVERTING A CAR INTO A COPTER... YOU ARE *GOOD!*
JUST DOING MY JOB.

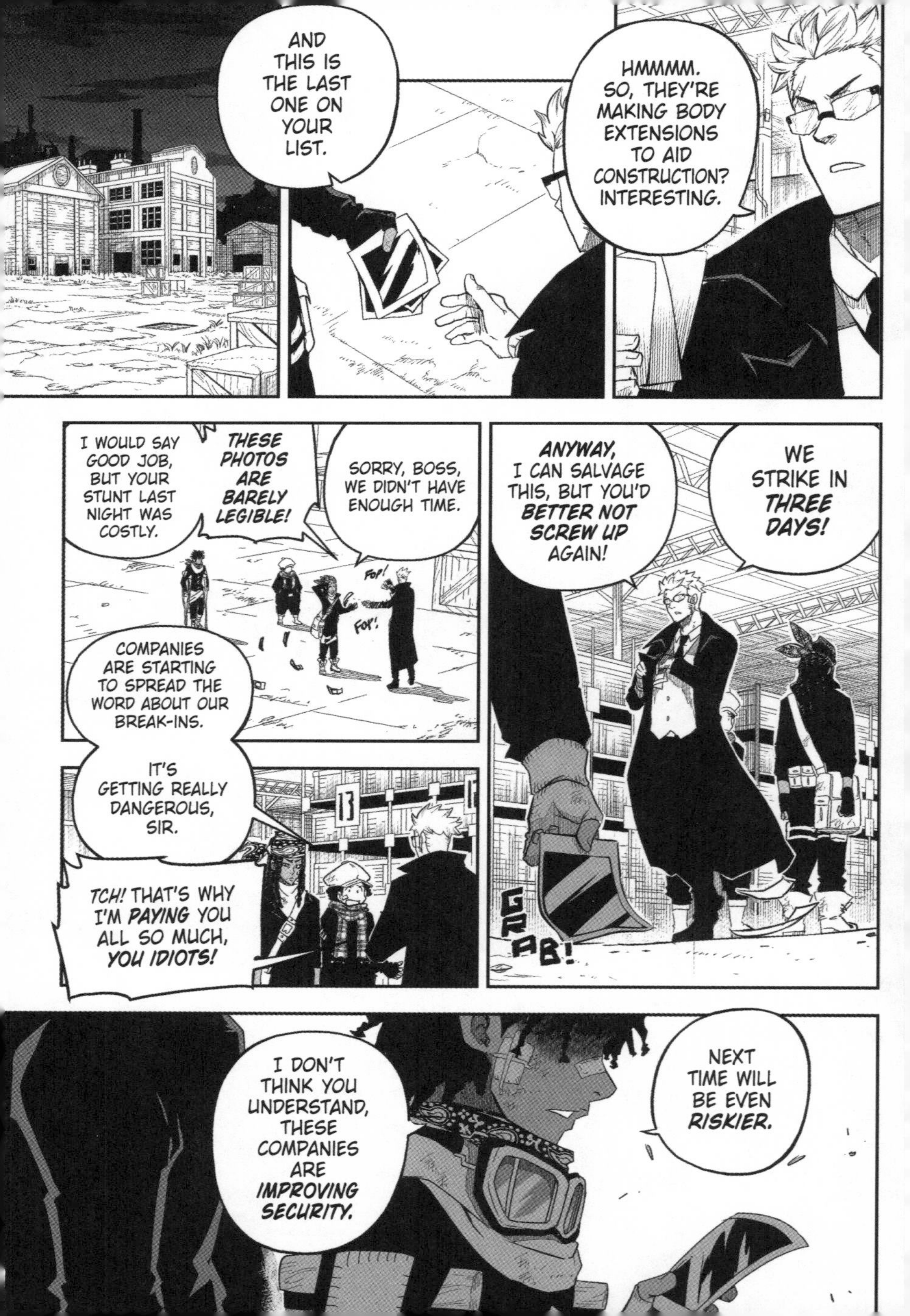
AND THIS IS THE LAST ONE ON YOUR LIST.
HMMMM. SO, THEY'RE MAKING BODY EXTENSIONS TO AID CONSTRUCTION? INTERESTING.
I WOULD SAY GOOD JOB, BUT YOUR STUNT LAST NIGHT WAS COSTLY.
THESE PHOTOS ARE BARELY LEGIBLE!
SORRY, BOSS, WE DIDN'T HAVE ENOUGH TIME.
FOP!
FOP!
COMPANIES ARE STARTING TO SPREAD THE WORD ABOUT OUR BREAK-INS.
IT'S GETTING REALLY DANGEROUS, SIR.
TCH! THAT'S WHY I'M PAYING YOU ALL SO MUCH, YOU IDIOTS!
ANYWAY, I CAN SALVAGE THIS, BUT YOU'D BETTER NOT SCREW UP AGAIN!
WE STRIKE IN THREE DAYS!
GRAB!
I DON'T THINK YOU UNDERSTAND, THESE COMPANIES ARE IMPROVING SECURITY.
NEXT TIME WILL BE EVEN RISKIER.

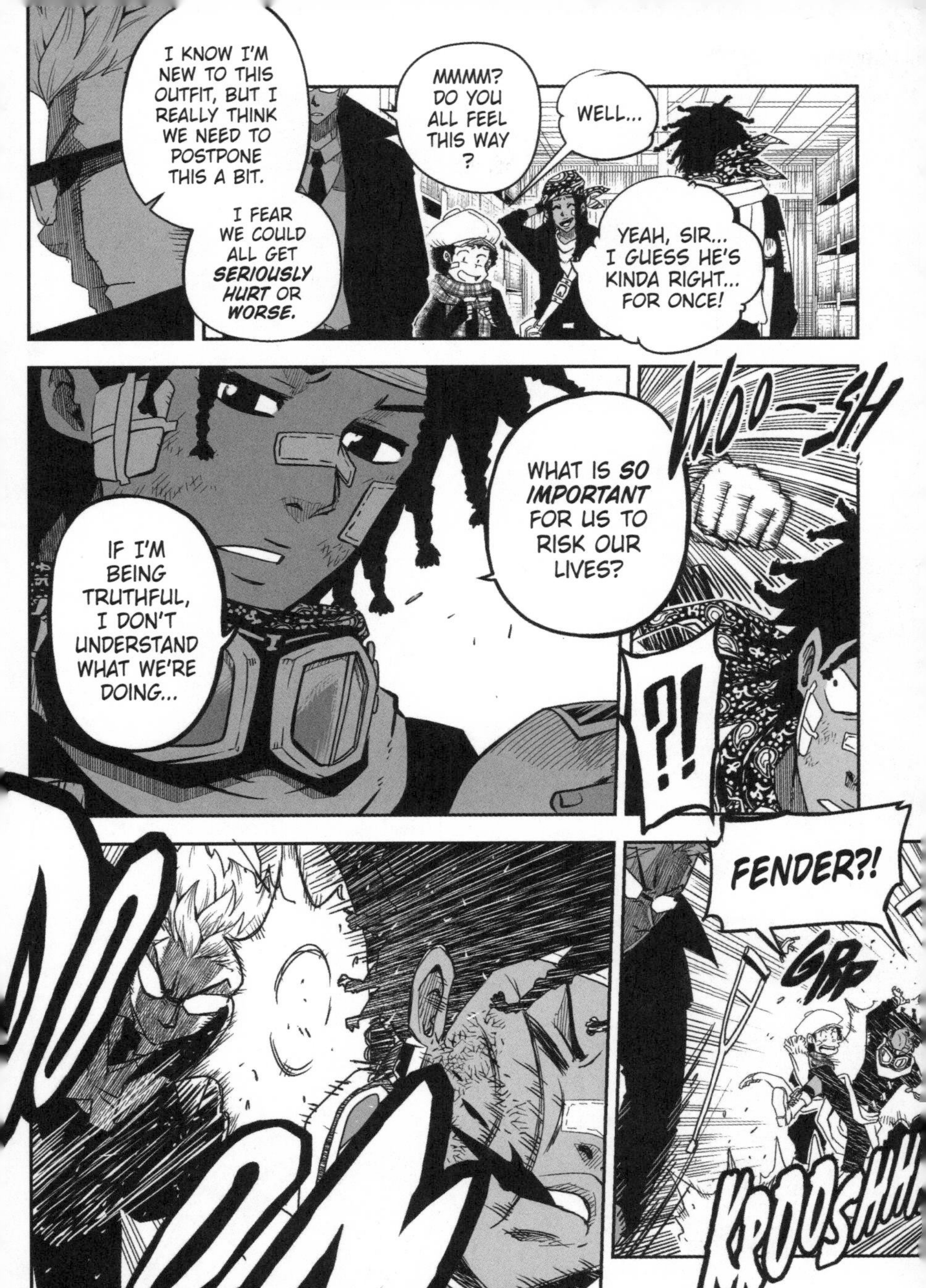
I KNOW I'M NEW TO THIS OUTFIT, BUT I REALLY THINK WE NEED TO POSTPONE THIS A BIT.
I FEAR WE COULD ALL GET SERIOUSLY HURT OR WORSE.
MMMM? DO YOU ALL FEEL THIS WAY?
WELL...
YEAH, SIR... I GUESS HE'S KINDA RIGHT... FOR ONCE!
IF I'M BEING TRUTHFUL, I DON'T UNDERSTAND WHAT WE'RE DOING...
WHAT IS SO IMPORTANT FOR US TO RISK OUR LIVES?
WOO-SH
?!
FENDER?!

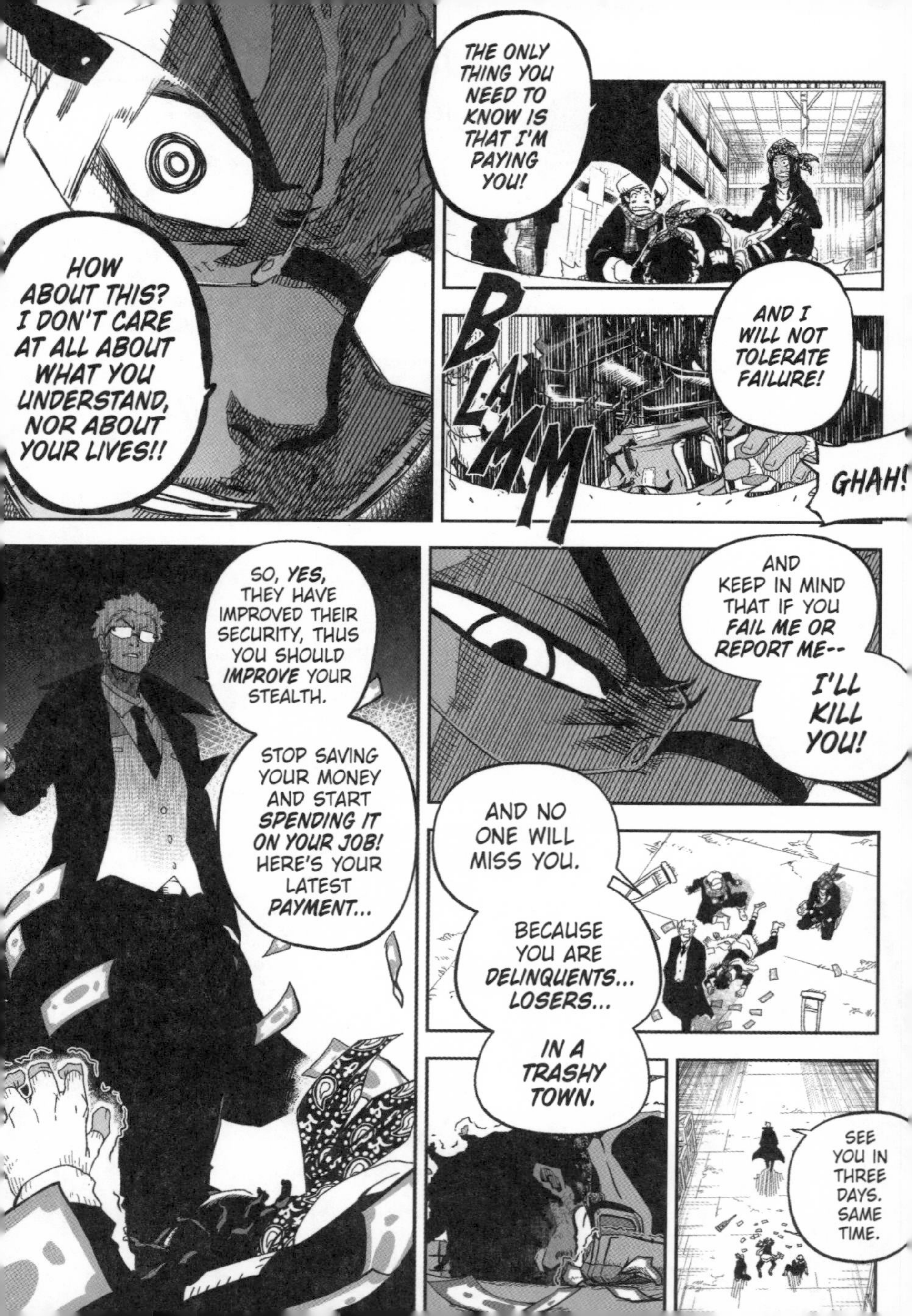
HOW ABOUT THIS? I DON'T CARE AT ALL ABOUT WHAT YOU UNDERSTAND, NOR ABOUT YOUR LIVES!!
THE ONLY THING YOU NEED TO KNOW IS THAT I'M PAYING YOU!
AND I WILL NOT TOLERATE FAILURE!
BLAMM
GHAH!
SO, YES, THEY HAVE IMPROVED THEIR SECURITY, THUS YOU SHOULD IMPROVE YOUR STEALTH.
STOP SAVING YOUR MONEY AND START SPENDING IT ON YOUR JOB! HERE'S YOUR LATEST PAYMENT...
AND KEEP IN MIND THAT IF YOU FAIL ME OR REPORT ME--
I'LL KILL YOU!
AND NO ONE WILL MISS YOU.
BECAUSE YOU ARE DELINQUENTS... LOSERS...
IN A TRASHY TOWN.
SEE YOU IN THREE DAYS. SAME TIME.

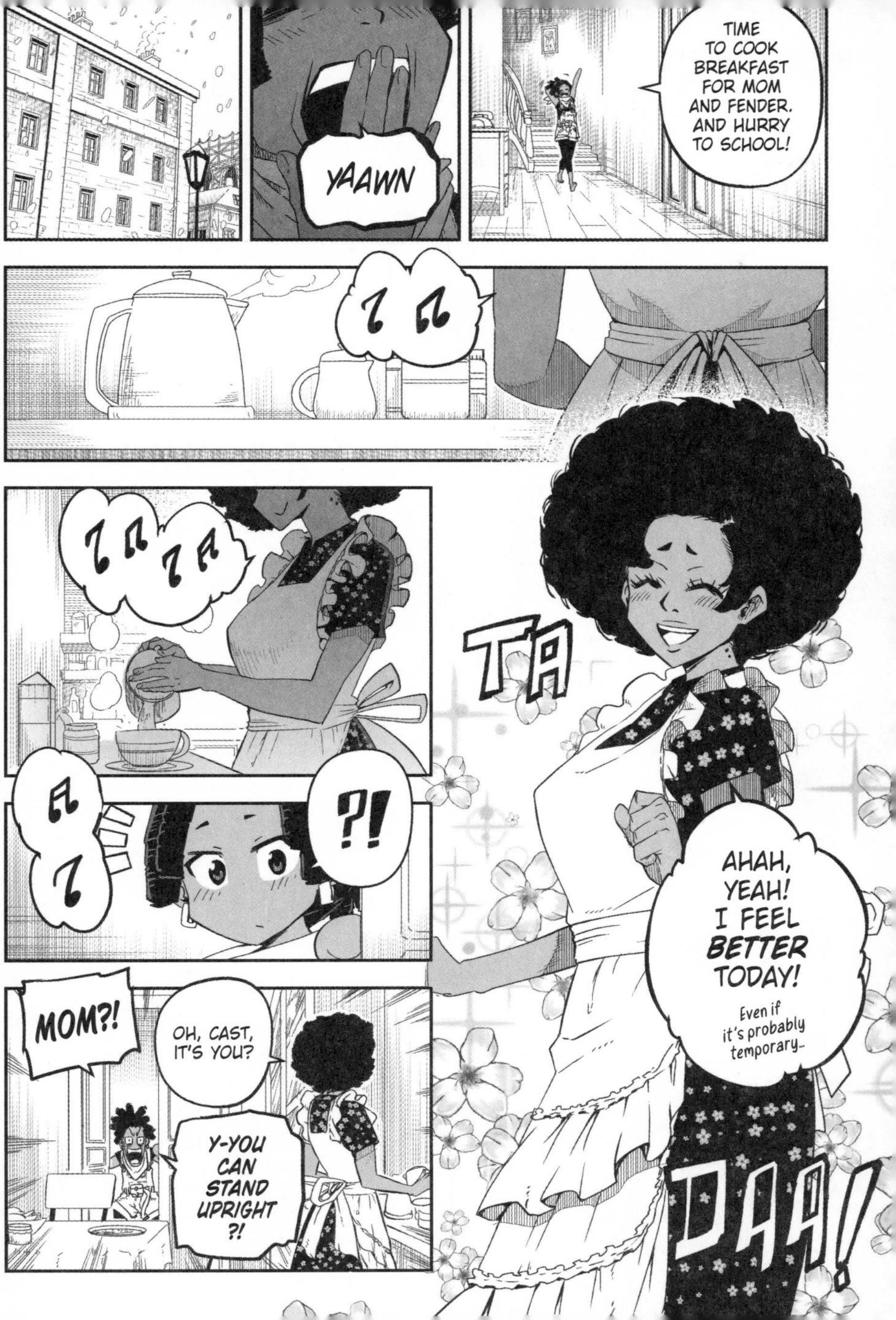
YAAWN
TIME TO COOK BREAKFAST FOR MOM AND FENDER. AND HURRY TO SCHOOL!
TA
AHAH, YEAH! I FEEL BETTER TODAY!
Even if it's probably temporary...
DAA!
?!
MOM?!
OH, CAST, IT'S YOU?
Y-YOU CAN STAND UPRIGHT ?!

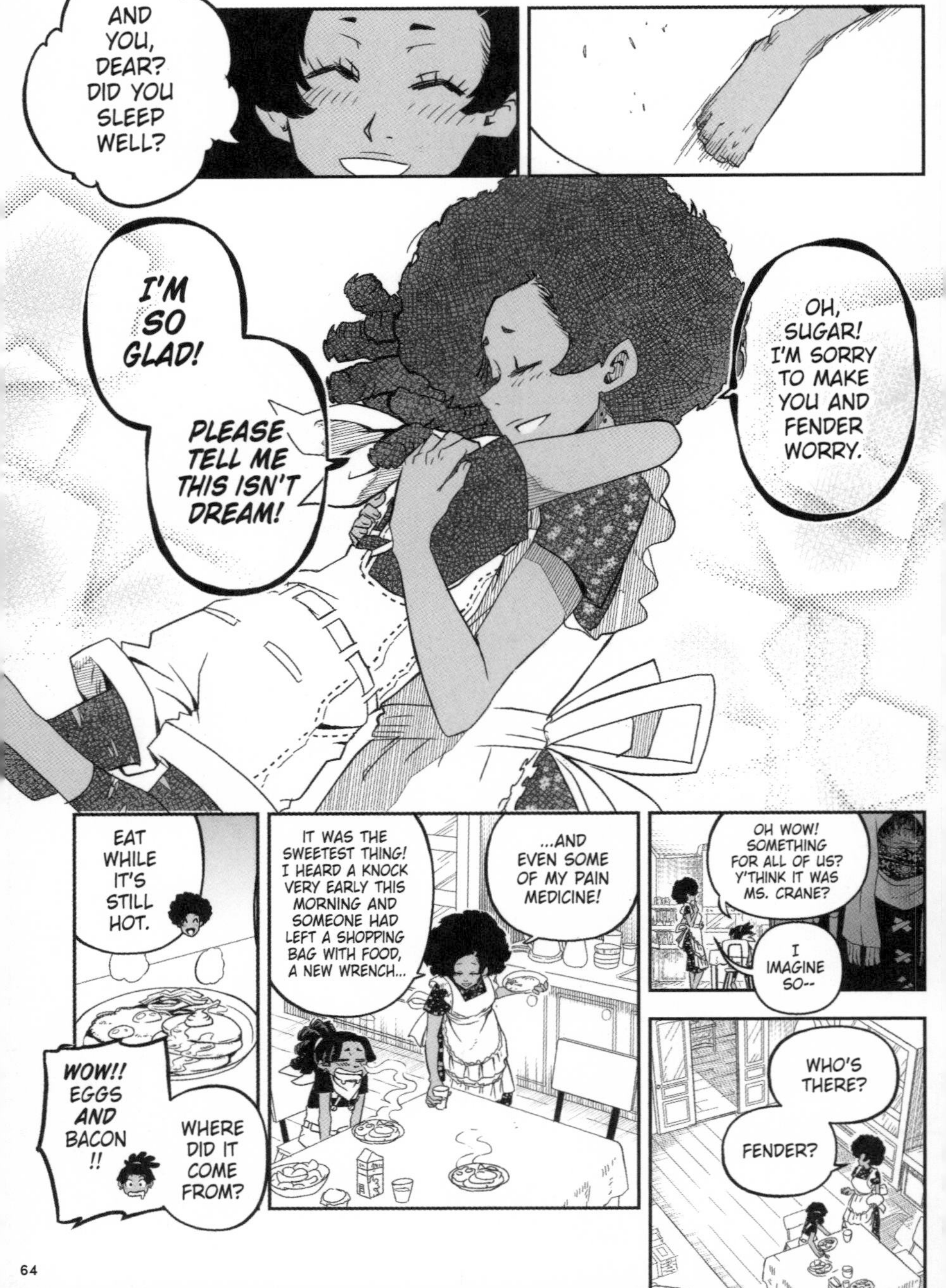

AND YOU, DEAR? DID YOU SLEEP WELL?
I'M SO GLAD!
PLEASE TELL ME THIS ISN'T DREAM!
OH, SUGAR! I'M SORRY TO MAKE YOU AND FENDER WORRY.
EAT WHILE IT'S STILL HOT.
WOW!! EGGS AND BACON !!
WHERE DID IT COME FROM?
IT WAS THE SWEETEST THING! I HEARD A KNOCK VERY EARLY THIS MORNING AND SOMEONE HAD LEFT A SHOPPING BAG WITH FOOD, A NEW WRENCH...
...AND EVEN SOME OF MY PAIN MEDICINE!
OH WOW! SOMETHING FOR ALL OF US? Y'THINK IT WAS MS. CRANE?
I IMAGINE SO--
WHO'S THERE?
FENDER?

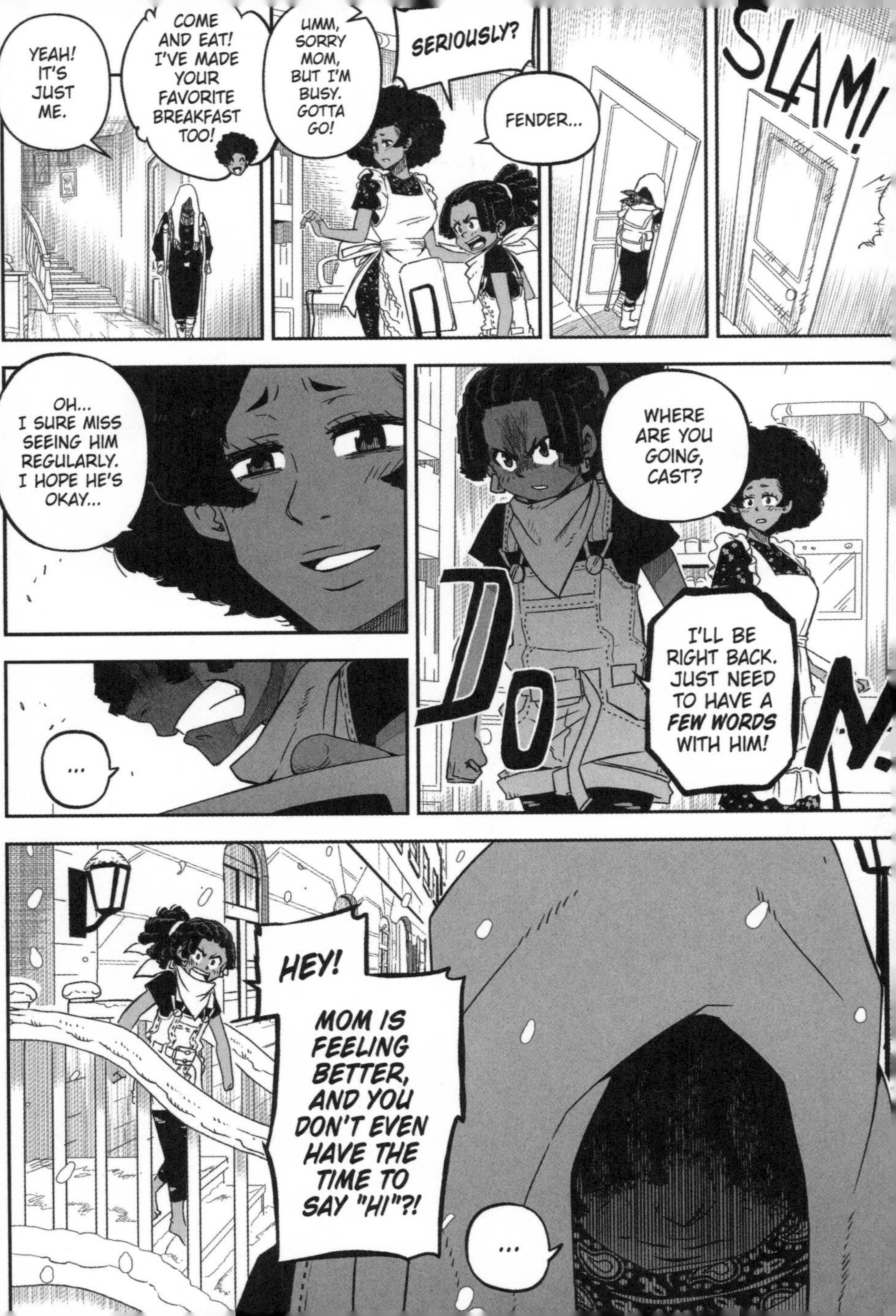
YEAH! IT'S JUST ME.
COME AND EAT! I'VE MADE YOUR FAVORITE BREAKFAST TOO!
UMM, SORRY MOM, BUT I'M BUSY. GOTTA GO!
SERIOUSLY?
FENDER...
SLAM!
OH... I SURE MISS SEEING HIM REGULARLY. I HOPE HE'S OKAY...
...
WHERE ARE YOU GOING, CAST?
DOM
I'LL BE RIGHT BACK. JUST NEED TO HAVE A FEW WORDS WITH HIM!
HEY!
MOM IS FEELING BETTER, AND YOU DON'T EVEN HAVE THE TIME TO SAY "HI"?!
...

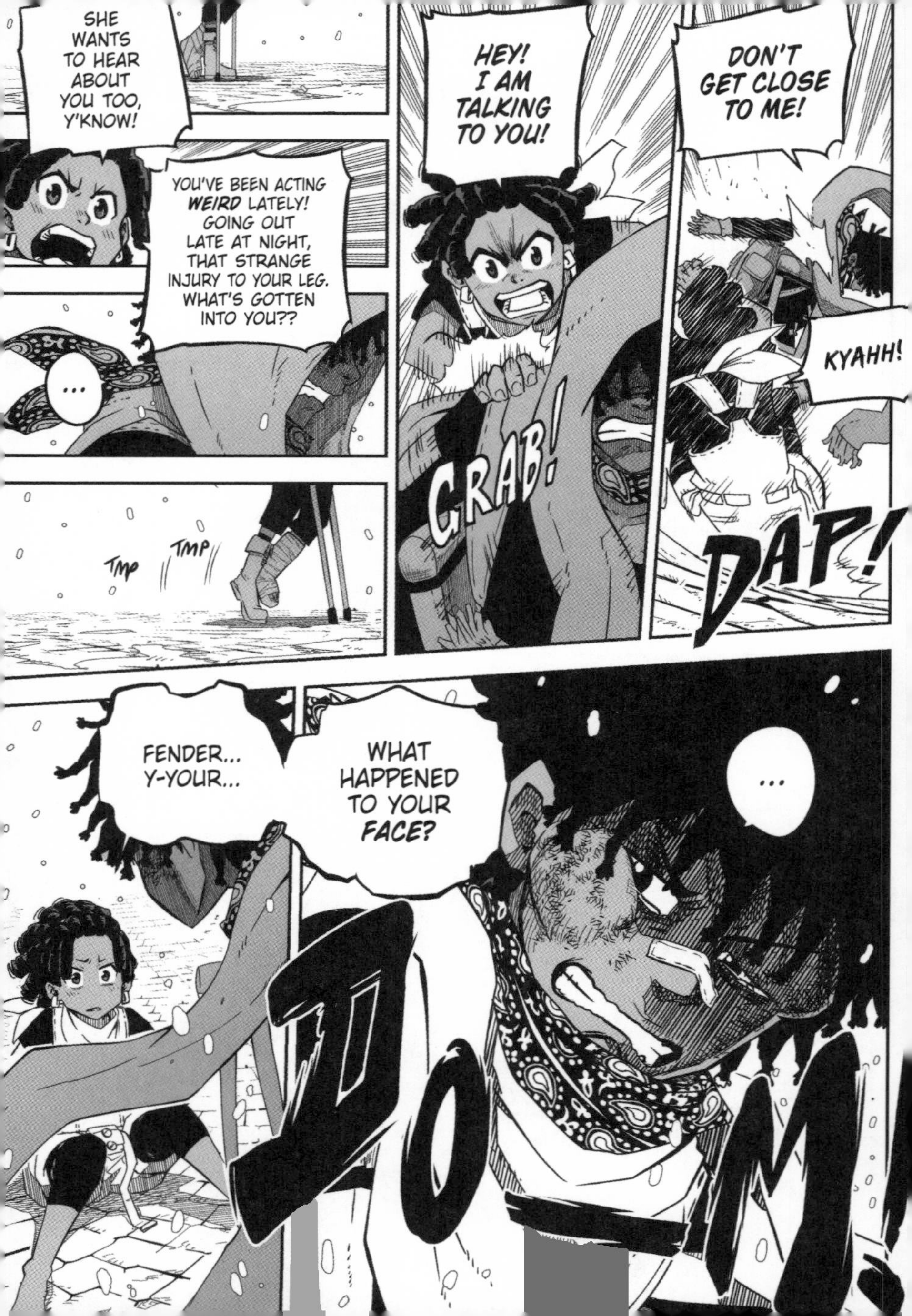
SHE WANTS TO HEAR ABOUT YOU TOO, Y'KNOW!
YOU'VE BEEN ACTING WEIRD LATELY! GOING OUT LATE AT NIGHT, THAT STRANGE INJURY TO YOUR LEG. WHAT'S GOTTEN INTO YOU??
...
TMP
TMP
HEY! I AM TALKING TO YOU!
GRAB!
DON'T GET CLOSE TO ME!
KYAHH!
DAP!
FENDER... Y-YOUR...
WHAT HAPPENED TO YOUR FACE?
...
DOOM!

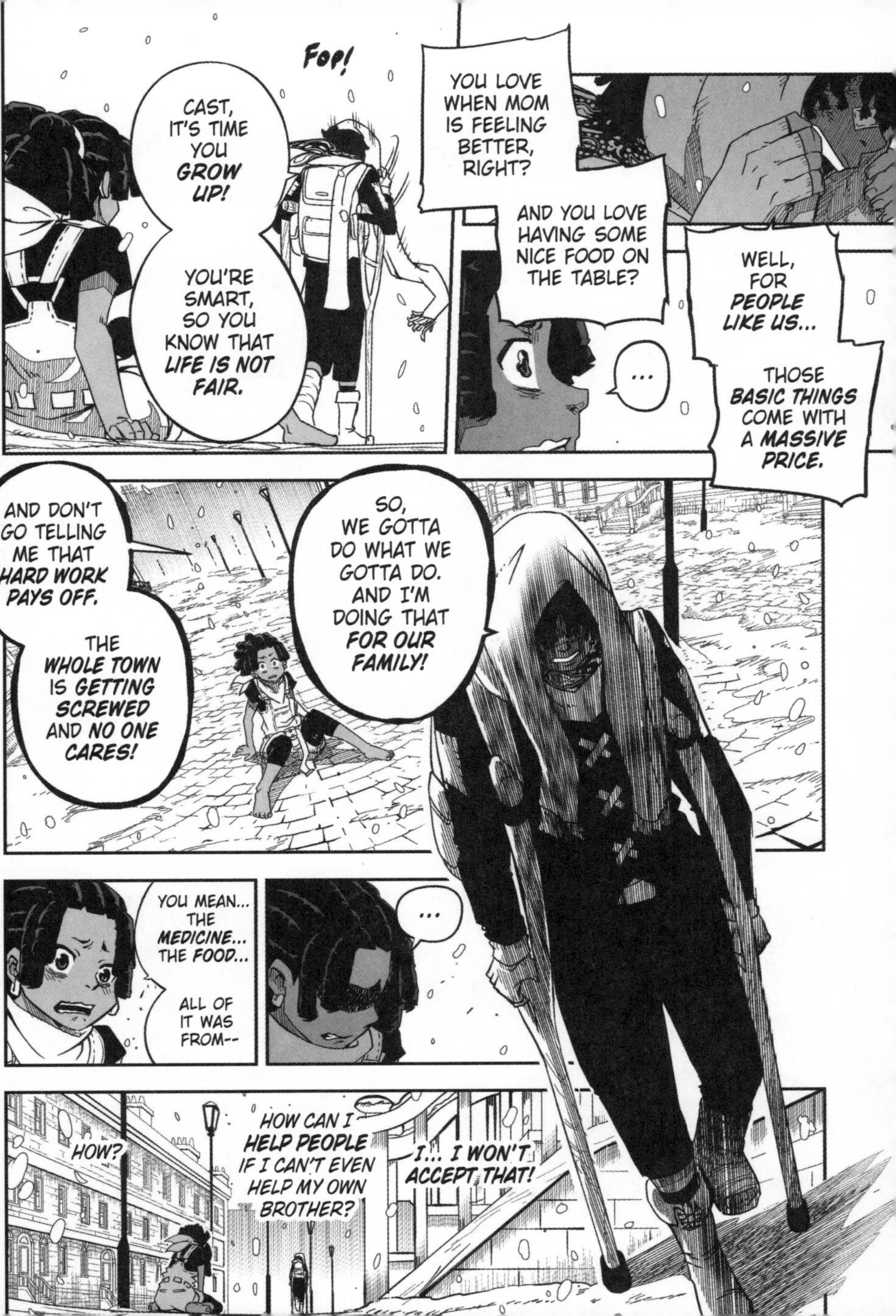
FOP!
CAST, IT'S TIME YOU GROW UP!
YOU'RE SMART, SO YOU KNOW THAT LIFE IS NOT FAIR.
YOU LOVE WHEN MOM IS FEELING BETTER, RIGHT?
AND YOU LOVE HAVING SOME NICE FOOD ON THE TABLE?
...
WELL, FOR PEOPLE LIKE US...
THOSE BASIC THINGS COME WITH A MASSIVE PRICE.
AND DON'T GO TELLING ME THAT HARD WORK PAYS OFF.
THE WHOLE TOWN IS GETTING SCREWED AND NO ONE CARES!
SO, WE GOTTA DO WHAT WE GOTTA DO. AND I'M DOING THAT FOR OUR FAMILY!
YOU MEAN... THE MEDICINE... THE FOOD...
ALL OF IT WAS FROM--
...
HOW?
HOW CAN I HELP PEOPLE IF I CAN'T EVEN HELP MY OWN BROTHER?
I... I WON'T ACCEPT THAT!

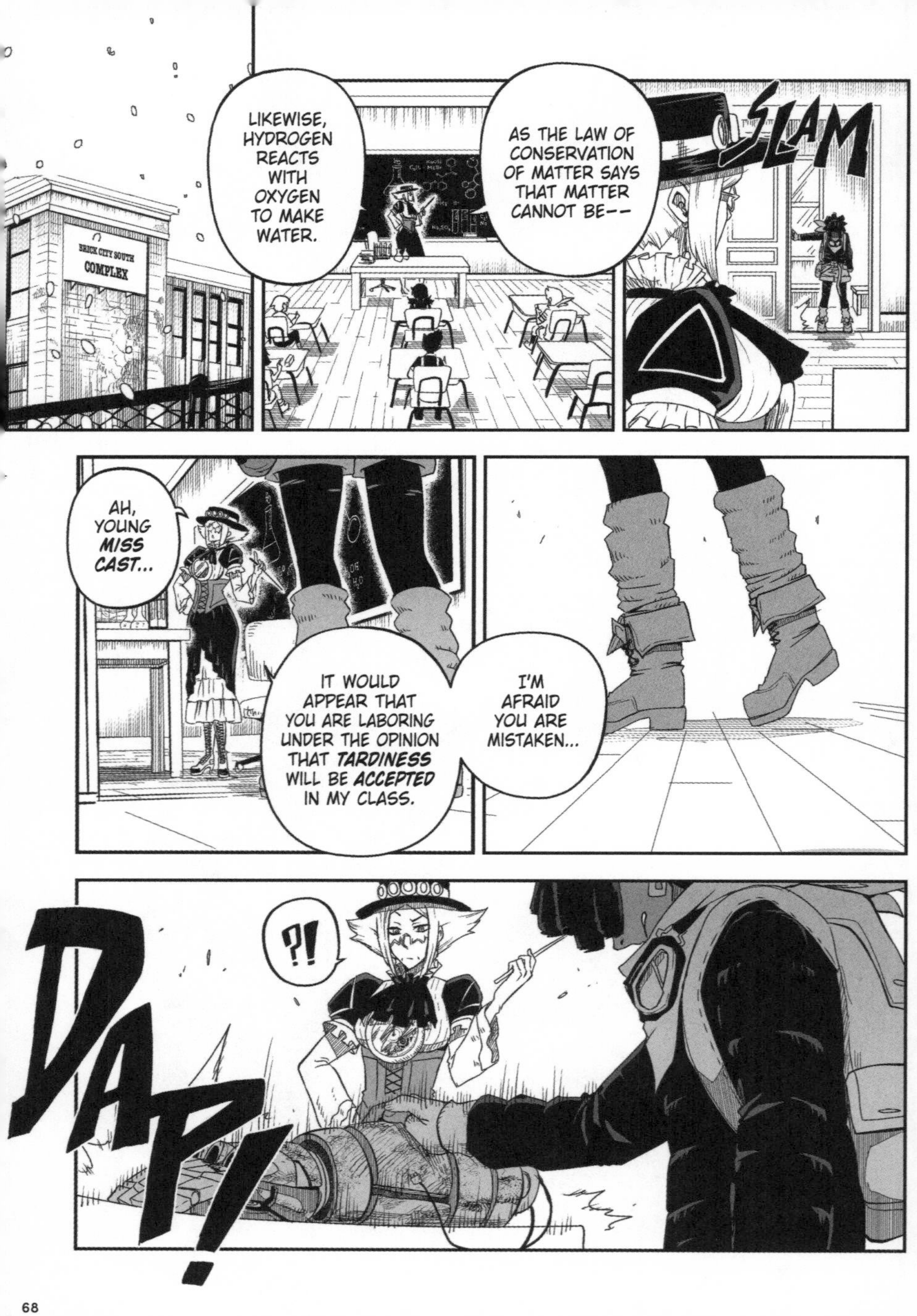
BRICK CITY SOUTH COMPLEX
LIKEWISE, HYDROGEN REACTS WITH OXYGEN TO MAKE WATER.
AS THE LAW OF CONSERVATION OF MATTER SAYS THAT MATTER CANNOT BE--
SLAM
AH, YOUNG MISS CAST...
IT WOULD APPEAR THAT YOU ARE LABORING UNDER THE OPINION THAT TARDINESS WILL BE ACCEPTED IN MY CLASS.
I'M AFRAID YOU ARE MISTAKEN...
?!
DAP!

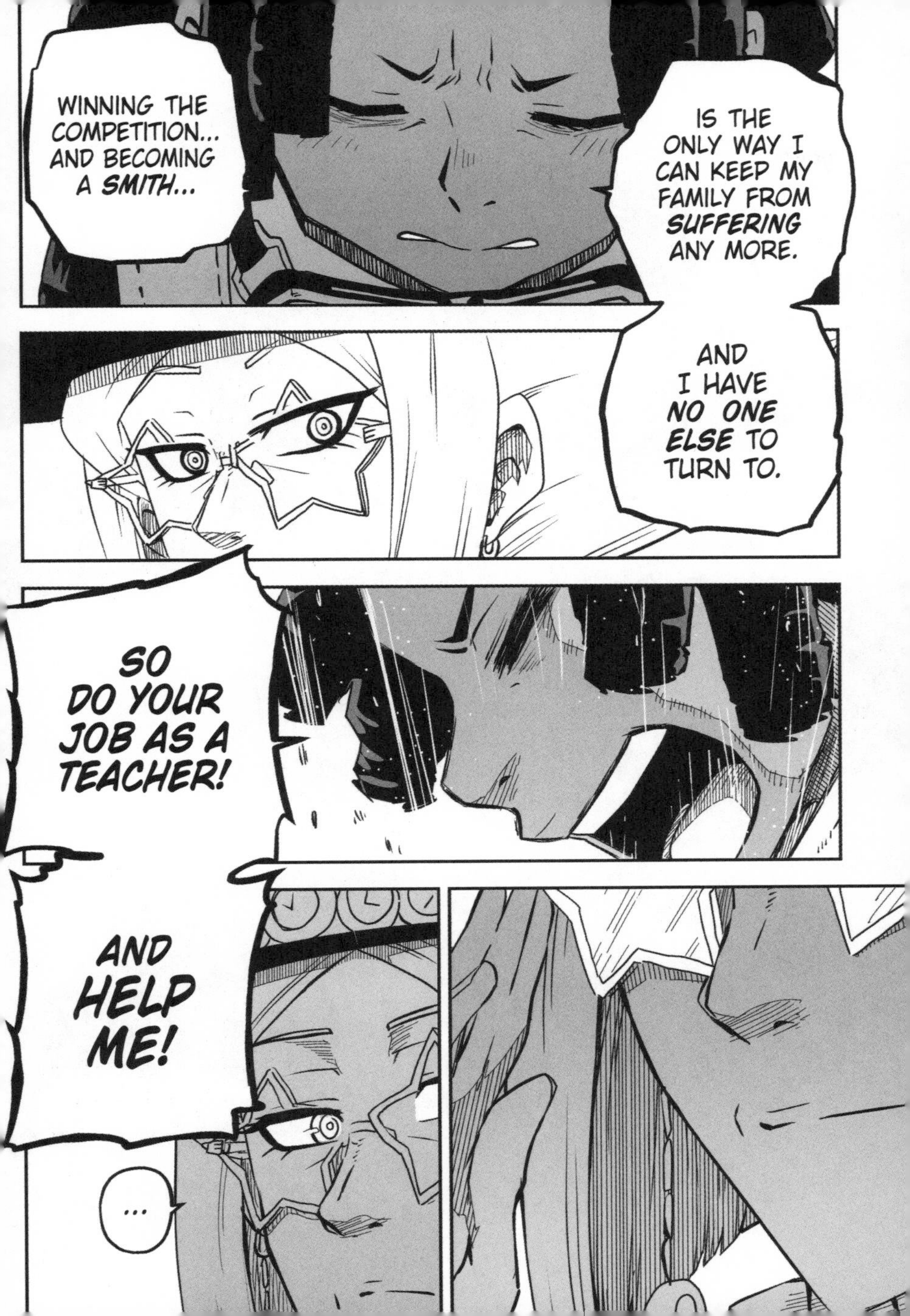
WINNING THE COMPETITION... AND BECOMING A SMITH...
IS THE ONLY WAY I CAN KEEP MY FAMILY FROM SUFFERING ANY MORE.
AND I HAVE NO ONE ELSE TO TURN TO.
SO DO YOUR JOB AS A TEACHER!
AND HELP ME!
...

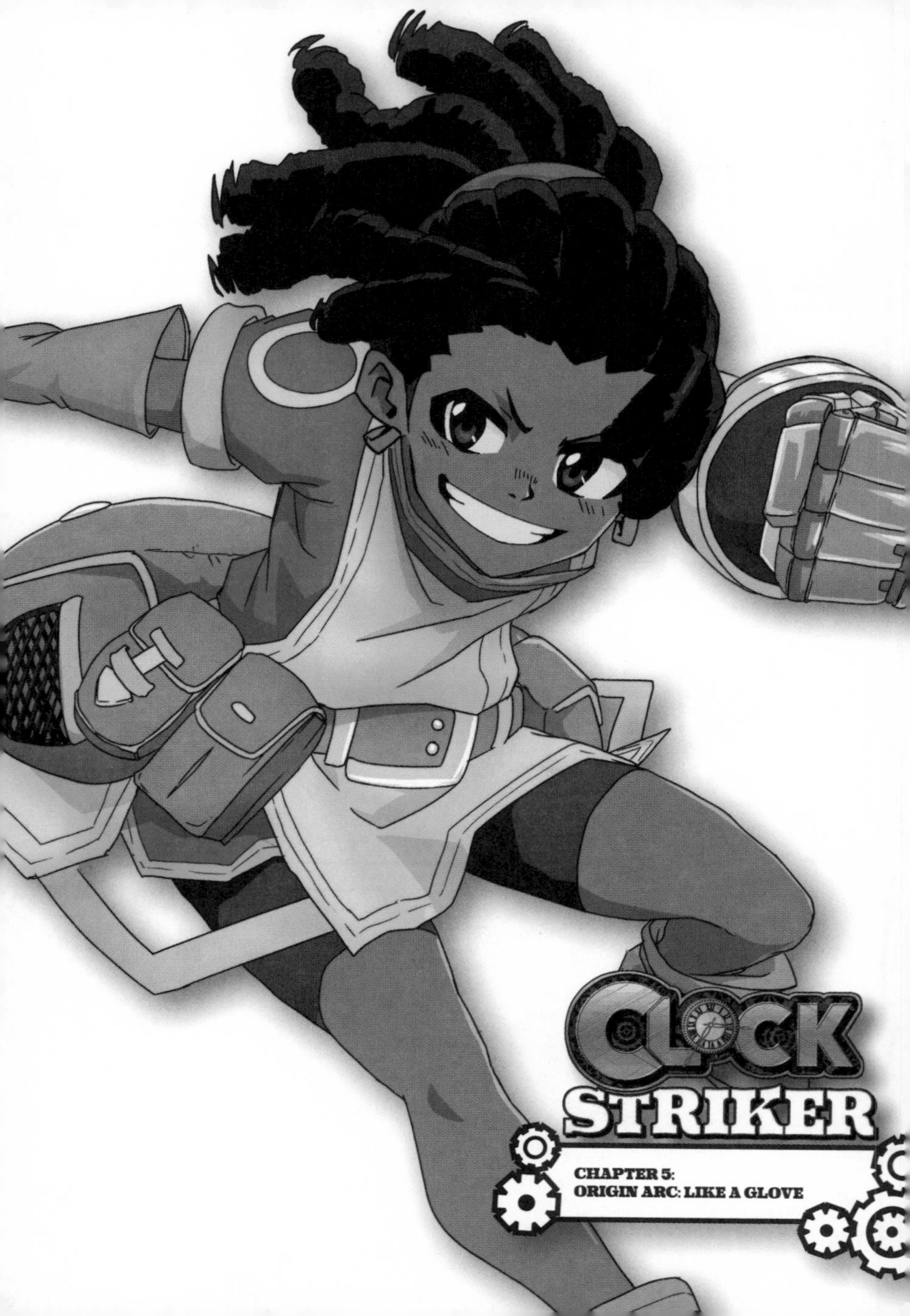
CLOCK
STRIKER
CHAPTER 5:
ORIGIN ARC: LIKE A GLOVE

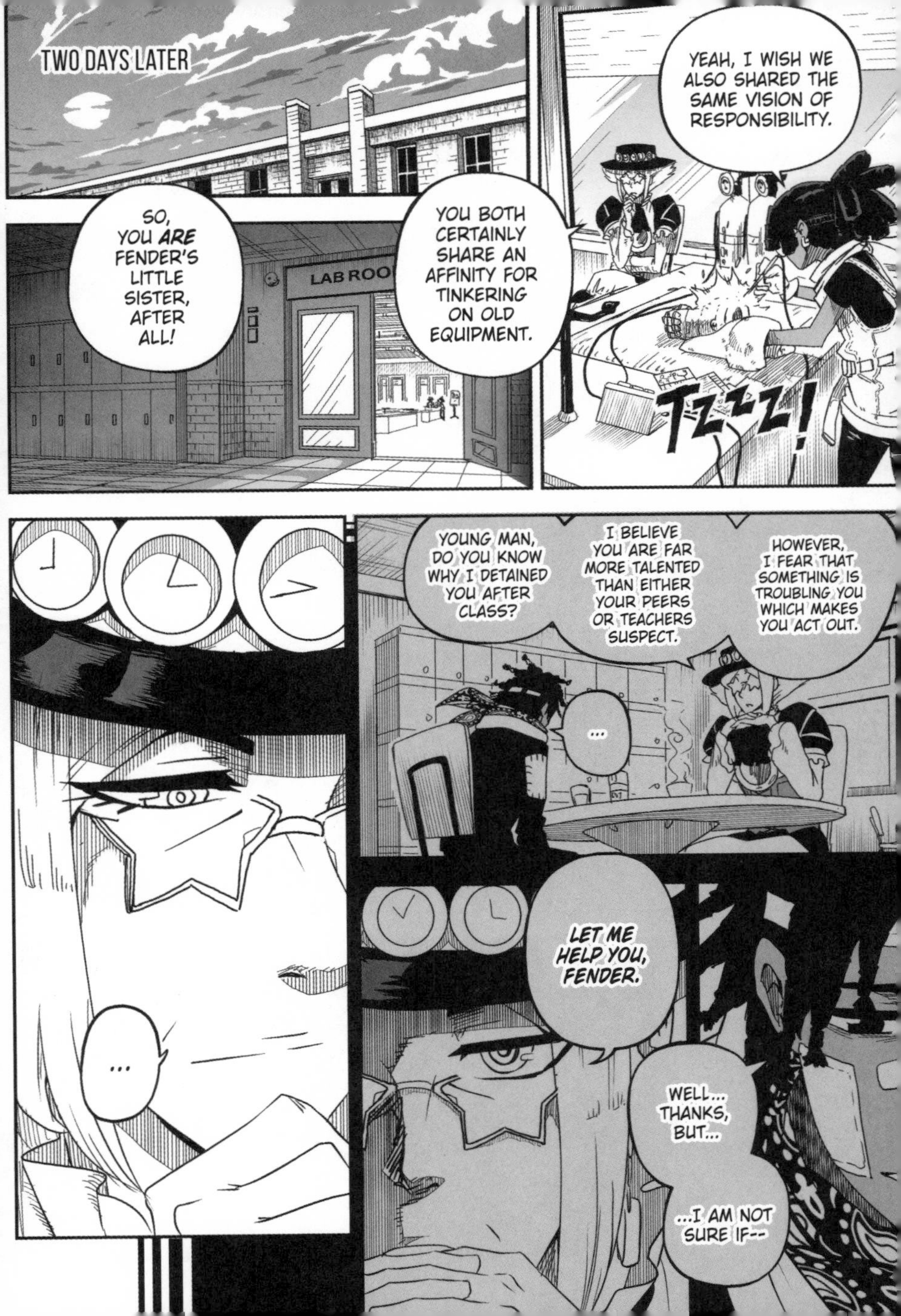
TWO DAYS LATER
YEAH, I WISH WE ALSO SHARED THE SAME VISION OF RESPONSIBILITY.
SO, YOU *ARE* FENDER'S LITTLE SISTER, AFTER ALL!
LAB ROO
YOU BOTH CERTAINLY SHARE AN AFFINITY FOR TINKERING ON OLD EQUIPMENT.
TZZZZ!
...
YOUNG MAN, DO YOU KNOW WHY I DETAINED YOU AFTER CLASS?
I BELIEVE YOU ARE FAR MORE TALENTED THAN EITHER YOUR PEERS OR TEACHERS SUSPECT.
HOWEVER, I FEAR THAT SOMETHING IS TROUBLING YOU WHICH MAKES YOU ACT OUT.
...
LET ME HELP YOU, FENDER.
WELL... THANKS, BUT...
...I AM NOT SURE IF--

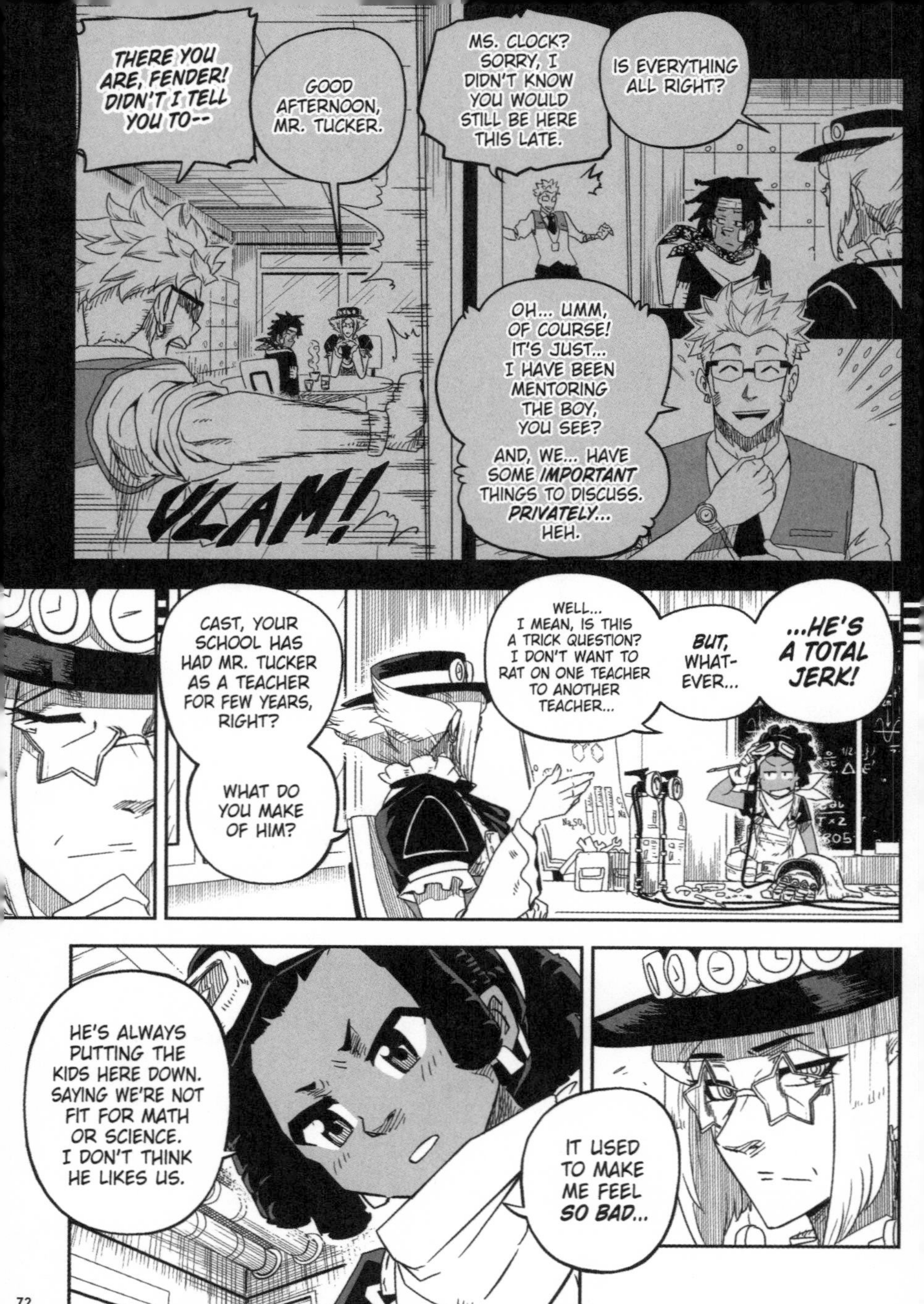

THERE YOU ARE, FENDER! DIDN'T I TELL YOU TO--
GOOD AFTERNOON, MR. TUCKER.
VLAM!
MS. CLOCK? SORRY, I DIDN'T KNOW YOU WOULD STILL BE HERE THIS LATE.
IS EVERYTHING ALL RIGHT?
OH... UMM, OF COURSE! IT'S JUST... I HAVE BEEN MENTORING THE BOY, YOU SEE?
AND, WE... HAVE SOME IMPORTANT THINGS TO DISCUSS. PRIVATELY... HEH.
CAST, YOUR SCHOOL HAS HAD MR. TUCKER AS A TEACHER FOR FEW YEARS, RIGHT?
WHAT DO YOU MAKE OF HIM?
WELL... I MEAN, IS THIS A TRICK QUESTION? I DON'T WANT TO RAT ON ONE TEACHER TO ANOTHER TEACHER...
BUT, WHAT-EVER...
...HE'S A TOTAL JERK!
HE'S ALWAYS PUTTING THE KIDS HERE DOWN. SAYING WE'RE NOT FIT FOR MATH OR SCIENCE. I DON'T THINK HE LIKES US.
IT USED TO MAKE ME FEEL SO BAD...

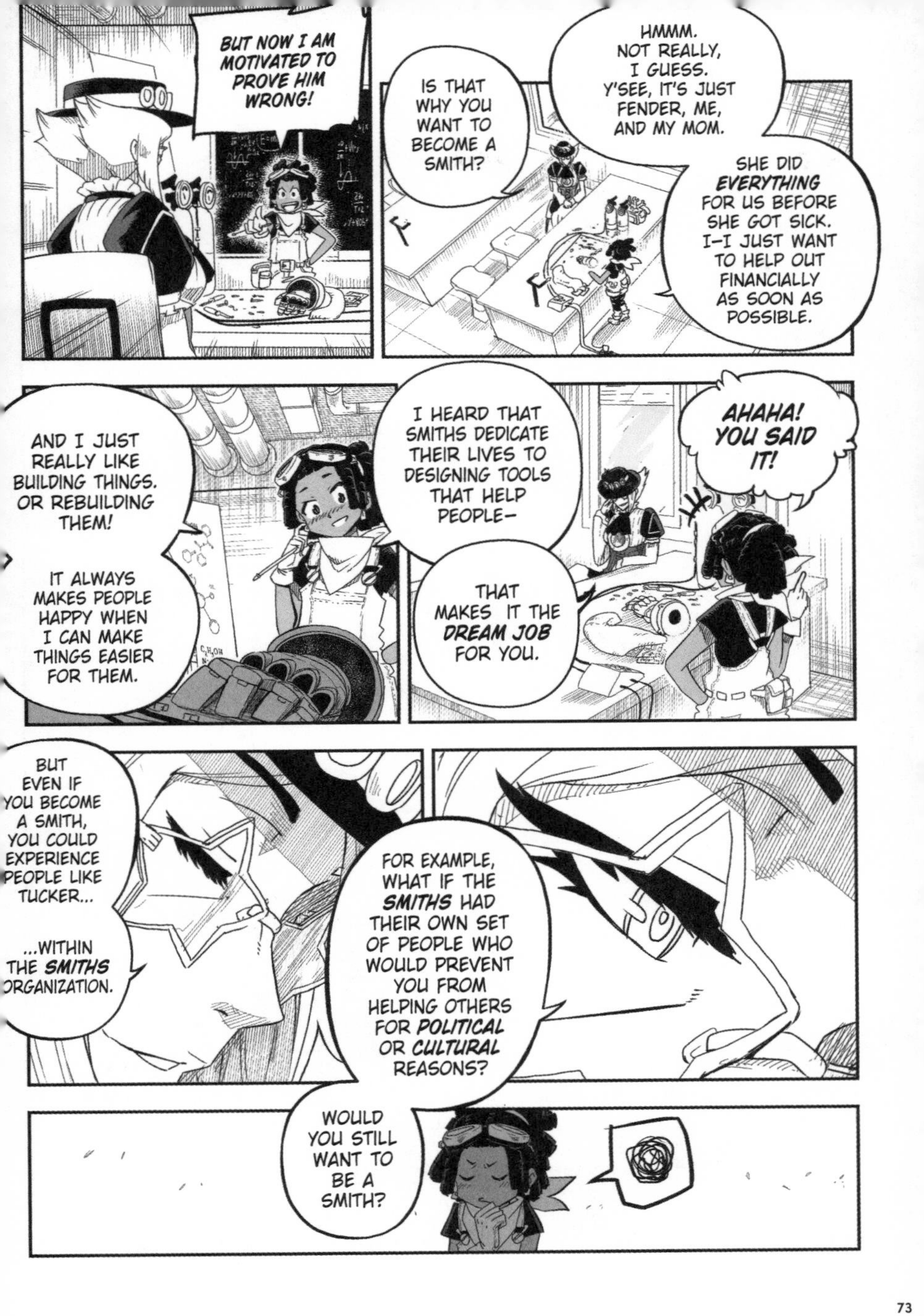
BUT NOW I AM MOTIVATED TO PROVE HIM WRONG!
IS THAT WHY YOU WANT TO BECOME A SMITH?
HMMM. NOT REALLY, I GUESS. Y'SEE, IT'S JUST FENDER, ME, AND MY MOM.
SHE DID EVERYTHING FOR US BEFORE SHE GOT SICK. I—I JUST WANT TO HELP OUT FINANCIALLY AS SOON AS POSSIBLE.
AND I JUST REALLY LIKE BUILDING THINGS. OR REBUILDING THEM!
IT ALWAYS MAKES PEOPLE HAPPY WHEN I CAN MAKE THINGS EASIER FOR THEM.
I HEARD THAT SMITHS DEDICATE THEIR LIVES TO DESIGNING TOOLS THAT HELP PEOPLE—
THAT MAKES IT THE DREAM JOB FOR YOU.
AHAHA! YOU SAID IT!
BUT EVEN IF YOU BECOME A SMITH, YOU COULD EXPERIENCE PEOPLE LIKE TUCKER...
...WITHIN THE SMITHS ORGANIZATION.
FOR EXAMPLE, WHAT IF THE SMITHS HAD THEIR OWN SET OF PEOPLE WHO WOULD PREVENT YOU FROM HELPING OTHERS FOR POLITICAL OR CULTURAL REASONS?
WOULD YOU STILL WANT TO BE A SMITH?

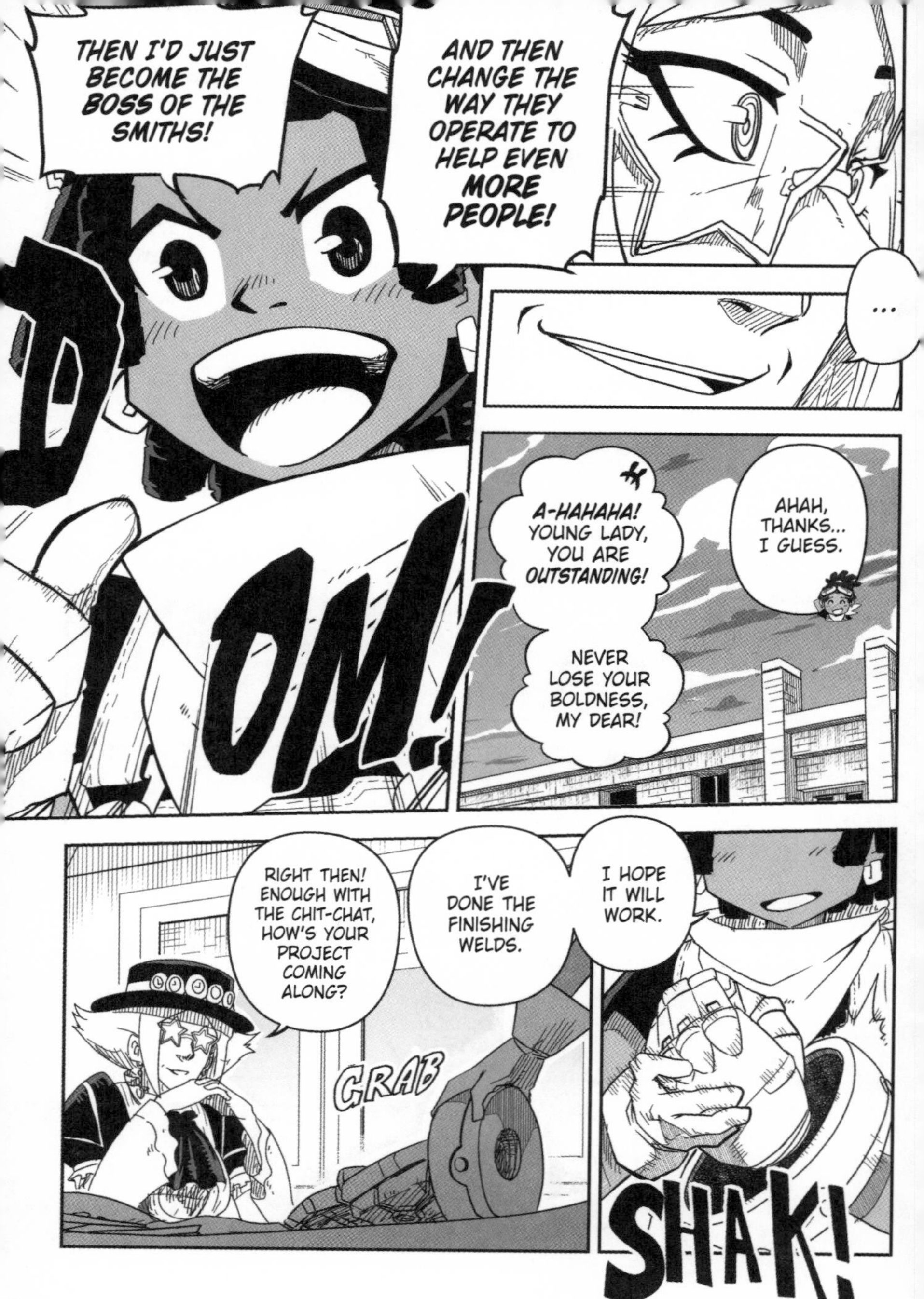
THEN I'D JUST BECOME THE BOSS OF THE SMITHS!
AND THEN CHANGE THE WAY THEY OPERATE TO HELP EVEN MORE PEOPLE!
...
A-HAHAHA! YOUNG LADY, YOU ARE OUTSTANDING!
AHAH, THANKS... I GUESS.
NEVER LOSE YOUR BOLDNESS, MY DEAR!
RIGHT THEN! ENOUGH WITH THE CHIT-CHAT, HOW'S YOUR PROJECT COMING ALONG?
GRAB
I'VE DONE THE FINISHING WELDS.
I HOPE IT WILL WORK.
SHAK!

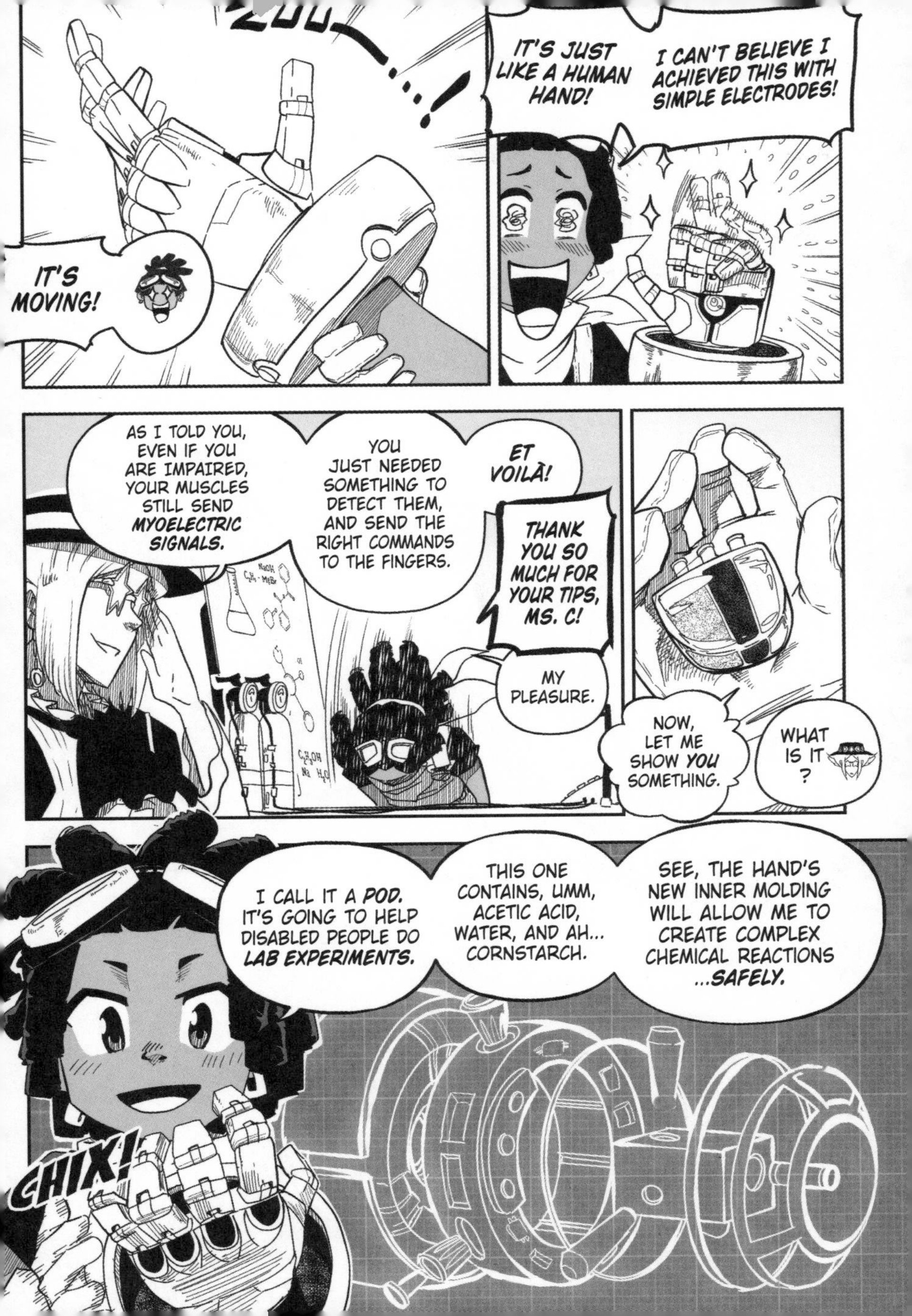
ZOO...!
IT'S MOVING!
IT'S JUST LIKE A HUMAN HAND!
I CAN'T BELIEVE I ACHIEVED THIS WITH SIMPLE ELECTRODES!
AS I TOLD YOU, EVEN IF YOU ARE IMPAIRED, YOUR MUSCLES STILL SEND MYOELECTRIC SIGNALS.
YOU JUST NEEDED SOMETHING TO DETECT THEM, AND SEND THE RIGHT COMMANDS TO THE FINGERS.
ET VOILÀ!
THANK YOU SO MUCH FOR YOUR TIPS, MS. C!
MY PLEASURE.
NOW, LET ME SHOW YOU SOMETHING.
WHAT IS IT ?
I CALL IT A POD. IT'S GOING TO HELP DISABLED PEOPLE DO LAB EXPERIMENTS.
THIS ONE CONTAINS, UMM, ACETIC ACID, WATER, AND AH... CORNSTARCH.
SEE, THE HAND'S NEW INNER MOLDING WILL ALLOW ME TO CREATE COMPLEX CHEMICAL REACTIONS ...SAFELY.
CHIK!

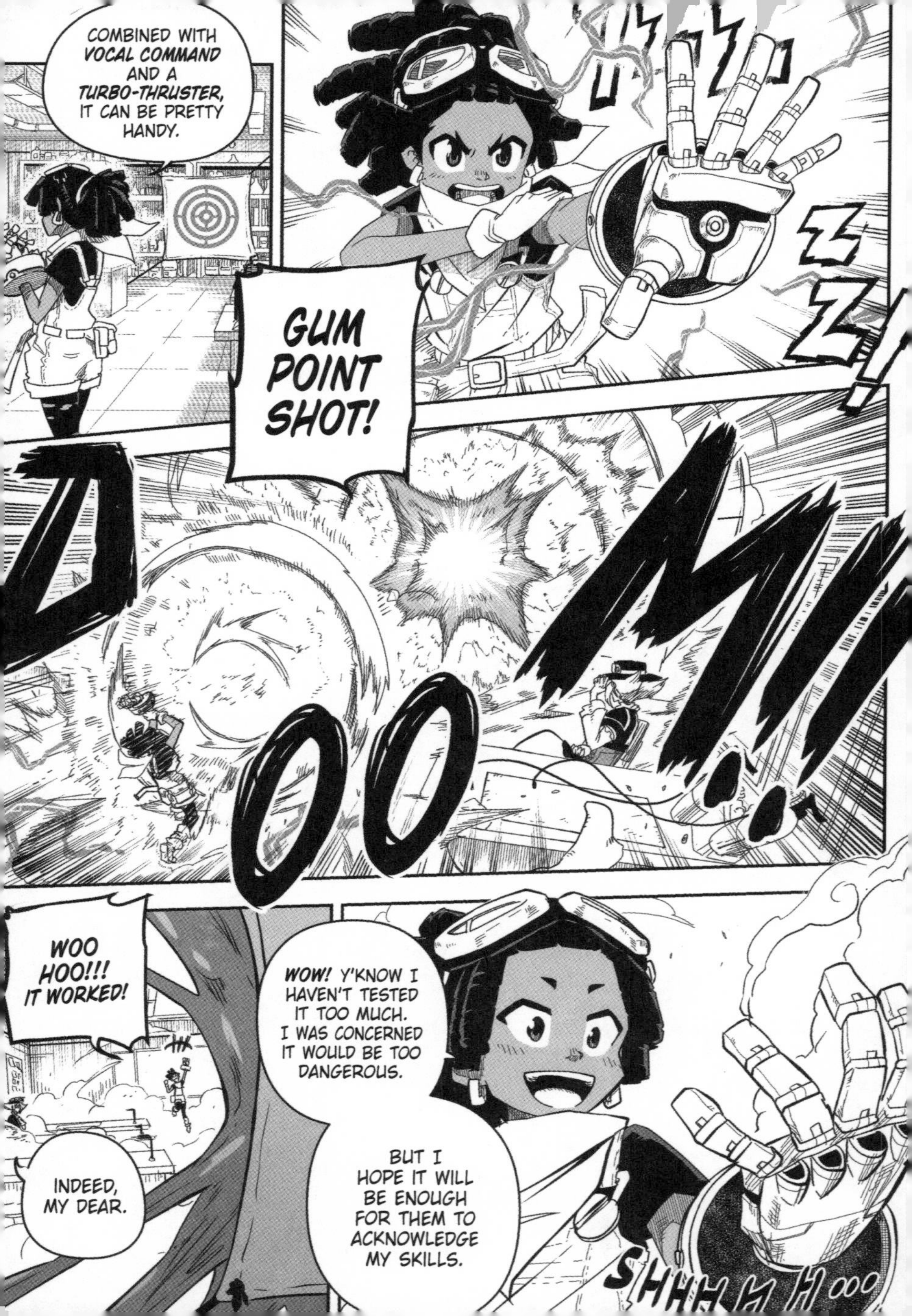
COMBINED WITH VOCAL COMMAND AND A TURBO-THRUSTER, IT CAN BE PRETTY HANDY.
ZZ!
GUM POINT SHOT!
DOOM!!
WOO HOO!!! IT WORKED!
INDEED, MY DEAR.
WOW! Y'KNOW I HAVEN'T TESTED IT TOO MUCH. I WAS CONCERNED IT WOULD BE TOO DANGEROUS.
BUT I HOPE IT WILL BE ENOUGH FOR THEM TO ACKNOWLEDGE MY SKILLS.
SHHHHH

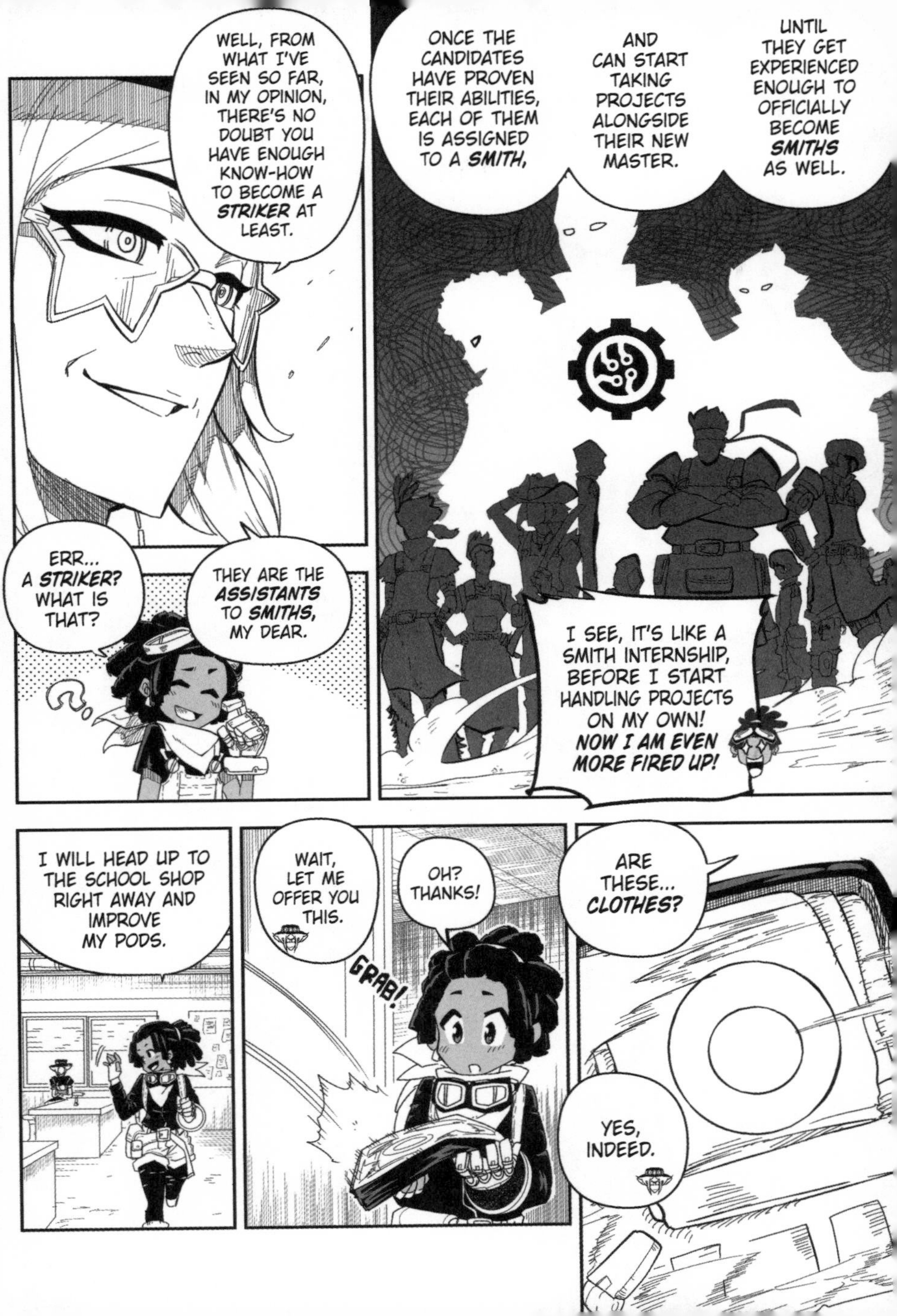
WELL, FROM WHAT I'VE SEEN SO FAR, IN MY OPINION, THERE'S NO DOUBT YOU HAVE ENOUGH KNOW-HOW TO BECOME A STRIKER AT LEAST.
ERR... A STRIKER? WHAT IS THAT?
THEY ARE THE ASSISTANTS TO SMITHS, MY DEAR.
ONCE THE CANDIDATES HAVE PROVEN THEIR ABILITIES, EACH OF THEM IS ASSIGNED TO A SMITH,
AND CAN START TAKING PROJECTS ALONGSIDE THEIR NEW MASTER.
UNTIL THEY GET EXPERIENCED ENOUGH TO OFFICIALLY BECOME SMITHS AS WELL.
I SEE, IT'S LIKE A SMITH INTERNSHIP, BEFORE I START HANDLING PROJECTS ON MY OWN! NOW I AM EVEN MORE FIRED UP!
I WILL HEAD UP TO THE SCHOOL SHOP RIGHT AWAY AND IMPROVE MY PODS.
WAIT, LET ME OFFER YOU THIS.
OH? THANKS!
GRAB!
ARE THESE... CLOTHES?
YES, INDEED.

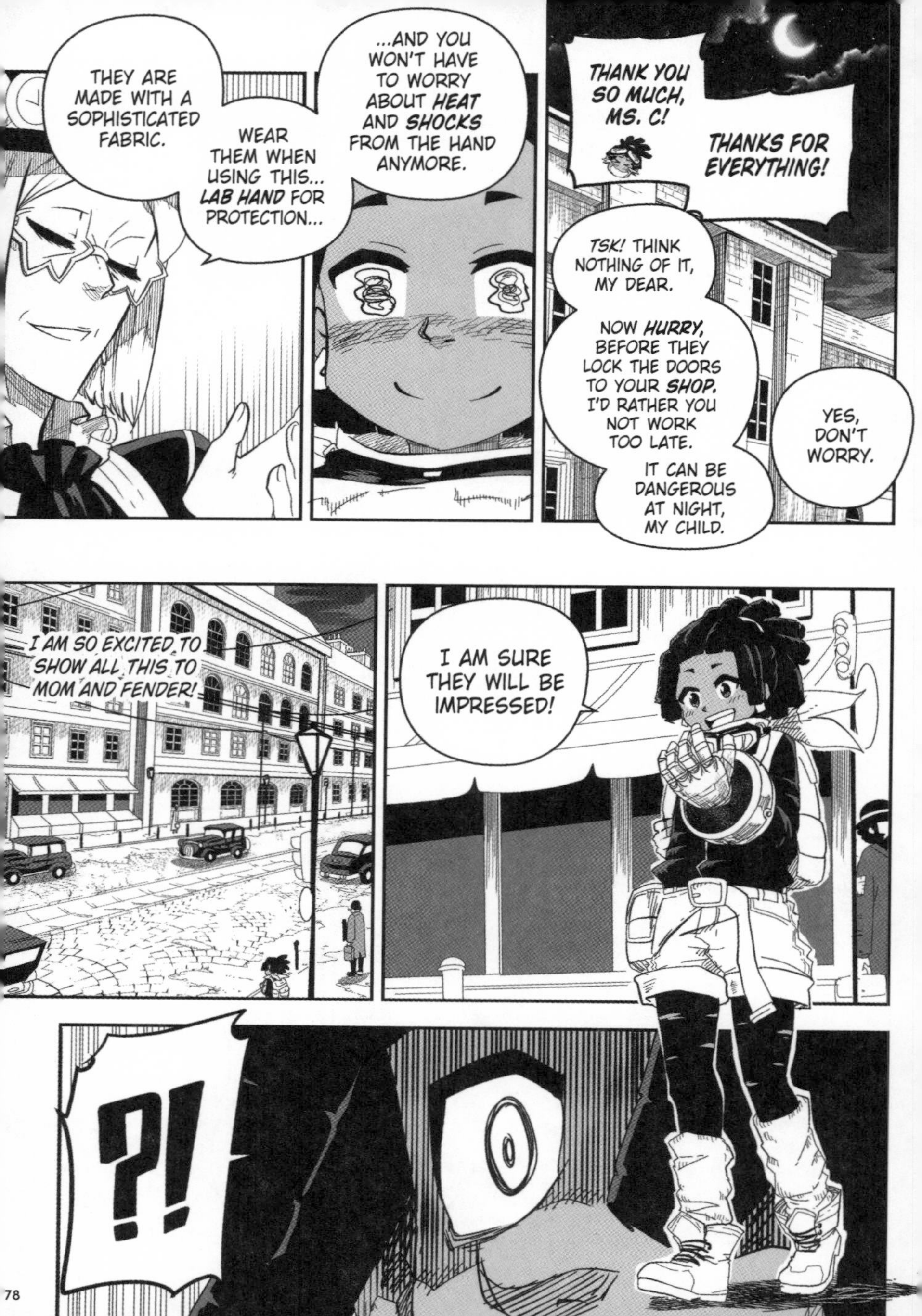
THEY ARE MADE WITH A SOPHISTICATED FABRIC.
WEAR THEM WHEN USING THIS... LAB HAND FOR PROTECTION...
...AND YOU WON'T HAVE TO WORRY ABOUT HEAT AND SHOCKS FROM THE HAND ANYMORE.
THANK YOU SO MUCH, MS. C!
THANKS FOR EVERYTHING!
TSK! THINK NOTHING OF IT, MY DEAR.
NOW HURRY, BEFORE THEY LOCK THE DOORS TO YOUR SHOP. I'D RATHER YOU NOT WORK TOO LATE.
IT CAN BE DANGEROUS AT NIGHT, MY CHILD.
YES, DON'T WORRY.
I AM SO EXCITED TO SHOW ALL THIS TO MOM AND FENDER!
I AM SURE THEY WILL BE IMPRESSED!
?!

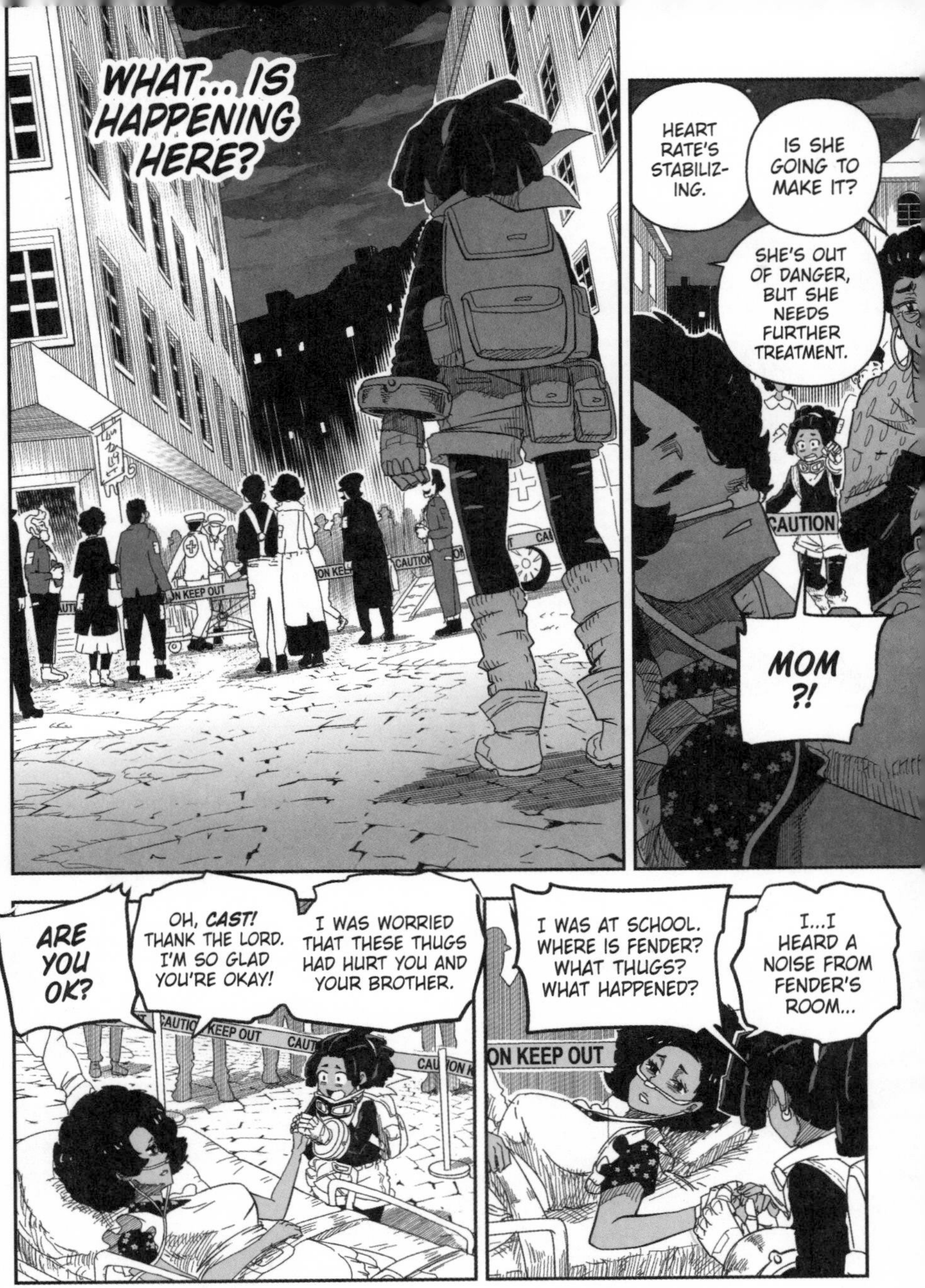
WHAT... IS HAPPENING HERE?
HEART RATE'S STABILIZ-ING.
IS SHE GOING TO MAKE IT?
SHE'S OUT OF DANGER, BUT SHE NEEDS FURTHER TREATMENT.
CAUTION
MOM ?!
ARE YOU OK?
OH, CAST! THANK THE LORD. I'M SO GLAD YOU'RE OKAY!
I WAS WORRIED THAT THESE THUGS HAD HURT YOU AND YOUR BROTHER.
I WAS AT SCHOOL. WHERE IS FENDER? WHAT THUGS? WHAT HAPPENED?
I...I HEARD A NOISE FROM FENDER'S ROOM...
ON KEEP OUT

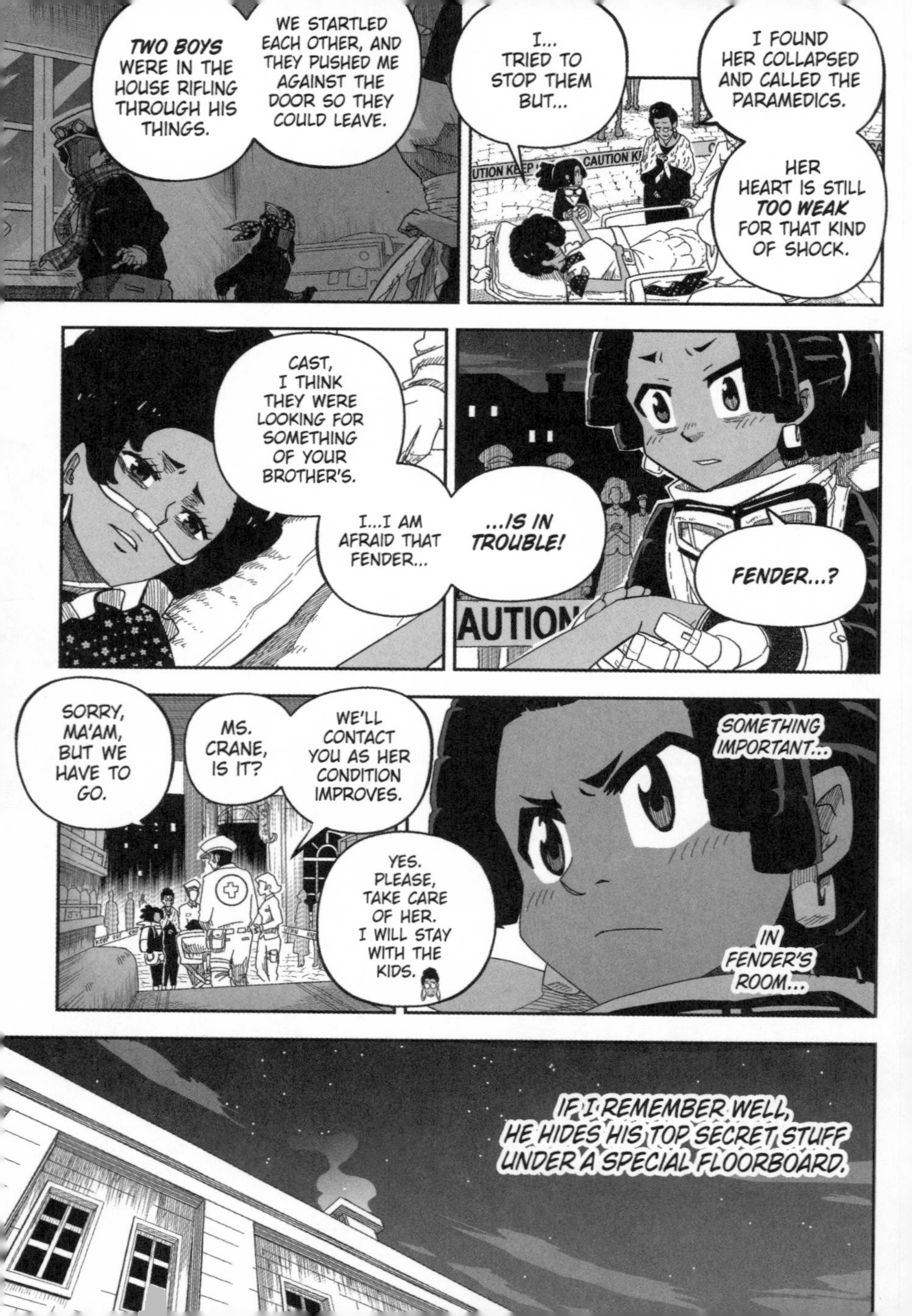
TWO BOYS WERE IN THE HOUSE RIFLING THROUGH HIS THINGS.
WE STARTLED EACH OTHER, AND THEY PUSHED ME AGAINST THE DOOR SO THEY COULD LEAVE.
I... TRIED TO STOP THEM BUT...
I FOUND HER COLLAPSED AND CALLED THE PARAMEDICS.
HER HEART IS STILL TOO WEAK FOR THAT KIND OF SHOCK.
CAST, I THINK THEY WERE LOOKING FOR SOMETHING OF YOUR BROTHER'S.
I...I AM AFRAID THAT FENDER...
...IS IN TROUBLE!
FENDER...?
SORRY, MA'AM, BUT WE HAVE TO GO.
MS. CRANE, IS IT?
WE'LL CONTACT YOU AS HER CONDITION IMPROVES.
YES. PLEASE, TAKE CARE OF HER. I WILL STAY WITH THE KIDS.
SOMETHING IMPORTANT...
IN FENDER'S ROOM...
IF I REMEMBER WELL, HE HIDES HIS TOP SECRET STUFF UNDER A SPECIAL FLOORBOARD.

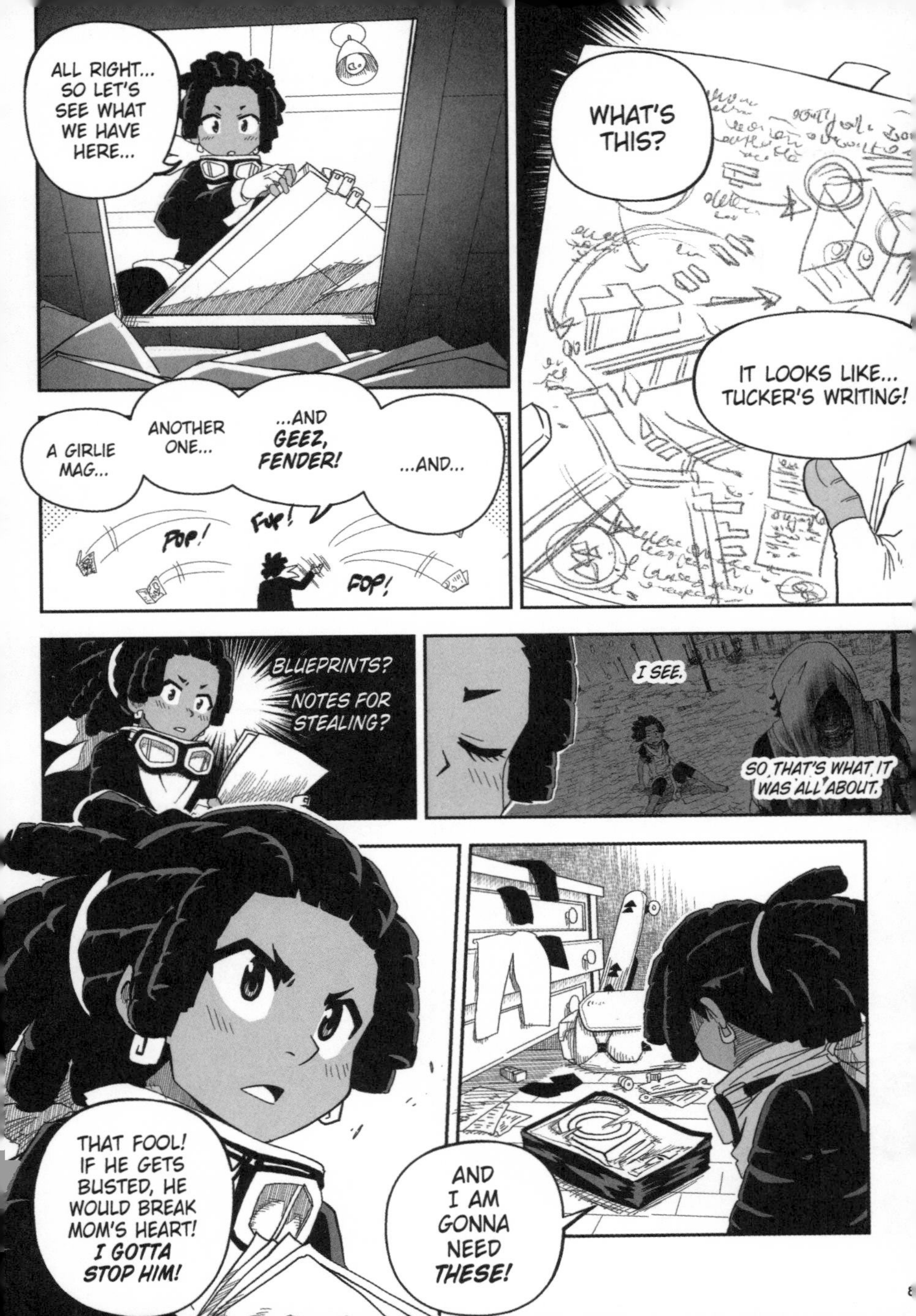
ALL RIGHT... SO LET'S SEE WHAT WE HAVE HERE...
A GIRLIE MAG...
ANOTHER ONE...
...AND GEEZ, FENDER!
...AND...
POP!
FUP!
FOP!
WHAT'S THIS?
IT LOOKS LIKE... TUCKER'S WRITING!
BLUEPRINTS?
NOTES FOR STEALING?
I SEE.
SO THAT'S WHAT IT WAS ALL ABOUT.
THAT FOOL! IF HE GETS BUSTED, HE WOULD BREAK MOM'S HEART! I GOTTA STOP HIM!
AND I AM GONNA NEED THESE!

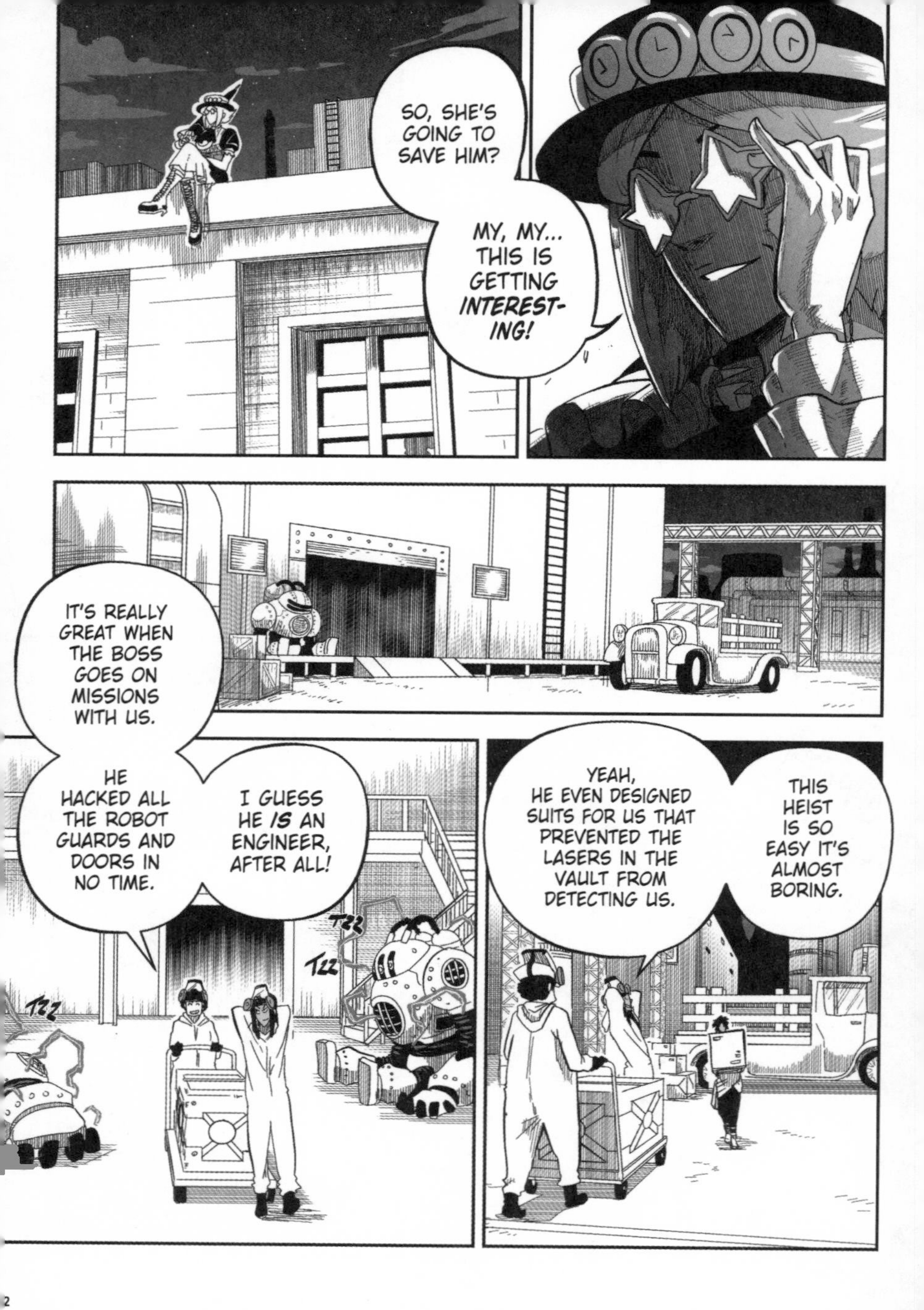
SO, SHE'S GOING TO SAVE HIM?
MY, MY... THIS IS GETTING *INTEREST-ING!*
IT'S REALLY GREAT WHEN THE BOSS GOES ON MISSIONS WITH US.
HE HACKED ALL THE ROBOT GUARDS AND DOORS IN NO TIME.
I GUESS HE *IS* AN ENGINEER, AFTER ALL!
TZZ
TZZ
TZZ
YEAH, HE EVEN DESIGNED SUITS FOR US THAT PREVENTED THE LASERS IN THE VAULT FROM DETECTING US.
THIS HEIST IS SO EASY IT'S ALMOST BORING.

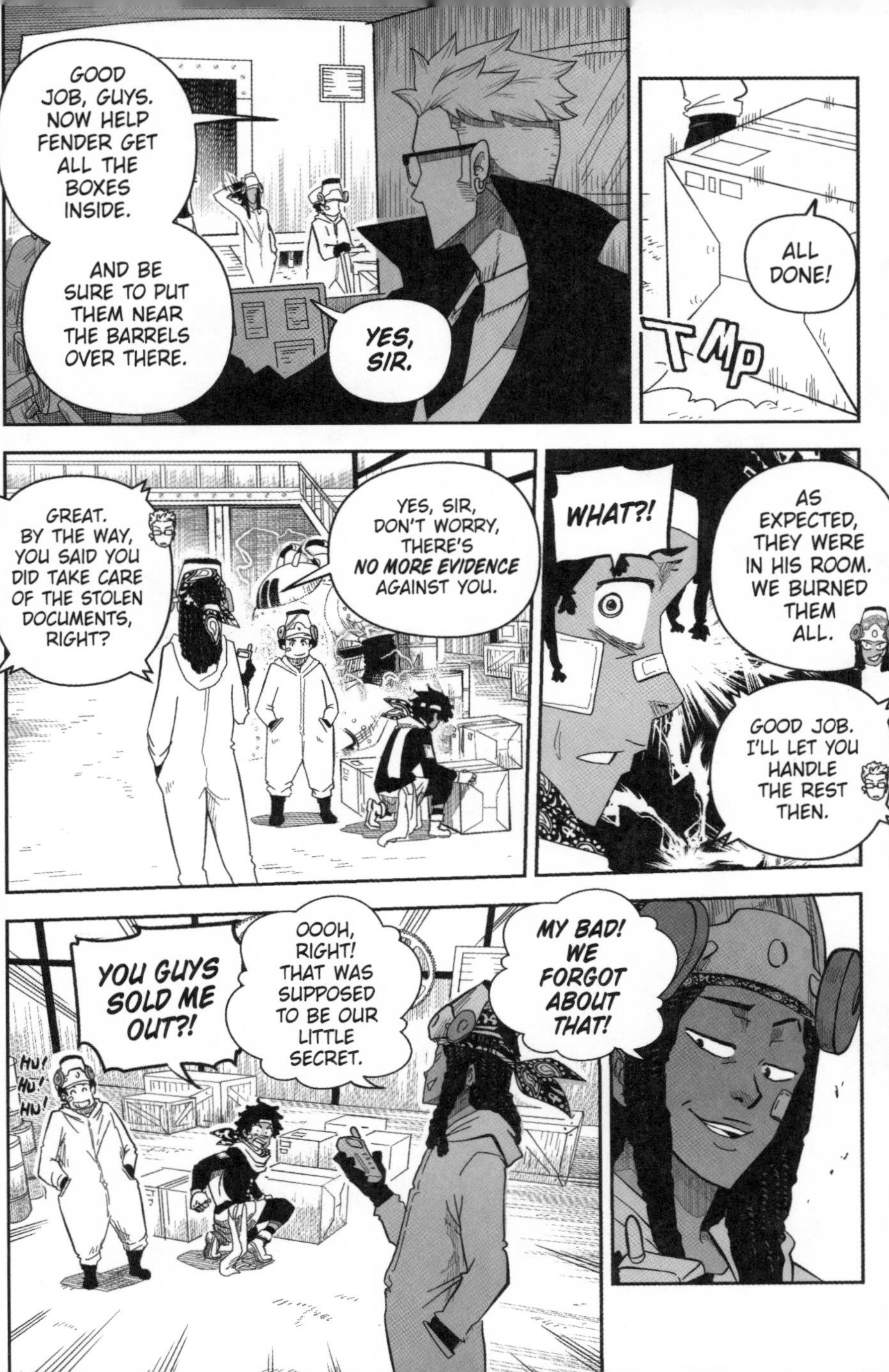
GOOD JOB, GUYS. NOW HELP FENDER GET ALL THE BOXES INSIDE.
AND BE SURE TO PUT THEM NEAR THE BARRELS OVER THERE.
YES, SIR.
ALL DONE!
TMP
GREAT. BY THE WAY, YOU SAID YOU DID TAKE CARE OF THE STOLEN DOCUMENTS, RIGHT?
YES, SIR, DON'T WORRY, THERE'S NO MORE EVIDENCE AGAINST YOU.
WHAT?!
AS EXPECTED, THEY WERE IN HIS ROOM. WE BURNED THEM ALL.
GOOD JOB. I'LL LET YOU HANDLE THE REST THEN.
YOU GUYS SOLD ME OUT?!
HU! HU! HU!
OOOH, RIGHT! THAT WAS SUPPOSED TO BE OUR LITTLE SECRET.
MY BAD! WE FORGOT ABOUT THAT!

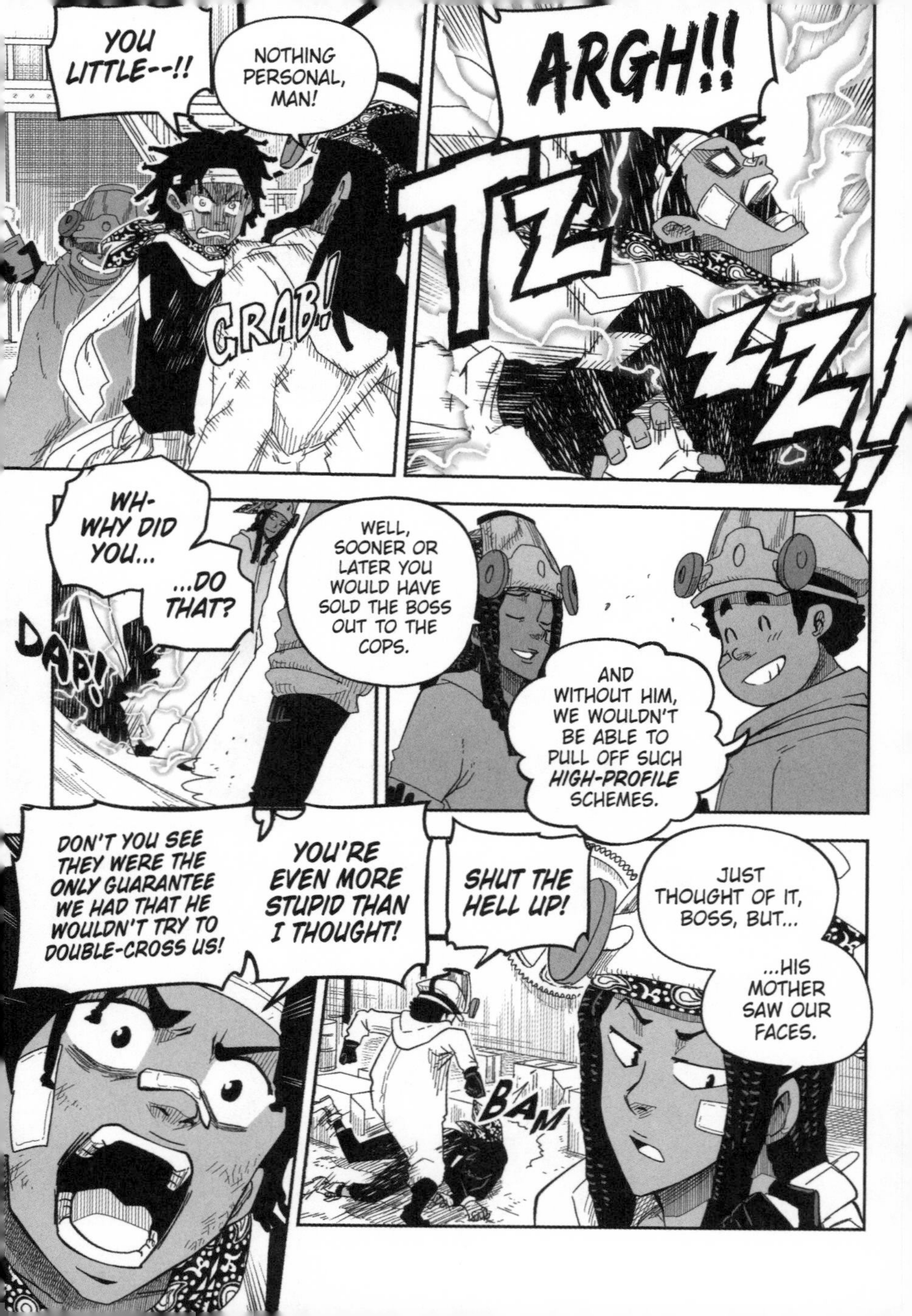
YOU LITTLE--!!
NOTHING PERSONAL, MAN!
GRAB!
ARGH!!
TZZZZ!!
WH- WHY DID YOU...
...DO THAT?
DAP!
WELL, SOONER OR LATER YOU WOULD HAVE SOLD THE BOSS OUT TO THE COPS.
AND WITHOUT HIM, WE WOULDN'T BE ABLE TO PULL OFF SUCH HIGH-PROFILE SCHEMES.
DON'T YOU SEE THEY WERE THE ONLY GUARANTEE WE HAD THAT HE WOULDN'T TRY TO DOUBLE-CROSS US!
YOU'RE EVEN MORE STUPID THAN I THOUGHT!
SHUT THE HELL UP!
JUST THOUGHT OF IT, BOSS, BUT...
...HIS MOTHER SAW OUR FACES.
BAM

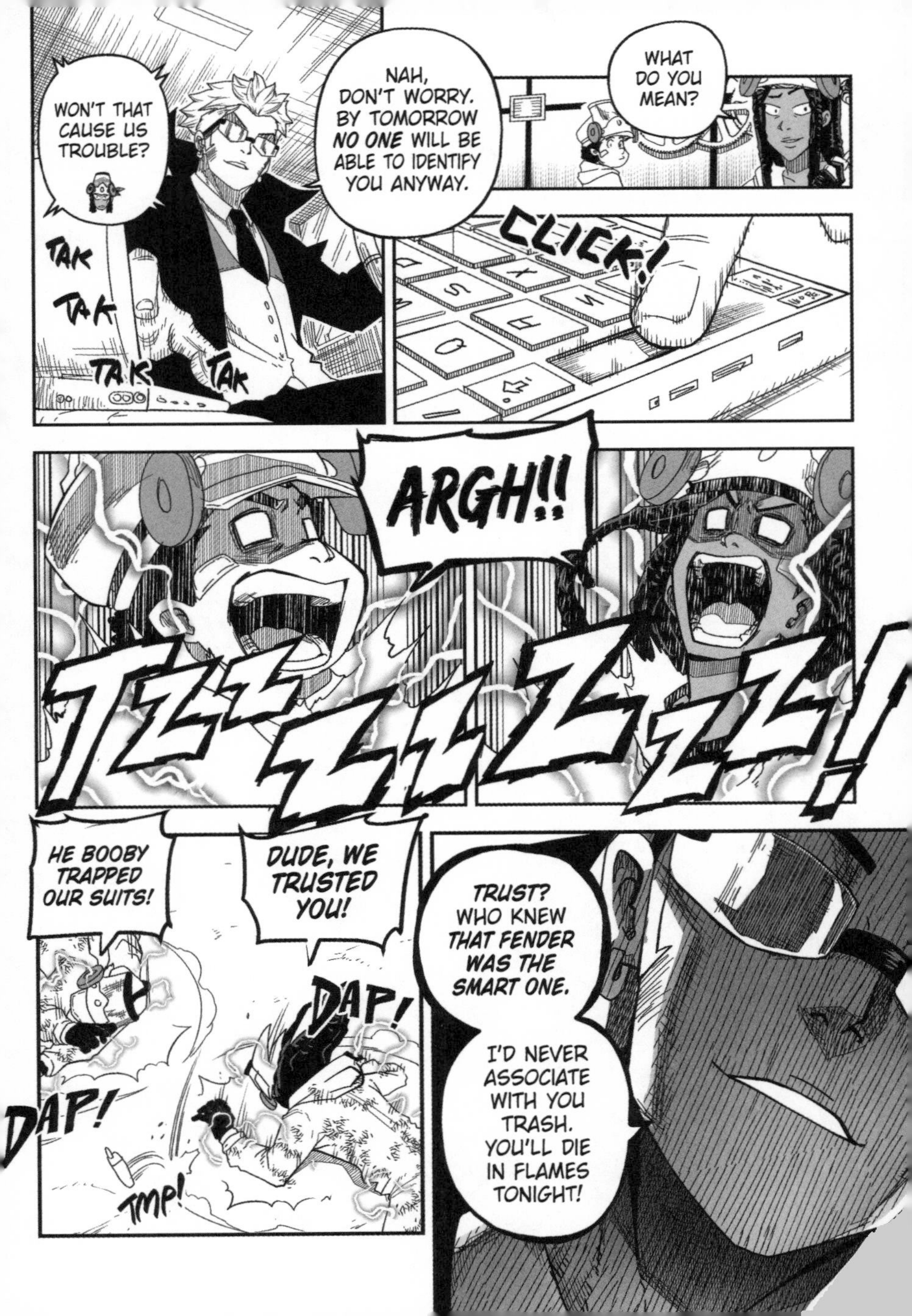
WON'T THAT CAUSE US TROUBLE?
NAH, DON'T WORRY. BY TOMORROW NO ONE WILL BE ABLE TO IDENTIFY YOU ANYWAY.
TAK
TAK
TAK
TAK
WHAT DO YOU MEAN?
CLICK!
ARGH!!
TZZZZZZZZ!
HE BOOBY TRAPPED OUR SUITS!
DUDE, WE TRUSTED YOU!
DAP!
DAP!
TMP!
TRUST? WHO KNEW THAT FENDER WAS THE SMART ONE.
I'D NEVER ASSOCIATE WITH YOU TRASH. YOU'LL DIE IN FLAMES TONIGHT!

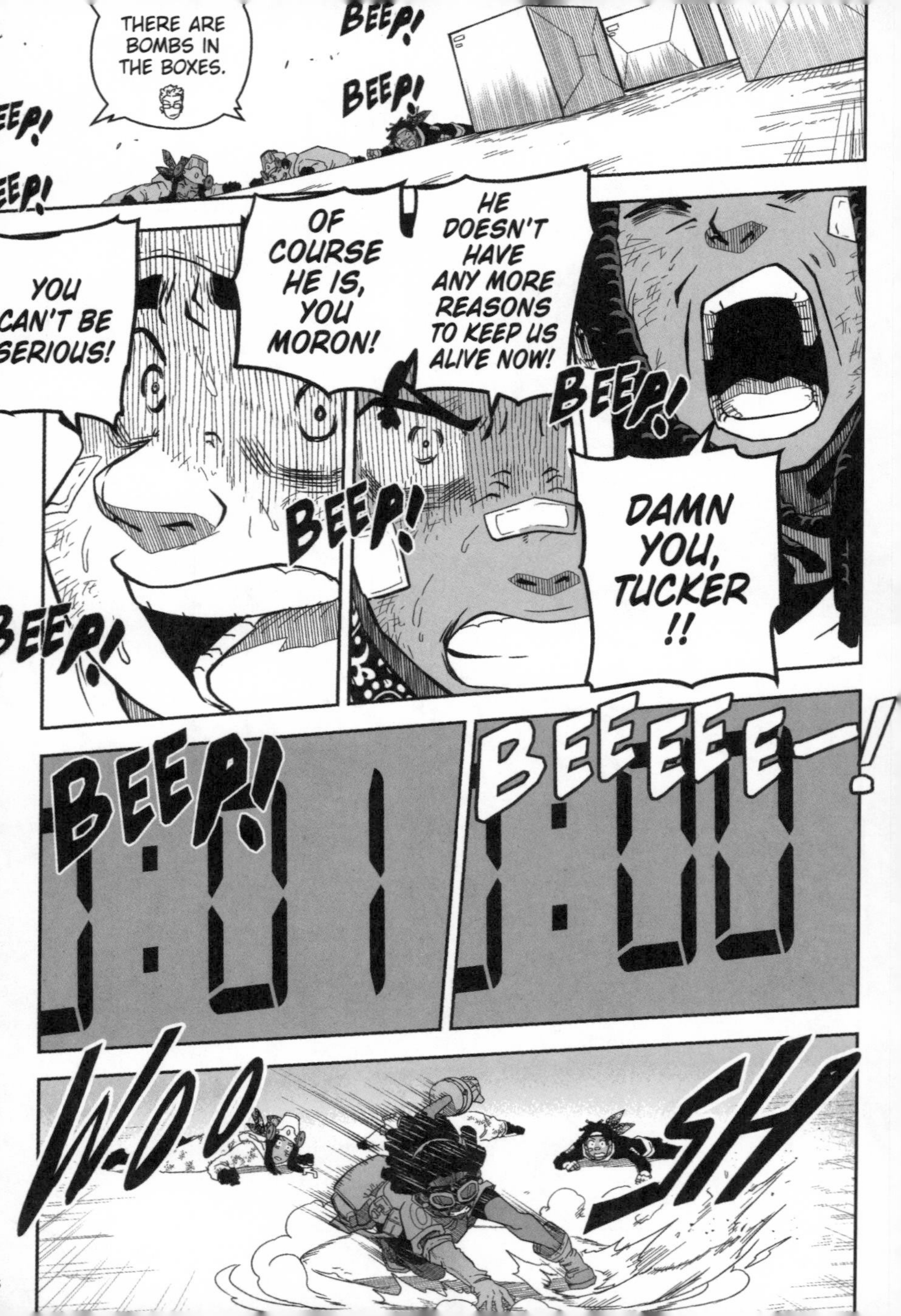
THERE ARE BOMBS IN THE BOXES.
BEEP!
BEEP!
EEP!
EEP!
YOU CAN'T BE SERIOUS!
OF COURSE HE IS, YOU MORON!
HE DOESN'T HAVE ANY MORE REASONS TO KEEP US ALIVE NOW!
BEEP!
BEEP!
BEEP!
DAMN YOU, TUCKER!!
BEEP!
BEEEEE—!
WOOSH

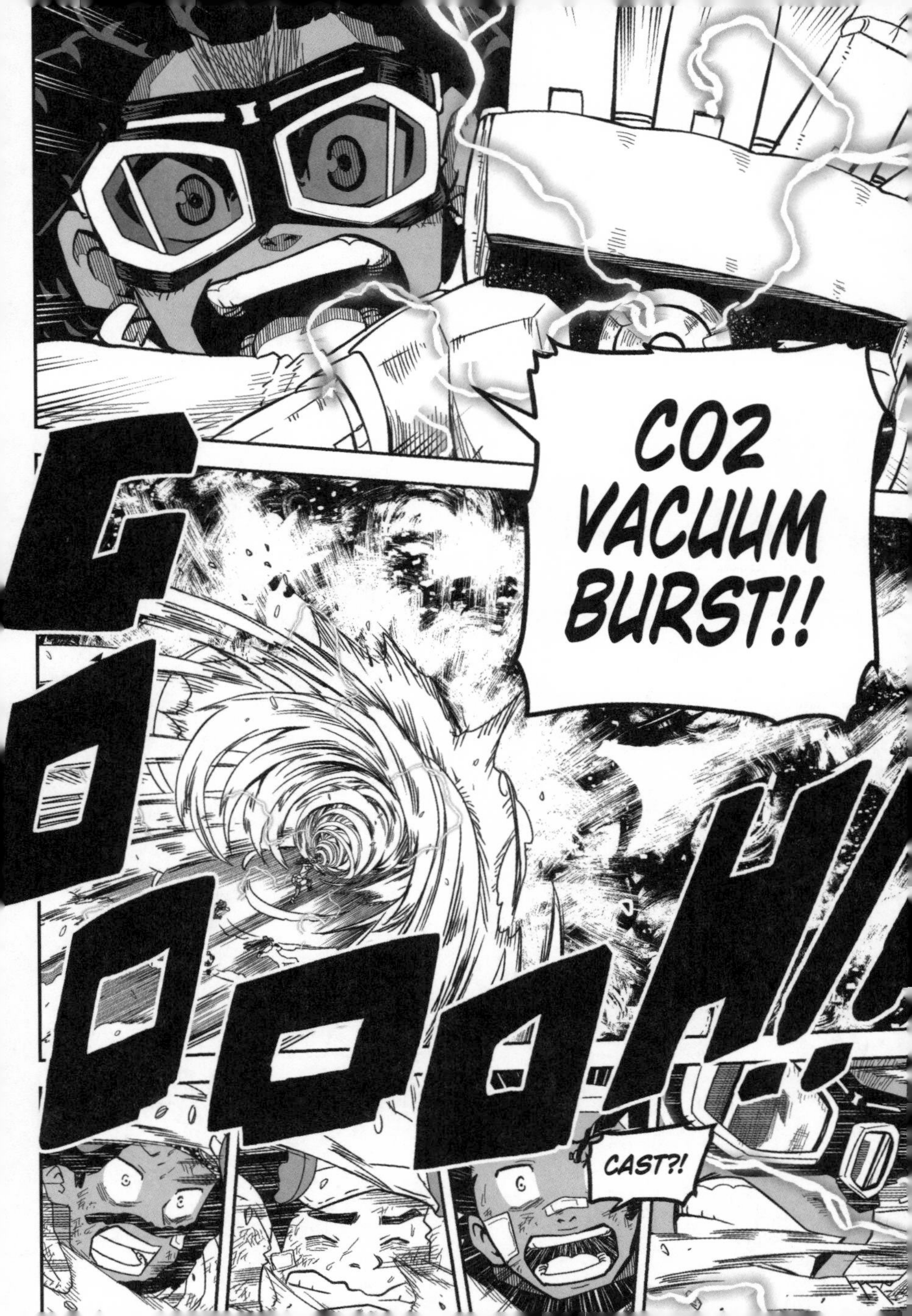
CO2 VACUUM BURST!!
CAST?!

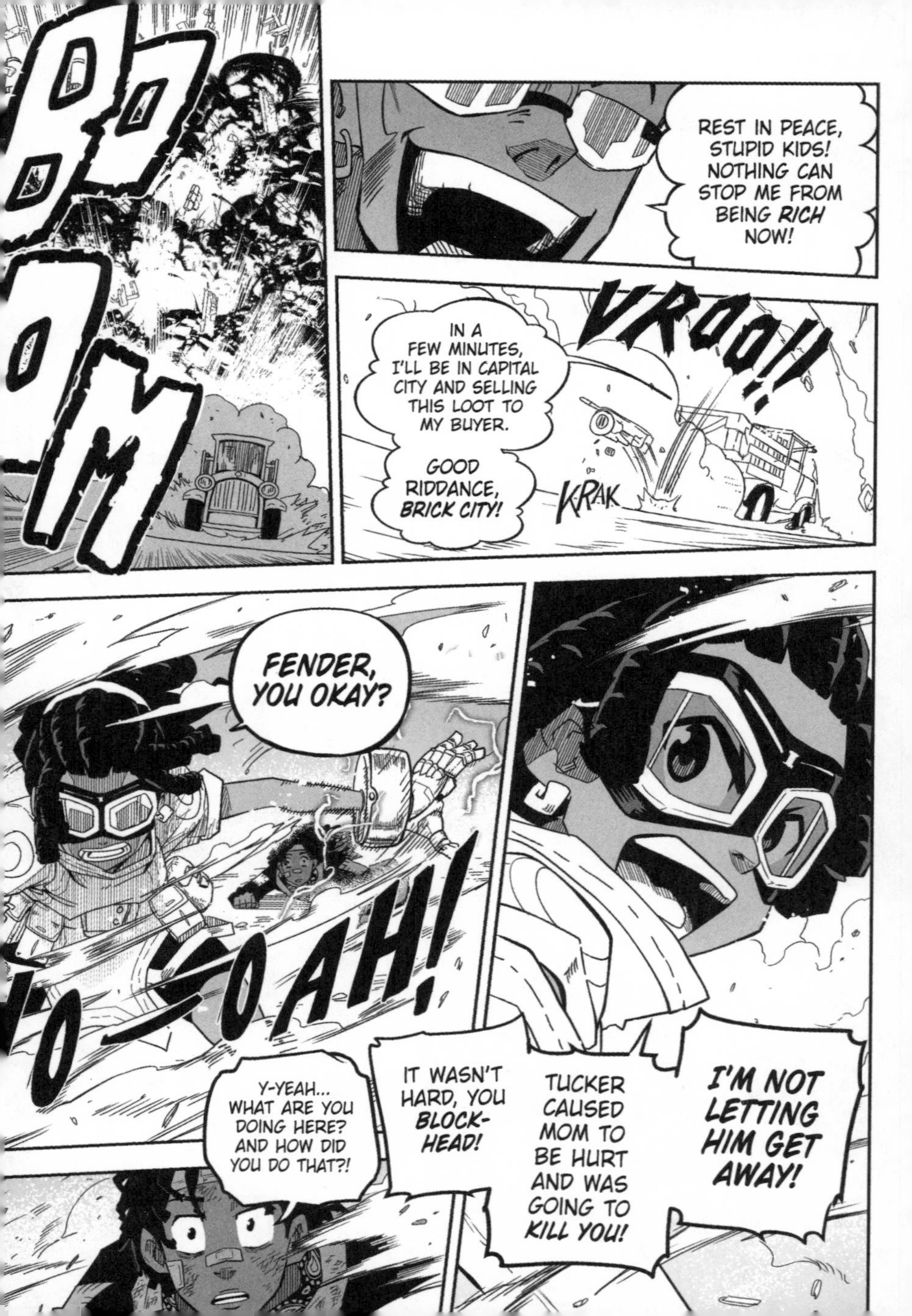
BOOM
REST IN PEACE, STUPID KIDS! NOTHING CAN STOP ME FROM BEING *RICH* NOW!
IN A FEW MINUTES, I'LL BE IN CAPITAL CITY AND SELLING THIS LOOT TO MY BUYER.
GOOD RIDDANCE, *BRICK CITY!*
VROO!!
K-RAK
FENDER, YOU OKAY?
O—OAH!
Y-YEAH... WHAT ARE YOU DOING HERE? AND HOW DID YOU DO THAT?!
IT WASN'T HARD, YOU *BLOCK-HEAD!*
TUCKER CAUSED MOM TO BE HURT AND WAS GOING TO *KILL YOU!*
I'M NOT LETTING HIM GET AWAY!

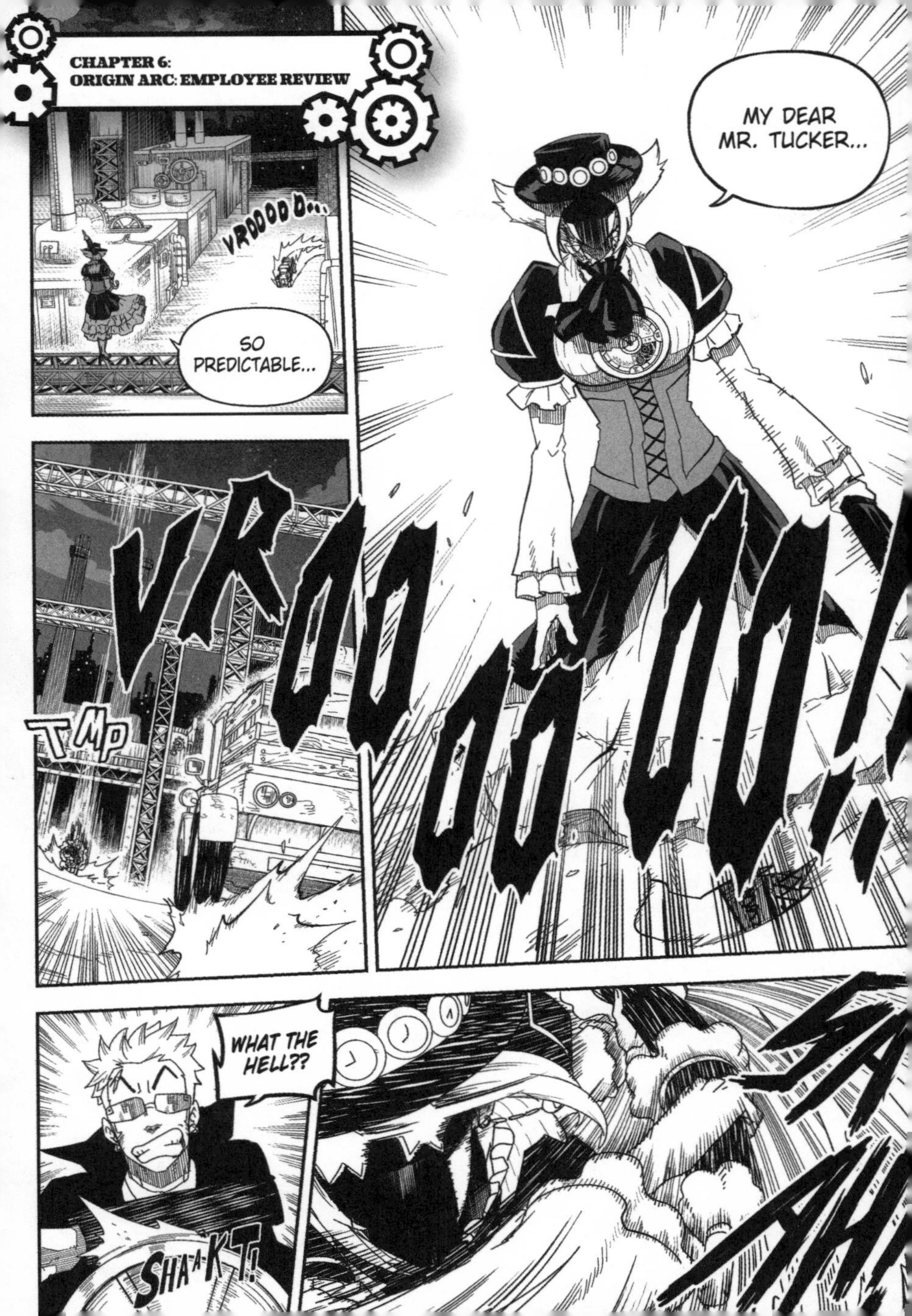
CHAPTER 6:
ORIGIN ARC: EMPLOYEE REVIEW
VROOOO O...
SO PREDICTABLE...
VROOOOOOOO!!
TMP
MY DEAR MR. TUCKER...
WHAT THE HELL??
SHA-A-KT!

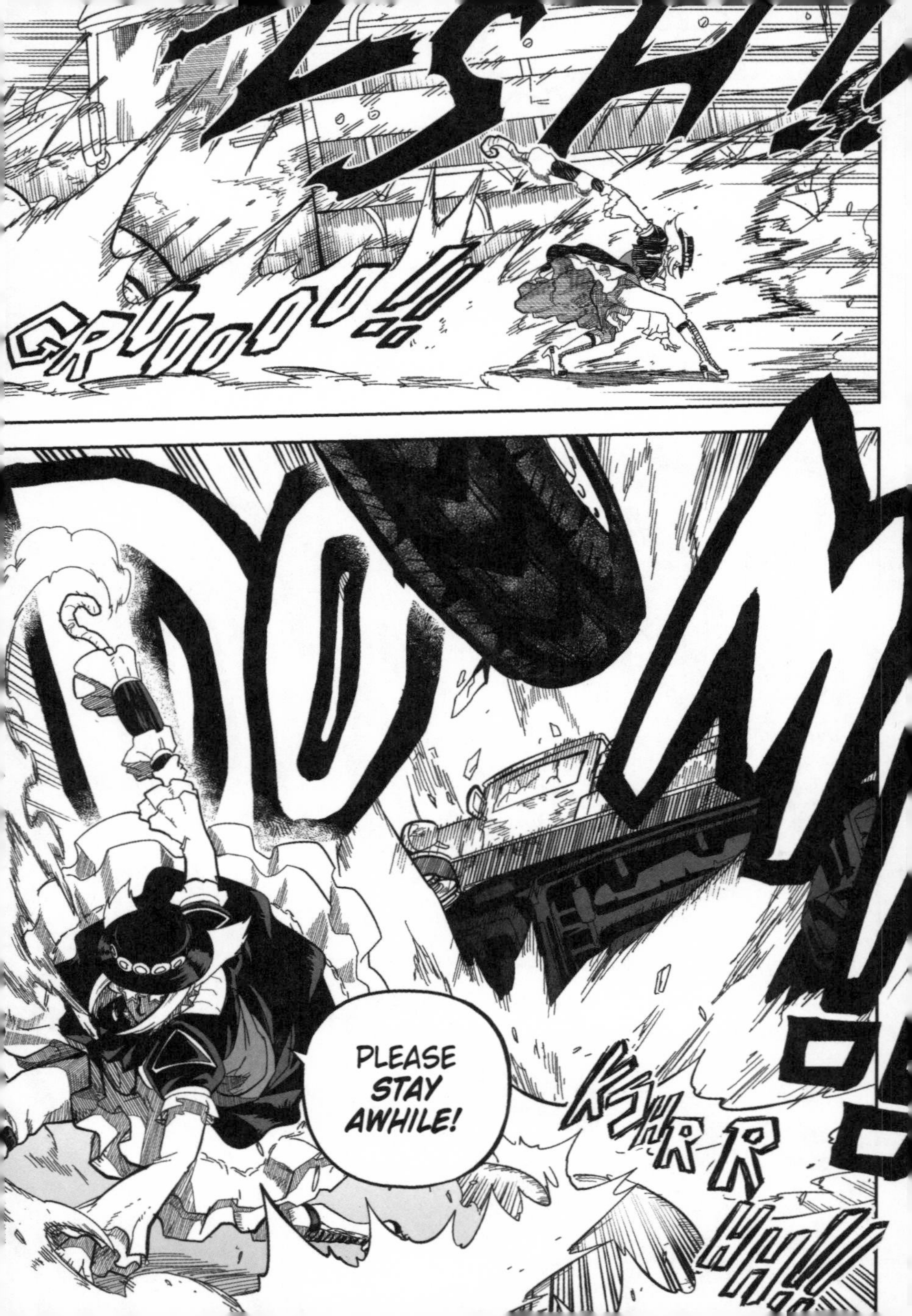
GRUOOOO!!
PLEASE STAY AWHILE!

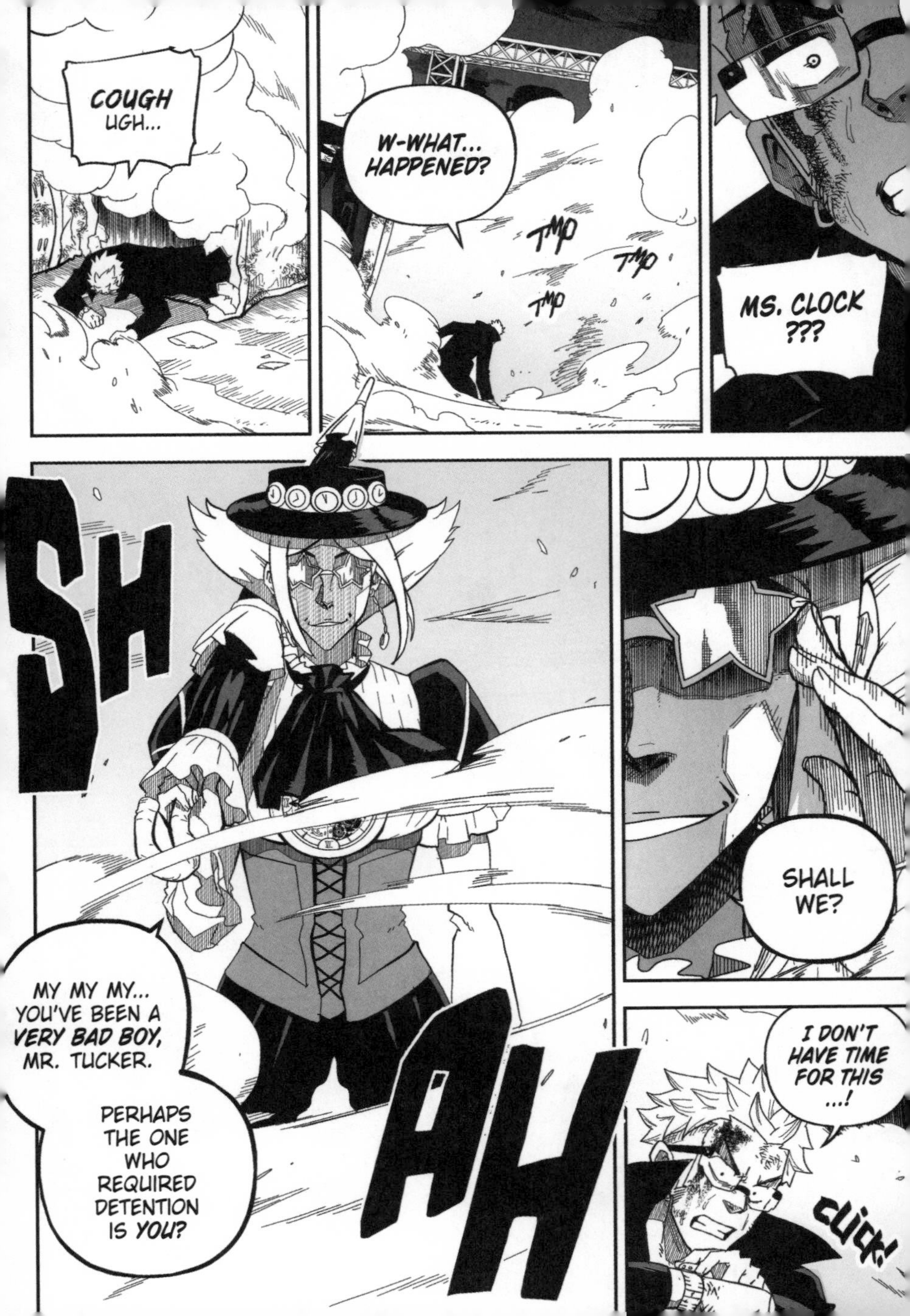
COUGH UGH...
W-WHAT... HAPPENED?
TMP
TMP
TMP
MS. CLOCK ???
SH
AH
MY MY MY... YOU'VE BEEN A *VERY BAD BOY,* MR. TUCKER.
PERHAPS THE ONE WHO REQUIRED DETENTION IS *YOU?*
SHALL WE?
I DON'T HAVE TIME FOR THIS ...!
CLICK!

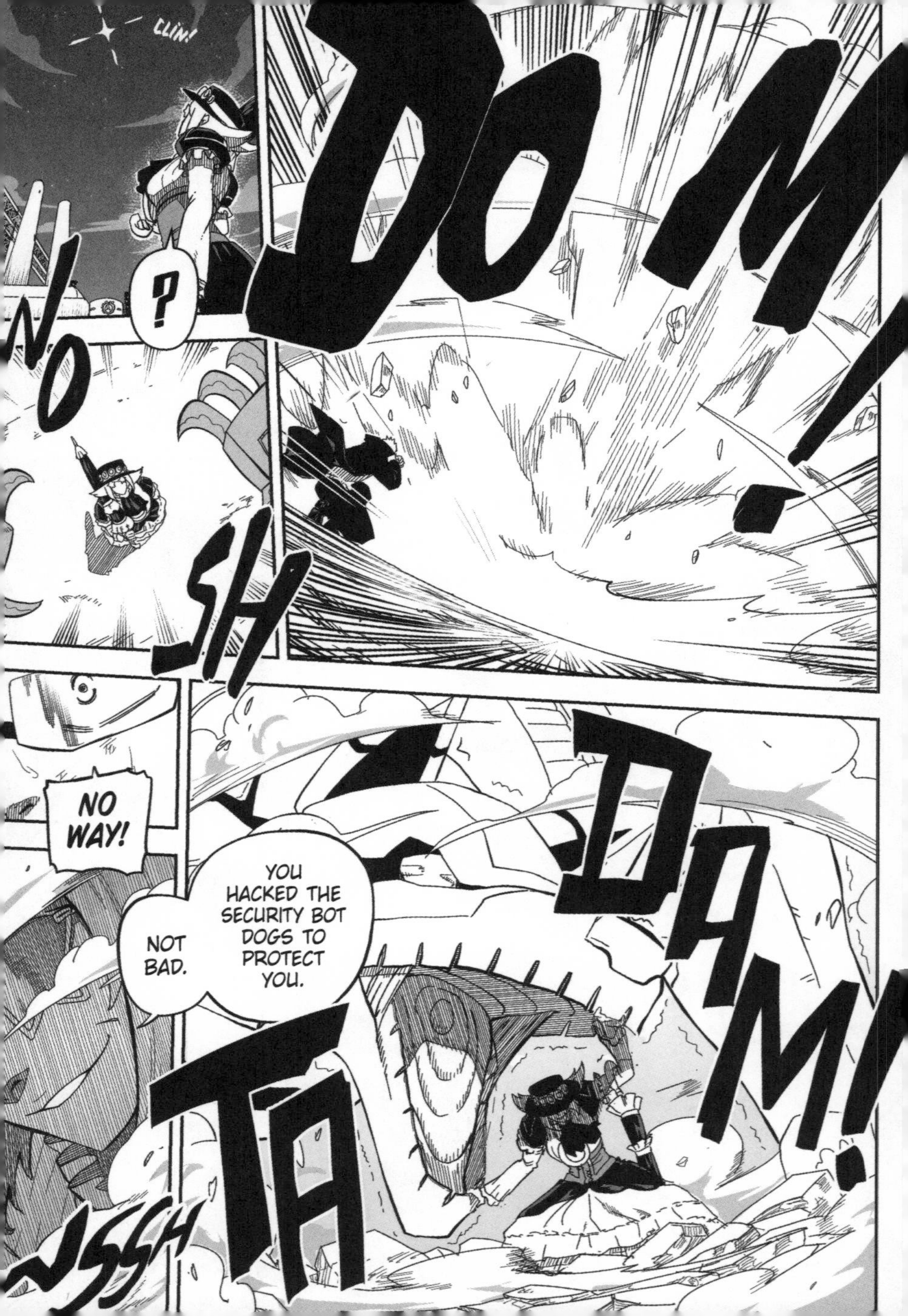

CLIN!
?
DOOM!
NO
SH
NO WAY!
DAM!
YOU HACKED THE SECURITY BOT DOGS TO PROTECT YOU.
NOT BAD.
TA
WSSH

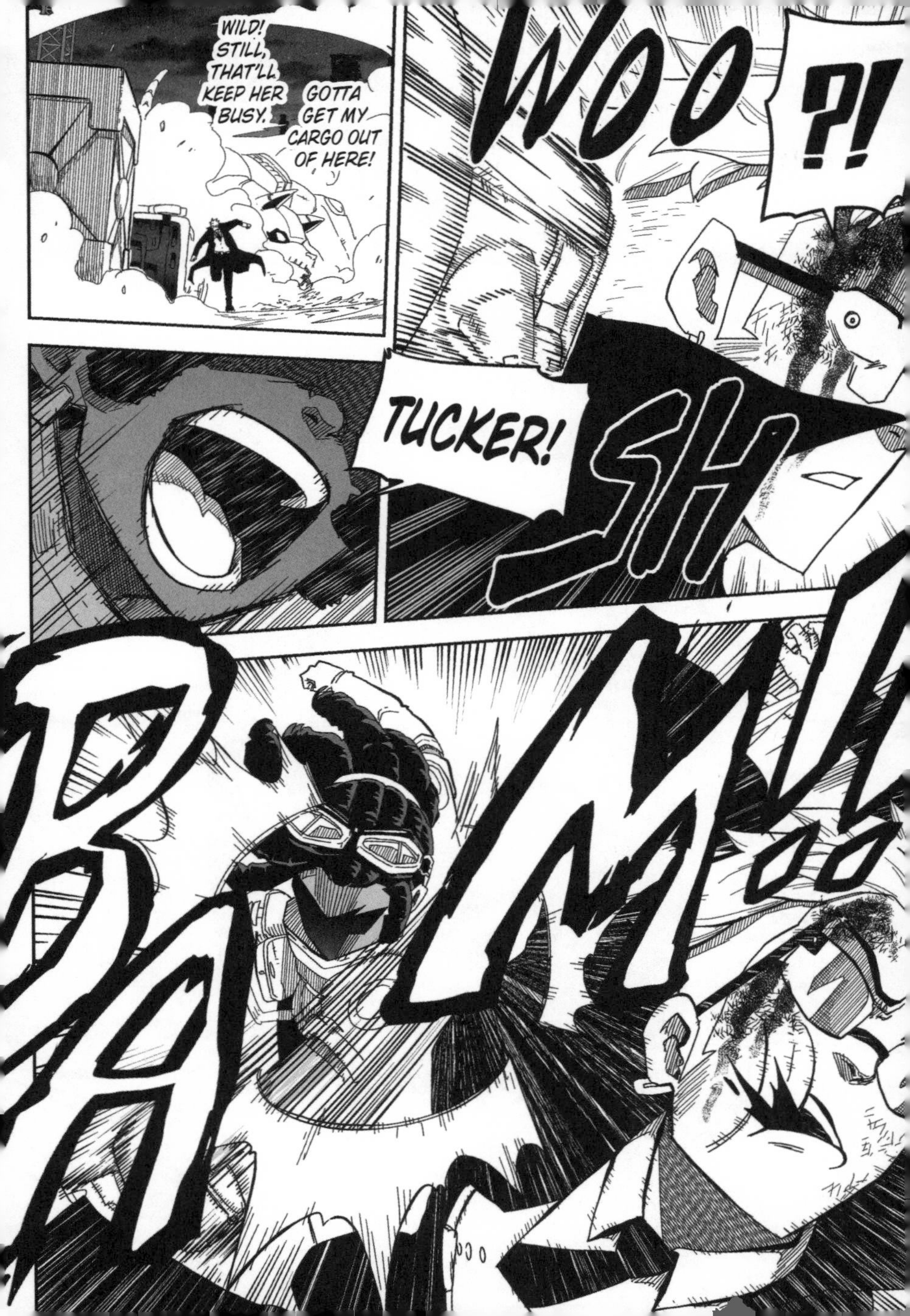
WILD! STILL, THAT'LL KEEP HER BUSY.
GOTTA GET MY CARGO OUT OF HERE!
WOO
?!
TUCKER!
SH
BAM

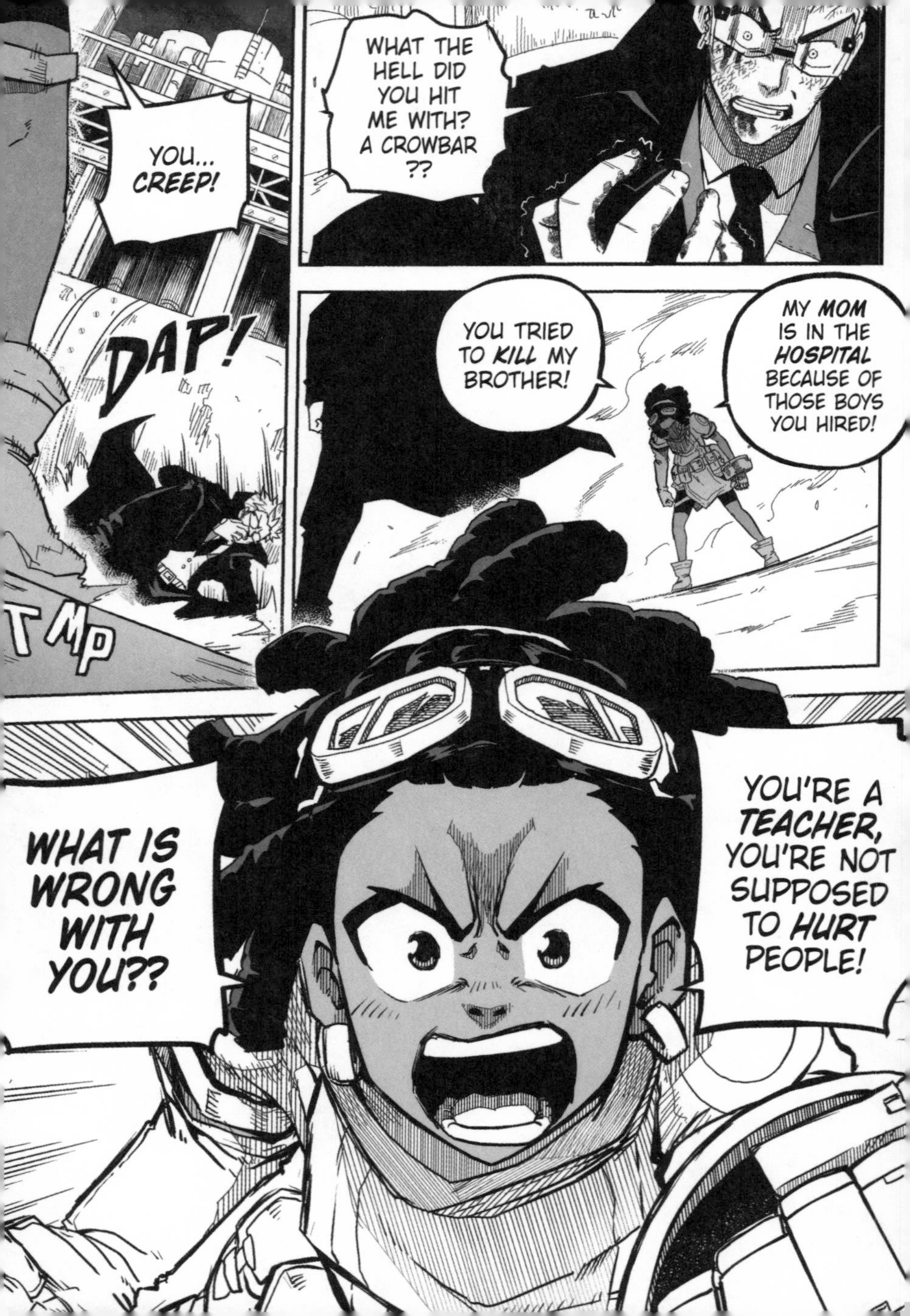
YOU... CREEP!
DAP!
TMP
WHAT THE HELL DID YOU HIT ME WITH? A CROWBAR ??
YOU TRIED TO KILL MY BROTHER!
MY MOM IS IN THE HOSPITAL BECAUSE OF THOSE BOYS YOU HIRED!
WHAT IS WRONG WITH YOU??
YOU'RE A TEACHER, YOU'RE NOT SUPPOSED TO HURT PEOPLE!

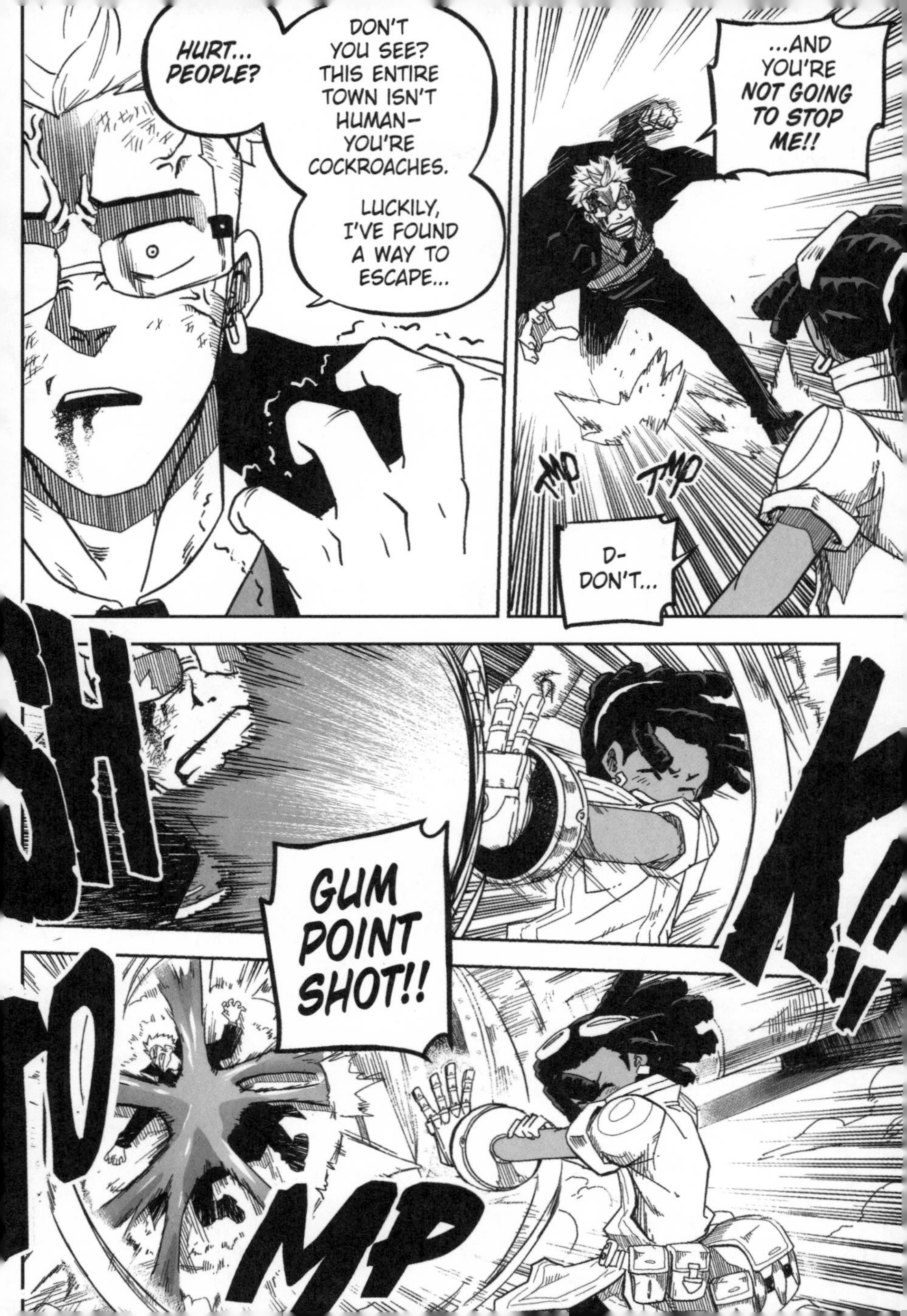
HURT... PEOPLE?
DON'T YOU SEE? THIS ENTIRE TOWN ISN'T HUMAN— YOU'RE COCKROACHES.
LUCKILY, I'VE FOUND A WAY TO ESCAPE...
...AND YOU'RE NOT GOING TO STOP ME!!
TMP
TMP
D- DON'T...
GUM POINT SHOT!!

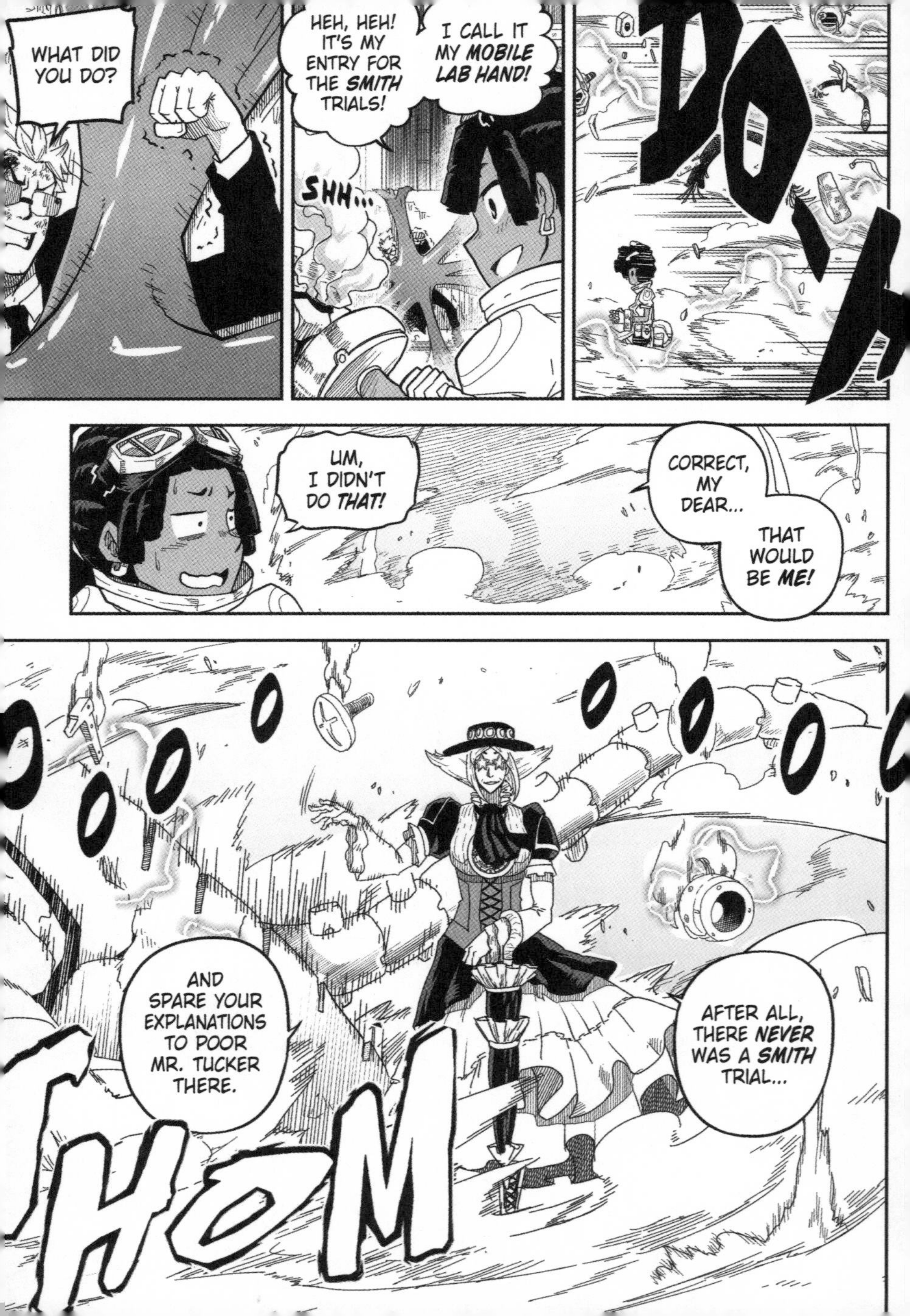
WHAT DID YOU DO?
HEH, HEH! IT'S MY ENTRY FOR THE SMITH TRIALS!
I CALL IT MY MOBILE LAB HAND!
SHH...
DO
UM, I DIDN'T DO THAT!
CORRECT, MY DEAR...
THAT WOULD BE ME!
AND SPARE YOUR EXPLANATIONS TO POOR MR. TUCKER THERE.
AFTER ALL, THERE NEVER WAS A SMITH TRIAL...
HOM

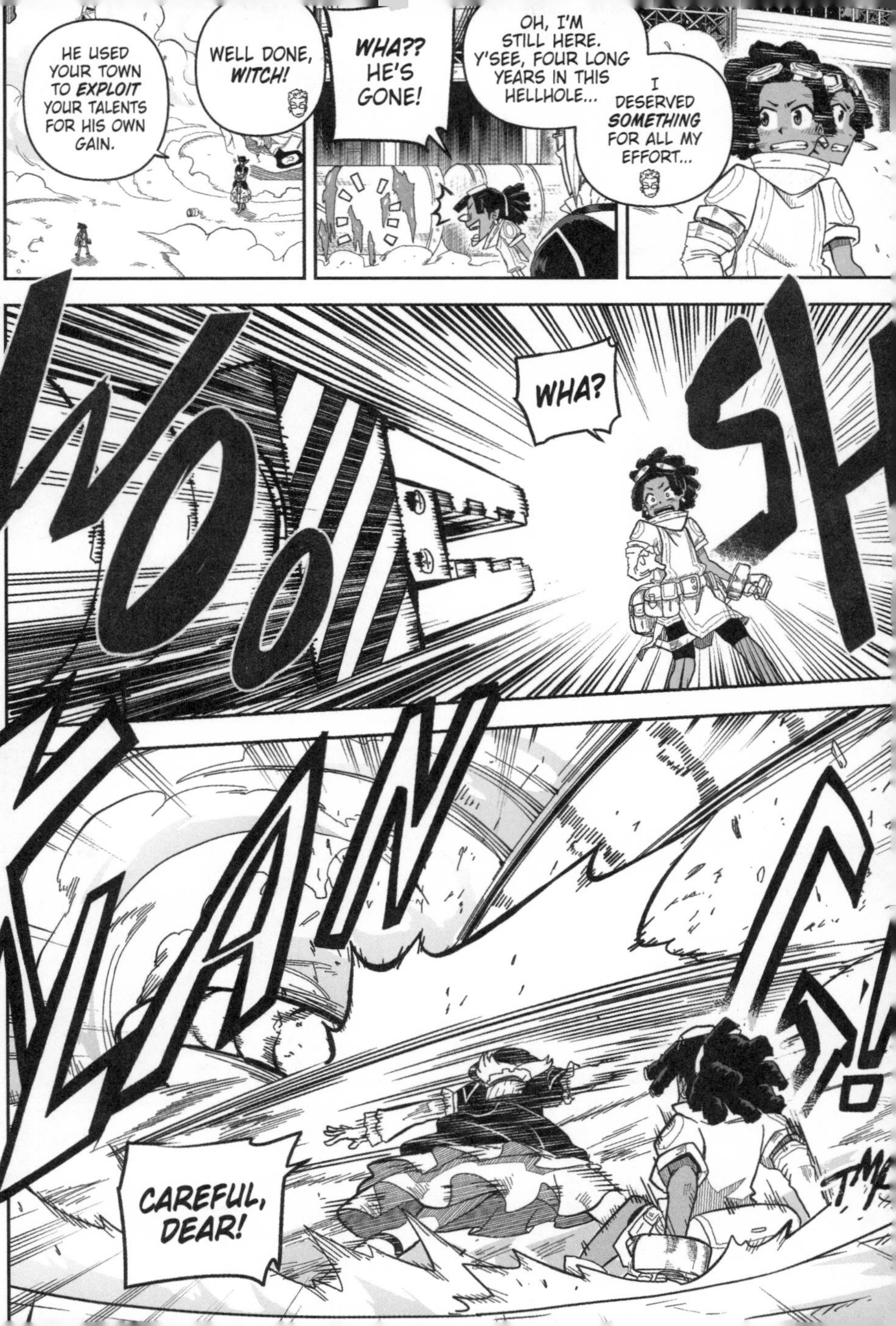
HE USED YOUR TOWN TO ***EXPLOIT*** YOUR TALENTS FOR HIS OWN GAIN.
WELL DONE, ***WITCH!***
WHA?? HE'S GONE!
OH, I'M STILL HERE. Y'SEE, FOUR LONG YEARS IN THIS HELLHOLE...
I DESERVED ***SOMETHING*** FOR ALL MY EFFORT...
WHA?
CAREFUL, DEAR!

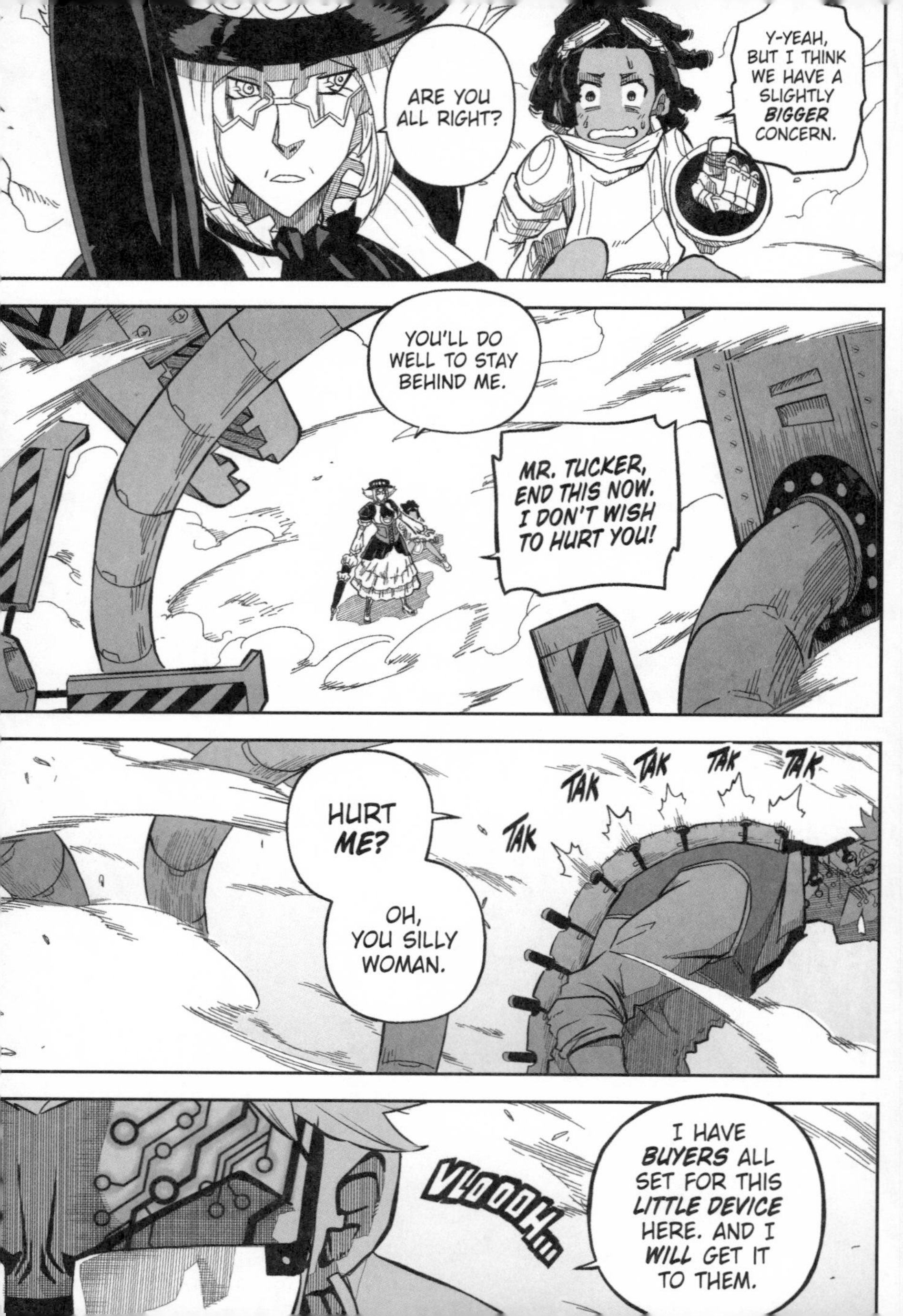
ARE YOU ALL RIGHT?
Y-YEAH, BUT I THINK WE HAVE A SLIGHTLY BIGGER CONCERN.
YOU'LL DO WELL TO STAY BEHIND ME.
MR. TUCKER, END THIS NOW. I DON'T WISH TO HURT YOU!
HURT ME?
OH, YOU SILLY WOMAN.
TAK
TAK
TAK
TAK
TAK
VLOOOH...
I HAVE BUYERS ALL SET FOR THIS LITTLE DEVICE HERE. AND I WILL GET IT TO THEM.

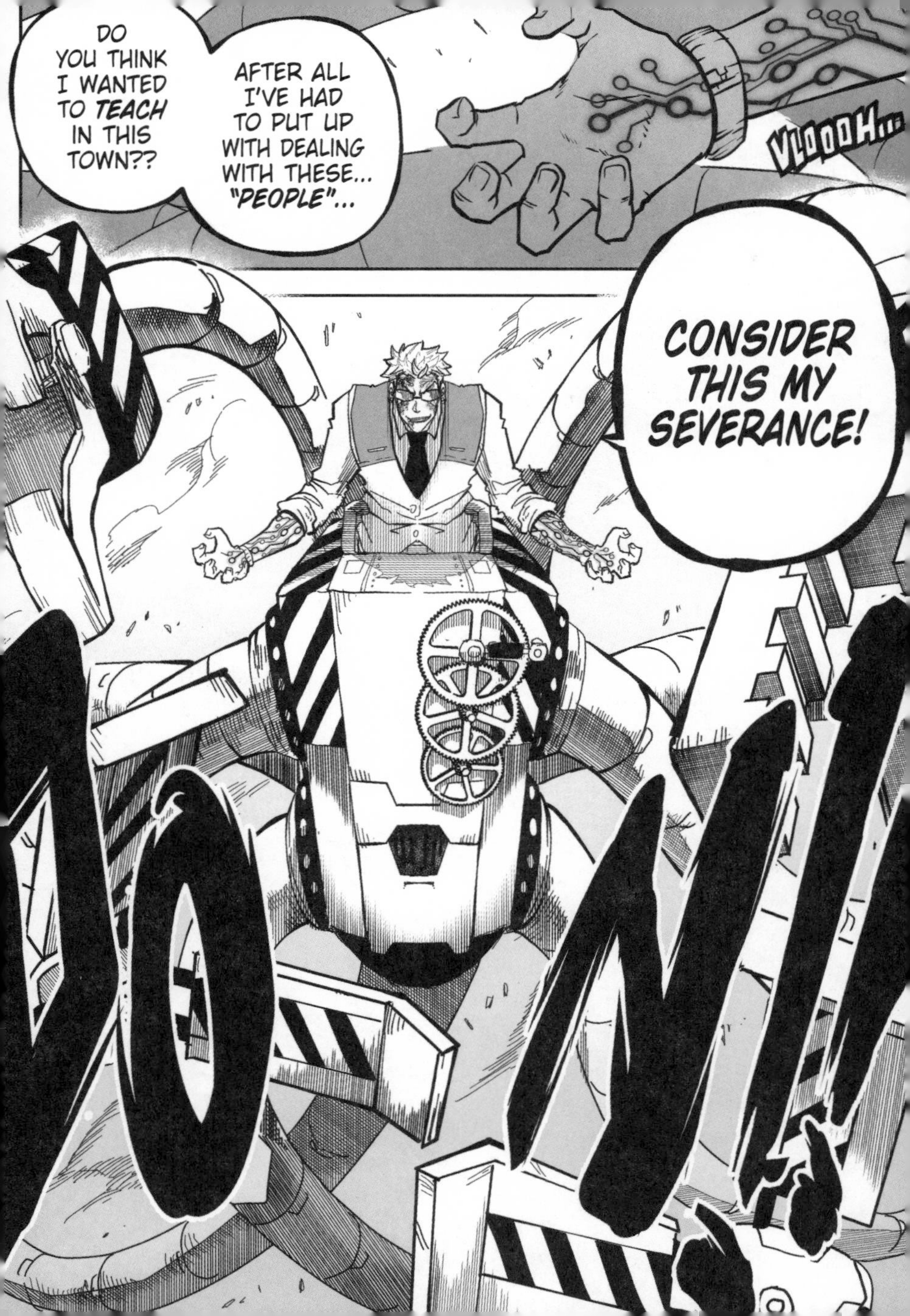
DO YOU THINK I WANTED TO *TEACH* IN THIS TOWN??
AFTER ALL I'VE HAD TO PUT UP WITH DEALING WITH THESE... *"PEOPLE"*...
VLOOOH...
CONSIDER THIS MY SEVERANCE!

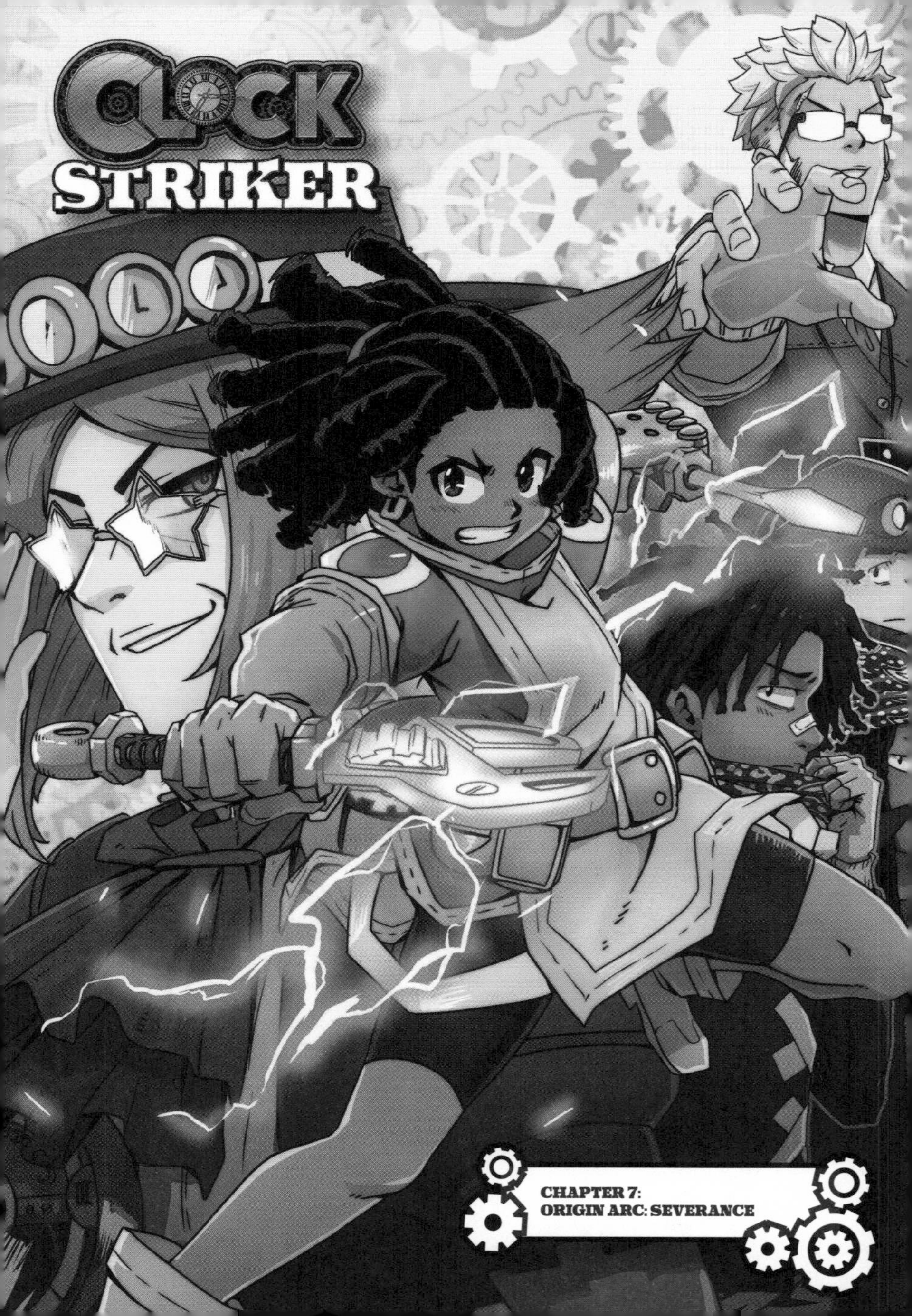
CLOCK
STRIKER
CHAPTER 7:
ORIGIN ARC: SEVERANCE

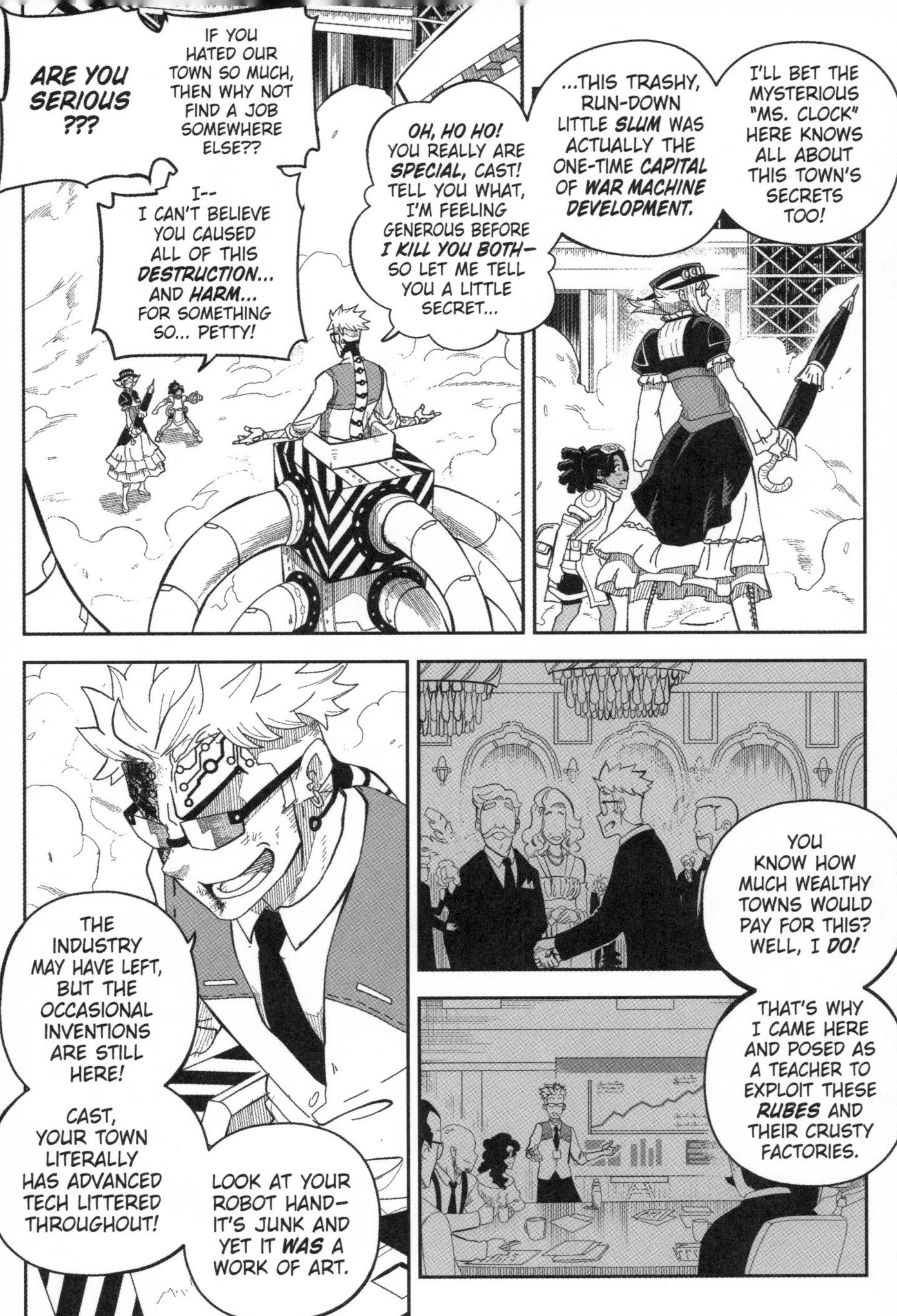
ARE YOU SERIOUS ???
IF YOU HATED OUR TOWN SO MUCH, THEN WHY NOT FIND A JOB SOMEWHERE ELSE??
I-- I CAN'T BELIEVE YOU CAUSED ALL OF THIS DESTRUCTION... AND HARM... FOR SOMETHING SO... PETTY!
OH, HO HO! YOU REALLY ARE SPECIAL, CAST! TELL YOU WHAT, I'M FEELING GENEROUS BEFORE I KILL YOU BOTH– SO LET ME TELL YOU A LITTLE SECRET...
...THIS TRASHY, RUN-DOWN LITTLE SLUM WAS ACTUALLY THE ONE-TIME CAPITAL OF WAR MACHINE DEVELOPMENT.
I'LL BET THE MYSTERIOUS "MS. CLOCK" HERE KNOWS ALL ABOUT THIS TOWN'S SECRETS TOO!
THE INDUSTRY MAY HAVE LEFT, BUT THE OCCASIONAL INVENTIONS ARE STILL HERE!
CAST, YOUR TOWN LITERALLY HAS ADVANCED TECH LITTERED THROUGHOUT!
LOOK AT YOUR ROBOT HAND– IT'S JUNK AND YET IT WAS A WORK OF ART.
YOU KNOW HOW MUCH WEALTHY TOWNS WOULD PAY FOR THIS? WELL, I DO!
THAT'S WHY I CAME HERE AND POSED AS A TEACHER TO EXPLOIT THESE RUBES AND THEIR CRUSTY FACTORIES.

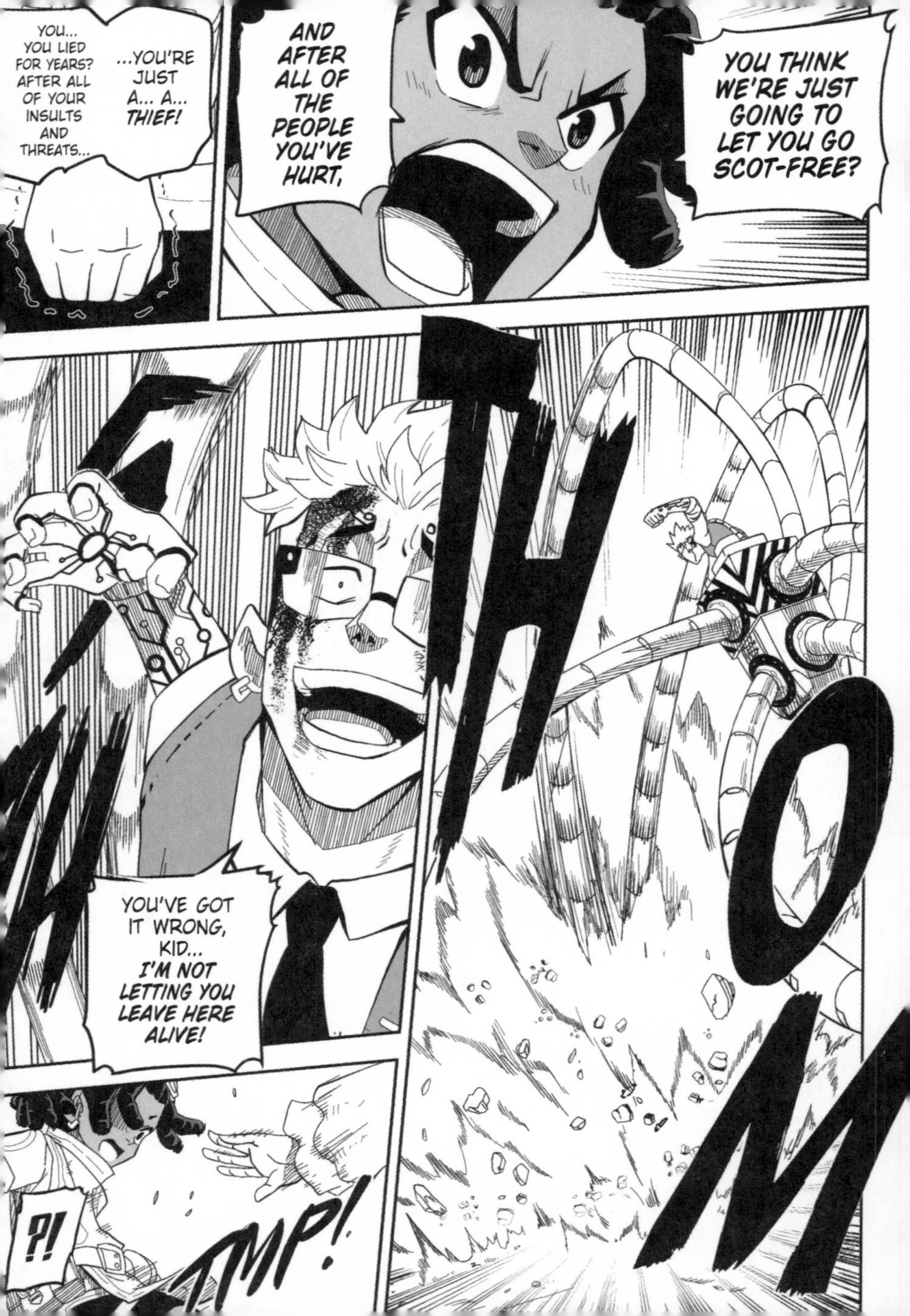
YOU... YOU LIED FOR YEARS? AFTER ALL OF YOUR INSULTS AND THREATS...
...YOU'RE JUST A... A... *THIEF!*
AND AFTER ALL OF THE PEOPLE YOU'VE HURT,
YOU THINK WE'RE JUST GOING TO LET YOU GO SCOT-FREE?
YOU'VE GOT IT WRONG, KID... *I'M NOT LETTING YOU LEAVE HERE ALIVE!*
?!
TMP!

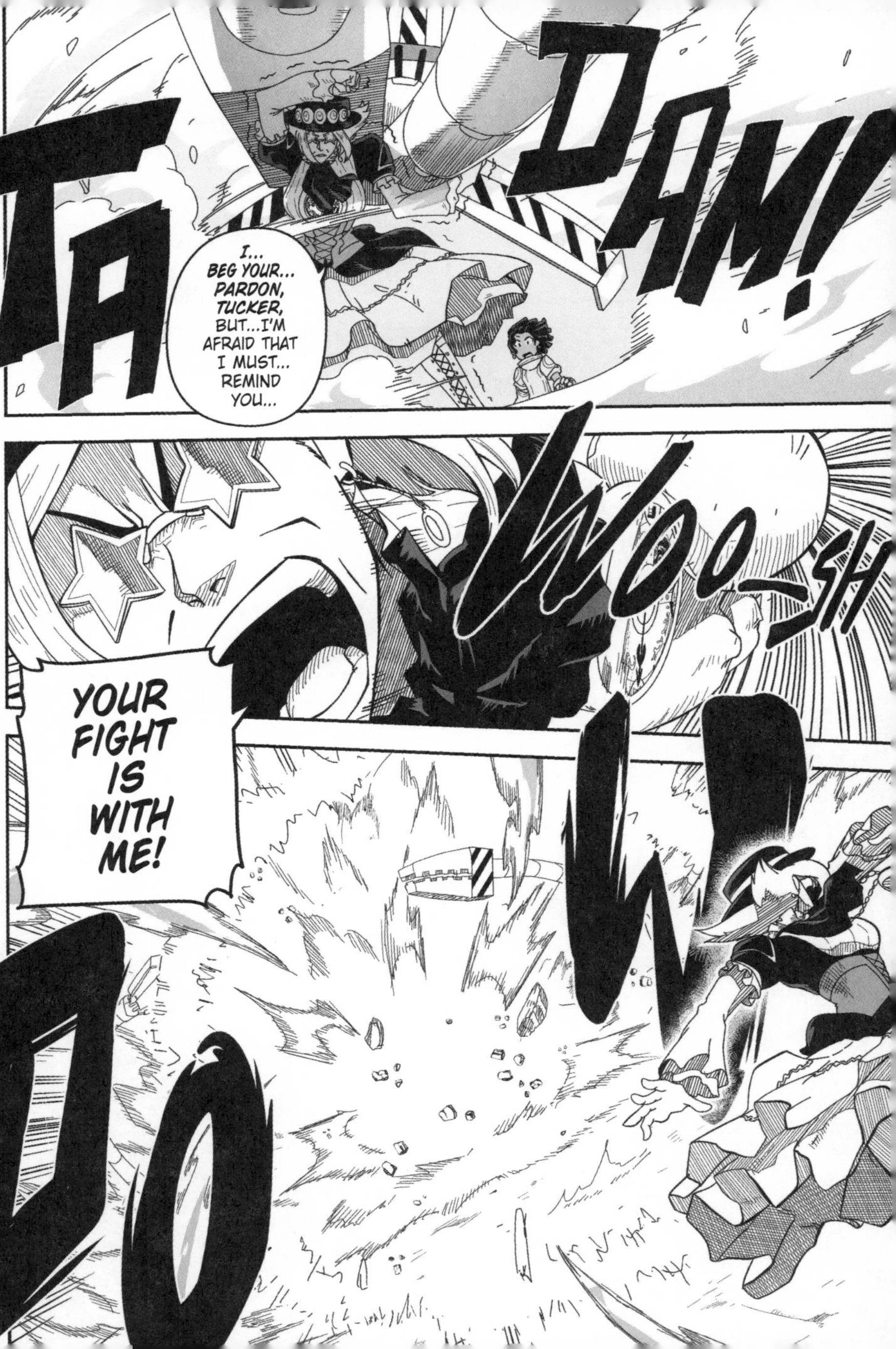
TA
DAM!
I... BEG YOUR... PARDON, TUCKER, BUT...I'M AFRAID THAT I MUST... REMIND YOU...
WOO-SH
YOUR FIGHT IS WITH ME!
DO
W

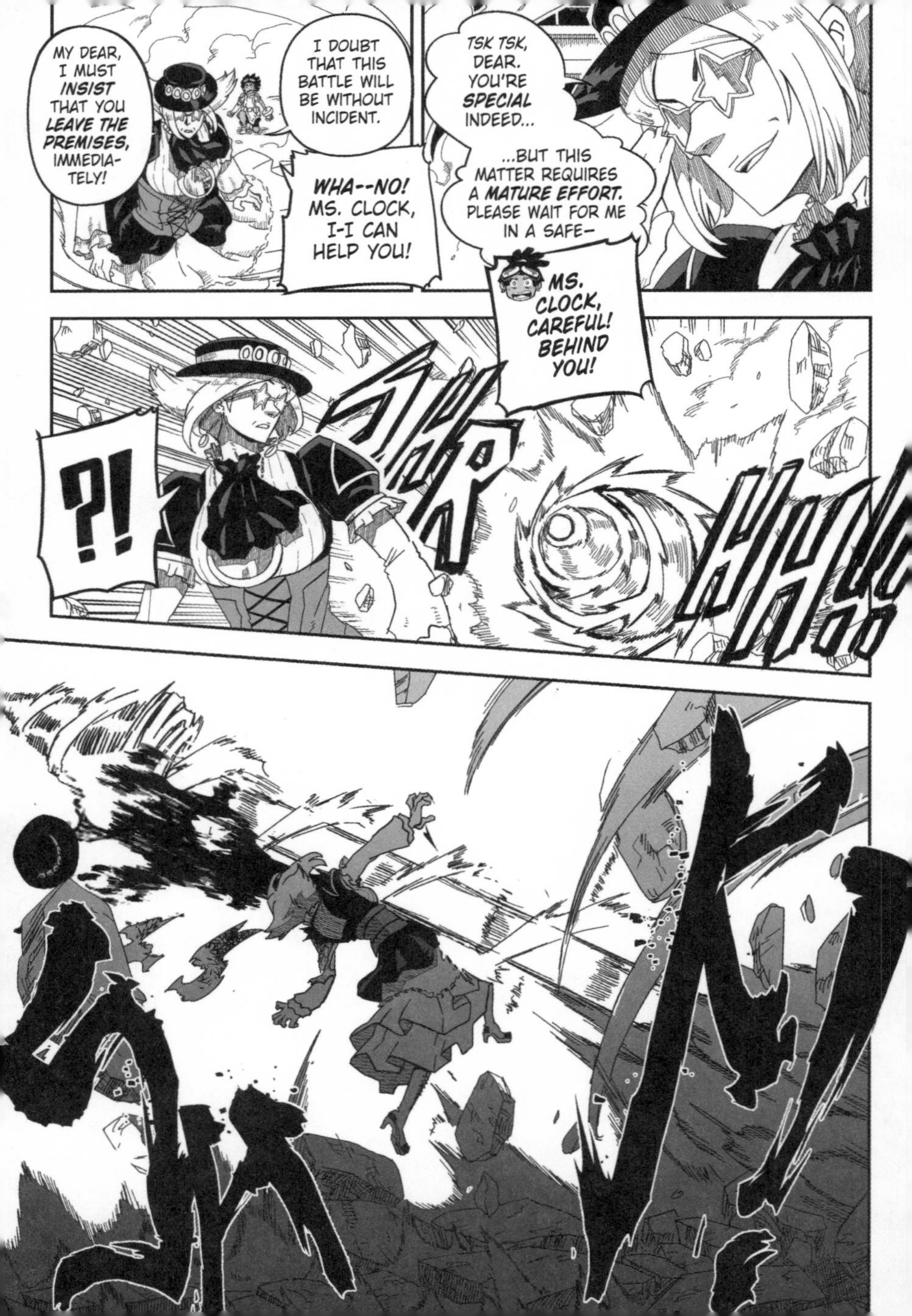
MY DEAR, I MUST INSIST THAT YOU LEAVE THE PREMISES, IMMEDIATELY!
I DOUBT THAT THIS BATTLE WILL BE WITHOUT INCIDENT.
WHA--NO! MS. CLOCK, I-I CAN HELP YOU!
TSK TSK, DEAR. YOU'RE SPECIAL INDEED...
...BUT THIS MATTER REQUIRES A MATURE EFFORT. PLEASE WAIT FOR ME IN A SAFE–
MS. CLOCK, CAREFUL! BEHIND YOU!
?!

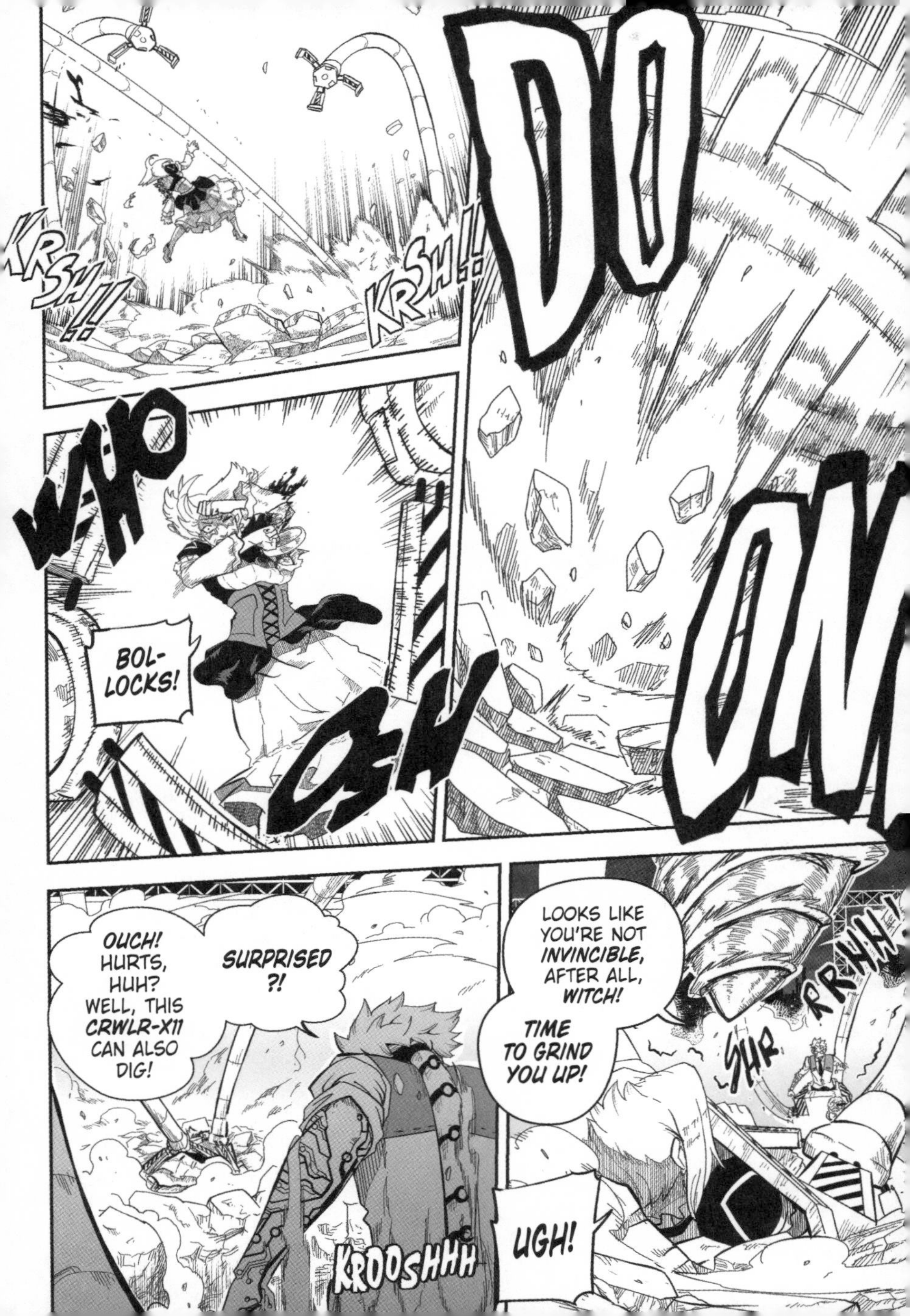
KRSH!!
KRSH!!
DOON
WHOOSH
BOL-LOCKS!
OUCH! HURTS, HUH? WELL, THIS CRWLR-X11 CAN ALSO DIG!
SURPRISED?!
KROOSHHH
LOOKS LIKE YOU'RE NOT INVINCIBLE, AFTER ALL, WITCH!
TIME TO GRIND YOU UP!
SHRRRHH!
UGH!

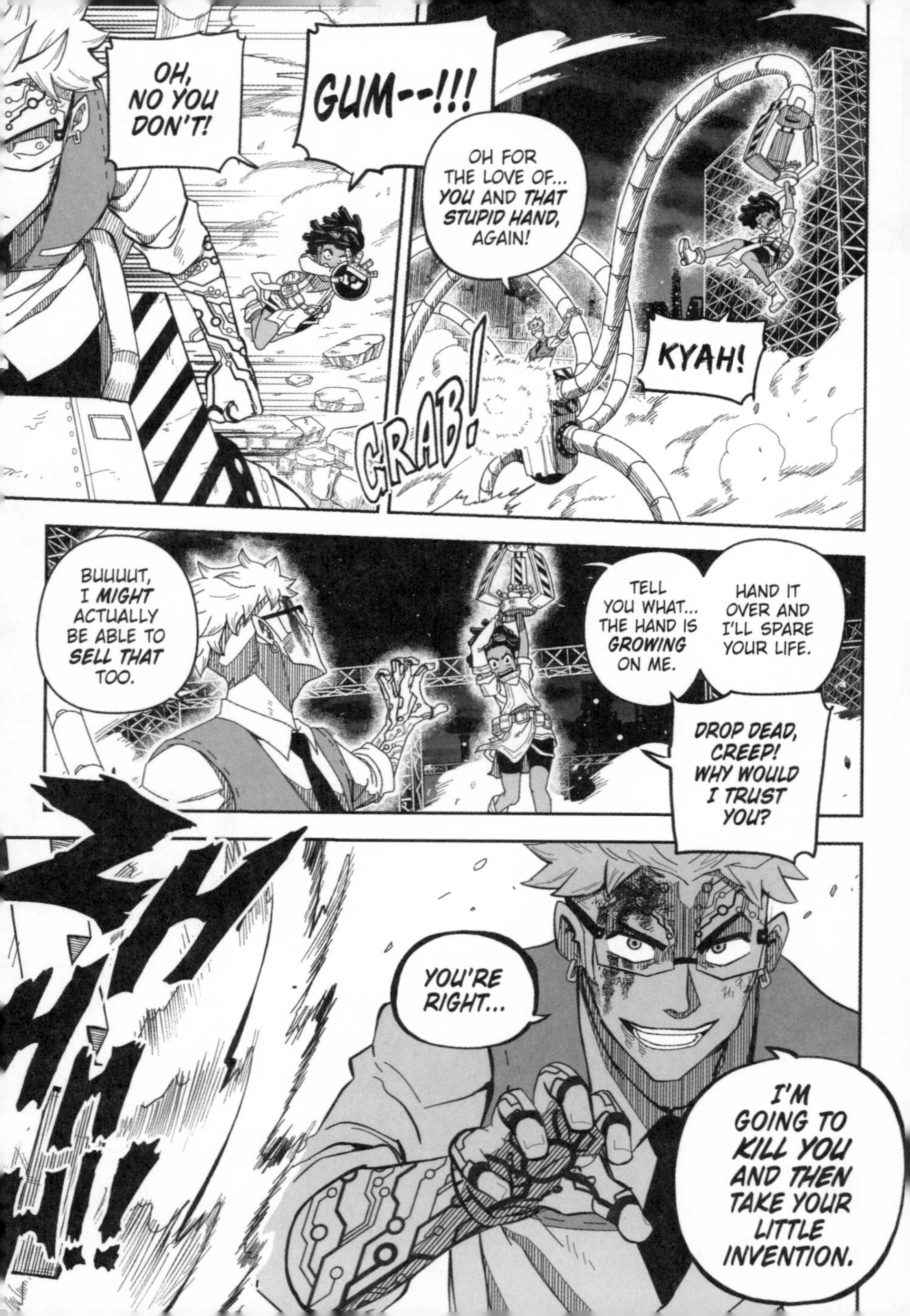
OH, NO YOU DON'T!
GUM--!!!
OH FOR THE LOVE OF... YOU AND THAT STUPID HAND, AGAIN!
GRAB!
KYAH!
BUUUUT, I MIGHT ACTUALLY BE ABLE TO SELL THAT TOO.
TELL YOU WHAT... THE HAND IS GROWING ON ME.
HAND IT OVER AND I'LL SPARE YOUR LIFE.
DROP DEAD, CREEP! WHY WOULD I TRUST YOU?
YOU'RE RIGHT...
I'M GOING TO KILL YOU AND THEN TAKE YOUR LITTLE INVENTION.

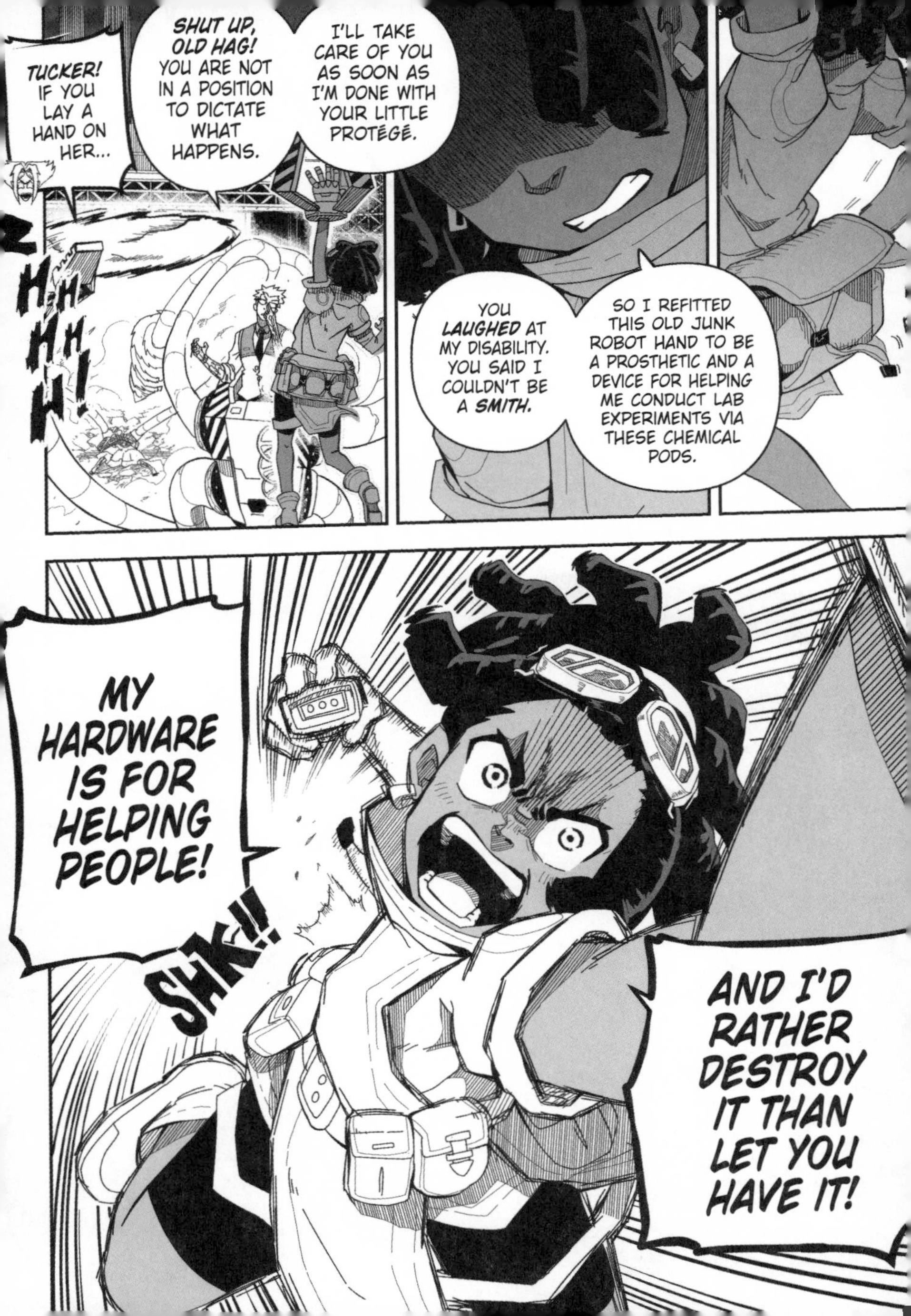
TUCKER! IF YOU LAY A HAND ON HER...
SHUT UP, OLD HAG! YOU ARE NOT IN A POSITION TO DICTATE WHAT HAPPENS.
I'LL TAKE CARE OF YOU AS SOON AS I'M DONE WITH YOUR LITTLE PROTÉGÉ.
YOU LAUGHED AT MY DISABILITY. YOU SAID I COULDN'T BE A SMITH.
SO I REFITTED THIS OLD JUNK ROBOT HAND TO BE A PROSTHETIC AND A DEVICE FOR HELPING ME CONDUCT LAB EXPERIMENTS VIA THESE CHEMICAL PODS.
MY HARDWARE IS FOR HELPING PEOPLE!
SHK!!
AND I'D RATHER DESTROY IT THAN LET YOU HAVE IT!

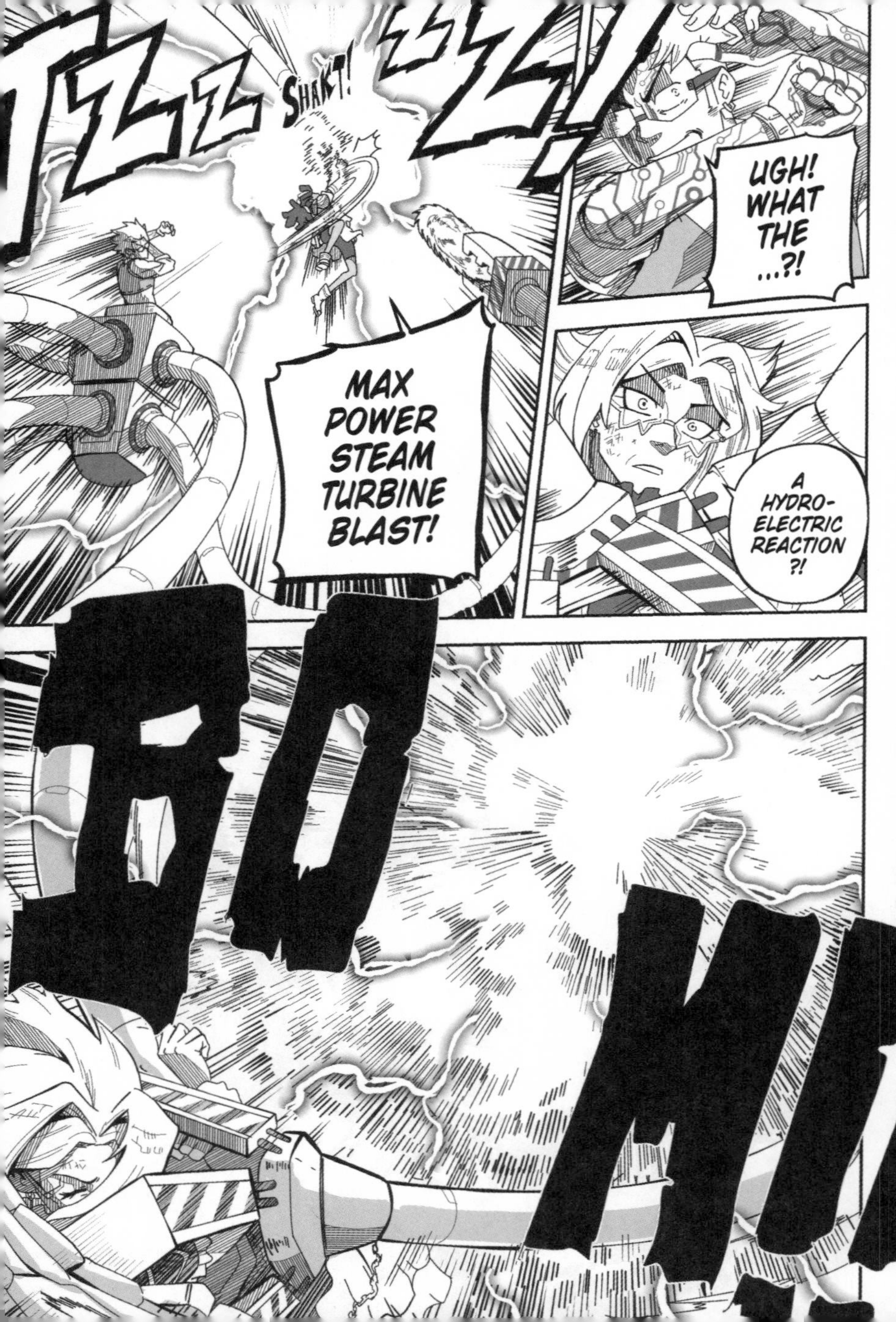

TZZZ
SHAKT!
ZZZZ!
MAX POWER STEAM TURBINE BLAST!
UGH! WHAT THE ...?!
A HYDRO-ELECTRIC REACTION?!
BO
M!!

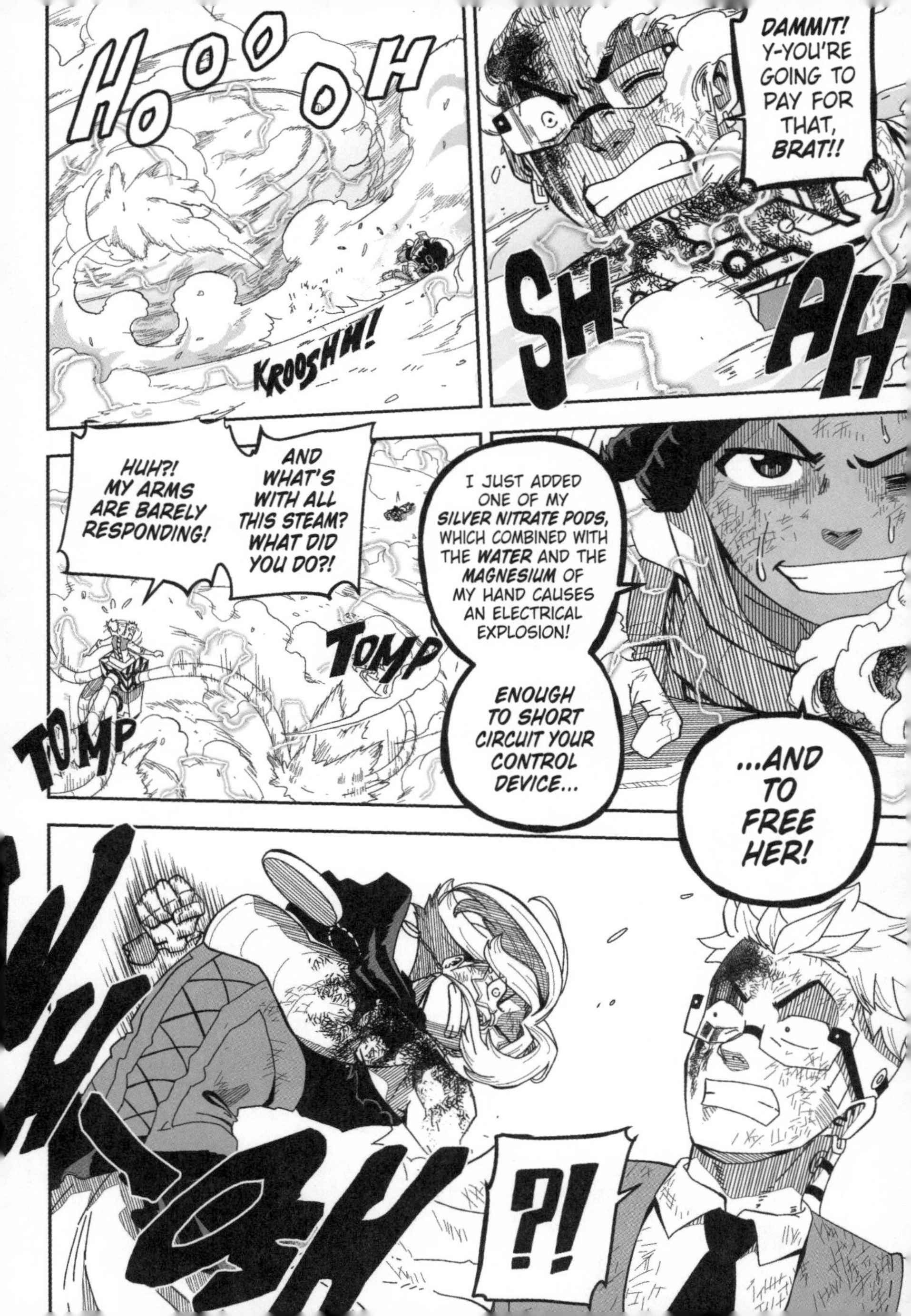
HOOOOH
KROOSHM!
DAMMIT! Y-YOU'RE GOING TO PAY FOR THAT, BRAT!!
SH
AH
HUH?! MY ARMS ARE BARELY RESPONDING!
AND WHAT'S WITH ALL THIS STEAM? WHAT DID YOU DO?!
TOMP
TOMP
I JUST ADDED ONE OF MY SILVER NITRATE PODS, WHICH COMBINED WITH THE WATER AND THE MAGNESIUM OF MY HAND CAUSES AN ELECTRICAL EXPLOSION!
ENOUGH TO SHORT CIRCUIT YOUR CONTROL DEVICE...
...AND TO FREE HER!
?!

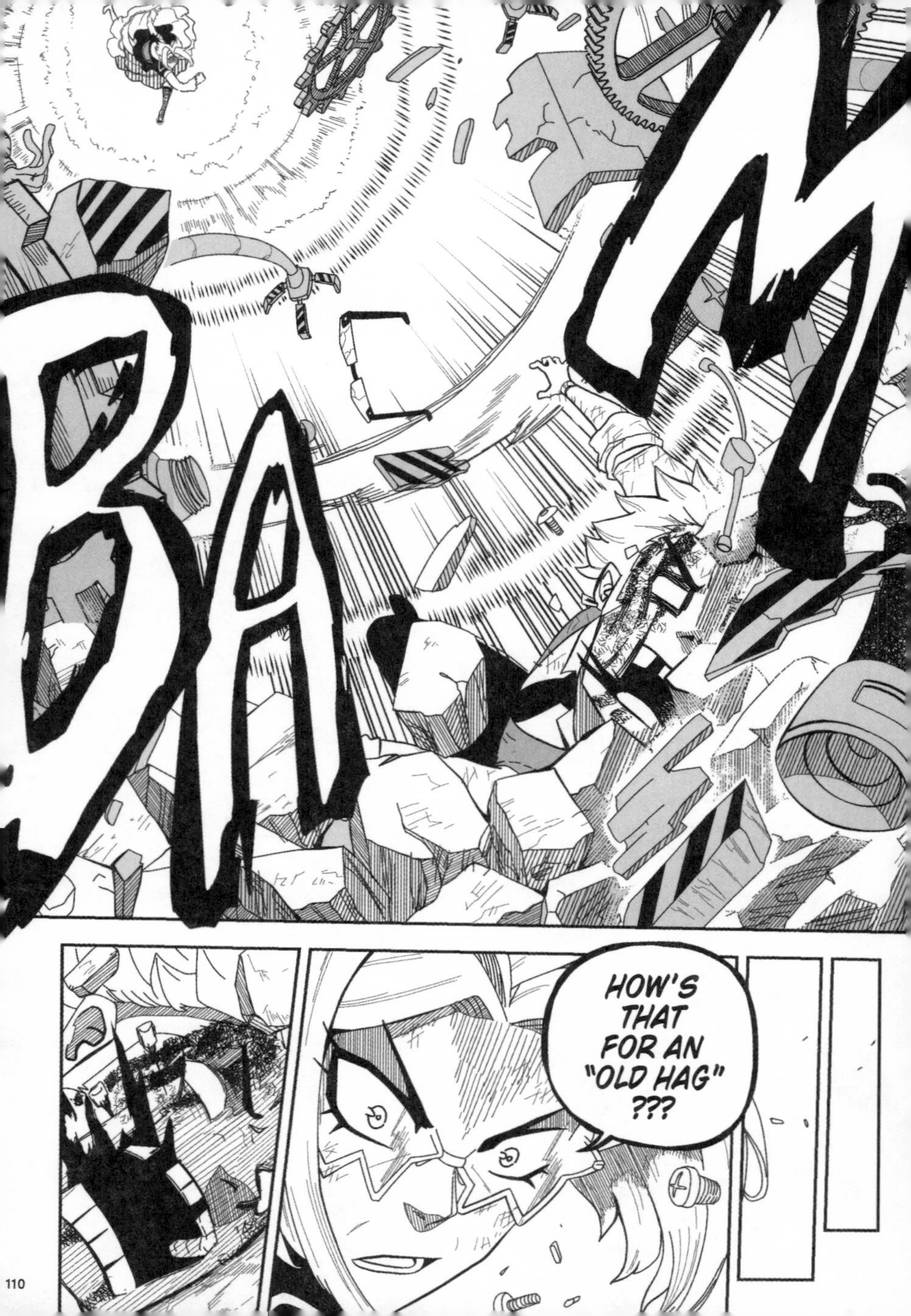
BAM
HOW'S THAT FOR AN "OLD HAG" ???

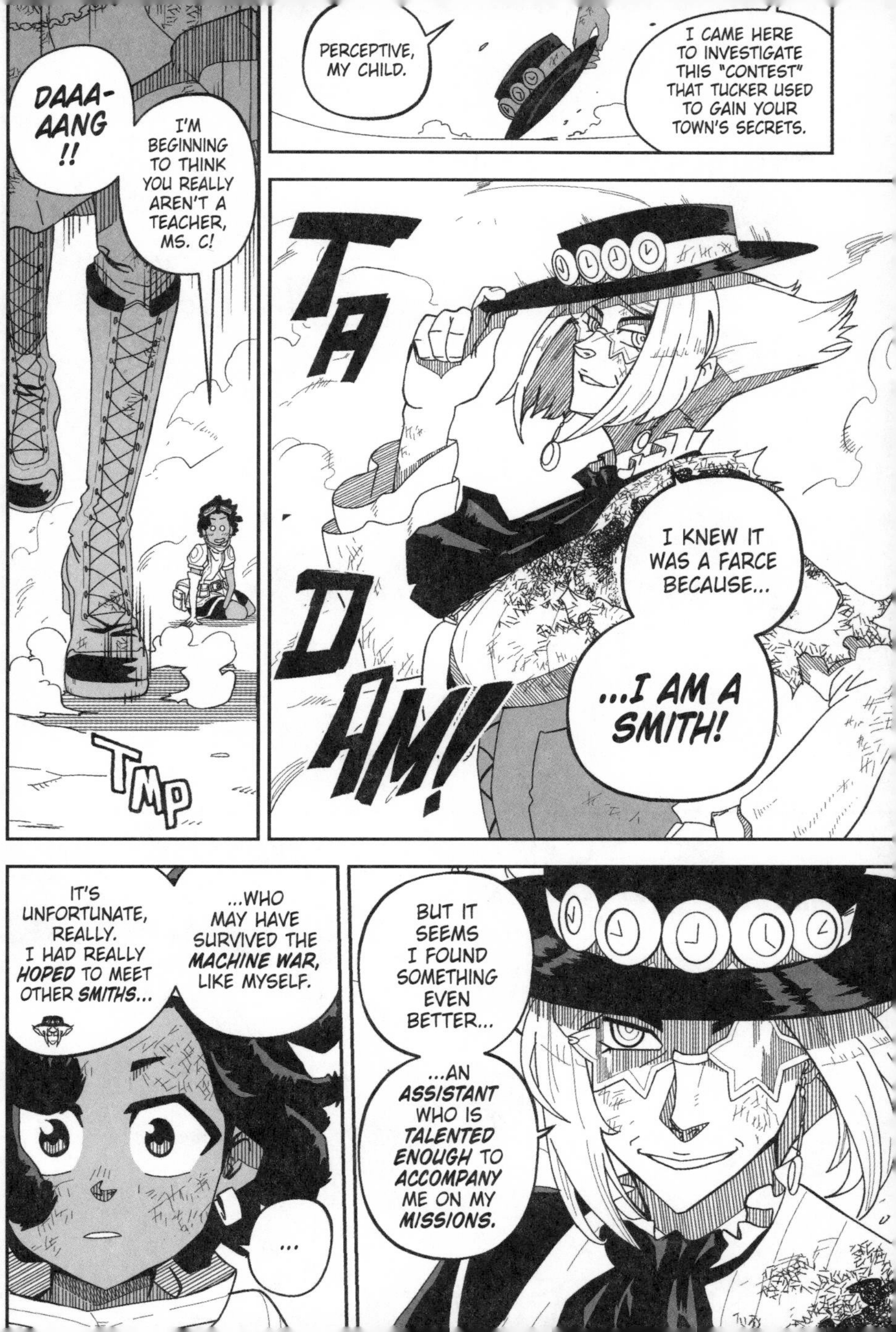
DAAA-AANG !!
I'M BEGINNING TO THINK YOU REALLY AREN'T A TEACHER, MS. C!
TMP
PERCEPTIVE, MY CHILD.
I CAME HERE TO INVESTIGATE THIS "CONTEST" THAT TUCKER USED TO GAIN YOUR TOWN'S SECRETS.
TA DAM!
I KNEW IT WAS A FARCE BECAUSE...
...I AM A SMITH!
IT'S UNFORTUNATE, REALLY. I HAD REALLY HOPED TO MEET OTHER SMITHS...
...WHO MAY HAVE SURVIVED THE MACHINE WAR, LIKE MYSELF.
...
BUT IT SEEMS I FOUND SOMETHING EVEN BETTER...
...AN ASSISTANT WHO IS TALENTED ENOUGH TO ACCOMPANY ME ON MY MISSIONS.

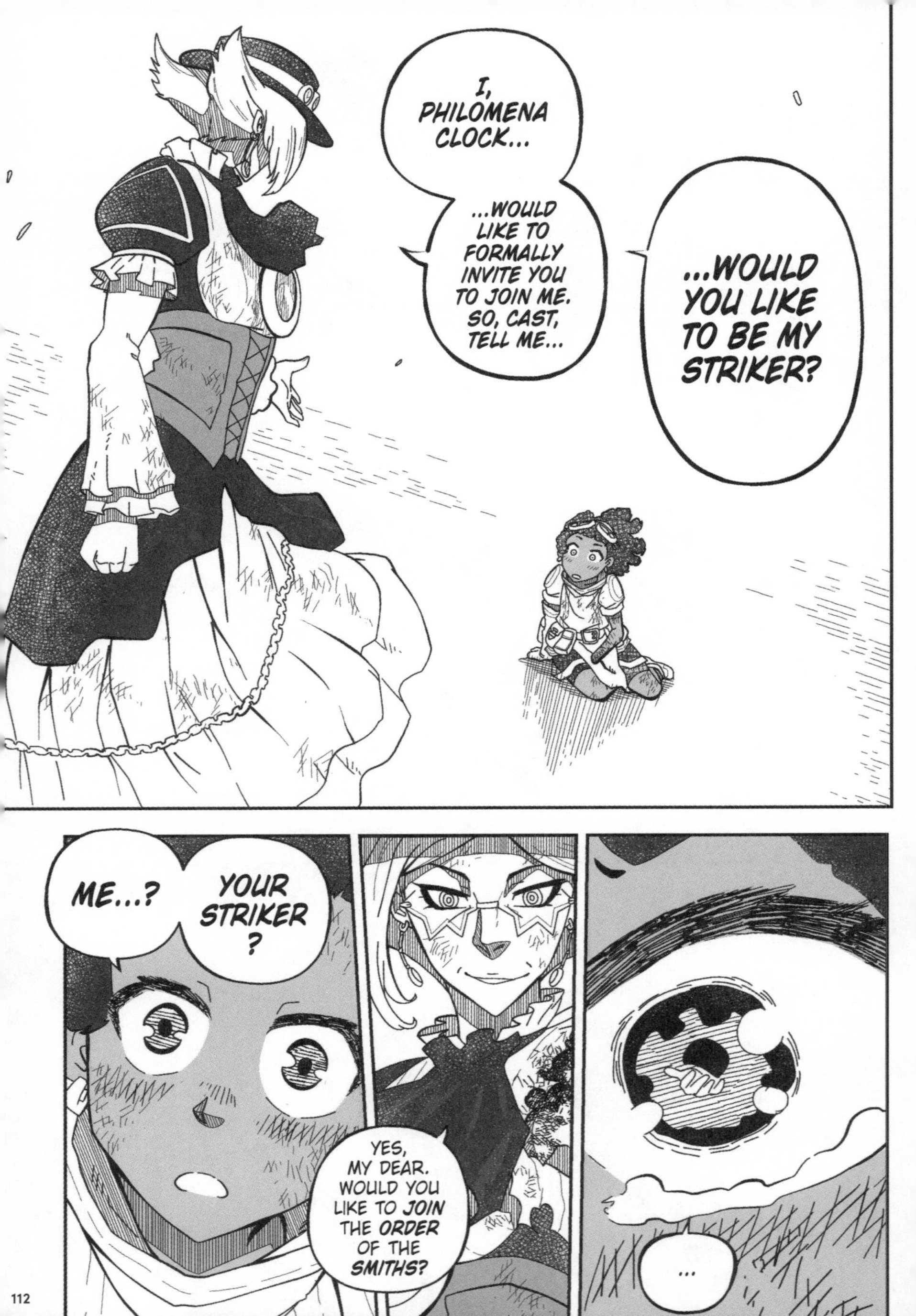
I, PHILOMENA CLOCK...
...WOULD LIKE TO FORMALLY INVITE YOU TO JOIN ME. SO, CAST, TELL ME...
...WOULD YOU LIKE TO BE MY STRIKER?
ME...?
YOUR STRIKER?
YES, MY DEAR. WOULD YOU LIKE TO JOIN THE ORDER OF THE SMITHS?
...

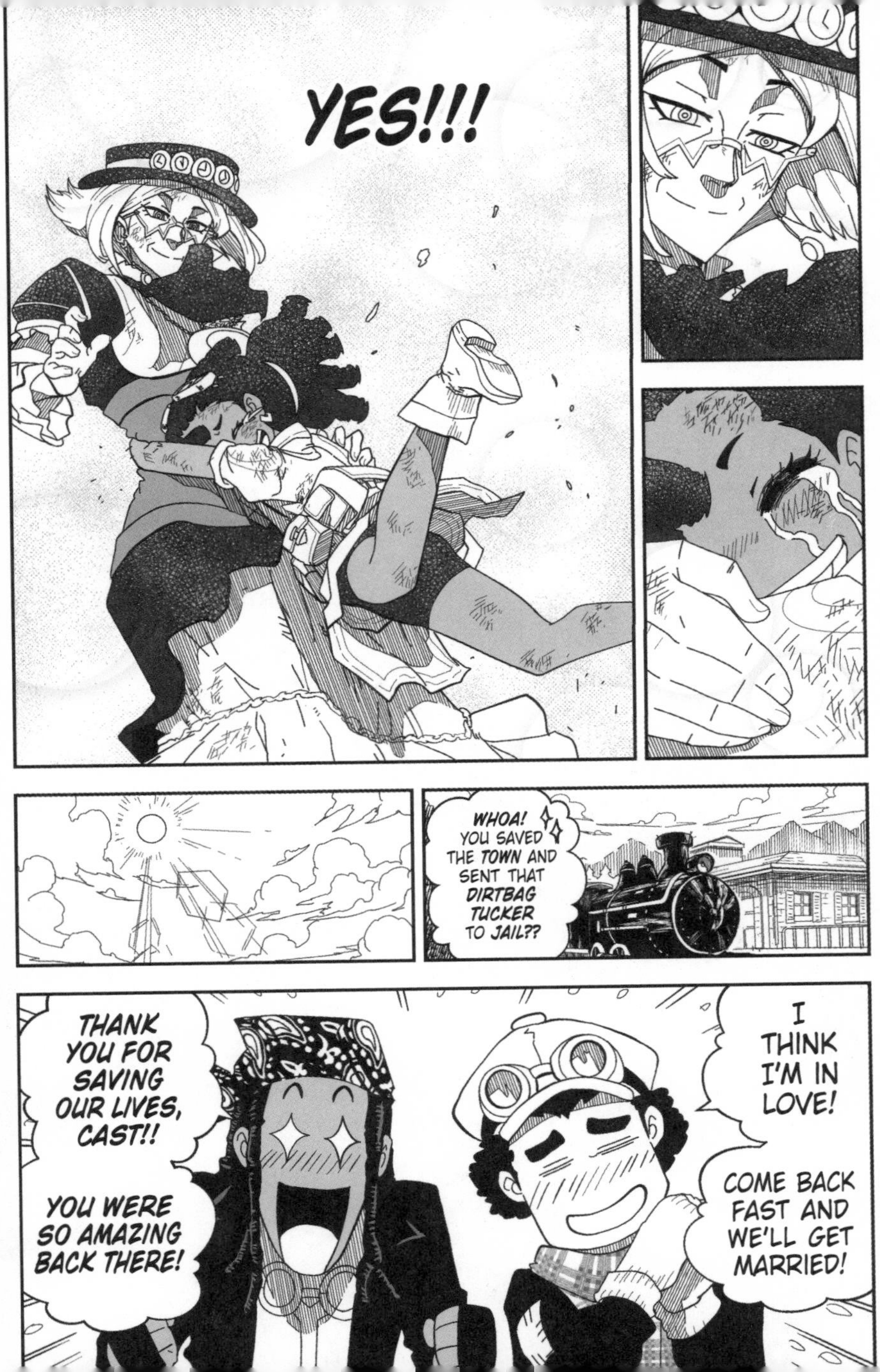
YES!!!
WHOA! YOU SAVED THE TOWN AND SENT THAT DIRTBAG TUCKER TO JAIL??
THANK YOU FOR SAVING OUR LIVES, CAST!!
YOU WERE SO AMAZING BACK THERE!
I THINK I'M IN LOVE!
COME BACK FAST AND WE'LL GET MARRIED!

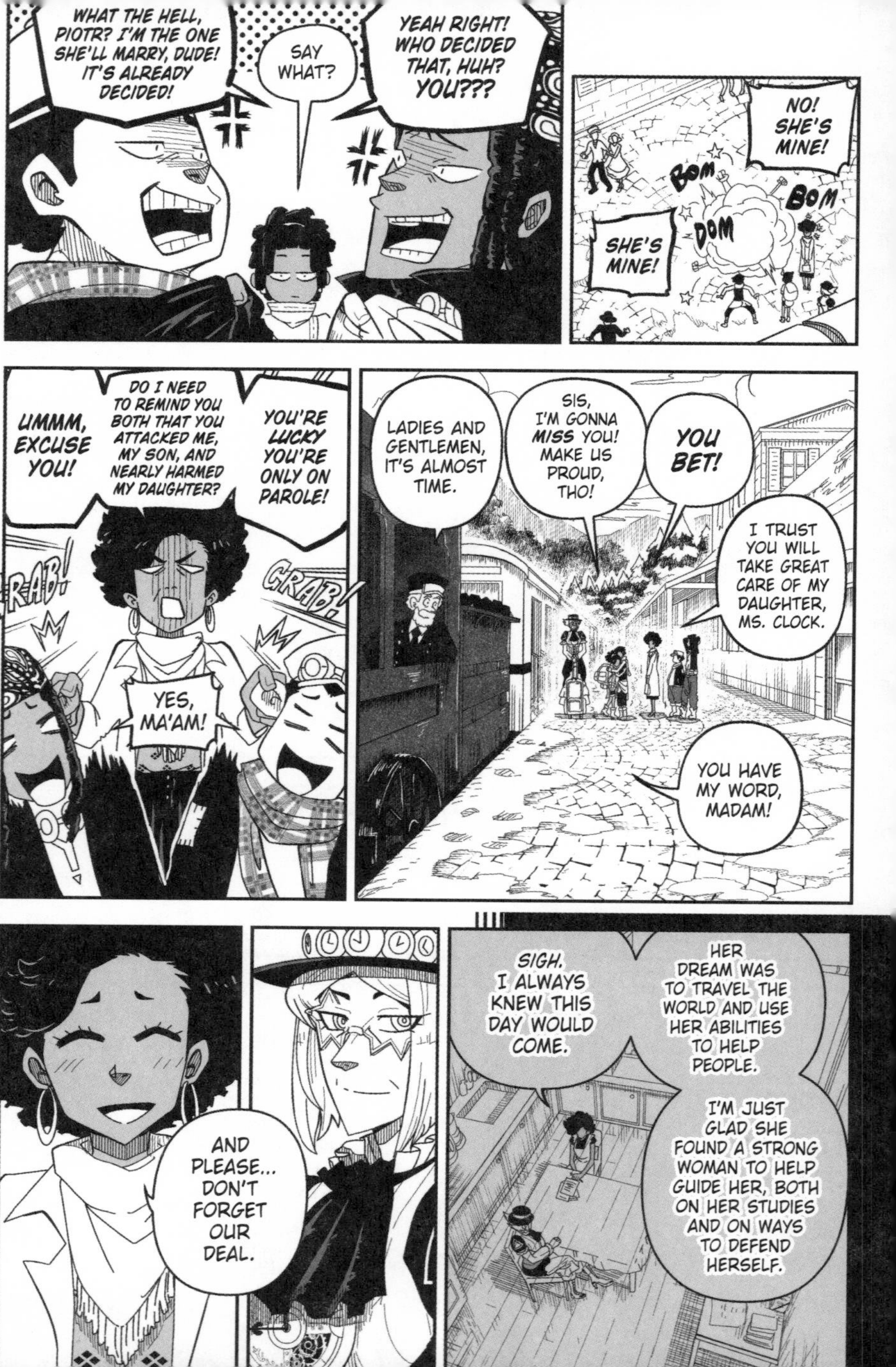
WHAT THE HELL, PIOTR? I'M THE ONE SHE'LL MARRY, DUDE! IT'S ALREADY DECIDED!
SAY WHAT?
YEAH RIGHT! WHO DECIDED THAT, HUH? YOU???
NO! SHE'S MINE!
BOM
BOM
DOM
SHE'S MINE!
UMMM, EXCUSE YOU!
DO I NEED TO REMIND YOU BOTH THAT YOU ATTACKED ME, MY SON, AND NEARLY HARMED MY DAUGHTER?
YOU'RE LUCKY YOU'RE ONLY ON PAROLE!
CRAB!
CRAB!
YES, MA'AM!
LADIES AND GENTLEMEN, IT'S ALMOST TIME.
SIS, I'M GONNA MISS YOU! MAKE US PROUD, THO!
YOU BET!
I TRUST YOU WILL TAKE GREAT CARE OF MY DAUGHTER, MS. CLOCK.
YOU HAVE MY WORD, MADAM!
AND PLEASE... DON'T FORGET OUR DEAL.
SIGH. I ALWAYS KNEW THIS DAY WOULD COME.
HER DREAM WAS TO TRAVEL THE WORLD AND USE HER ABILITIES TO HELP PEOPLE.
I'M JUST GLAD SHE FOUND A STRONG WOMAN TO HELP GUIDE HER, BOTH ON HER STUDIES AND ON WAYS TO DEFEND HERSELF.

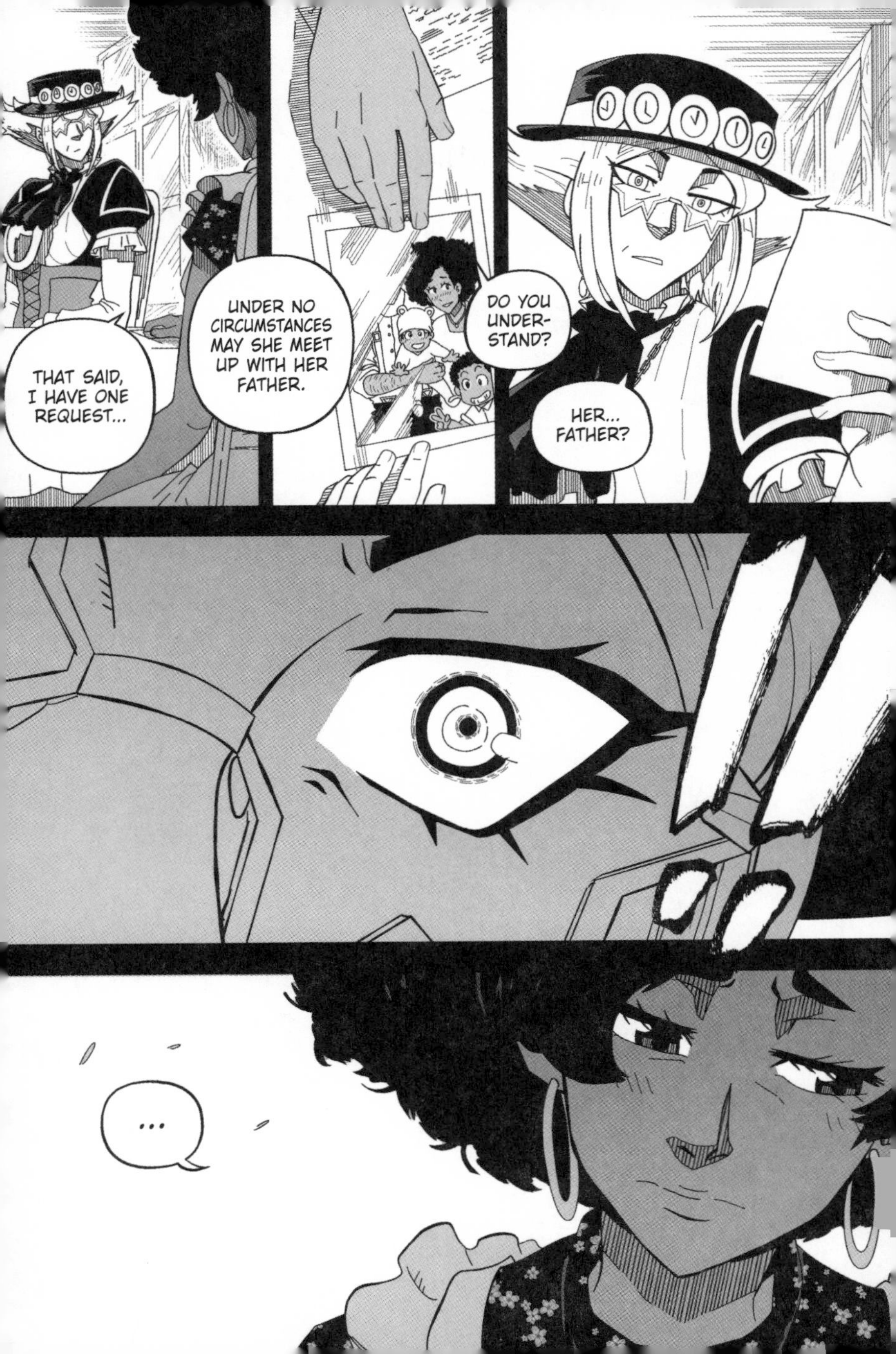
THAT SAID, I HAVE ONE REQUEST...
UNDER NO CIRCUMSTANCES MAY SHE MEET UP WITH HER FATHER.
DO YOU UNDER-STAND?
HER... FATHER?
...

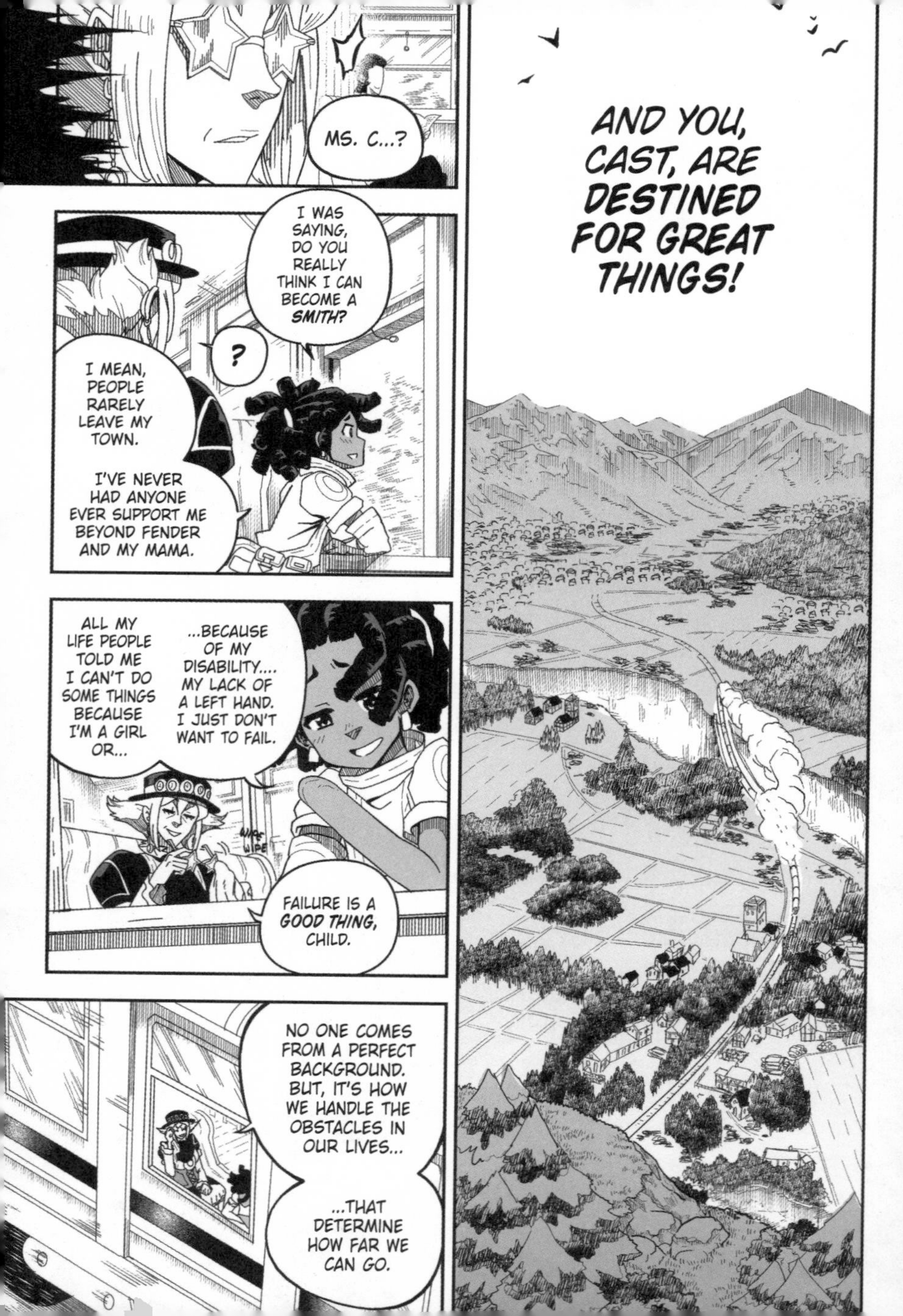
MS. C...?
I WAS SAYING, DO YOU REALLY THINK I CAN BECOME A *SMITH*?
?
I MEAN, PEOPLE RARELY LEAVE MY TOWN.
I'VE NEVER HAD ANYONE EVER SUPPORT ME BEYOND FENDER AND MY MAMA.
ALL MY LIFE PEOPLE TOLD ME I CAN'T DO SOME THINGS BECAUSE I'M A GIRL OR...
...BECAUSE OF MY DISABILITY.... MY LACK OF A LEFT HAND. I JUST DON'T WANT TO FAIL.
WIPE WIPE
FAILURE IS A *GOOD THING*, CHILD.
NO ONE COMES FROM A PERFECT BACKGROUND. BUT, IT'S HOW WE HANDLE THE OBSTACLES IN OUR LIVES...
...THAT DETERMINE HOW FAR WE CAN GO.
AND YOU, CAST, ARE DESTINED FOR GREAT THINGS!

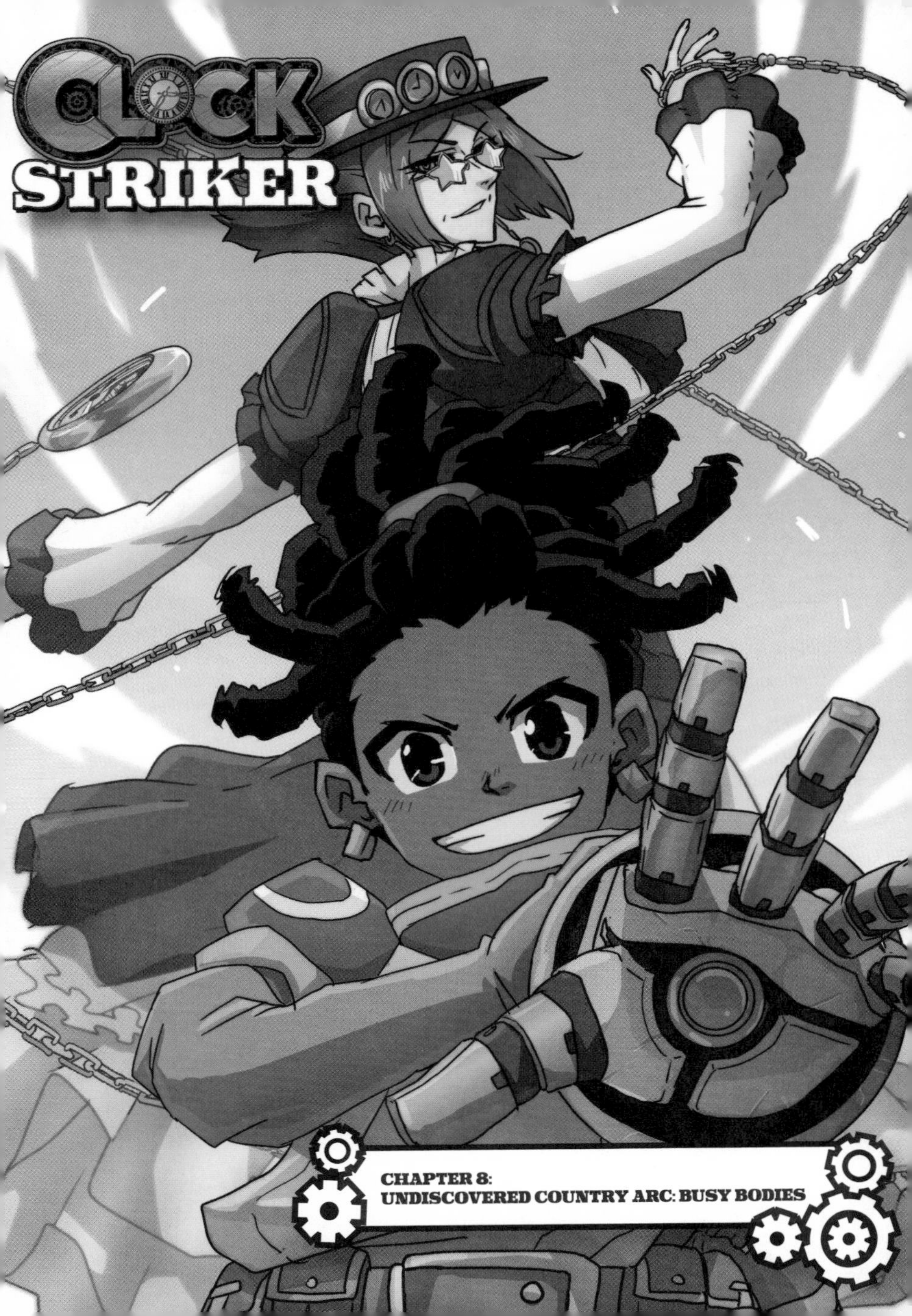
CLOCK STRIKER
CHAPTER 8:
UNDISCOVERED COUNTRY ARC: BUSY BODIES

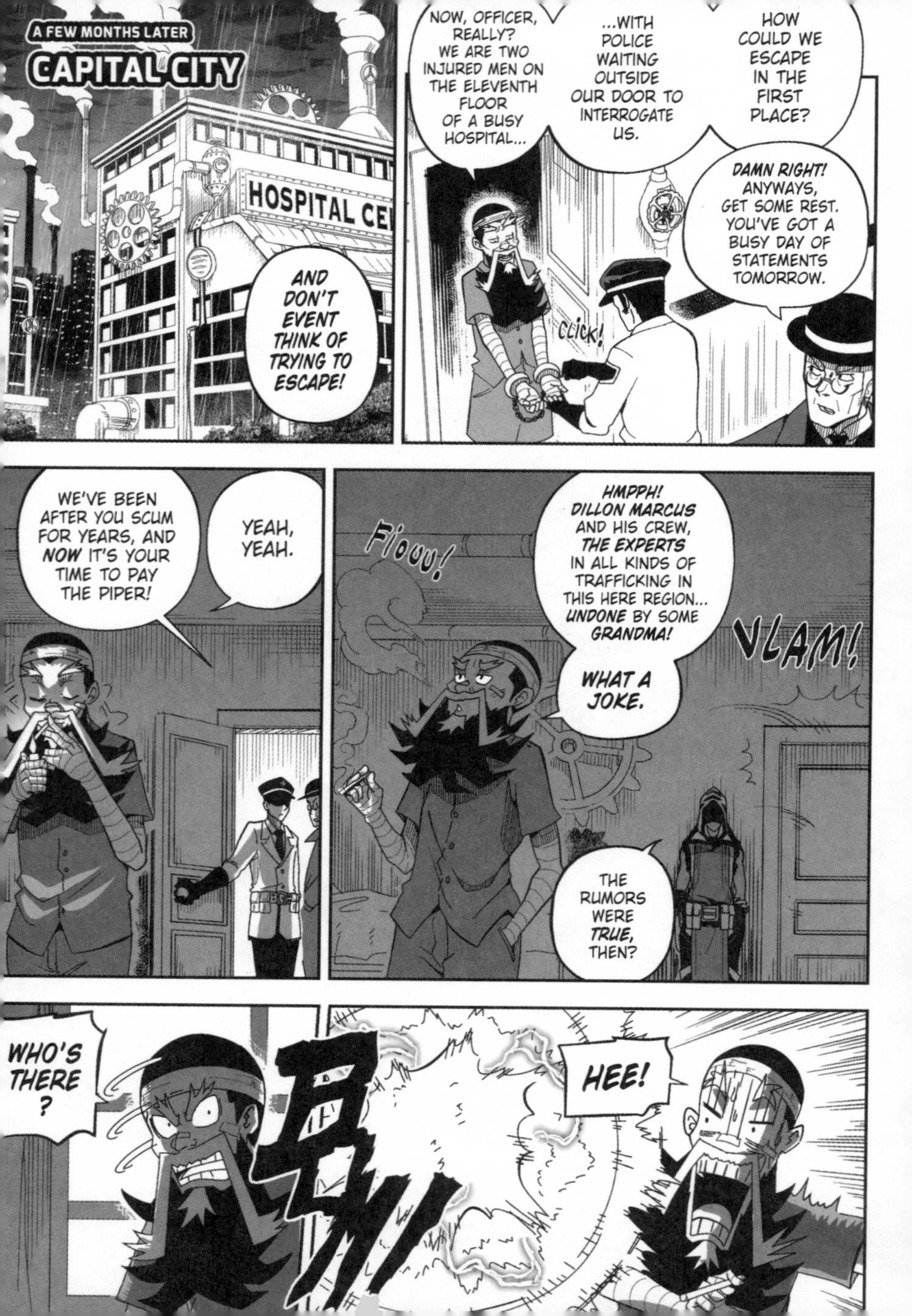
A FEW MONTHS LATER
CAPITAL CITY
HOSPITAL CE
AND DON'T EVENT THINK OF TRYING TO ESCAPE!
NOW, OFFICER, REALLY? WE ARE TWO INJURED MEN ON THE ELEVENTH FLOOR OF A BUSY HOSPITAL...
...WITH POLICE WAITING OUTSIDE OUR DOOR TO INTERROGATE US.
HOW COULD WE ESCAPE IN THE FIRST PLACE?
CLICK!
DAMN RIGHT! ANYWAYS, GET SOME REST. YOU'VE GOT A BUSY DAY OF STATEMENTS TOMORROW.
WE'VE BEEN AFTER YOU SCUM FOR YEARS, AND NOW IT'S YOUR TIME TO PAY THE PIPER!
YEAH, YEAH.
Fiouu!
HMPPH! DILLON MARCUS AND HIS CREW, THE EXPERTS IN ALL KINDS OF TRAFFICKING IN THIS HERE REGION... UNDONE BY SOME GRANDMA!
WHAT A JOKE.
VLAM!
THE RUMORS WERE TRUE, THEN?
WHO'S THERE ?
HEE!

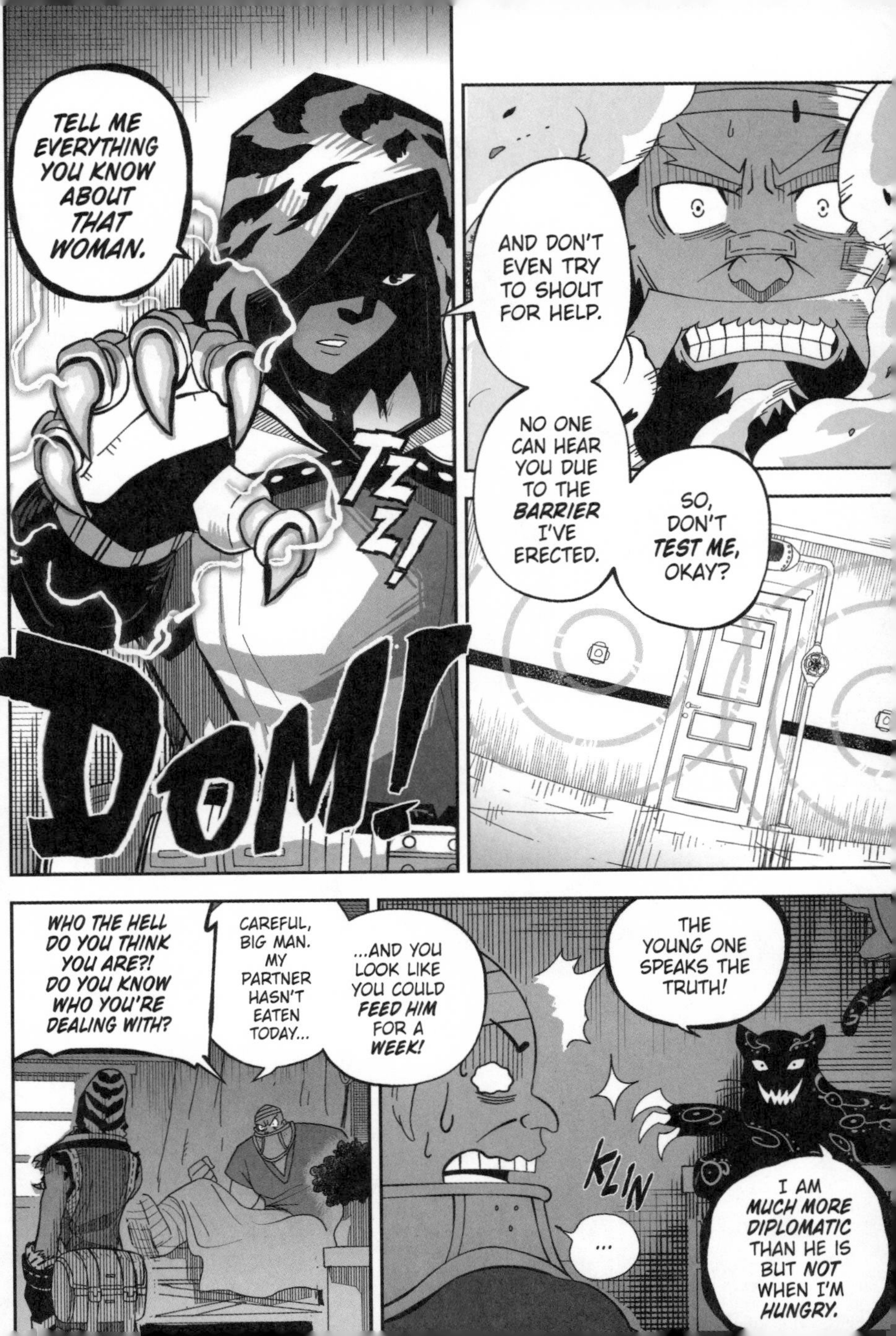
TELL ME EVERYTHING YOU KNOW ABOUT THAT WOMAN.
TZZZ!
DOM!
AND DON'T EVEN TRY TO SHOUT FOR HELP.
NO ONE CAN HEAR YOU DUE TO THE BARRIER I'VE ERECTED.
SO, DON'T TEST ME, OKAY?
WHO THE HELL DO YOU THINK YOU ARE?! DO YOU KNOW WHO YOU'RE DEALING WITH?
CAREFUL, BIG MAN. MY PARTNER HASN'T EATEN TODAY...
...AND YOU LOOK LIKE YOU COULD FEED HIM FOR A WEEK!
THE YOUNG ONE SPEAKS THE TRUTH!
KLIN
...
I AM MUCH MORE DIPLOMATIC THAN HE IS BUT NOT WHEN I'M HUNGRY.

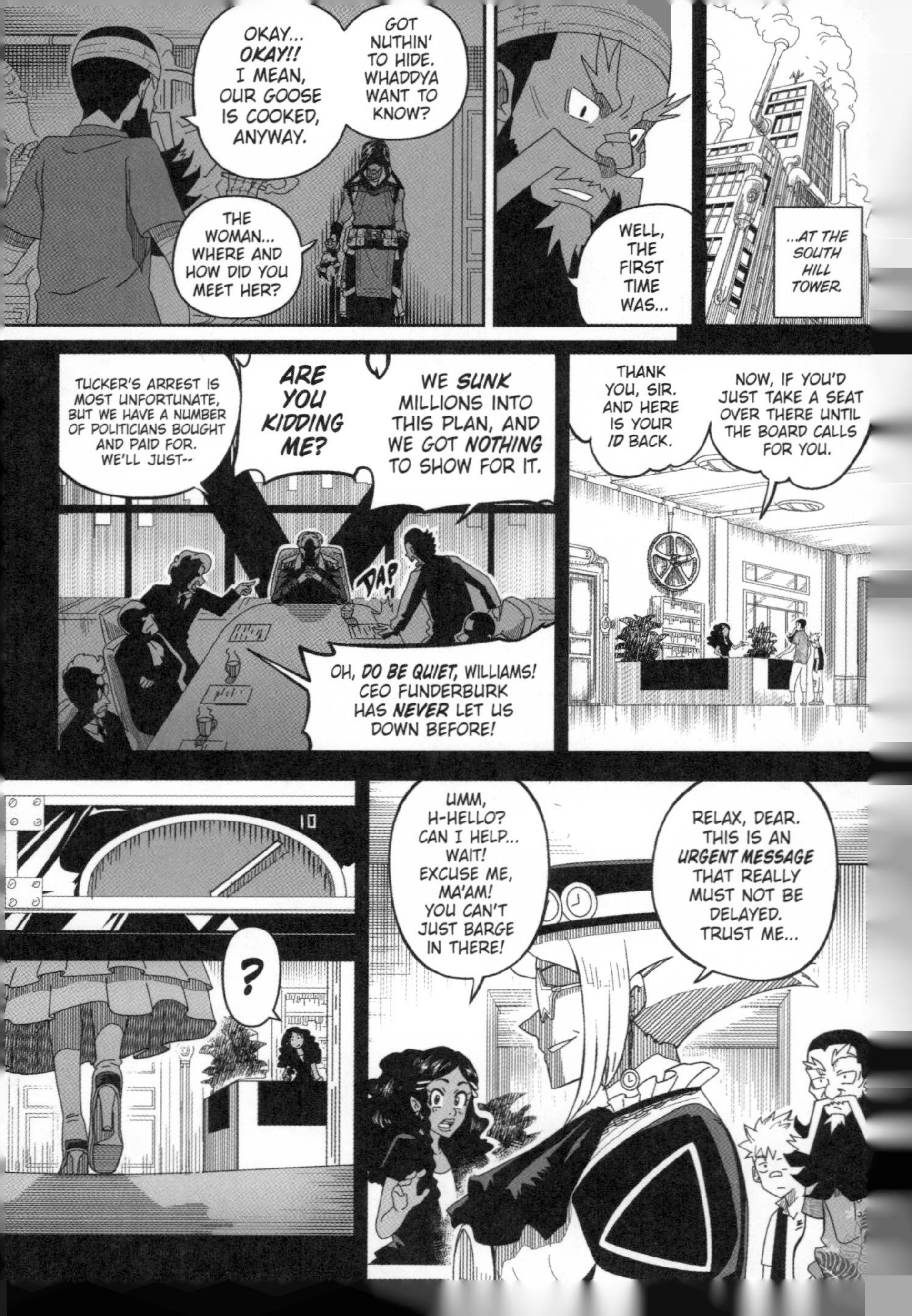
OKAY... OKAY!! I MEAN, OUR GOOSE IS COOKED, ANYWAY.
GOT NUTHIN' TO HIDE. WHADDYA WANT TO KNOW?
THE WOMAN... WHERE AND HOW DID YOU MEET HER?
WELL, THE FIRST TIME WAS...
...AT THE SOUTH HILL TOWER.
TUCKER'S ARREST IS MOST UNFORTUNATE, BUT WE HAVE A NUMBER OF POLITICIANS BOUGHT AND PAID FOR. WE'LL JUST--
ARE YOU KIDDING ME?
WE SUNK MILLIONS INTO THIS PLAN, AND WE GOT NOTHING TO SHOW FOR IT.
DAP
OH, DO BE QUIET, WILLIAMS! CEO FUNDERBURK HAS NEVER LET US DOWN BEFORE!
THANK YOU, SIR. AND HERE IS YOUR ID BACK.
NOW, IF YOU'D JUST TAKE A SEAT OVER THERE UNTIL THE BOARD CALLS FOR YOU.
10
?
UMM, H-HELLO? CAN I HELP... WAIT! EXCUSE ME, MA'AM! YOU CAN'T JUST BARGE IN THERE!
RELAX, DEAR. THIS IS AN URGENT MESSAGE THAT REALLY MUST NOT BE DELAYED. TRUST ME...

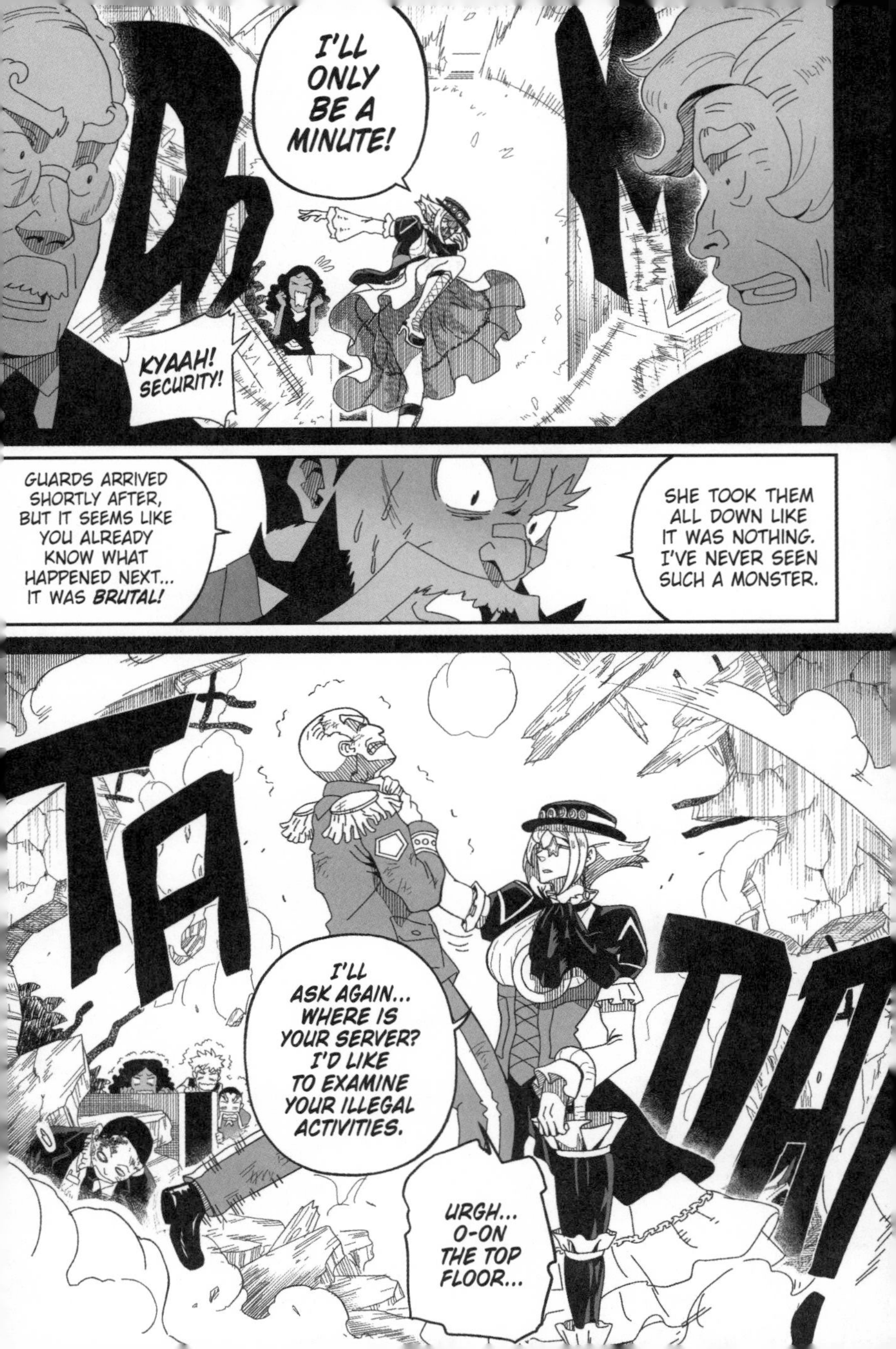
I'LL ONLY BE A MINUTE!
KYAAH! SECURITY!
GUARDS ARRIVED SHORTLY AFTER, BUT IT SEEMS LIKE YOU ALREADY KNOW WHAT HAPPENED NEXT... IT WAS BRUTAL!
SHE TOOK THEM ALL DOWN LIKE IT WAS NOTHING. I'VE NEVER SEEN SUCH A MONSTER.
TA
I'LL ASK AGAIN... WHERE IS YOUR SERVER? I'D LIKE TO EXAMINE YOUR ILLEGAL ACTIVITIES.
URGH... O-ON THE TOP FLOOR...
DA!

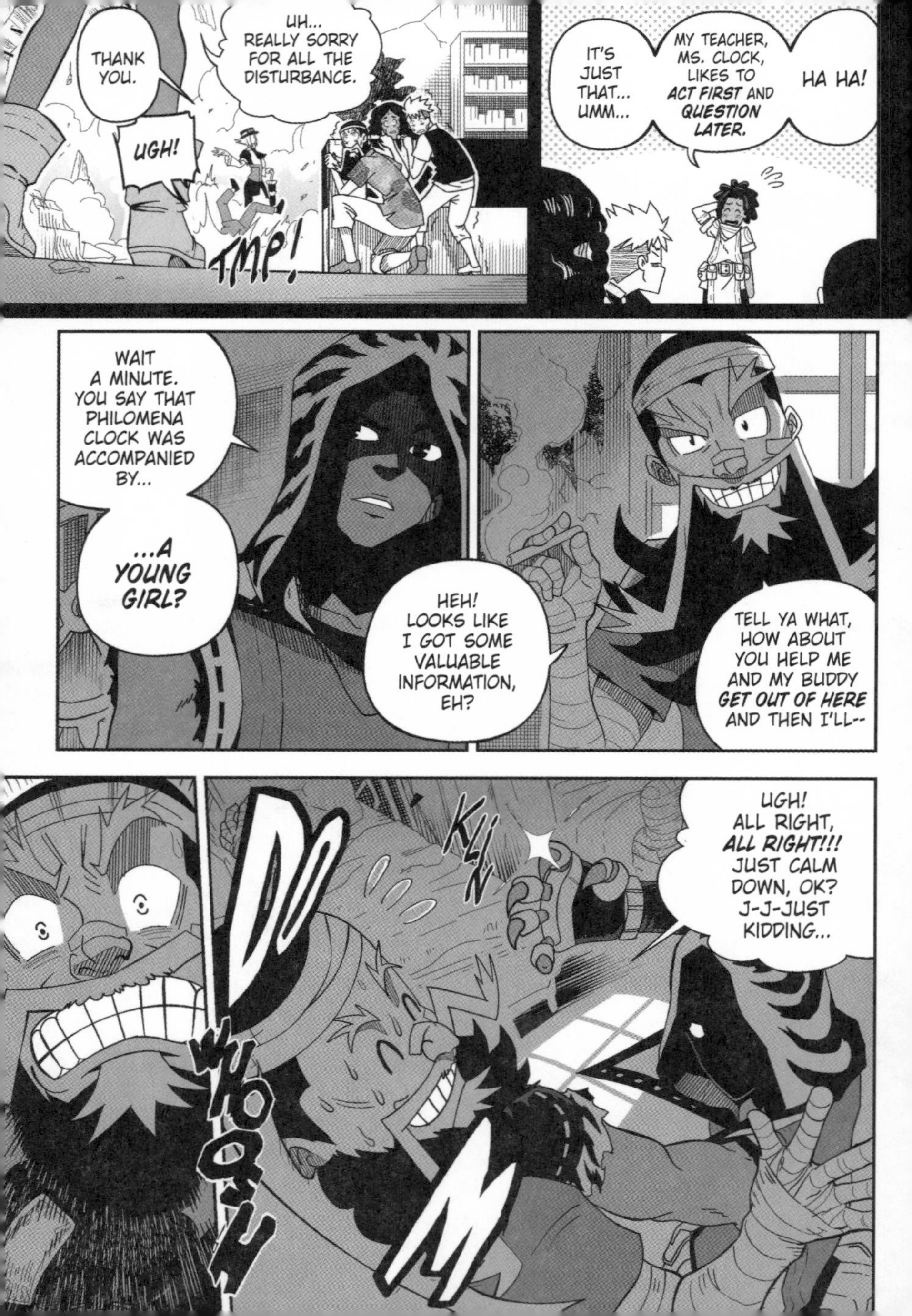
THANK YOU.
UH... REALLY SORRY FOR ALL THE DISTURBANCE.
UGH!
TMP!
IT'S JUST THAT... UMM...
MY TEACHER, MS. CLOCK, LIKES TO ACT FIRST AND QUESTION LATER.
HA HA!
WAIT A MINUTE. YOU SAY THAT PHILOMENA CLOCK WAS ACCOMPANIED BY...
...A YOUNG GIRL?
HEH! LOOKS LIKE I GOT SOME VALUABLE INFORMATION, EH?
TELL YA WHAT, HOW ABOUT YOU HELP ME AND MY BUDDY GET OUT OF HERE AND THEN I'LL--
DOOM
KLIN
UGH! ALL RIGHT, ALL RIGHT!!! JUST CALM DOWN, OK? J-J-JUST KIDDING...
WHOOM

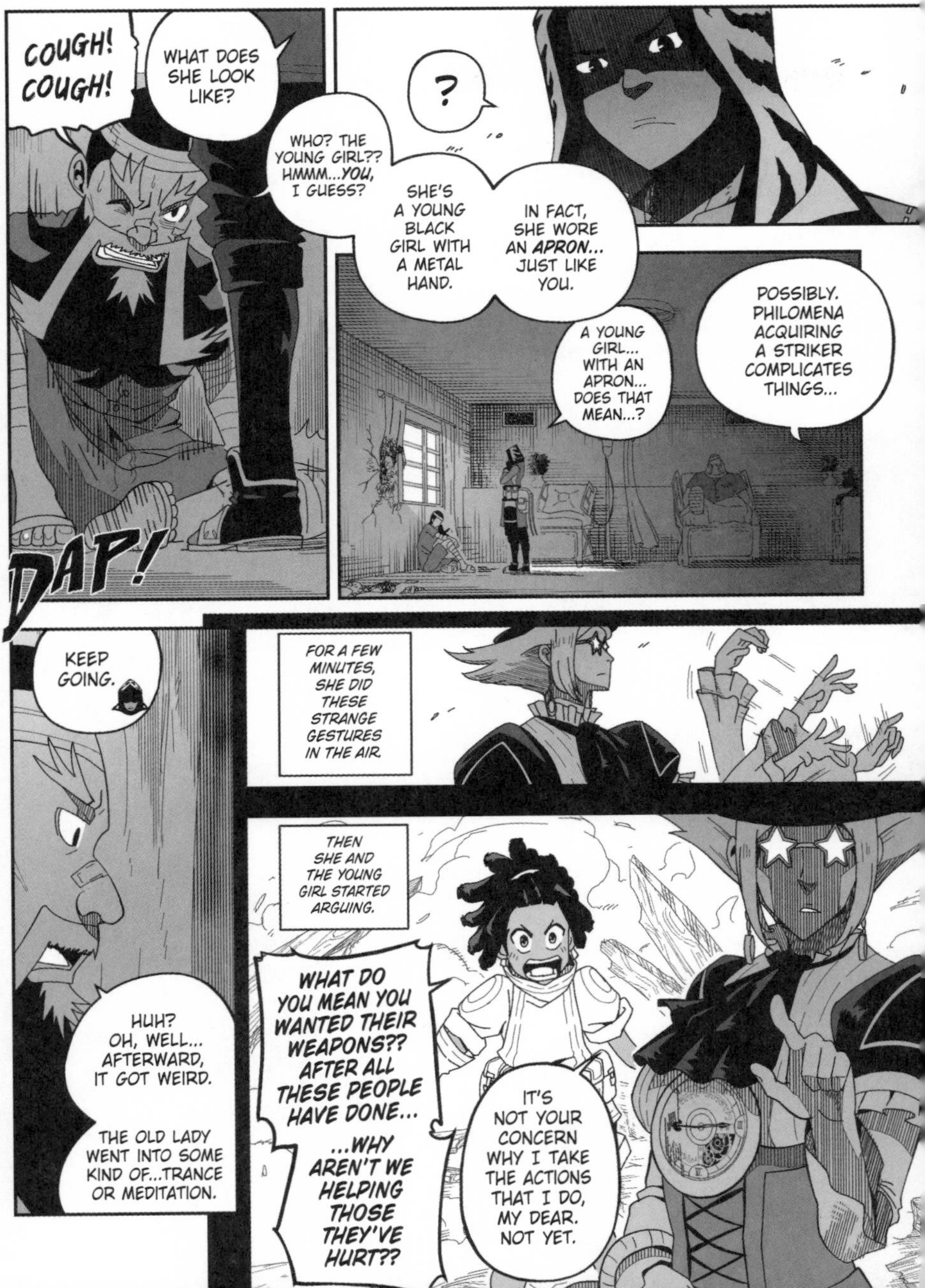

COUGH! COUGH!
WHAT DOES SHE LOOK LIKE?
DAP!
?
WHO? THE YOUNG GIRL?? HMMM...YOU, I GUESS?
SHE'S A YOUNG BLACK GIRL WITH A METAL HAND.
IN FACT, SHE WORE AN APRON... JUST LIKE YOU.
A YOUNG GIRL... WITH AN APRON... DOES THAT MEAN...?
POSSIBLY. PHILOMENA ACQUIRING A STRIKER COMPLICATES THINGS...
KEEP GOING.
HUH? OH, WELL... AFTERWARD, IT GOT WEIRD.
THE OLD LADY WENT INTO SOME KIND OF...TRANCE OR MEDITATION.
FOR A FEW MINUTES, SHE DID THESE STRANGE GESTURES IN THE AIR.
THEN SHE AND THE YOUNG GIRL STARTED ARGUING.
WHAT DO YOU MEAN YOU WANTED THEIR WEAPONS?? AFTER ALL THESE PEOPLE HAVE DONE...
...WHY AREN'T WE HELPING THOSE THEY'VE HURT??
IT'S NOT YOUR CONCERN WHY I TAKE THE ACTIONS THAT I DO, MY DEAR. NOT YET.

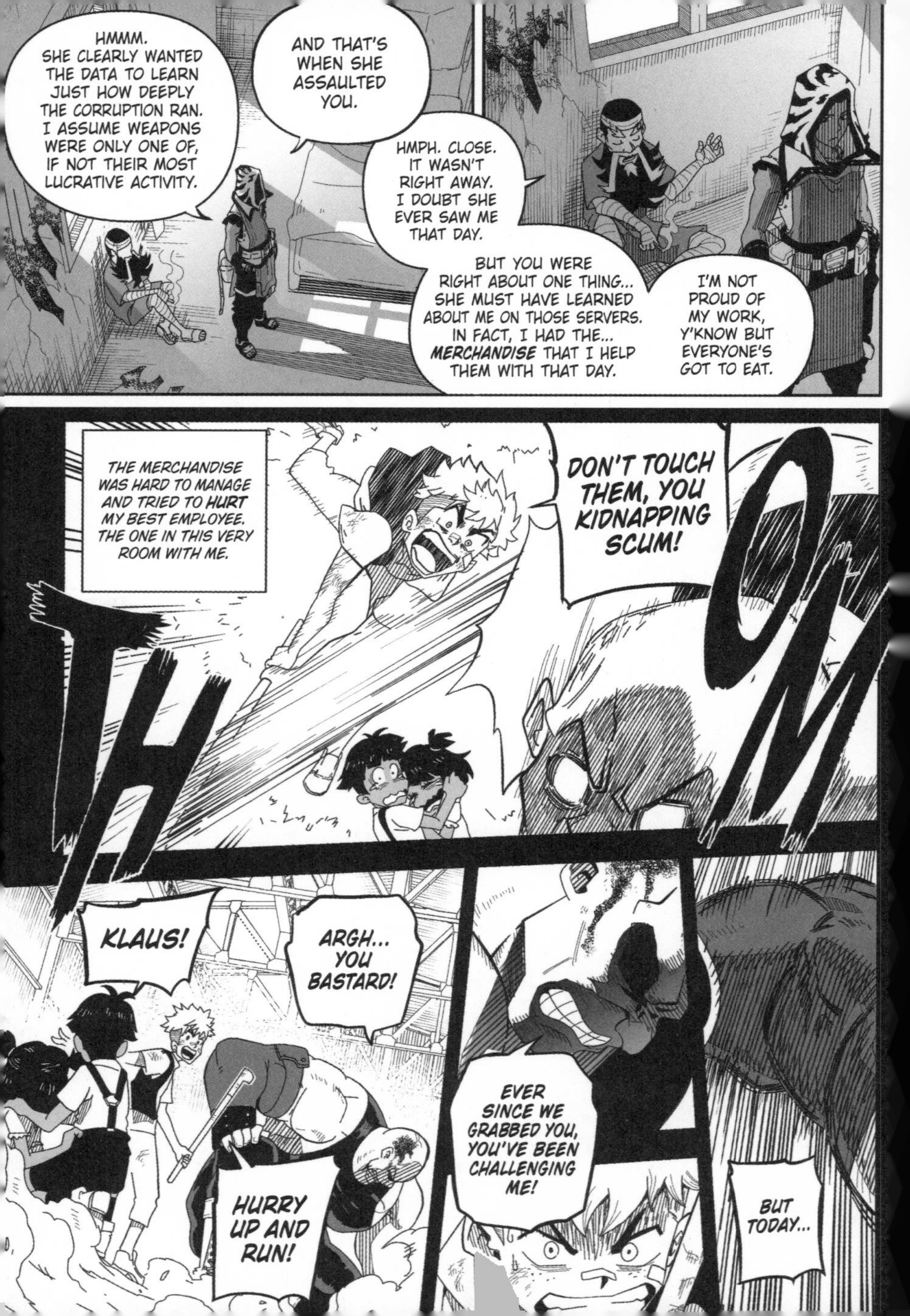
HMMM. SHE CLEARLY WANTED THE DATA TO LEARN JUST HOW DEEPLY THE CORRUPTION RAN. I ASSUME WEAPONS WERE ONLY ONE OF, IF NOT THEIR MOST LUCRATIVE ACTIVITY.
AND THAT'S WHEN SHE ASSAULTED YOU.
HMPH. CLOSE. IT WASN'T RIGHT AWAY. I DOUBT SHE EVER SAW ME THAT DAY.
BUT YOU WERE RIGHT ABOUT ONE THING... SHE MUST HAVE LEARNED ABOUT ME ON THOSE SERVERS. IN FACT, I HAD THE... MERCHANDISE THAT I HELP THEM WITH THAT DAY.
I'M NOT PROUD OF MY WORK, Y'KNOW BUT EVERYONE'S GOT TO EAT.
THE MERCHANDISE WAS HARD TO MANAGE AND TRIED TO HURT MY BEST EMPLOYEE. THE ONE IN THIS VERY ROOM WITH ME.
DON'T TOUCH THEM, YOU KIDNAPPING SCUM!
THOM
KLAUS!
ARGH... YOU BASTARD!
HURRY UP AND RUN!
EVER SINCE WE GRABBED YOU, YOU'VE BEEN CHALLENGING ME!
BUT TODAY...

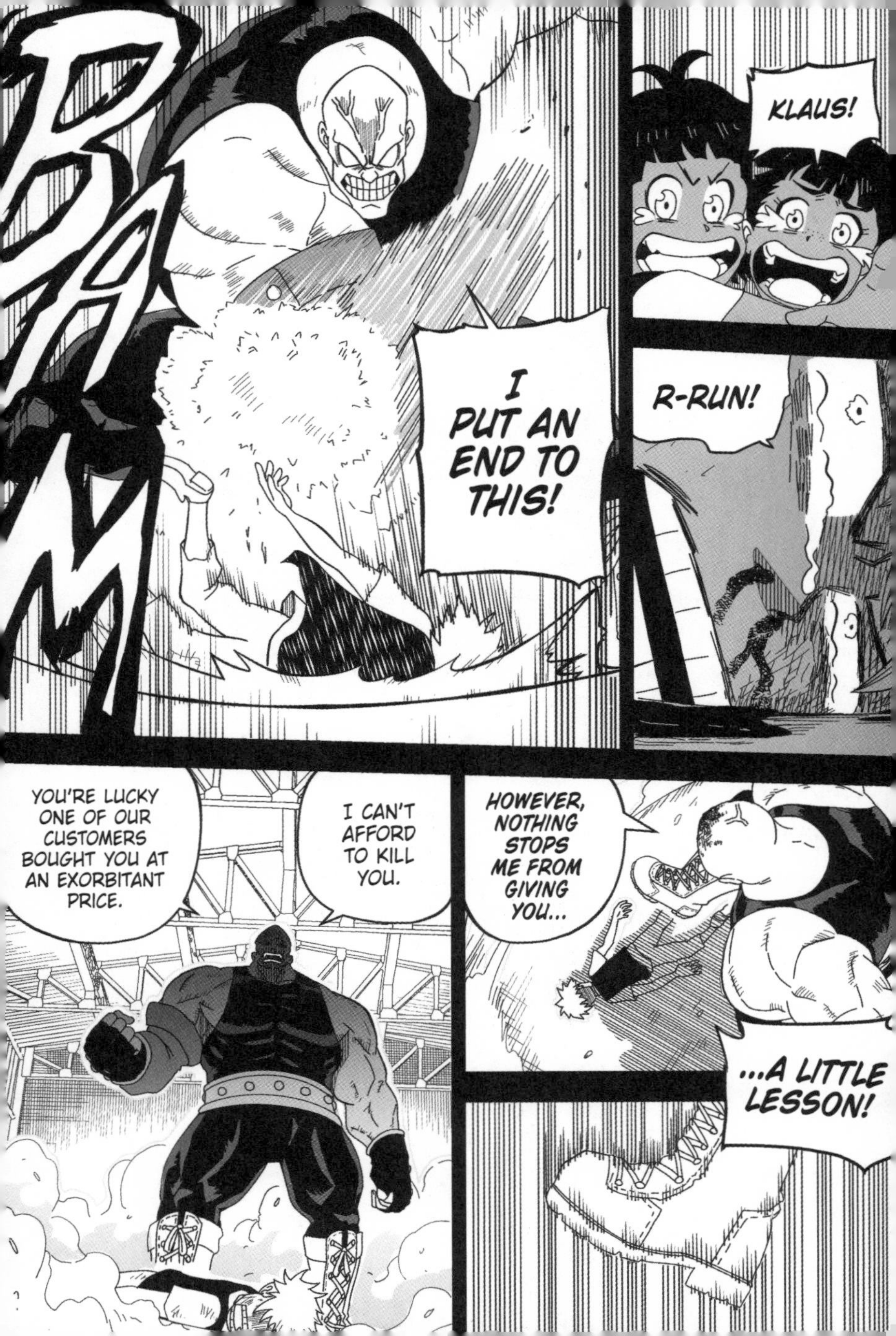
I PUT AN END TO THIS!
KLAUS!
R-RUN!
YOU'RE LUCKY ONE OF OUR CUSTOMERS BOUGHT YOU AT AN EXORBITANT PRICE.
I CAN'T AFFORD TO KILL YOU.
HOWEVER, NOTHING STOPS ME FROM GIVING YOU...
...A LITTLE LESSON!

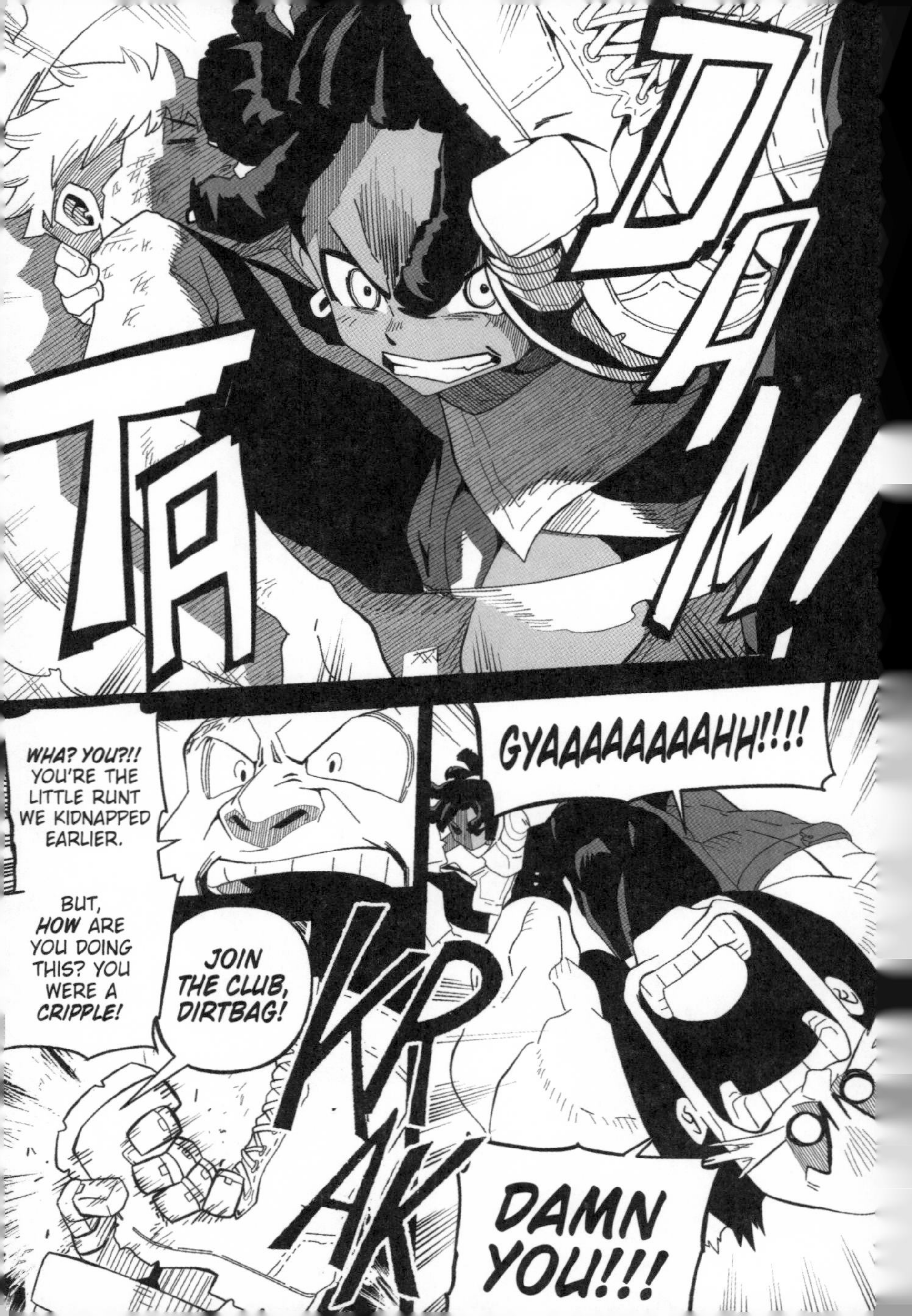
TA
DAM!
WHA? YOU?!! YOU'RE THE LITTLE RUNT WE KIDNAPPED EARLIER.
BUT, HOW ARE YOU DOING THIS? YOU WERE A CRIPPLE!
JOIN THE CLUB, DIRTBAG!
KRAK
GYAAAAAAAAHH!!!!
DAMN YOU!!!

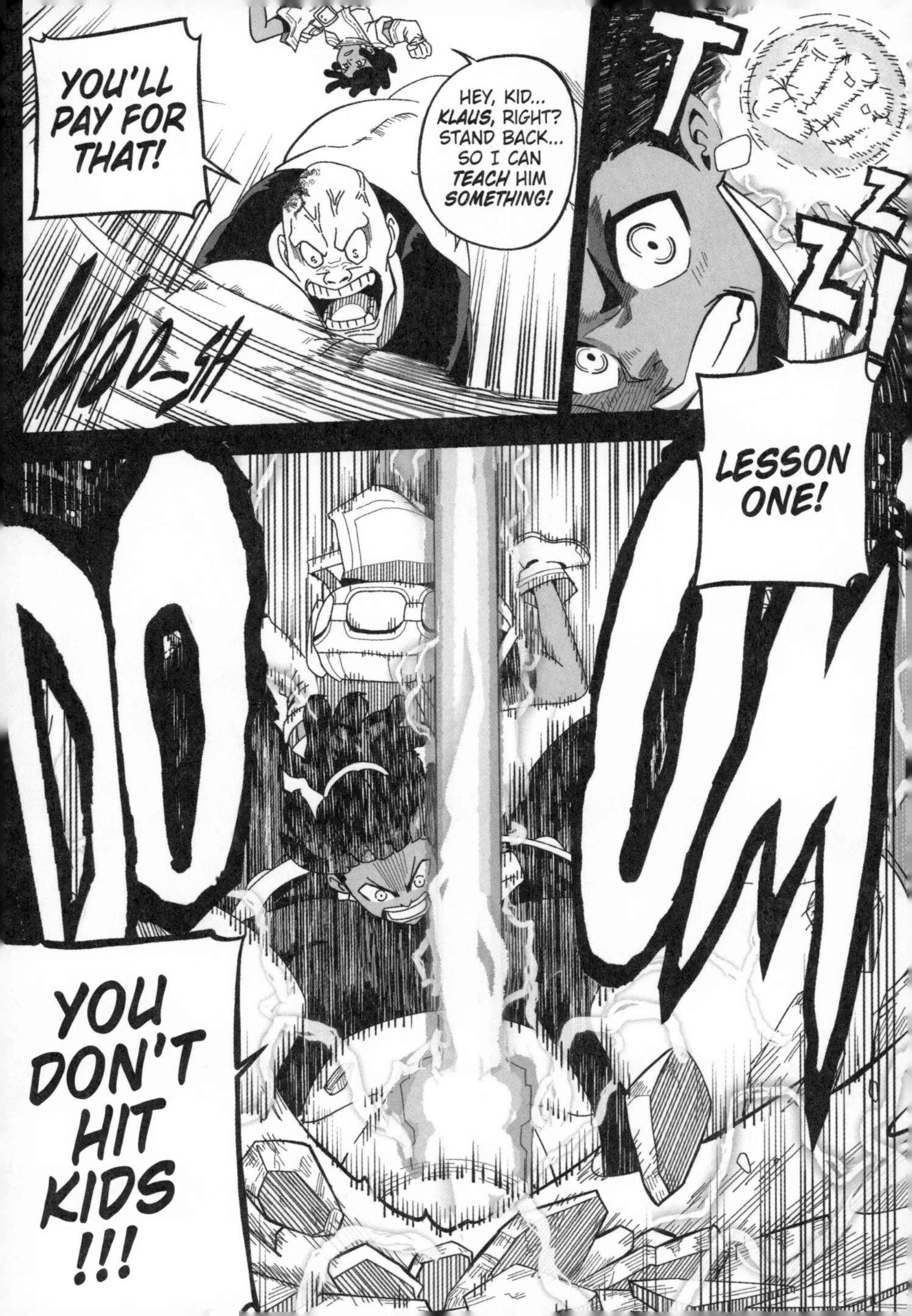
YOU'LL PAY FOR THAT!
HEY, KID... KLAUS, RIGHT? STAND BACK... SO I CAN TEACH HIM SOMETHING!
WHOO-SH
LESSON ONE!
DOOM
YOU DON'T HIT KIDS!!!

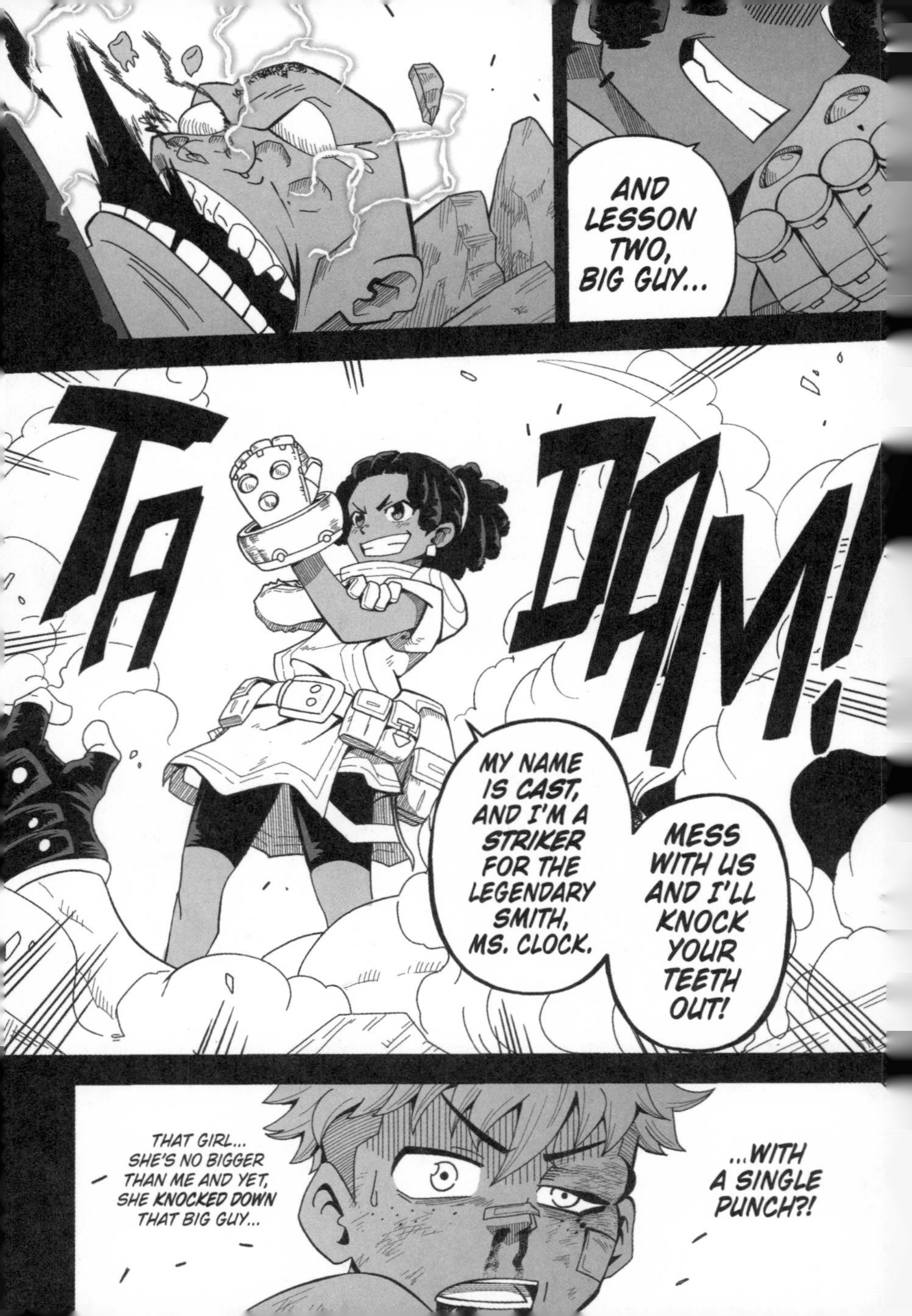
AND LESSON TWO, BIG GUY...
TA DAM!
MY NAME IS CAST, AND I'M A STRIKER FOR THE LEGENDARY SMITH, MS. CLOCK.
MESS WITH US AND I'LL KNOCK YOUR TEETH OUT!
THAT GIRL... SHE'S NO BIGGER THAN ME AND YET, SHE KNOCKED DOWN THAT BIG GUY...
...WITH A SINGLE PUNCH?!

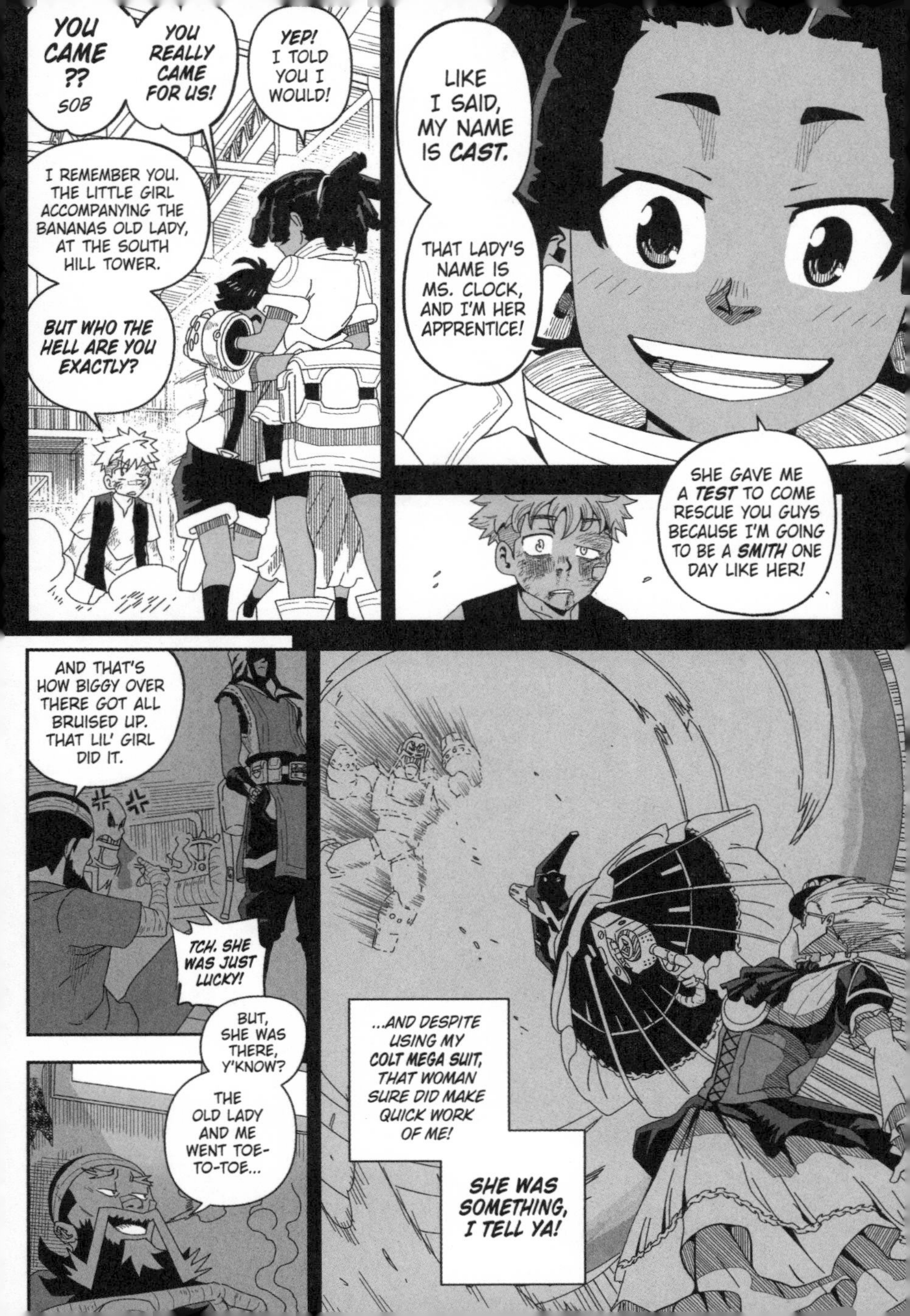
YOU CAME ?? SOB
YOU REALLY CAME FOR US!
YEP! I TOLD YOU I WOULD!
I REMEMBER YOU. THE LITTLE GIRL ACCOMPANYING THE BANANAS OLD LADY, AT THE SOUTH HILL TOWER.
BUT WHO THE HELL ARE YOU EXACTLY?
LIKE I SAID, MY NAME IS CAST.
THAT LADY'S NAME IS MS. CLOCK, AND I'M HER APPRENTICE!
SHE GAVE ME A TEST TO COME RESCUE YOU GUYS BECAUSE I'M GOING TO BE A SMITH ONE DAY LIKE HER!
AND THAT'S HOW BIGGY OVER THERE GOT ALL BRUISED UP. THAT LIL' GIRL DID IT.
TCH. SHE WAS JUST LUCKY!
BUT, SHE WAS THERE, Y'KNOW?
THE OLD LADY AND ME WENT TOE-TO-TOE...
...AND DESPITE USING MY COLT MEGA SUIT, THAT WOMAN SURE DID MAKE QUICK WORK OF ME!
SHE WAS SOMETHING, I TELL YA!

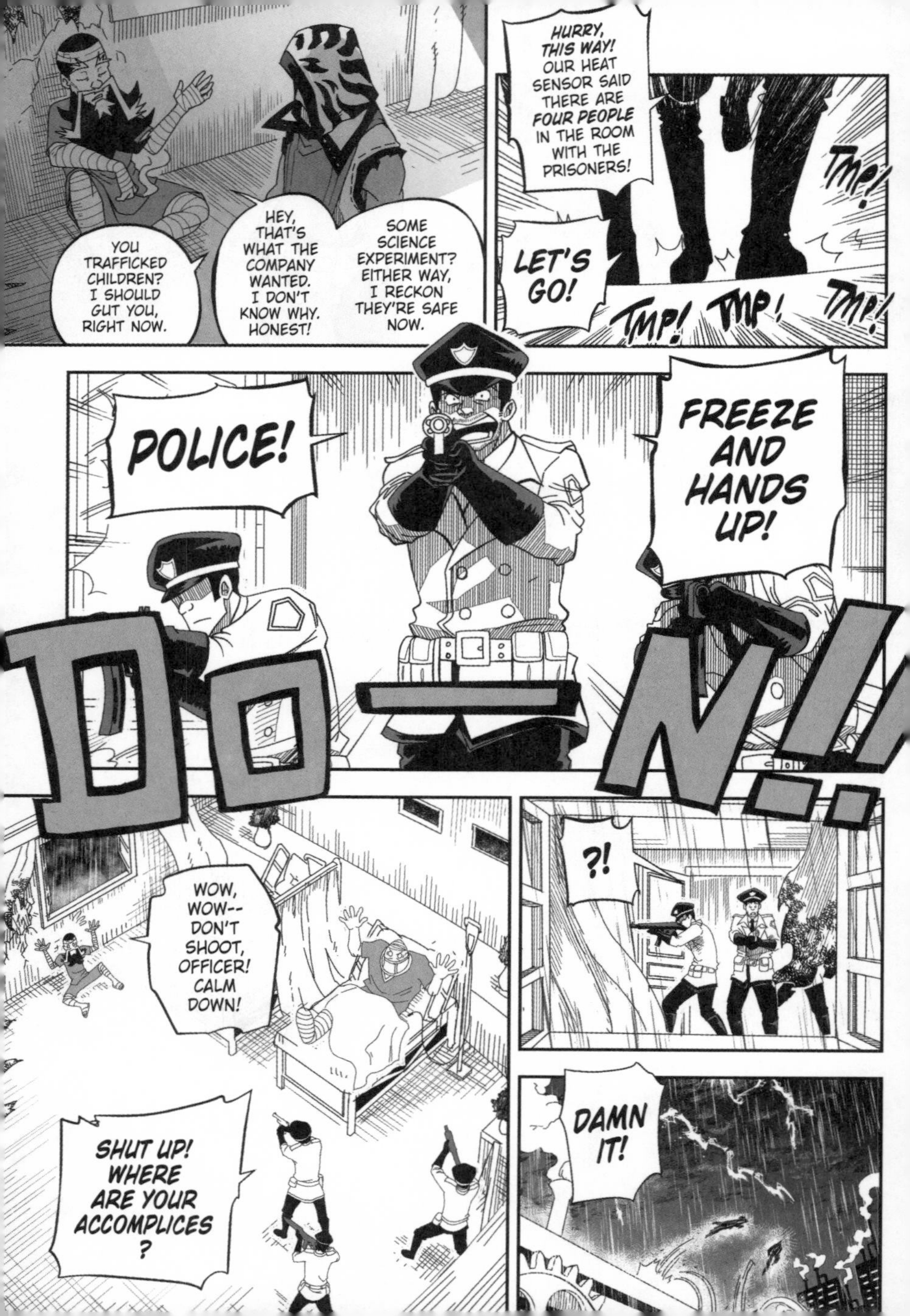
YOU TRAFFICKED CHILDREN? I SHOULD GUT YOU, RIGHT NOW.
HEY, THAT'S WHAT THE COMPANY WANTED. I DON'T KNOW WHY. HONEST!
SOME SCIENCE EXPERIMENT? EITHER WAY, I RECKON THEY'RE SAFE NOW.
HURRY, THIS WAY! OUR HEAT SENSOR SAID THERE ARE FOUR PEOPLE IN THE ROOM WITH THE PRISONERS!
TMP!
LET'S GO!
TMP! TMP! TMP!
POLICE!
FREEZE AND HANDS UP!
DO—N!!
WOW, WOW-- DON'T SHOOT, OFFICER! CALM DOWN!
SHUT UP! WHERE ARE YOUR ACCOMPLICES?
?!
DAMN IT!

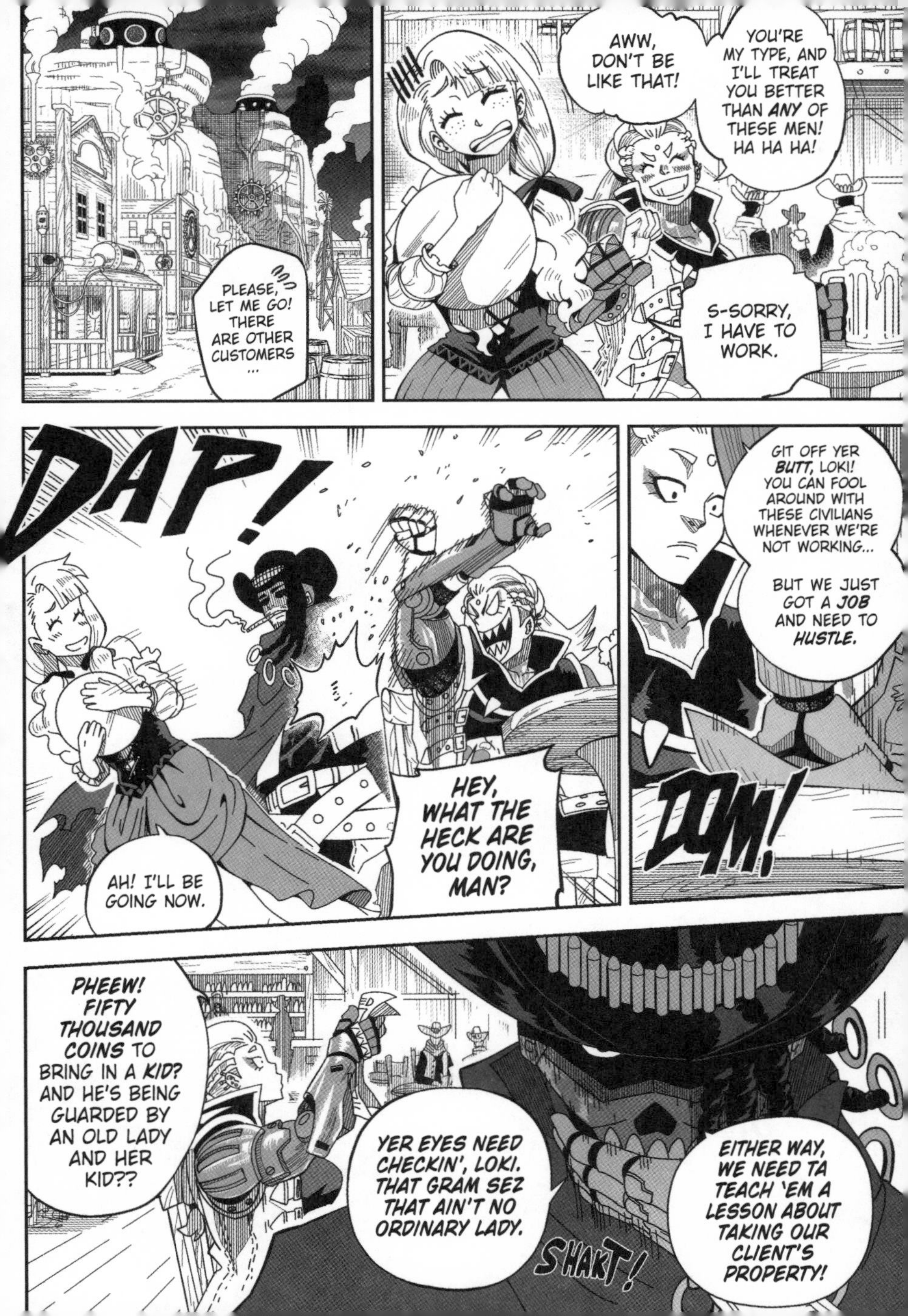
PLEASE, LET ME GO! THERE ARE OTHER CUSTOMERS ...
AWW, DON'T BE LIKE THAT!
YOU'RE MY TYPE, AND I'LL TREAT YOU BETTER THAN ANY OF THESE MEN! HA HA HA!
S-SORRY, I HAVE TO WORK.
DAP!
HEY, WHAT THE HECK ARE YOU DOING, MAN?
AH! I'LL BE GOING NOW.
GIT OFF YER BUTT, LOKI! YOU CAN FOOL AROUND WITH THESE CIVILIANS WHENEVER WE'RE NOT WORKING...
BUT WE JUST GOT A JOB AND NEED TO HUSTLE.
DOM!
PHEEW! FIFTY THOUSAND COINS TO BRING IN A KID? AND HE'S BEING GUARDED BY AN OLD LADY AND HER KID??
YER EYES NEED CHECKIN', LOKI. THAT GRAM SEZ THAT AIN'T NO ORDINARY LADY.
EITHER WAY, WE NEED TA TEACH 'EM A LESSON ABOUT TAKING OUR CLIENT'S PROPERTY!
SHAKT!

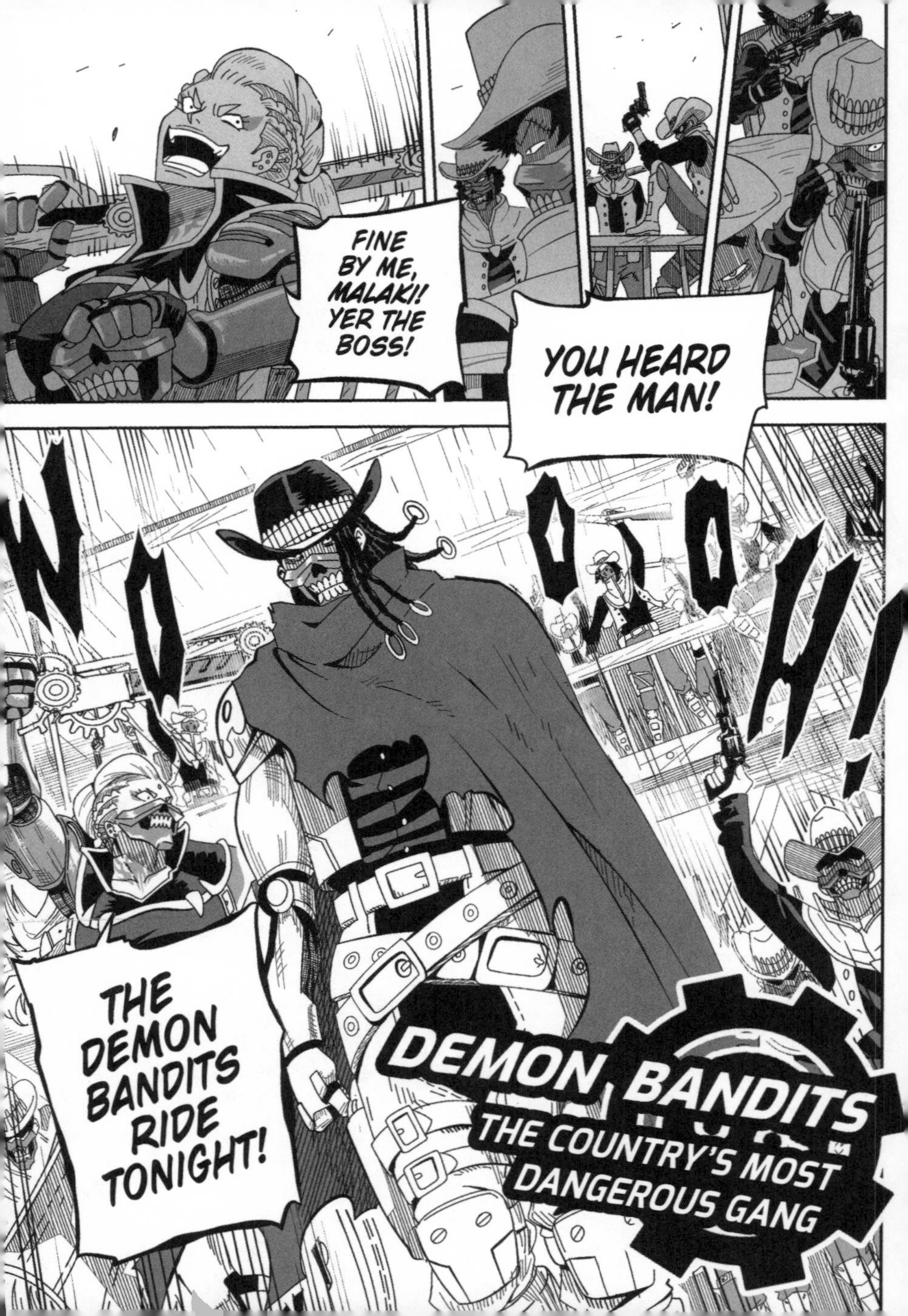
FINE BY ME, MALAKI! YER THE BOSS!
YOU HEARD THE MAN!
WOOOOOH!!
THE DEMON BANDITS RIDE TONIGHT!
DEMON BANDITS
THE COUNTRY'S MOST DANGEROUS GANG

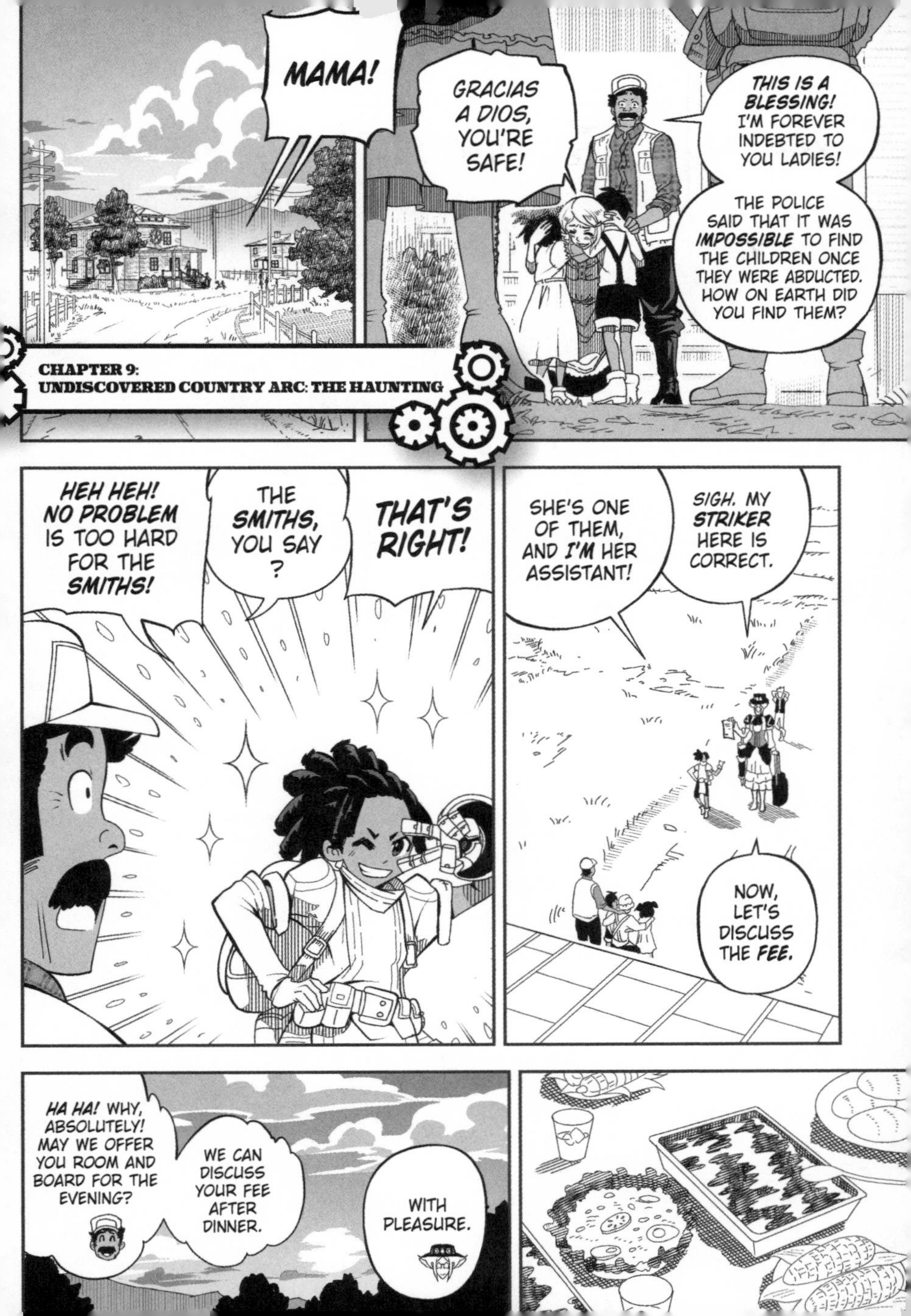
MAMA!
GRACIAS A DIOS, YOU'RE SAFE!
THIS IS A BLESSING! I'M FOREVER INDEBTED TO YOU LADIES!
THE POLICE SAID THAT IT WAS IMPOSSIBLE TO FIND THE CHILDREN ONCE THEY WERE ABDUCTED. HOW ON EARTH DID YOU FIND THEM?
CHAPTER 9: UNDISCOVERED COUNTRY ARC: THE HAUNTING
HEH HEH! NO PROBLEM IS TOO HARD FOR THE SMITHS!
THE SMITHS, YOU SAY?
THAT'S RIGHT!
SHE'S ONE OF THEM, AND I'M HER ASSISTANT!
SIGH. MY STRIKER HERE IS CORRECT.
NOW, LET'S DISCUSS THE FEE.
HA HA! WHY, ABSOLUTELY! MAY WE OFFER YOU ROOM AND BOARD FOR THE EVENING?
WE CAN DISCUSS YOUR FEE AFTER DINNER.
WITH PLEASURE.

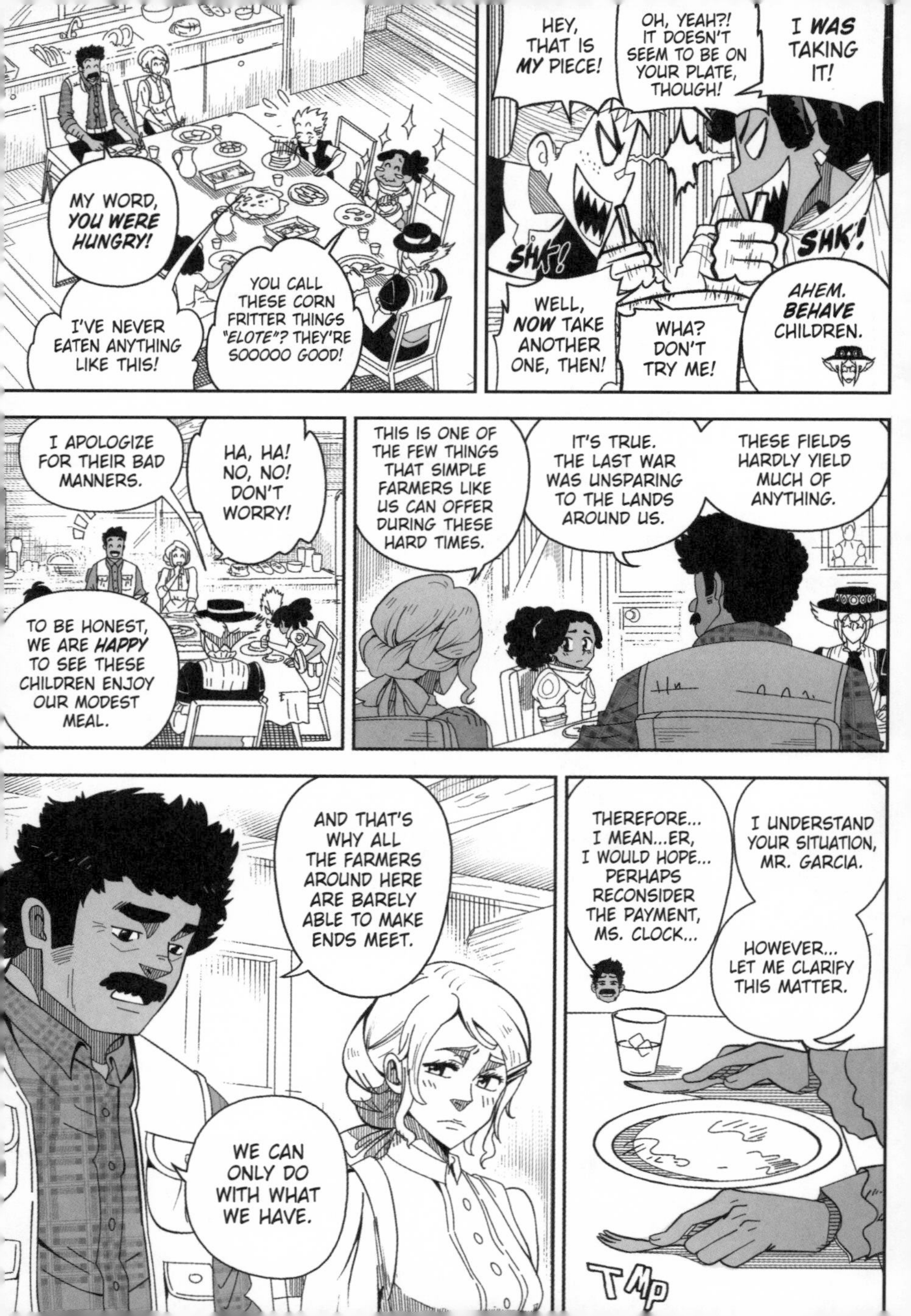
MY WORD, YOU WERE HUNGRY!
I'VE NEVER EATEN ANYTHING LIKE THIS!
YOU CALL THESE CORN FRITTER THINGS "ELOTE"? THEY'RE SOOOOO GOOD!
HEY, THAT IS MY PIECE!
OH, YEAH?! IT DOESN'T SEEM TO BE ON YOUR PLATE, THOUGH!
I WAS TAKING IT!
SHK!
SHK!
WELL, NOW TAKE ANOTHER ONE, THEN!
WHA? DON'T TRY ME!
AHEM. BEHAVE CHILDREN.
I APOLOGIZE FOR THEIR BAD MANNERS.
HA, HA! NO, NO! DON'T WORRY!
TO BE HONEST, WE ARE HAPPY TO SEE THESE CHILDREN ENJOY OUR MODEST MEAL.
THIS IS ONE OF THE FEW THINGS THAT SIMPLE FARMERS LIKE US CAN OFFER DURING THESE HARD TIMES.
IT'S TRUE. THE LAST WAR WAS UNSPARING TO THE LANDS AROUND US.
THESE FIELDS HARDLY YIELD MUCH OF ANYTHING.
AND THAT'S WHY ALL THE FARMERS AROUND HERE ARE BARELY ABLE TO MAKE ENDS MEET.
WE CAN ONLY DO WITH WHAT WE HAVE.
THEREFORE... I MEAN...ER, I WOULD HOPE... PERHAPS RECONSIDER THE PAYMENT, MS. CLOCK...
I UNDERSTAND YOUR SITUATION, MR. GARCIA.
HOWEVER... LET ME CLARIFY THIS MATTER.
TMP

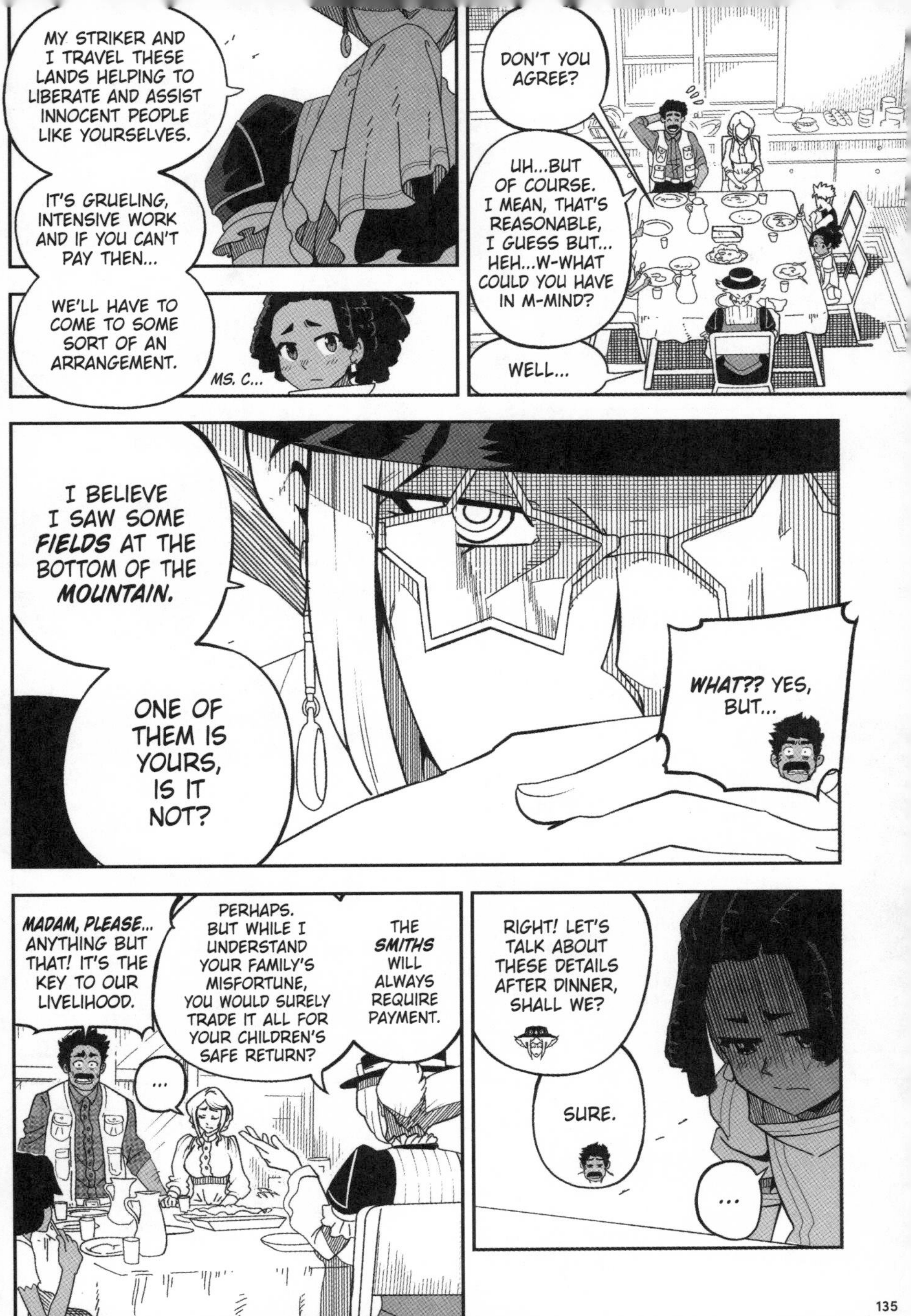
MY STRIKER AND I TRAVEL THESE LANDS HELPING TO LIBERATE AND ASSIST INNOCENT PEOPLE LIKE YOURSELVES.
IT'S GRUELING, INTENSIVE WORK AND IF YOU CAN'T PAY THEN...
WE'LL HAVE TO COME TO SOME SORT OF AN ARRANGEMENT.
MS. C...
DON'T YOU AGREE?
UH...BUT OF COURSE. I MEAN, THAT'S REASONABLE, I GUESS BUT... HEH...W-WHAT COULD YOU HAVE IN M-MIND?
WELL...
I BELIEVE I SAW SOME FIELDS AT THE BOTTOM OF THE MOUNTAIN.
ONE OF THEM IS YOURS, IS IT NOT?
WHAT?? YES, BUT...
MADAM, PLEASE... ANYTHING BUT THAT! IT'S THE KEY TO OUR LIVELIHOOD.
PERHAPS. BUT WHILE I UNDERSTAND YOUR FAMILY'S MISFORTUNE, YOU WOULD SURELY TRADE IT ALL FOR YOUR CHILDREN'S SAFE RETURN?
THE SMITHS WILL ALWAYS REQUIRE PAYMENT.
...
RIGHT! LET'S TALK ABOUT THESE DETAILS AFTER DINNER, SHALL WE?
SURE.
...

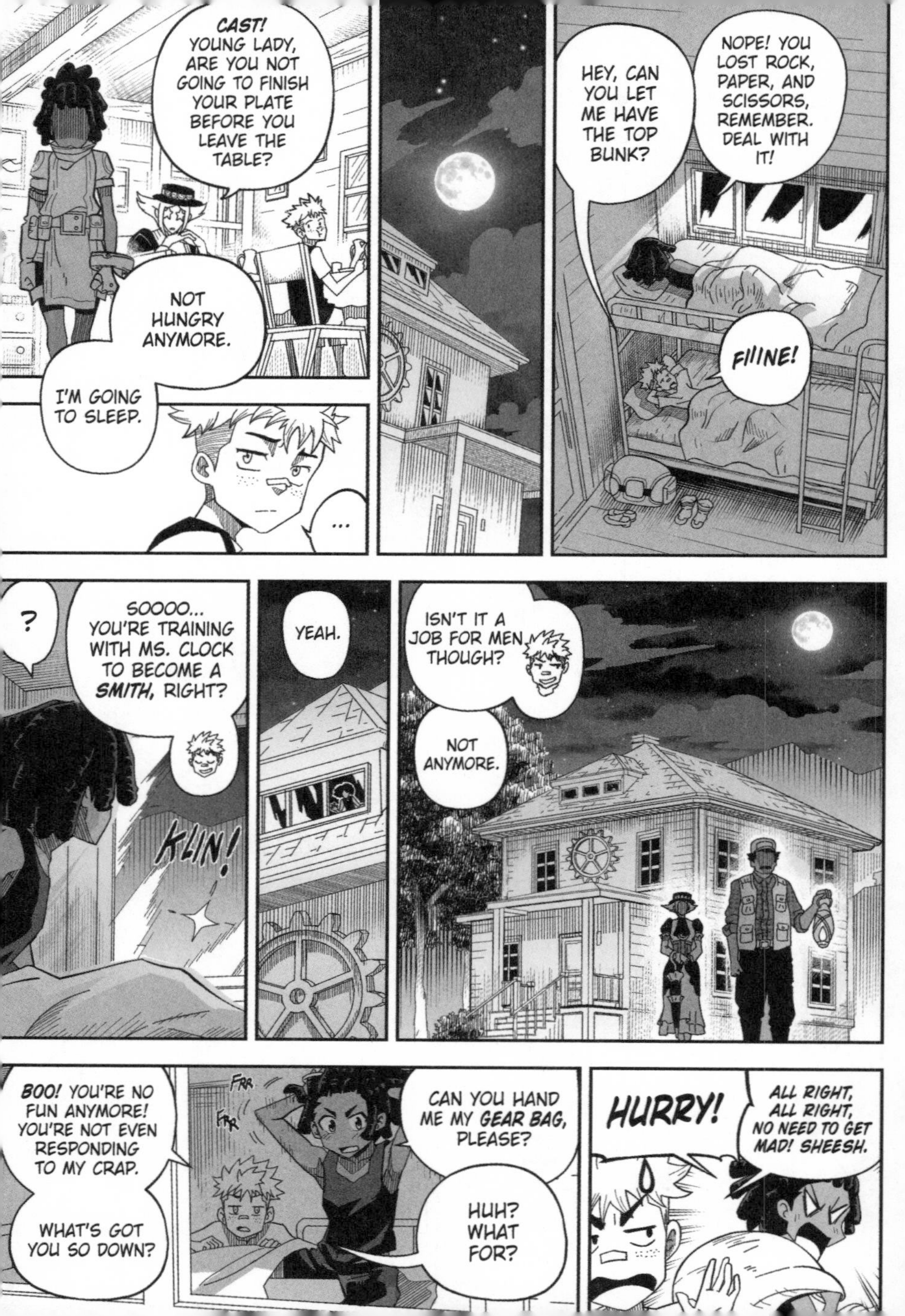
CAST! YOUNG LADY, ARE YOU NOT GOING TO FINISH YOUR PLATE BEFORE YOU LEAVE THE TABLE?
NOT HUNGRY ANYMORE.
I'M GOING TO SLEEP.
...
HEY, CAN YOU LET ME HAVE THE TOP BUNK?
NOPE! YOU LOST ROCK, PAPER, AND SCISSORS, REMEMBER. DEAL WITH IT!
FIIINE!
?
SOOOO... YOU'RE TRAINING WITH MS. CLOCK TO BECOME A SMITH, RIGHT?
KLIN!
YEAH.
ISN'T IT A JOB FOR MEN THOUGH?
NOT ANYMORE.
BOO! YOU'RE NO FUN ANYMORE! YOU'RE NOT EVEN RESPONDING TO MY CRAP.
WHAT'S GOT YOU SO DOWN?
FRR
FRR
CAN YOU HAND ME MY GEAR BAG, PLEASE?
HUH? WHAT FOR?
HURRY!
ALL RIGHT, ALL RIGHT, NO NEED TO GET MAD! SHEESH.

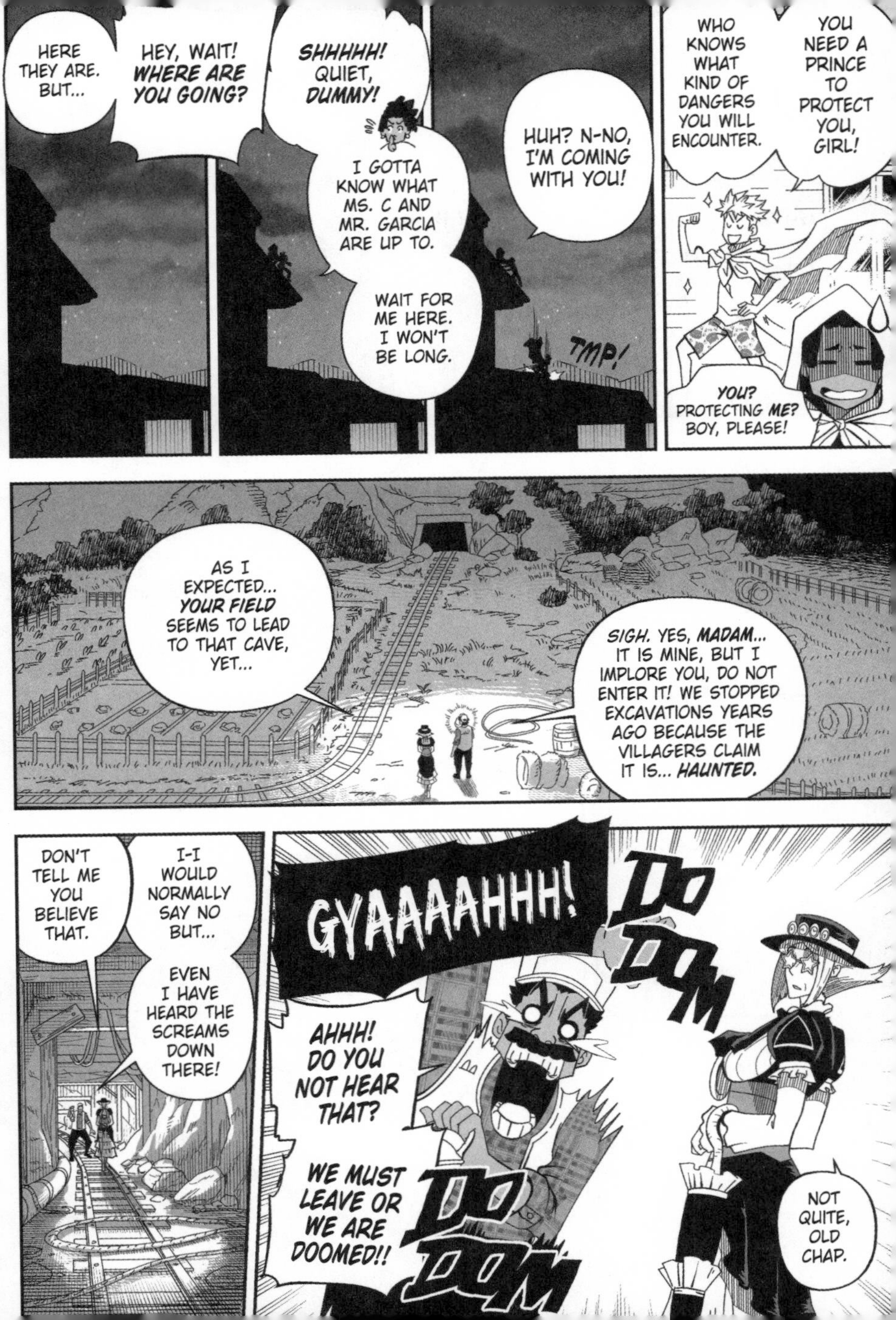
HERE THEY ARE. BUT...
HEY, WAIT! WHERE ARE YOU GOING?
SHHHHH! QUIET, DUMMY!
I GOTTA KNOW WHAT MS. C AND MR. GARCIA ARE UP TO.
WAIT FOR ME HERE. I WON'T BE LONG.
HUH? N-NO, I'M COMING WITH YOU!
TMP!
WHO KNOWS WHAT KIND OF DANGERS YOU WILL ENCOUNTER.
YOU NEED A PRINCE TO PROTECT YOU, GIRL!
YOU? PROTECTING ME? BOY, PLEASE!
AS I EXPECTED... YOUR FIELD SEEMS TO LEAD TO THAT CAVE, YET...
SIGH. YES, MADAM... IT IS MINE, BUT I IMPLORE YOU, DO NOT ENTER IT! WE STOPPED EXCAVATIONS YEARS AGO BECAUSE THE VILLAGERS CLAIM IT IS... HAUNTED.
DON'T TELL ME YOU BELIEVE THAT.
I-I WOULD NORMALLY SAY NO BUT...
EVEN I HAVE HEARD THE SCREAMS DOWN THERE!
GYAAAAHHH!
DO DOM
AHHH! DO YOU NOT HEAR THAT?
WE MUST LEAVE OR WE ARE DOOMED!!
DO DOM
NOT QUITE, OLD CHAP.

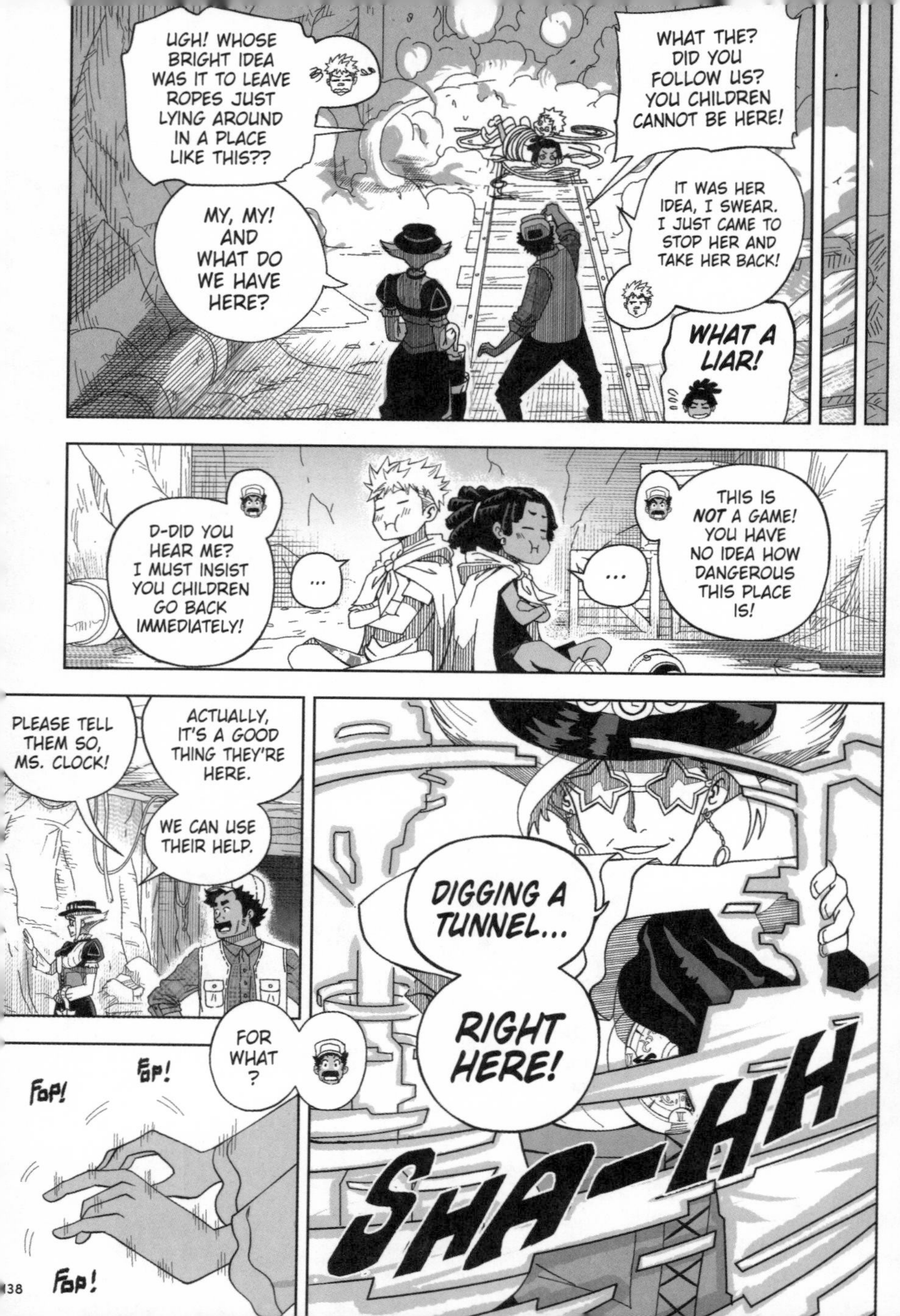
UGH! WHOSE BRIGHT IDEA WAS IT TO LEAVE ROPES JUST LYING AROUND IN A PLACE LIKE THIS??
WHAT THE? DID YOU FOLLOW US? YOU CHILDREN CANNOT BE HERE!
MY, MY! AND WHAT DO WE HAVE HERE?
IT WAS HER IDEA, I SWEAR. I JUST CAME TO STOP HER AND TAKE HER BACK!
WHAT A LIAR!
D-DID YOU HEAR ME? I MUST INSIST YOU CHILDREN GO BACK IMMEDIATELY!
...
...
THIS IS NOT A GAME! YOU HAVE NO IDEA HOW DANGEROUS THIS PLACE IS!
PLEASE TELL THEM SO, MS. CLOCK!
ACTUALLY, IT'S A GOOD THING THEY'RE HERE.
WE CAN USE THEIR HELP.
FOP!
FOP!
FOP!
FOR WHAT?
DIGGING A TUNNEL...
RIGHT HERE!
SHA-HH

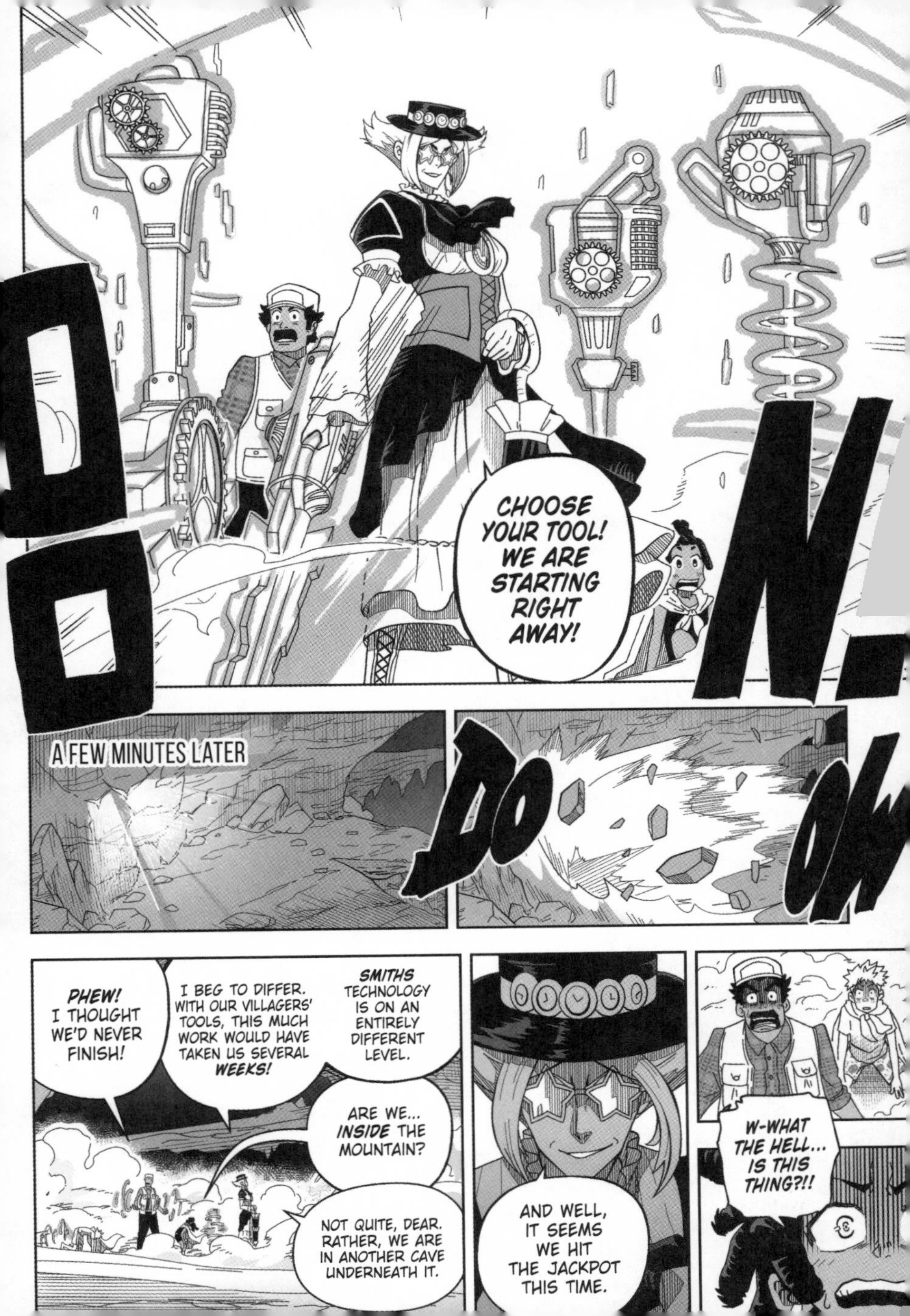
CHOOSE YOUR TOOL! WE ARE STARTING RIGHT AWAY!
A FEW MINUTES LATER
DO
PHEW! I THOUGHT WE'D NEVER FINISH!
I BEG TO DIFFER. WITH OUR VILLAGERS' TOOLS, THIS MUCH WORK WOULD HAVE TAKEN US SEVERAL WEEKS!
SMITHS TECHNOLOGY IS ON AN ENTIRELY DIFFERENT LEVEL.
ARE WE... INSIDE THE MOUNTAIN?
NOT QUITE, DEAR. RATHER, WE ARE IN ANOTHER CAVE UNDERNEATH IT.
AND WELL, IT SEEMS WE HIT THE JACKPOT THIS TIME.
W-WHAT THE HELL... IS THIS THING?!!

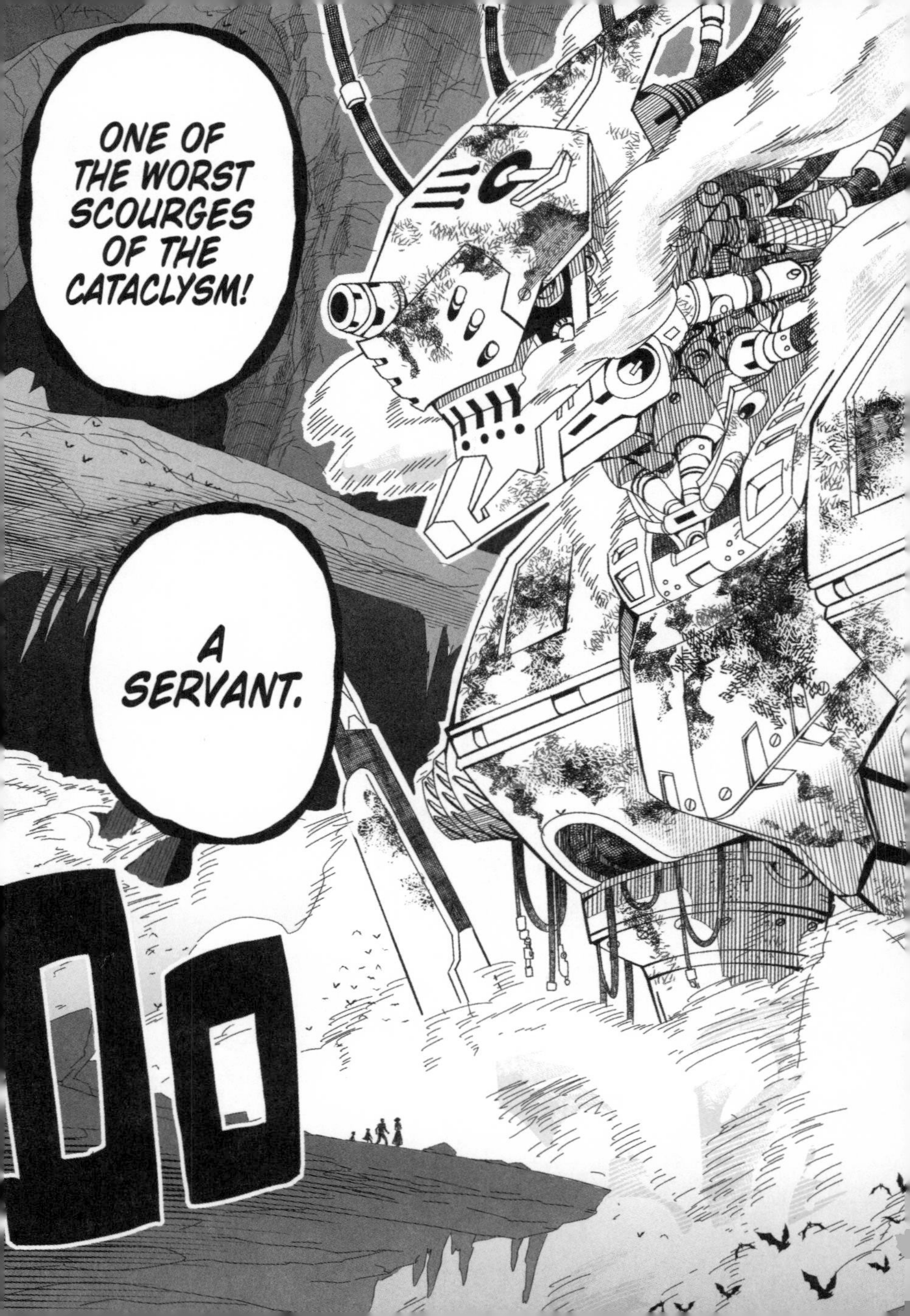
ONE OF THE WORST SCOURGES OF THE CATACLYSM!
A SERVANT.

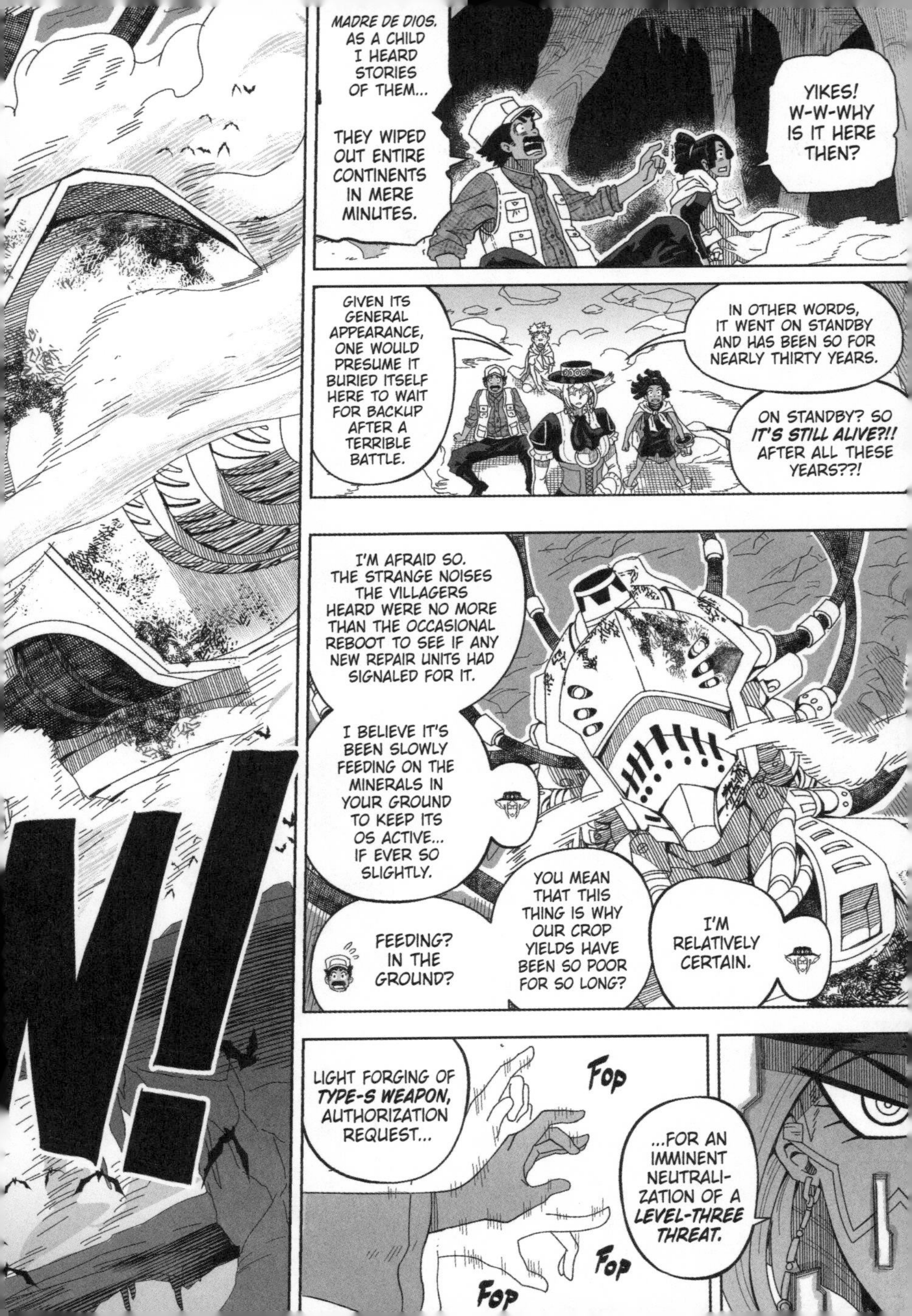

MADRE DE DIOS. AS A CHILD I HEARD STORIES OF THEM...
THEY WIPED OUT ENTIRE CONTINENTS IN MERE MINUTES.
YIKES! W-W-WHY IS IT HERE THEN?
GIVEN ITS GENERAL APPEARANCE, ONE WOULD PRESUME IT BURIED ITSELF HERE TO WAIT FOR BACKUP AFTER A TERRIBLE BATTLE.
IN OTHER WORDS, IT WENT ON STANDBY AND HAS BEEN SO FOR NEARLY THIRTY YEARS.
ON STANDBY? SO IT'S STILL ALIVE?!! AFTER ALL THESE YEARS??!
I'M AFRAID SO. THE STRANGE NOISES THE VILLAGERS HEARD WERE NO MORE THAN THE OCCASIONAL REBOOT TO SEE IF ANY NEW REPAIR UNITS HAD SIGNALED FOR IT.
I BELIEVE IT'S BEEN SLOWLY FEEDING ON THE MINERALS IN YOUR GROUND TO KEEP ITS OS ACTIVE... IF EVER SO SLIGHTLY.
FEEDING? IN THE GROUND?
YOU MEAN THAT THIS THING IS WHY OUR CROP YIELDS HAVE BEEN SO POOR FOR SO LONG?
I'M RELATIVELY CERTAIN.
LIGHT FORGING OF TYPE-S WEAPON, AUTHORIZATION REQUEST...
FOP
FOP
FOP
...FOR AN IMMINENT NEUTRALIZATION OF A LEVEL-THREE THREAT.

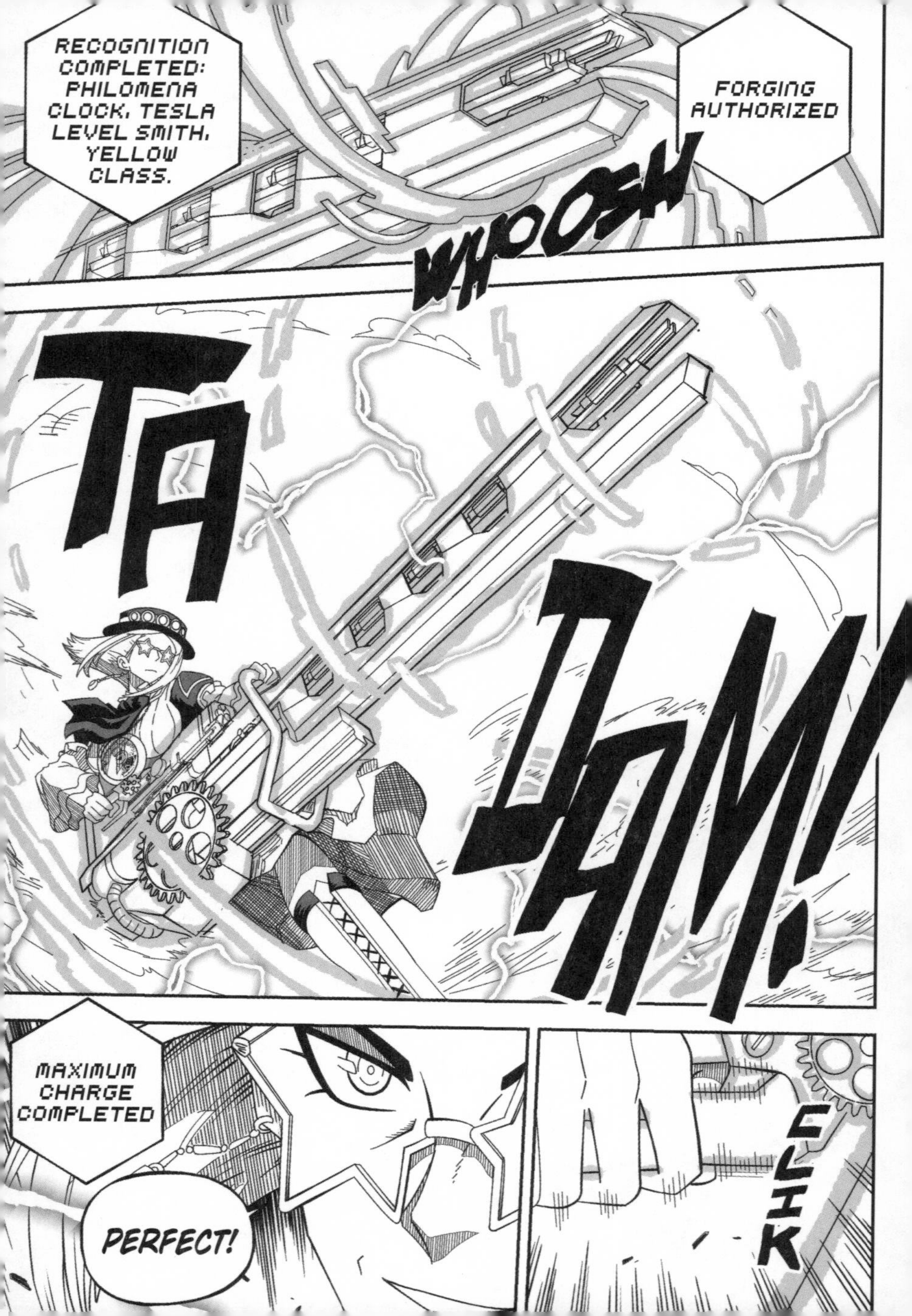
RECOGNITION COMPLETED: PHILOMENA CLOCK, TESLA LEVEL SMITH, YELLOW CLASS.
FORGING AUTHORIZED
WHOOSH
TA
DAM!
MAXIMUM CHARGE COMPLETED
PERFECT!
CLIK

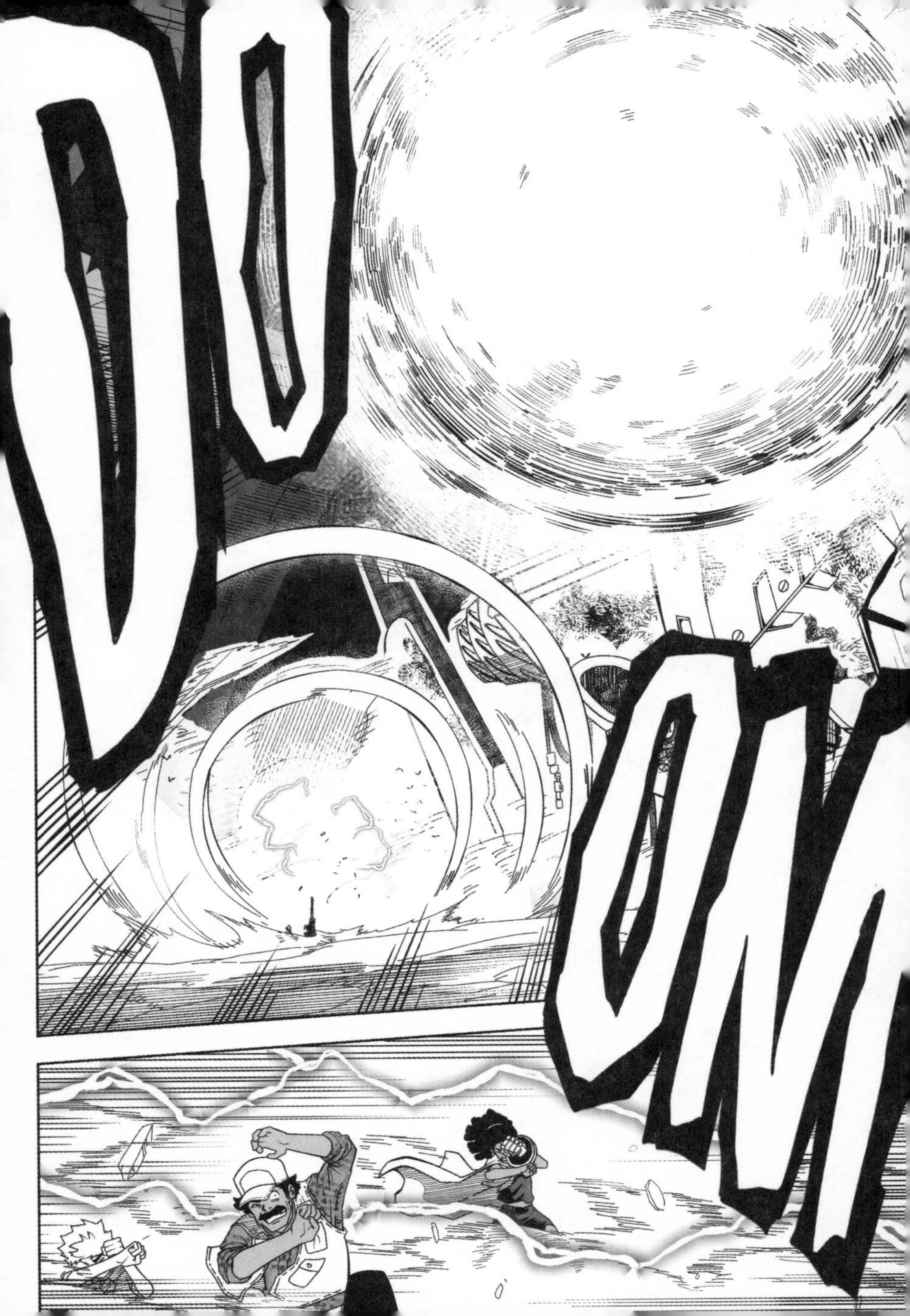

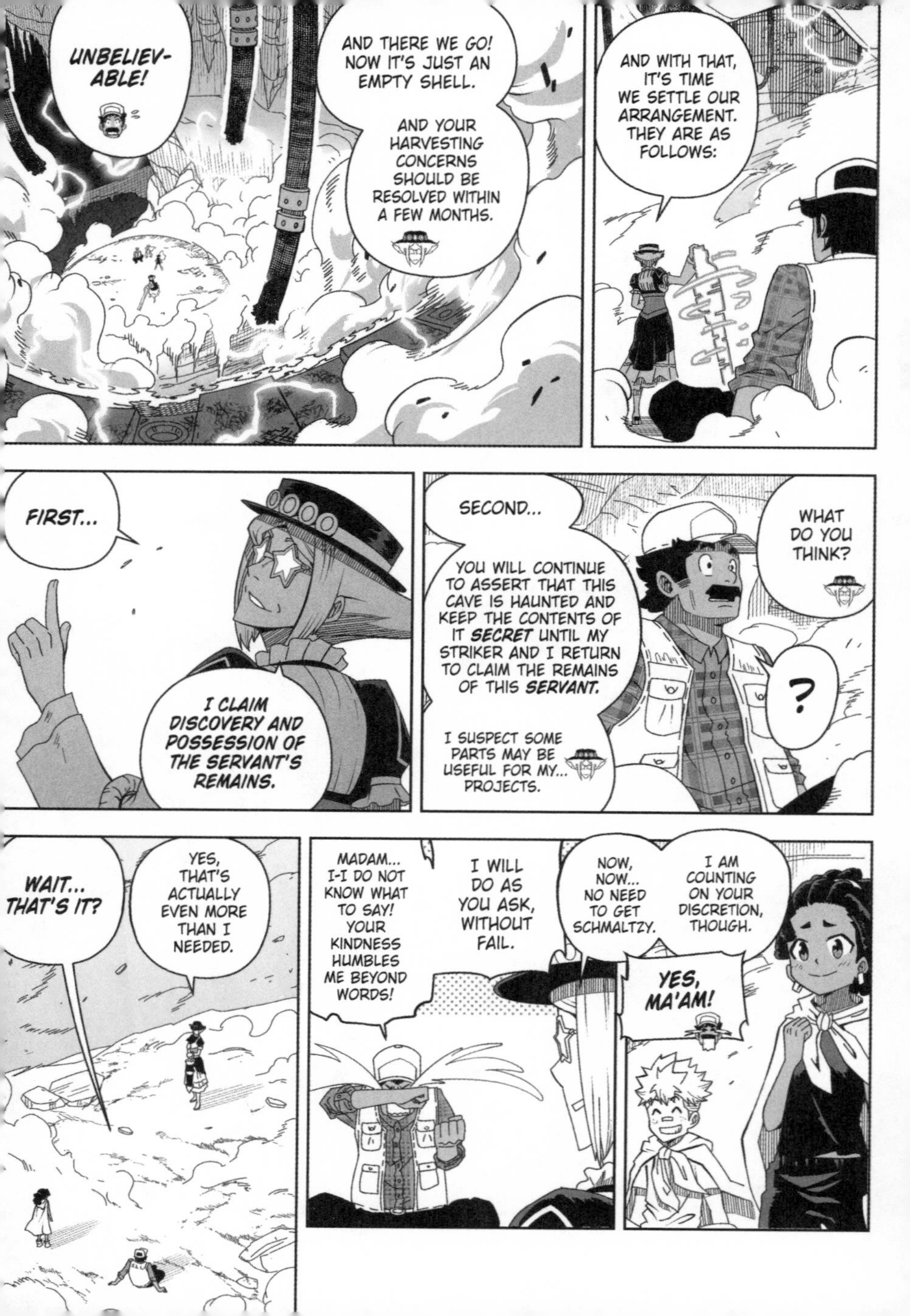
UNBELIEV-ABLE!
AND THERE WE GO! NOW IT'S JUST AN EMPTY SHELL.
AND YOUR HARVESTING CONCERNS SHOULD BE RESOLVED WITHIN A FEW MONTHS.
AND WITH THAT, IT'S TIME WE SETTLE OUR ARRANGEMENT. THEY ARE AS FOLLOWS:
FIRST...
I CLAIM DISCOVERY AND POSSESSION OF THE SERVANT'S REMAINS.
SECOND...
YOU WILL CONTINUE TO ASSERT THAT THIS CAVE IS HAUNTED AND KEEP THE CONTENTS OF IT SECRET UNTIL MY STRIKER AND I RETURN TO CLAIM THE REMAINS OF THIS SERVANT.
I SUSPECT SOME PARTS MAY BE USEFUL FOR MY... PROJECTS.
WHAT DO YOU THINK?
?
WAIT... THAT'S IT?
YES, THAT'S ACTUALLY EVEN MORE THAN I NEEDED.
MADAM... I-I DO NOT KNOW WHAT TO SAY! YOUR KINDNESS HUMBLES ME BEYOND WORDS!
I WILL DO AS YOU ASK, WITHOUT FAIL.
NOW, NOW... NO NEED TO GET SCHMALTZY.
I AM COUNTING ON YOUR DISCRETION, THOUGH.
YES, MA'AM!

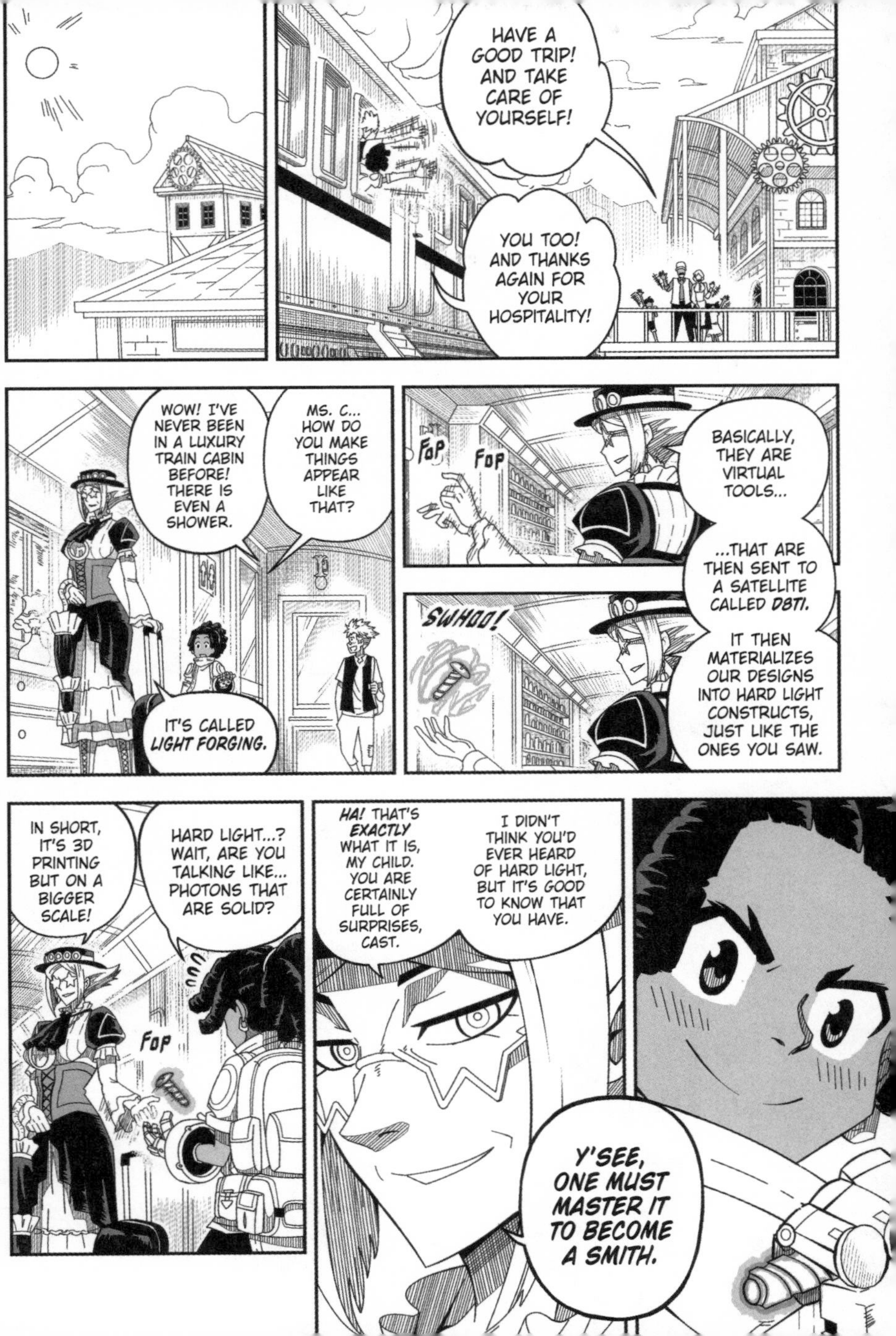
HAVE A GOOD TRIP! AND TAKE CARE OF YOURSELF!
YOU TOO! AND THANKS AGAIN FOR YOUR HOSPITALITY!
WOW! I'VE NEVER BEEN IN A LUXURY TRAIN CABIN BEFORE! THERE IS EVEN A SHOWER.
MS. C... HOW DO YOU MAKE THINGS APPEAR LIKE THAT?
IT'S CALLED *LIGHT FORGING.*
FOP
FOP
BASICALLY, THEY ARE VIRTUAL TOOLS...
...THAT ARE THEN SENT TO A SATELLITE CALLED *D8TI.*
SWHOO!
IT THEN MATERIALIZES OUR DESIGNS INTO HARD LIGHT CONSTRUCTS, JUST LIKE THE ONES YOU SAW.
IN SHORT, IT'S 3D PRINTING BUT ON A BIGGER SCALE!
HARD LIGHT...? WAIT, ARE YOU TALKING LIKE... PHOTONS THAT ARE SOLID?
FOP
HA! THAT'S *EXACTLY* WHAT IT IS, MY CHILD. YOU ARE CERTAINLY FULL OF SURPRISES, CAST.
I DIDN'T THINK YOU'D EVER HEARD OF HARD LIGHT, BUT IT'S GOOD TO KNOW THAT YOU HAVE.
Y'SEE, ONE MUST MASTER IT TO BECOME A SMITH.

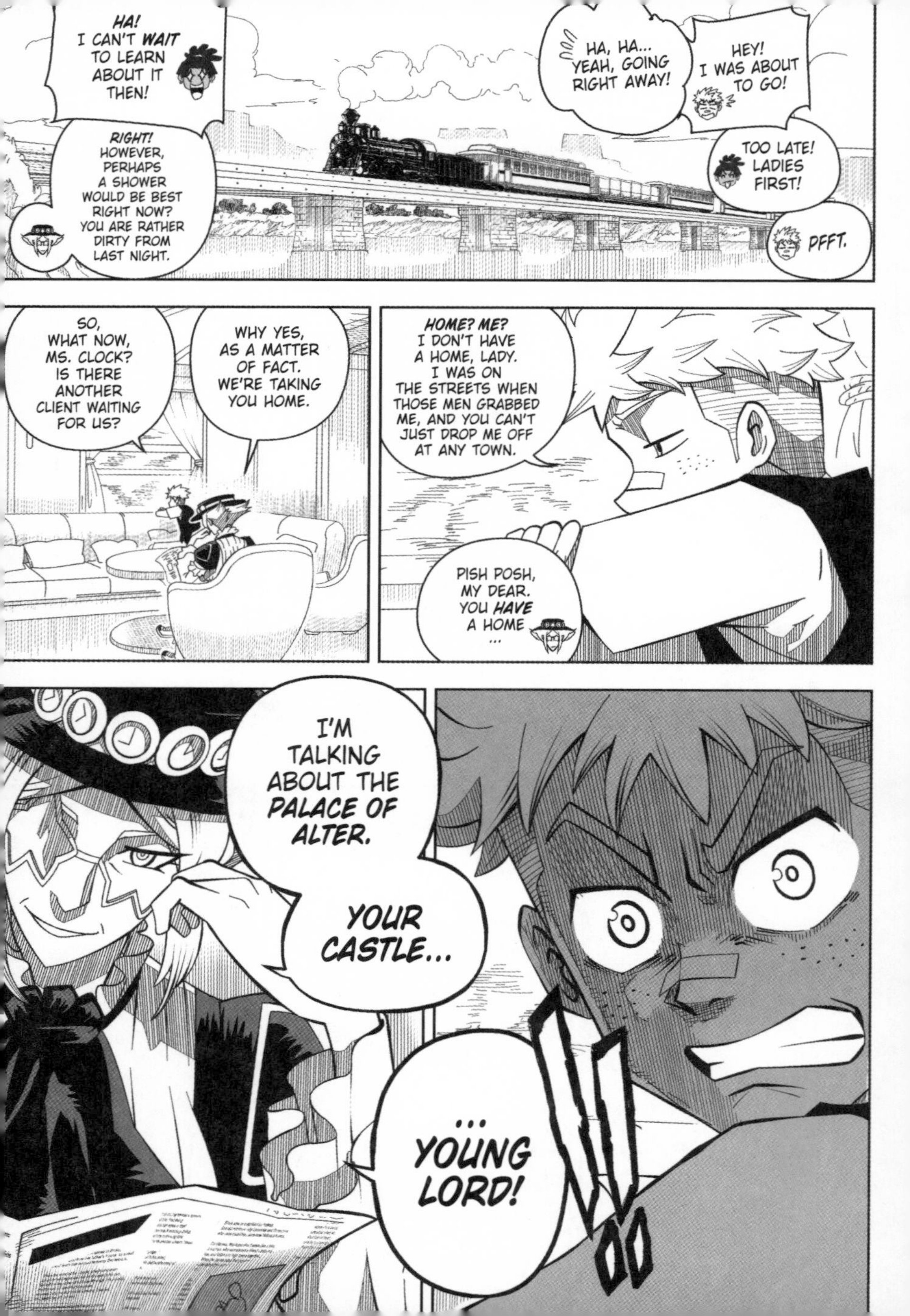
HA! I CAN'T WAIT TO LEARN ABOUT IT THEN!
RIGHT! HOWEVER, PERHAPS A SHOWER WOULD BE BEST RIGHT NOW? YOU ARE RATHER DIRTY FROM LAST NIGHT.
HA, HA... YEAH, GOING RIGHT AWAY!
HEY! I WAS ABOUT TO GO!
TOO LATE! LADIES FIRST!
PFFT.
SO, WHAT NOW, MS. CLOCK? IS THERE ANOTHER CLIENT WAITING FOR US?
WHY YES, AS A MATTER OF FACT. WE'RE TAKING YOU HOME.
HOME? ME? I DON'T HAVE A HOME, LADY. I WAS ON THE STREETS WHEN THOSE MEN GRABBED ME, AND YOU CAN'T JUST DROP ME OFF AT ANY TOWN.
PISH POSH, MY DEAR. YOU HAVE A HOME ...
I'M TALKING ABOUT THE PALACE OF ALTER.
YOUR CASTLE...
... YOUNG LORD!

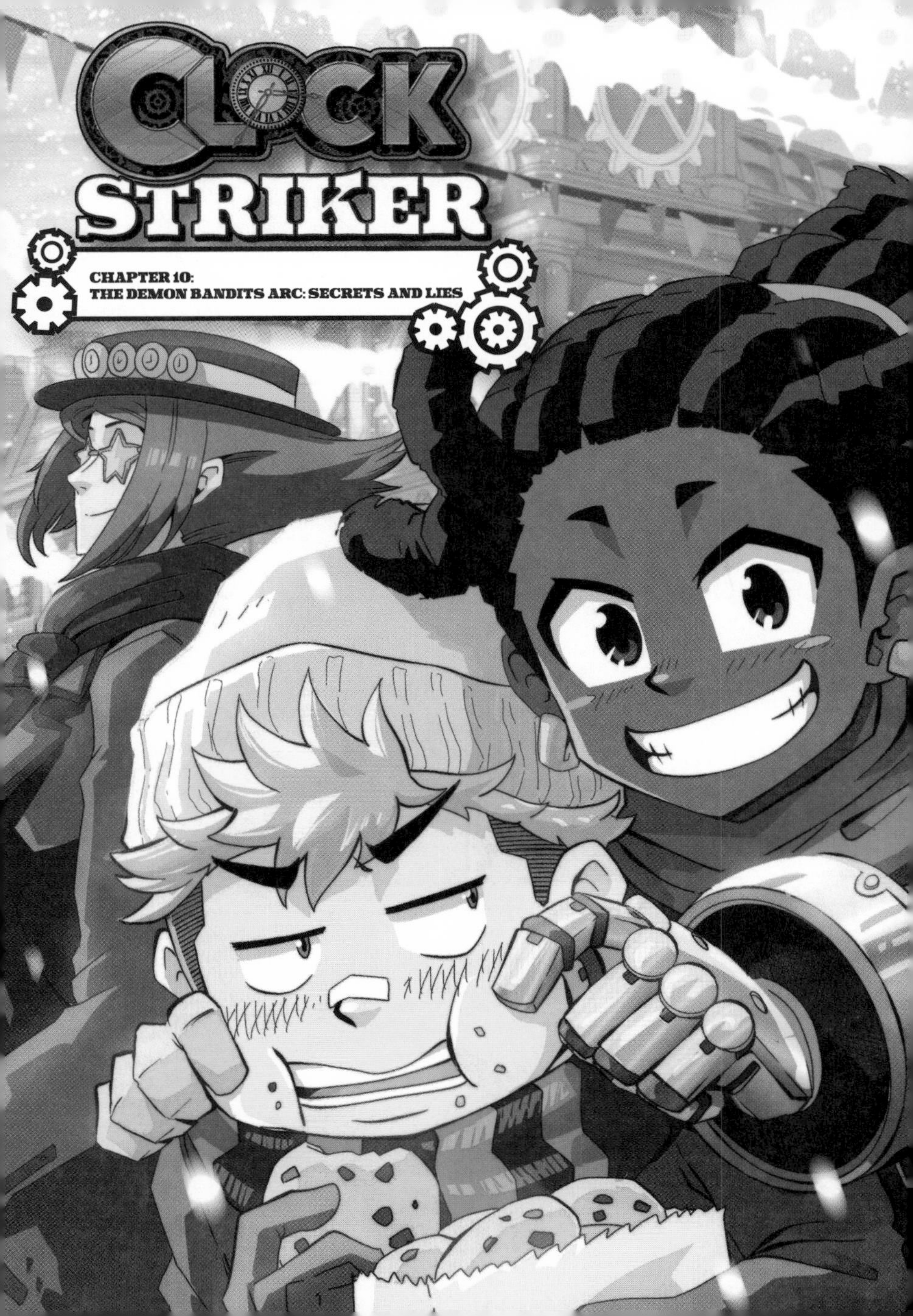
CLOCK STRIKER
CHAPTER 10:
THE DEMON BANDITS ARC: SECRETS AND LIES

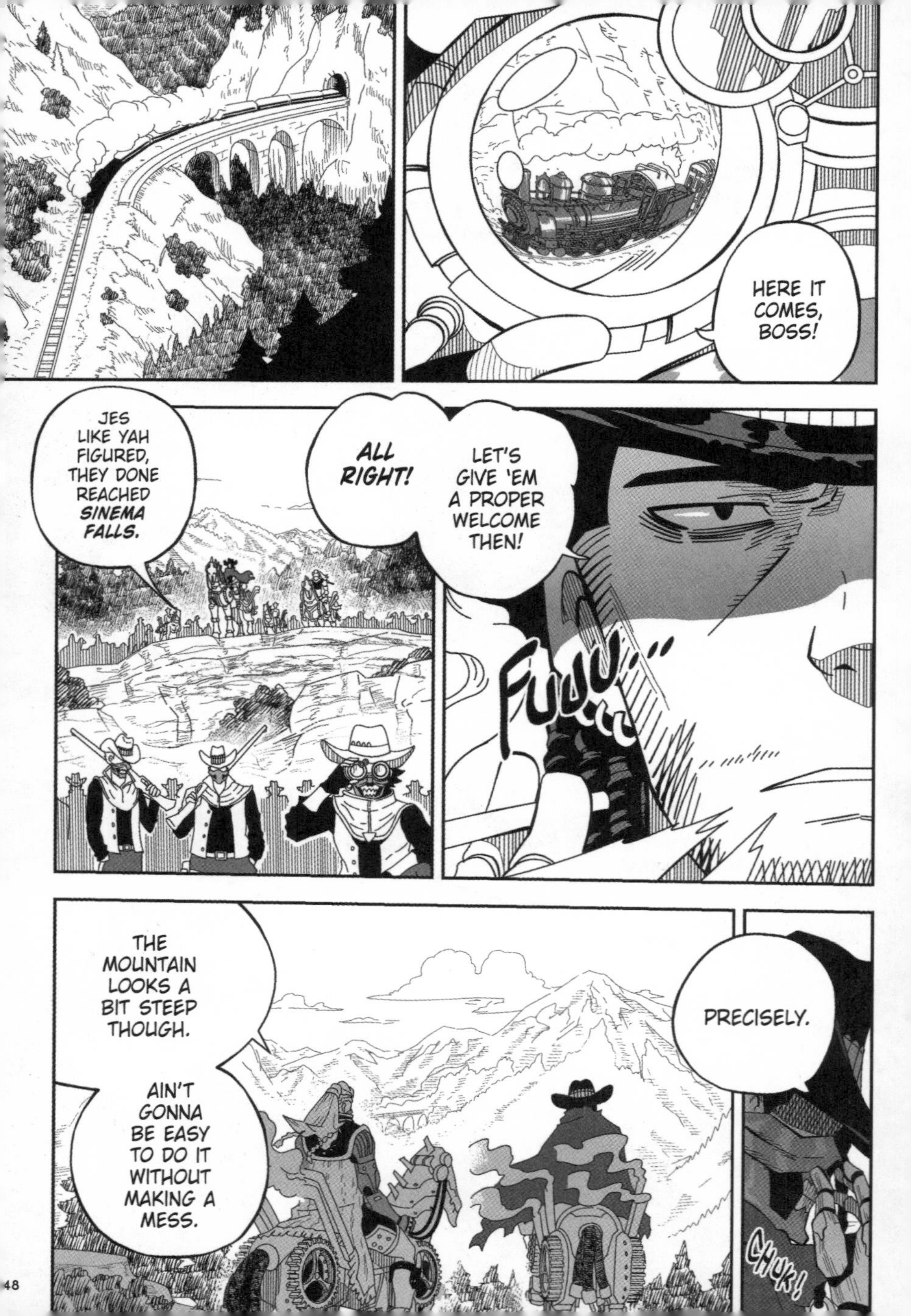
HERE IT COMES, BOSS!
JES LIKE YAH FIGURED, THEY DONE REACHED SINEMA FALLS.
ALL RIGHT!
LET'S GIVE 'EM A PROPER WELCOME THEN!
FUUU...
THE MOUNTAIN LOOKS A BIT STEEP THOUGH.
AIN'T GONNA BE EASY TO DO IT WITHOUT MAKING A MESS.
PRECISELY.
CHAK!

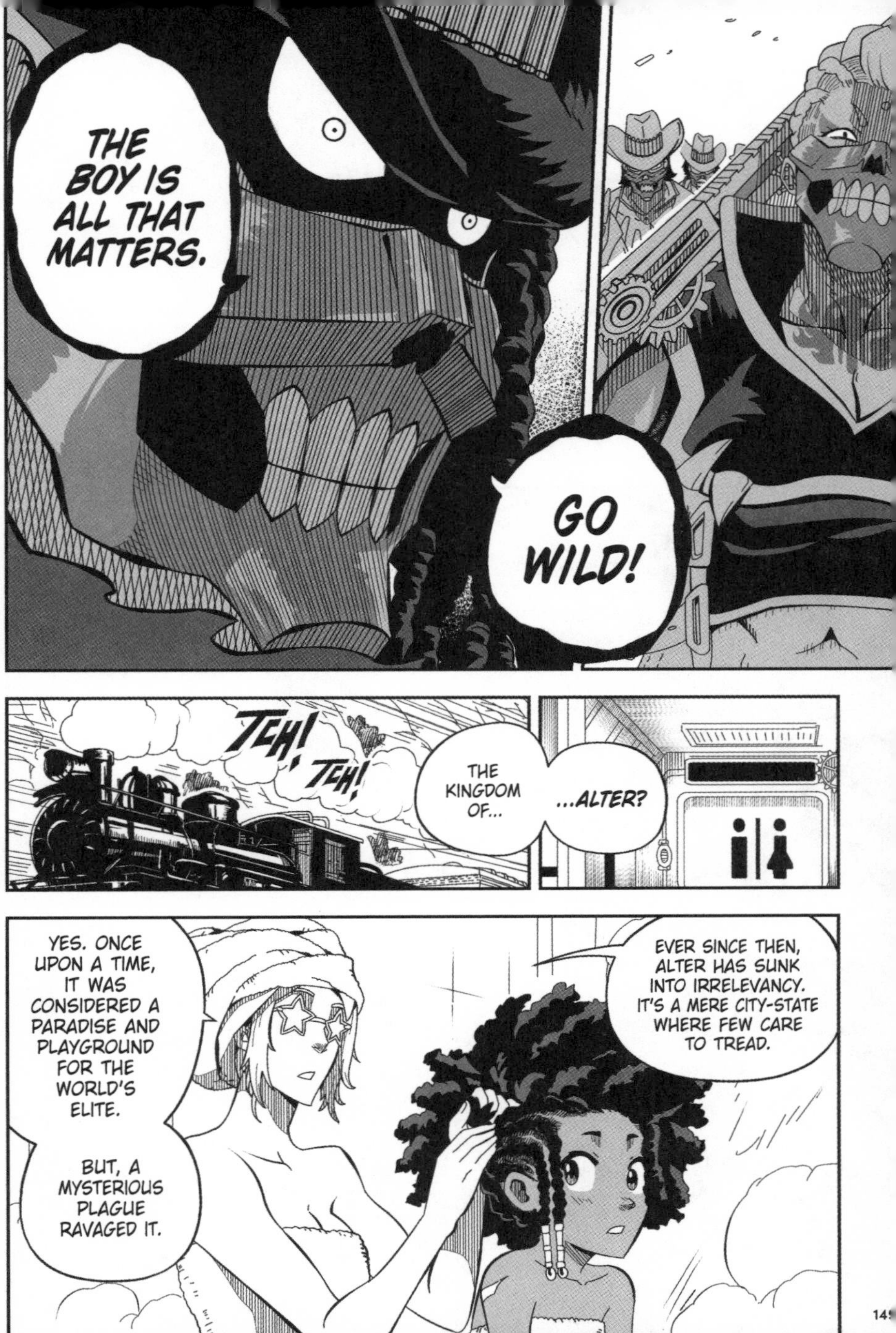
THE BOY IS ALL THAT MATTERS.
GO WILD!
TCH! TCH!
THE KINGDOM OF...
...ALTER?
YES. ONCE UPON A TIME, IT WAS CONSIDERED A PARADISE AND PLAYGROUND FOR THE WORLD'S ELITE.
BUT, A MYSTERIOUS PLAGUE RAVAGED IT.
EVER SINCE THEN, ALTER HAS SUNK INTO IRRELEVANCY. IT'S A MERE CITY-STATE WHERE FEW CARE TO TREAD.

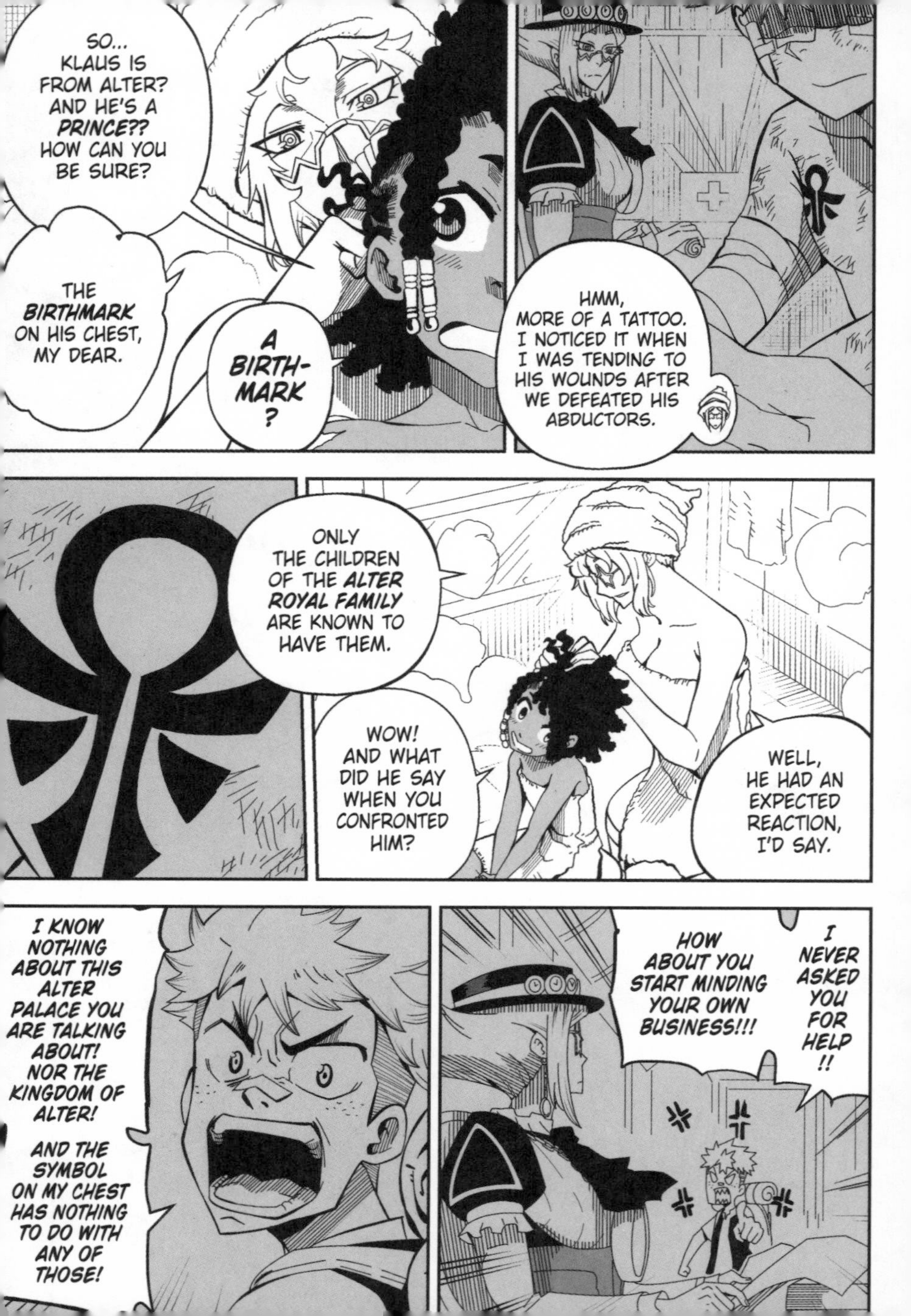
SO... KLAUS IS FROM ALTER? AND HE'S A PRINCE?? HOW CAN YOU BE SURE?
THE BIRTHMARK ON HIS CHEST, MY DEAR.
A BIRTH-MARK?
HMM, MORE OF A TATTOO. I NOTICED IT WHEN I WAS TENDING TO HIS WOUNDS AFTER WE DEFEATED HIS ABDUCTORS.
ONLY THE CHILDREN OF THE ALTER ROYAL FAMILY ARE KNOWN TO HAVE THEM.
WOW! AND WHAT DID HE SAY WHEN YOU CONFRONTED HIM?
WELL, HE HAD AN EXPECTED REACTION, I'D SAY.
I KNOW NOTHING ABOUT THIS ALTER PALACE YOU ARE TALKING ABOUT! NOR THE KINGDOM OF ALTER!
AND THE SYMBOL ON MY CHEST HAS NOTHING TO DO WITH ANY OF THOSE!
HOW ABOUT YOU START MINDING YOUR OWN BUSINESS!!!
I NEVER ASKED YOU FOR HELP!!

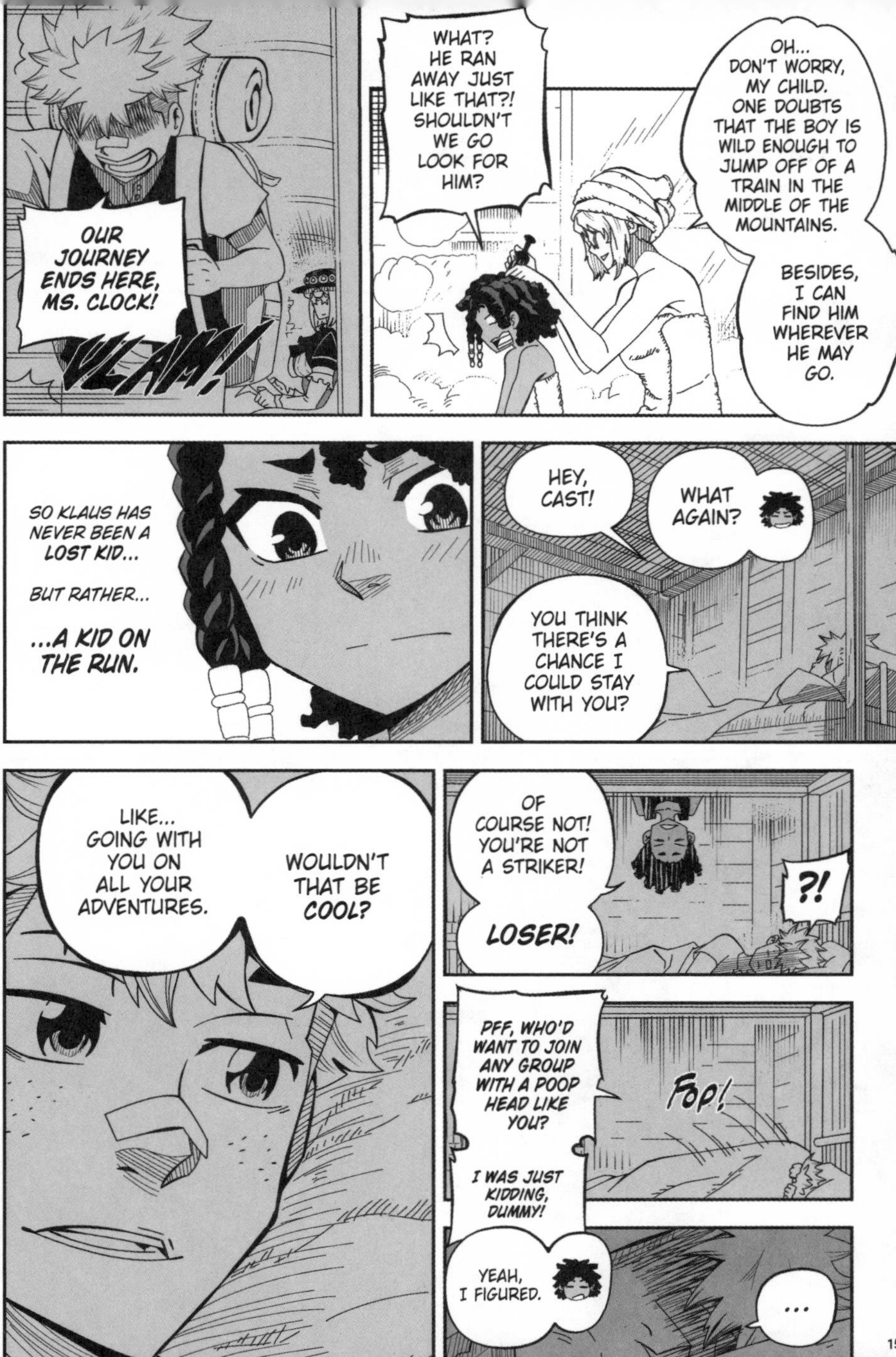
OUR JOURNEY ENDS HERE, MS. CLOCK!
VLAM!
WHAT? HE RAN AWAY JUST LIKE THAT?! SHOULDN'T WE GO LOOK FOR HIM?
OH... DON'T WORRY, MY CHILD. ONE DOUBTS THAT THE BOY IS WILD ENOUGH TO JUMP OFF OF A TRAIN IN THE MIDDLE OF THE MOUNTAINS.
BESIDES, I CAN FIND HIM WHEREVER HE MAY GO.
SO KLAUS HAS NEVER BEEN A LOST KID...
BUT RATHER...
...A KID ON THE RUN.
HEY, CAST!
WHAT AGAIN?
YOU THINK THERE'S A CHANCE I COULD STAY WITH YOU?
LIKE... GOING WITH YOU ON ALL YOUR ADVENTURES.
WOULDN'T THAT BE COOL?
OF COURSE NOT! YOU'RE NOT A STRIKER!
LOSER!
?!
PFF, WHO'D WANT TO JOIN ANY GROUP WITH A POOP HEAD LIKE YOU?
FOP!
I WAS JUST KIDDING, DUMMY!
YEAH, I FIGURED.
...

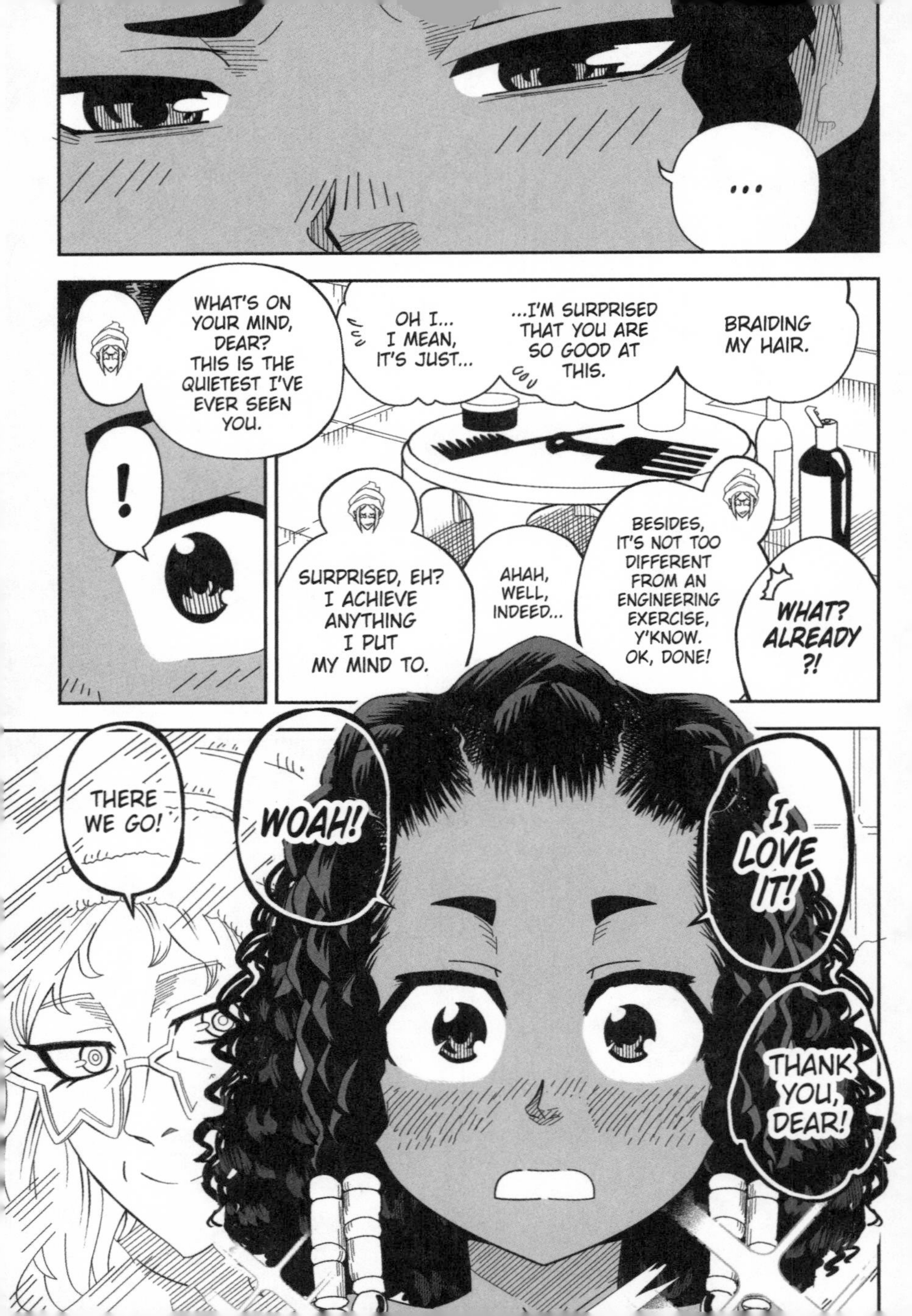
...
WHAT'S ON YOUR MIND, DEAR? THIS IS THE QUIETEST I'VE EVER SEEN YOU.
!
OH I... I MEAN, IT'S JUST...
...I'M SURPRISED THAT YOU ARE SO GOOD AT THIS.
BRAIDING MY HAIR.
SURPRISED, EH? I ACHIEVE ANYTHING I PUT MY MIND TO.
AHAH, WELL, INDEED...
BESIDES, IT'S NOT TOO DIFFERENT FROM AN ENGINEERING EXERCISE, Y'KNOW. OK, DONE!
WHAT? ALREADY ?!
THERE WE GO!
WOAH!
I LOVE IT!
THANK YOU, DEAR!

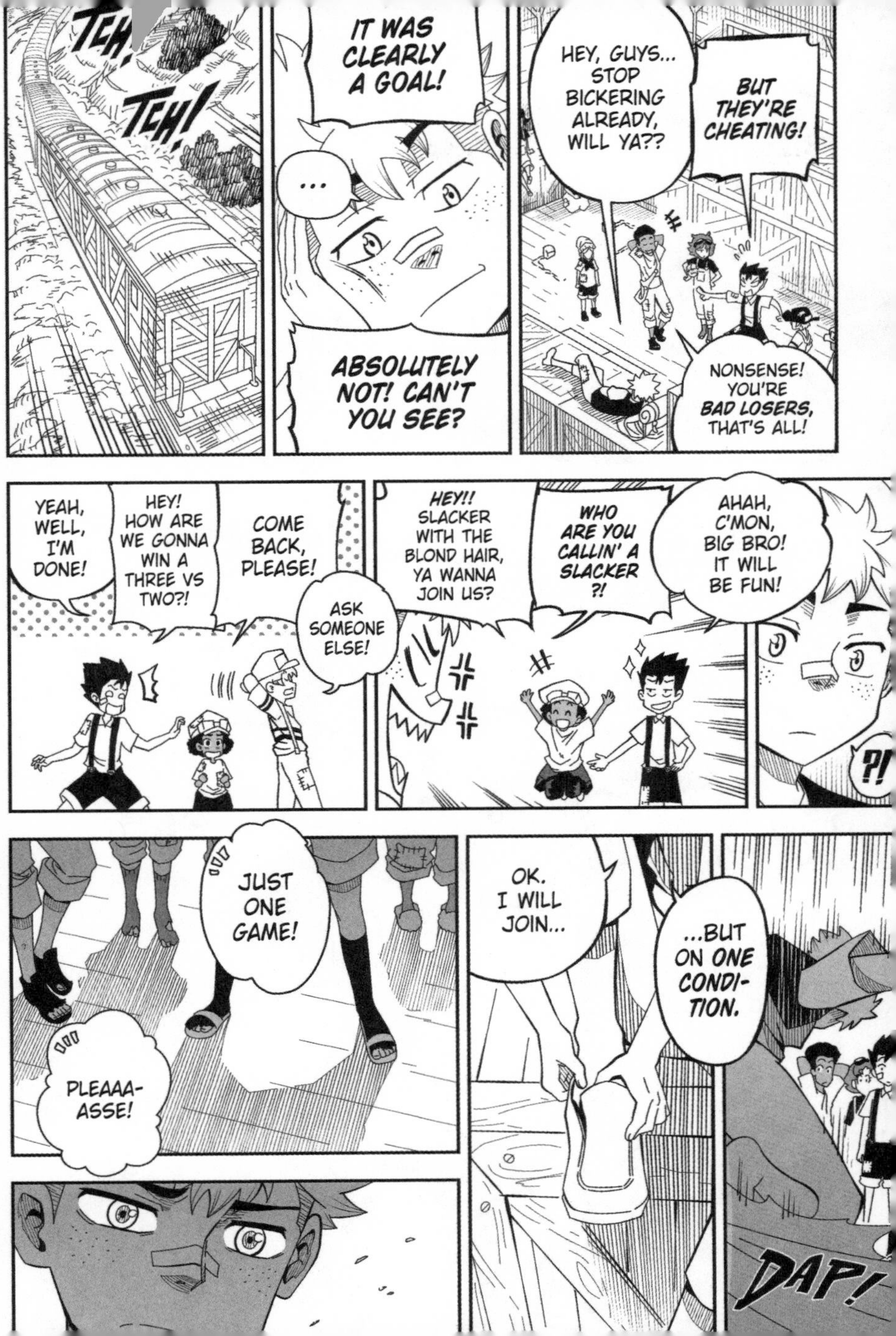
TCH! TCH!
IT WAS CLEARLY A GOAL!
...
ABSOLUTELY NOT! CAN'T YOU SEE?
HEY, GUYS... STOP BICKERING ALREADY, WILL YA??
BUT THEY'RE CHEATING!
NONSENSE! YOU'RE BAD LOSERS, THAT'S ALL!
YEAH, WELL, I'M DONE!
HEY! HOW ARE WE GONNA WIN A THREE VS TWO?!
COME BACK, PLEASE!
ASK SOMEONE ELSE!
HEY!! SLACKER WITH THE BLOND HAIR, YA WANNA JOIN US?
WHO ARE YOU CALLIN' A SLACKER ?!
AHAH, C'MON, BIG BRO! IT WILL BE FUN!
?!
JUST ONE GAME!
PLEAAA-ASSE!
OK. I WILL JOIN...
...BUT ON ONE CONDITION.
DAP!

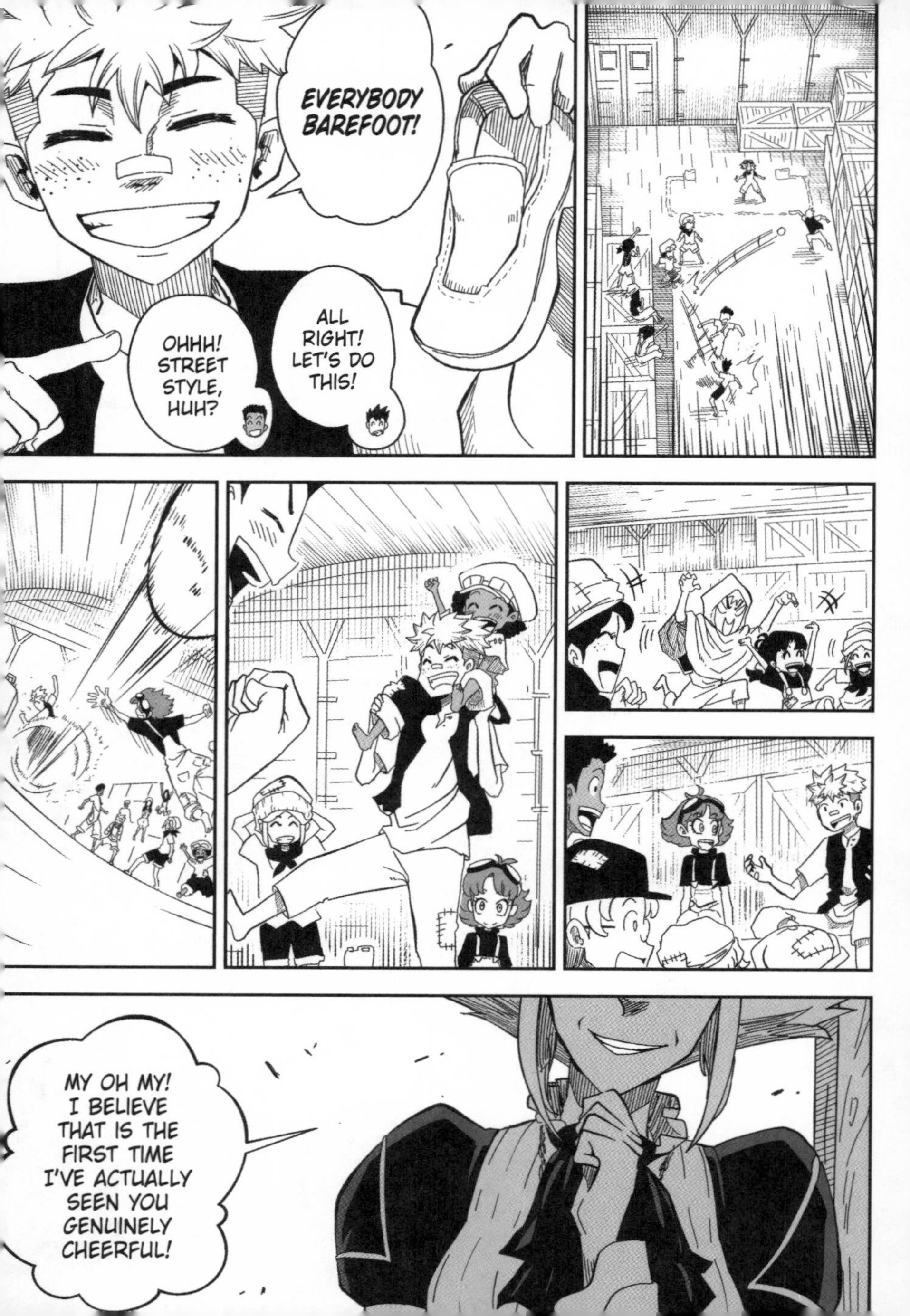
EVERYBODY BAREFOOT!
OHHH! STREET STYLE, HUH?
ALL RIGHT! LET'S DO THIS!
MY OH MY! I BELIEVE THAT IS THE FIRST TIME I'VE ACTUALLY SEEN YOU GENUINELY CHEERFUL!

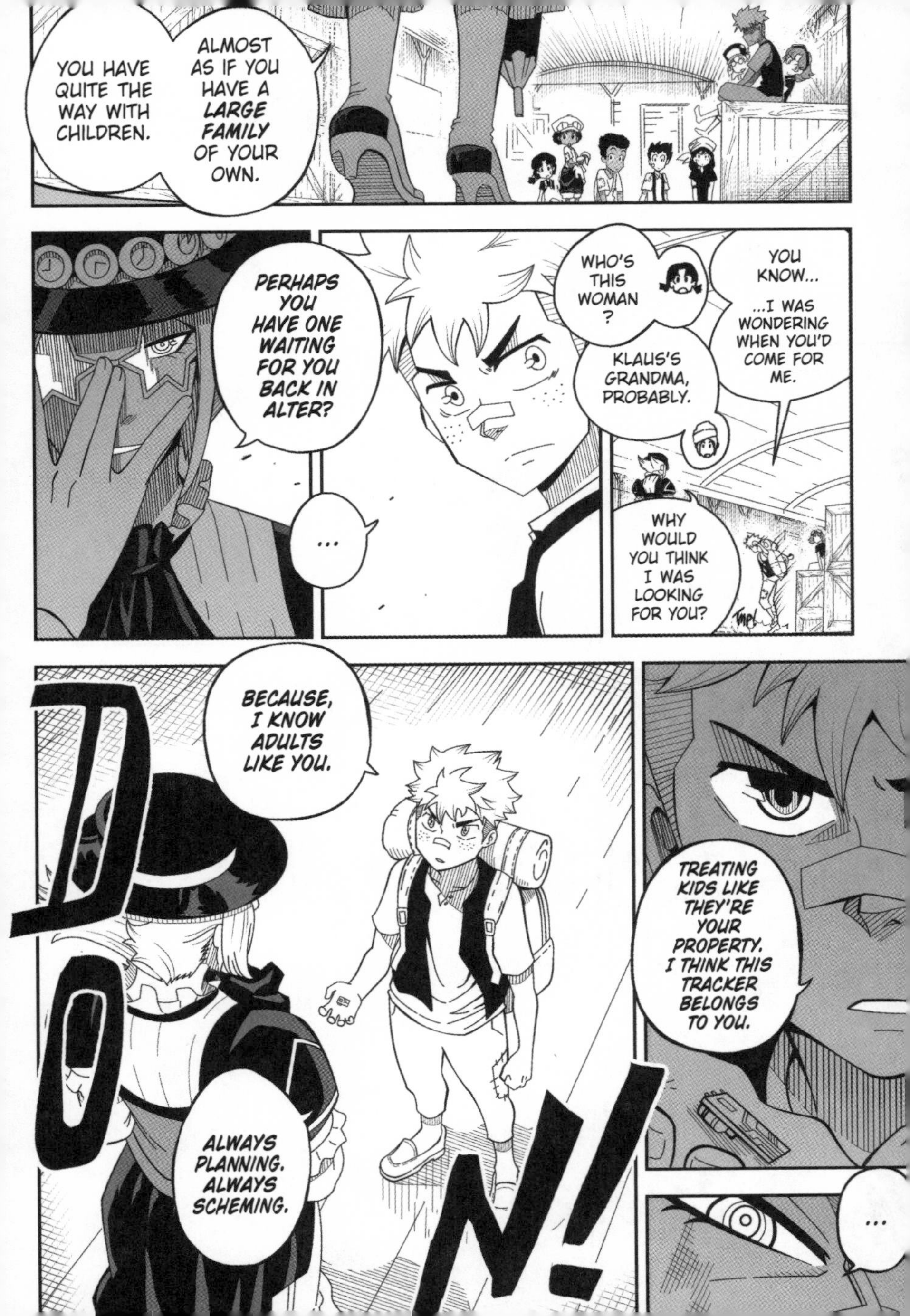
YOU HAVE QUITE THE WAY WITH CHILDREN.
ALMOST AS IF YOU HAVE A *LARGE FAMILY* OF YOUR OWN.
PERHAPS YOU HAVE ONE WAITING FOR YOU BACK IN ALTER?
...
WHO'S THIS WOMAN?
YOU KNOW...
...I WAS WONDERING WHEN YOU'D COME FOR ME.
KLAUS'S GRANDMA, PROBABLY.
WHY WOULD YOU THINK I WAS LOOKING FOR YOU?
TMP!
BECAUSE, I KNOW ADULTS LIKE YOU.
DOON!
ALWAYS PLANNING. ALWAYS SCHEMING.
TREATING KIDS LIKE THEY'RE YOUR PROPERTY. I THINK THIS TRACKER BELONGS TO YOU.
...

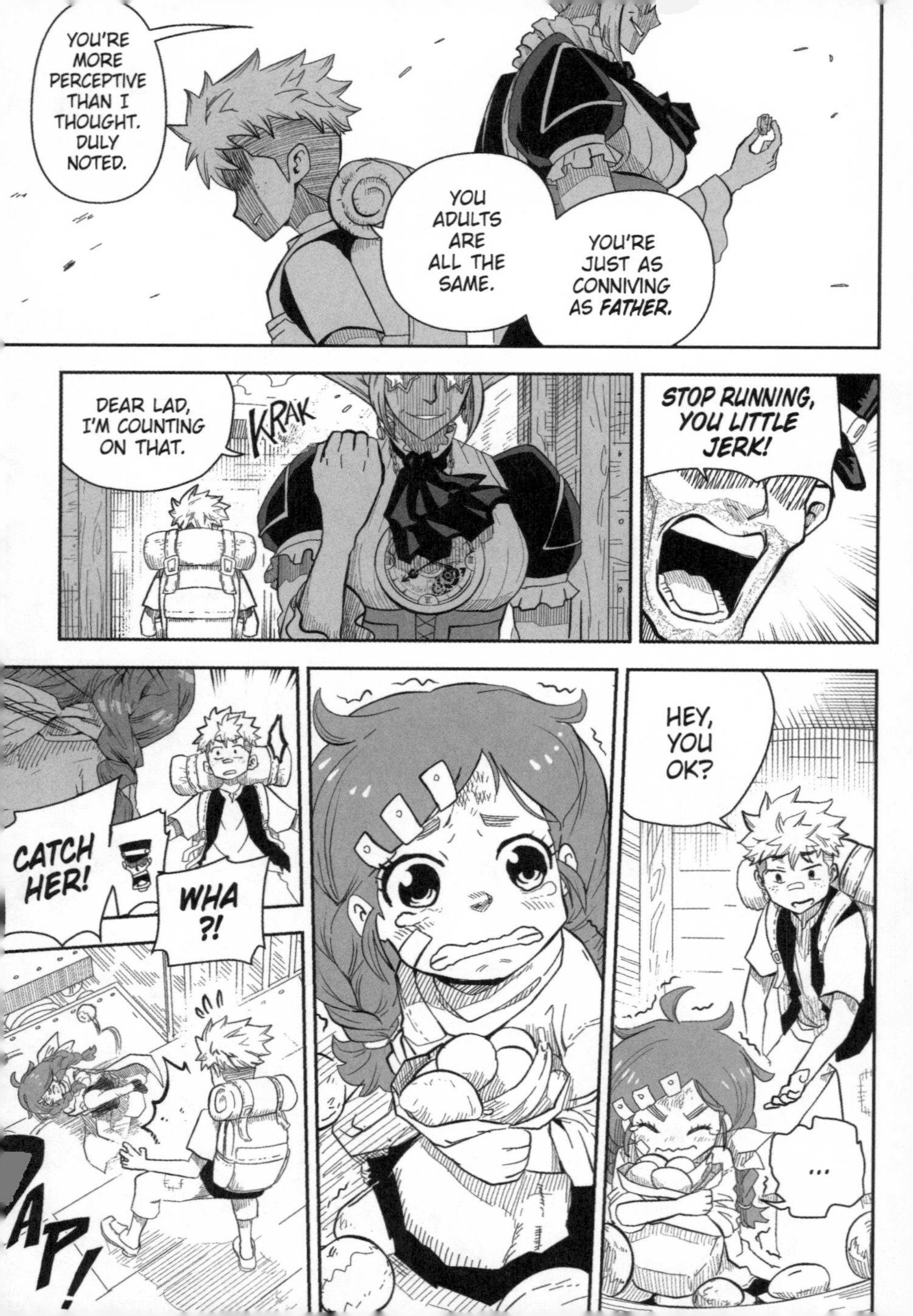
YOU'RE MORE PERCEPTIVE THAN I THOUGHT. DULY NOTED.
YOU ADULTS ARE ALL THE SAME.
YOU'RE JUST AS CONNIVING AS FATHER.
DEAR LAD, I'M COUNTING ON THAT.
KRAK
STOP RUNNING, YOU LITTLE JERK!
CATCH HER!
WHA ?!
AP!
HEY, YOU OK?
...

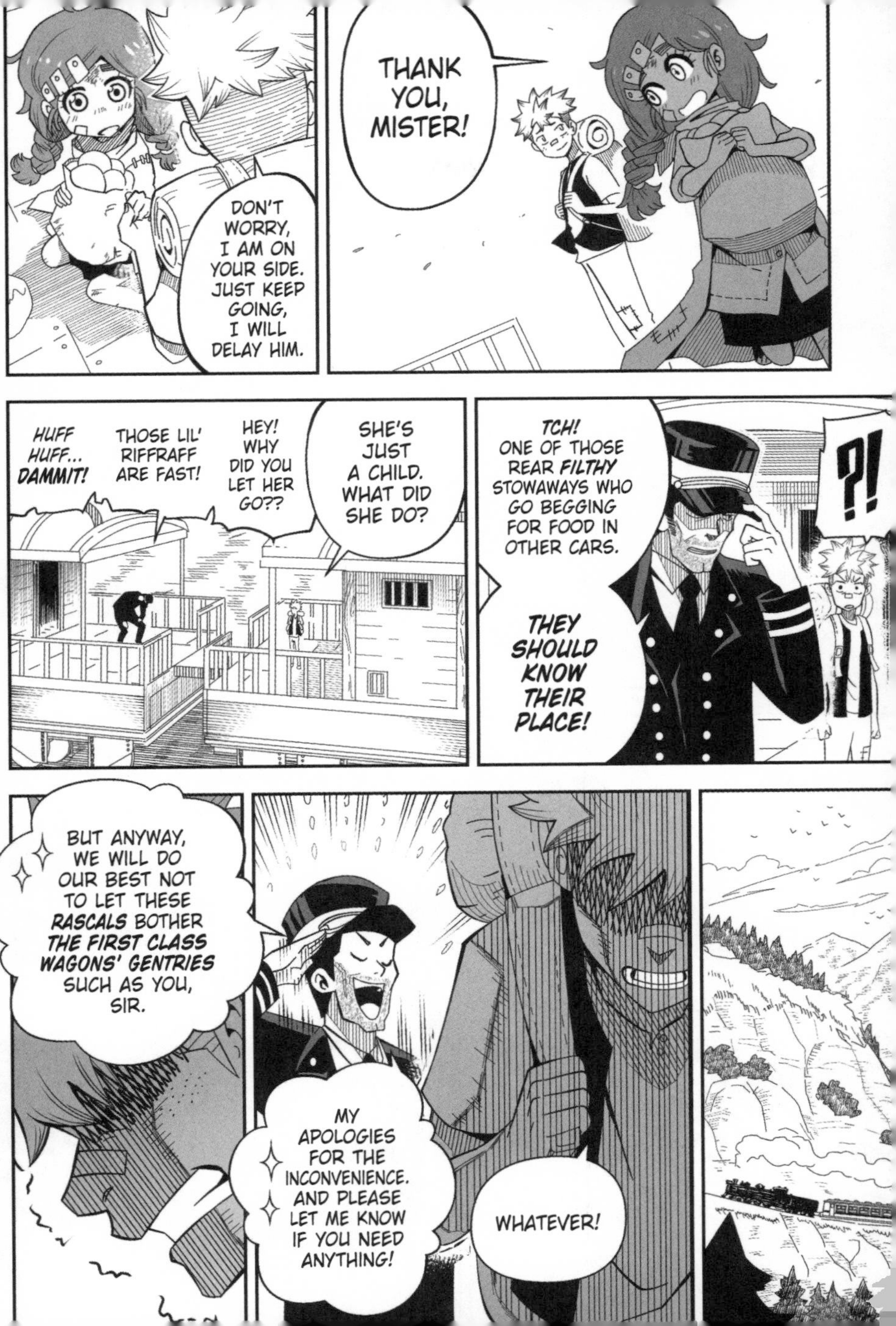
DON'T WORRY, I AM ON YOUR SIDE. JUST KEEP GOING, I WILL DELAY HIM.
THANK YOU, MISTER!
HUFF HUFF... DAMMIT!
THOSE LIL' RIFFRAFF ARE FAST!
HEY! WHY DID YOU LET HER GO??
SHE'S JUST A CHILD. WHAT DID SHE DO?
TCH! ONE OF THOSE REAR FILTHY STOWAWAYS WHO GO BEGGING FOR FOOD IN OTHER CARS.
THEY SHOULD KNOW THEIR PLACE!
?!
BUT ANYWAY, WE WILL DO OUR BEST NOT TO LET THESE RASCALS BOTHER THE FIRST CLASS WAGONS' GENTRIES SUCH AS YOU, SIR.
MY APOLOGIES FOR THE INCONVENIENCE. AND PLEASE LET ME KNOW IF YOU NEED ANYTHING!
WHATEVER!

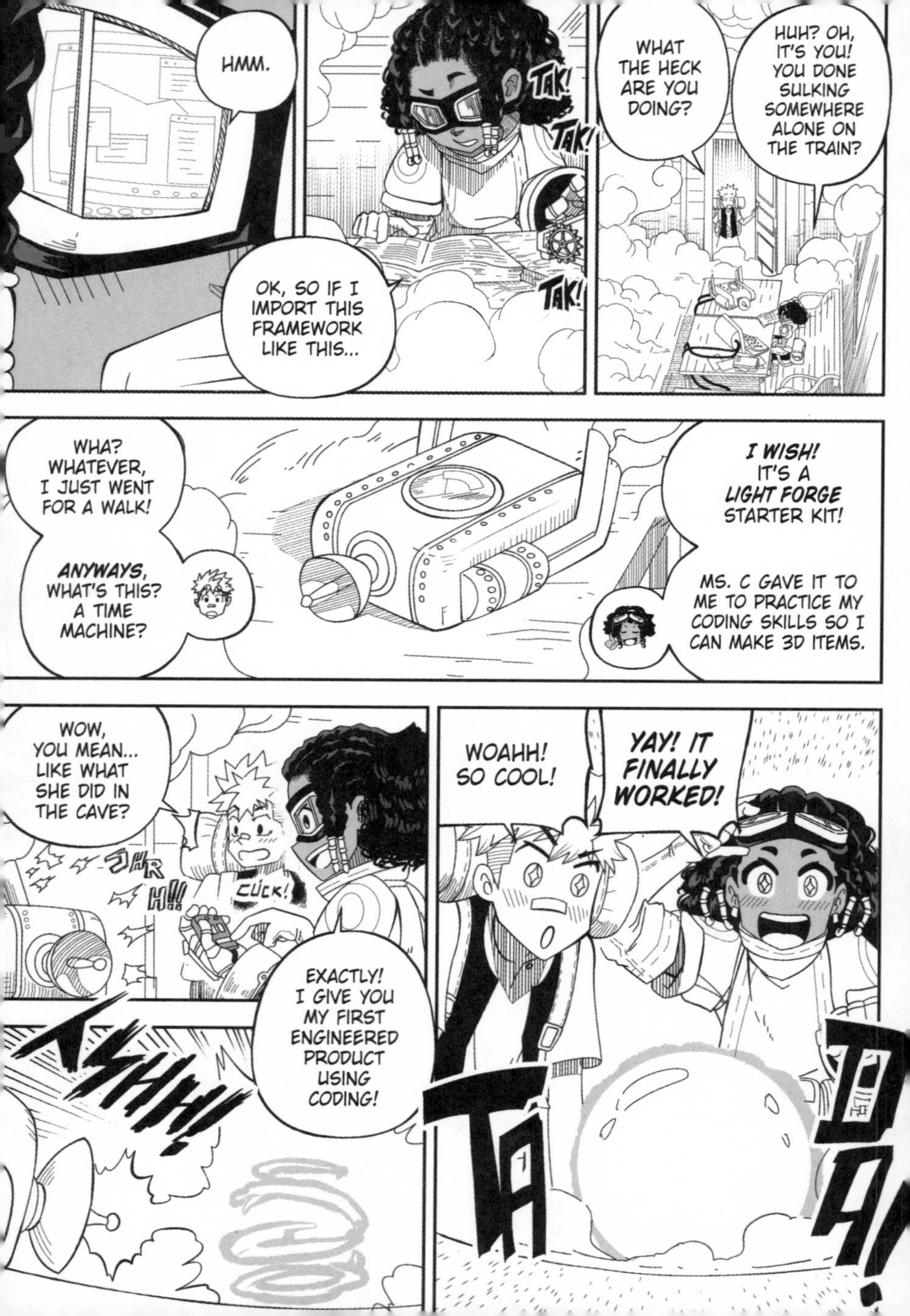
HMM.
TAK!
TAK!
OK, SO IF I IMPORT THIS FRAMEWORK LIKE THIS...
TAK!
WHAT THE HECK ARE YOU DOING?
HUH? OH, IT'S YOU! YOU DONE SULKING SOMEWHERE ALONE ON THE TRAIN?
WHA? WHATEVER, I JUST WENT FOR A WALK!
ANYWAYS, WHAT'S THIS? A TIME MACHINE?
I WISH! IT'S A *LIGHT FORGE* STARTER KIT!
MS. C GAVE IT TO ME TO PRACTICE MY CODING SKILLS SO I CAN MAKE 3D ITEMS.
WOW, YOU MEAN... LIKE WHAT SHE DID IN THE CAVE?
CLICK!
EXACTLY! I GIVE YOU MY FIRST ENGINEERED PRODUCT USING CODING!
WOAHH! SO COOL!
YAY! IT FINALLY WORKED!

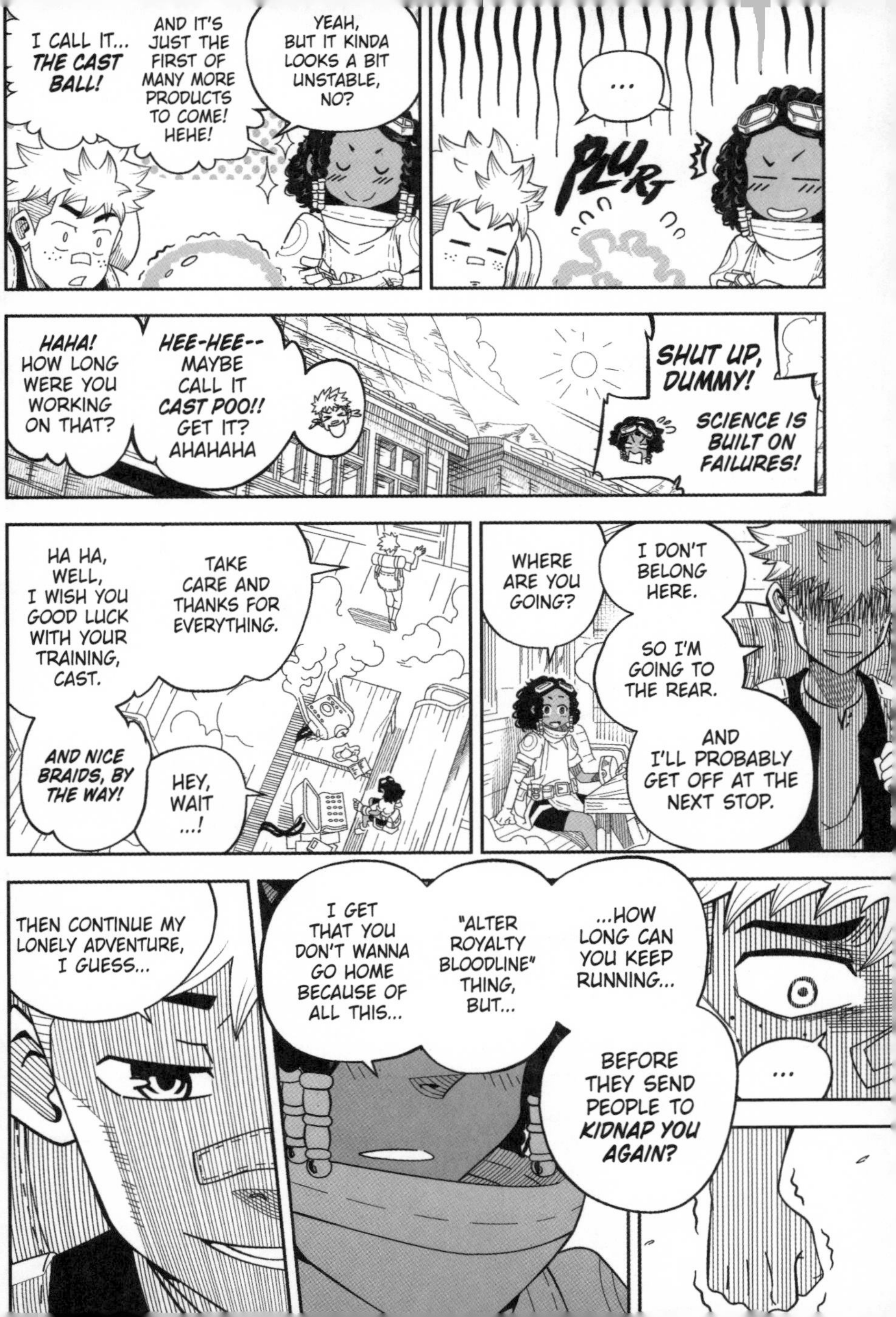
I CALL IT... THE CAST BALL!
AND IT'S JUST THE FIRST OF MANY MORE PRODUCTS TO COME! HEHE!
YEAH, BUT IT KINDA LOOKS A BIT UNSTABLE, NO?
...
PLURT
HAHA! HOW LONG WERE YOU WORKING ON THAT?
HEE-HEE-- MAYBE CALL IT CAST POO!! GET IT? AHAHAHA
SHUT UP, DUMMY!
SCIENCE IS BUILT ON FAILURES!
HA HA, WELL, I WISH YOU GOOD LUCK WITH YOUR TRAINING, CAST.
TAKE CARE AND THANKS FOR EVERYTHING.
AND NICE BRAIDS, BY THE WAY!
HEY, WAIT ...!
WHERE ARE YOU GOING?
I DON'T BELONG HERE.
SO I'M GOING TO THE REAR.
AND I'LL PROBABLY GET OFF AT THE NEXT STOP.
THEN CONTINUE MY LONELY ADVENTURE, I GUESS...
I GET THAT YOU DON'T WANNA GO HOME BECAUSE OF ALL THIS...
"ALTER ROYALTY BLOODLINE" THING, BUT...
...HOW LONG CAN YOU KEEP RUNNING...
BEFORE THEY SEND PEOPLE TO KIDNAP YOU AGAIN?
...

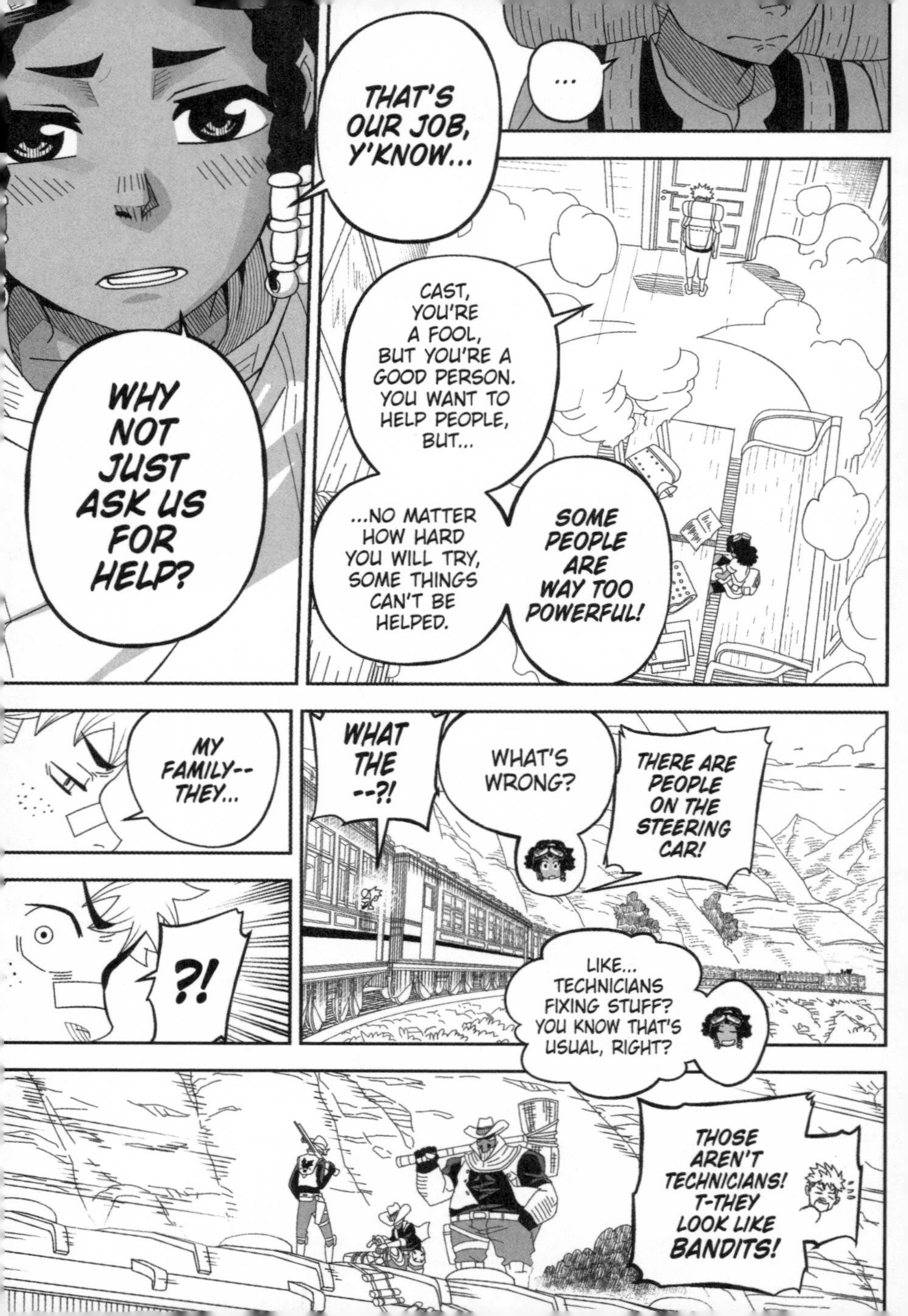
THAT'S OUR JOB, Y'KNOW...
...
WHY NOT JUST ASK US FOR HELP?
CAST, YOU'RE A FOOL, BUT YOU'RE A GOOD PERSON. YOU WANT TO HELP PEOPLE, BUT...
...NO MATTER HOW HARD YOU WILL TRY, SOME THINGS CAN'T BE HELPED.
SOME PEOPLE ARE WAY TOO POWERFUL!
MY FAMILY-- THEY...
?!
WHAT THE --?!
WHAT'S WRONG?
THERE ARE PEOPLE ON THE STEERING CAR!
LIKE... TECHNICIANS FIXING STUFF? YOU KNOW THAT'S USUAL, RIGHT?
THOSE AREN'T TECHNICIANS! T-THEY LOOK LIKE BANDITS!

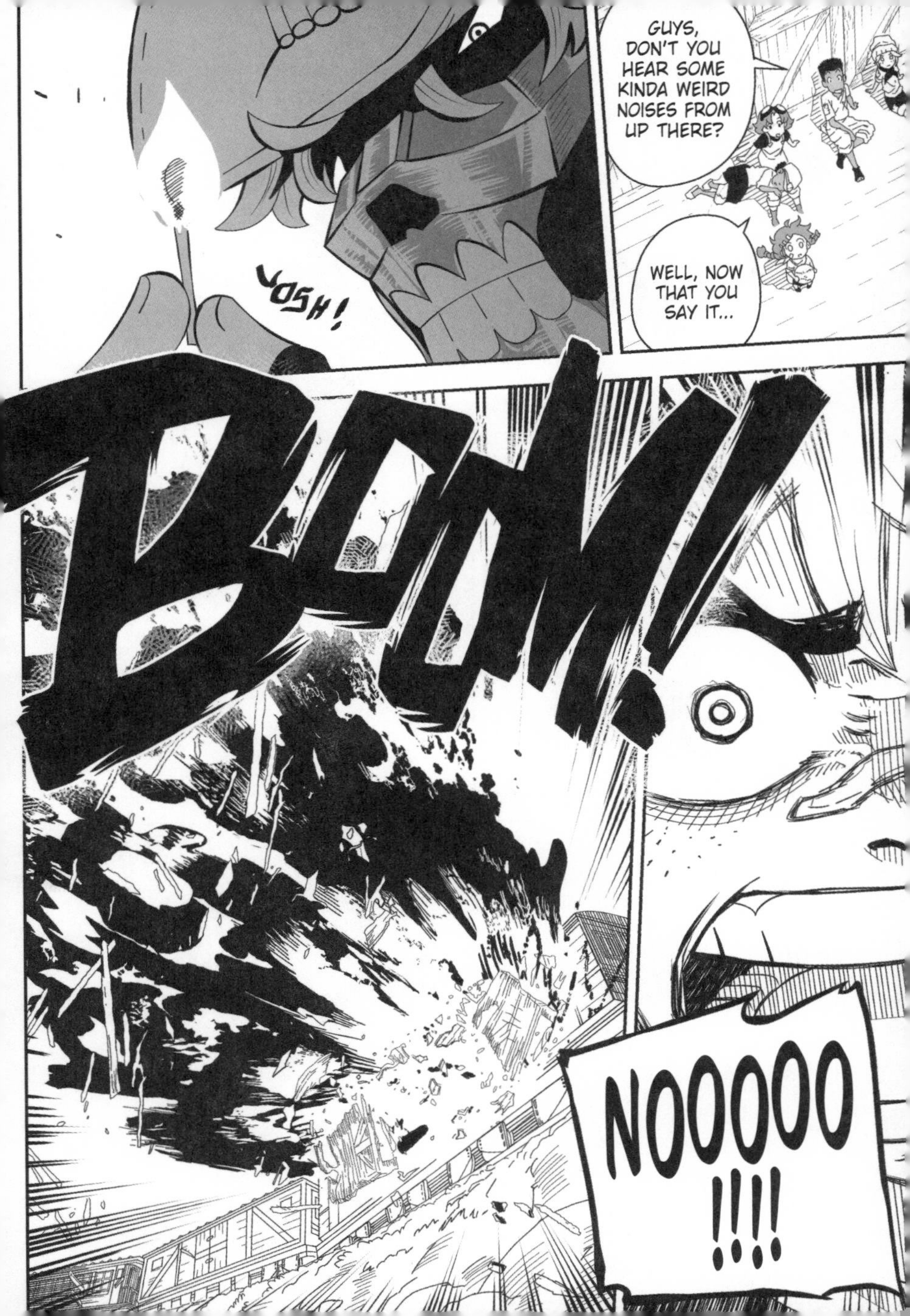
VOSH!
GUYS, DON'T YOU HEAR SOME KINDA WEIRD NOISES FROM UP THERE?
WELL, NOW THAT YOU SAY IT...
BOOM!
NOOOOO!!!!!

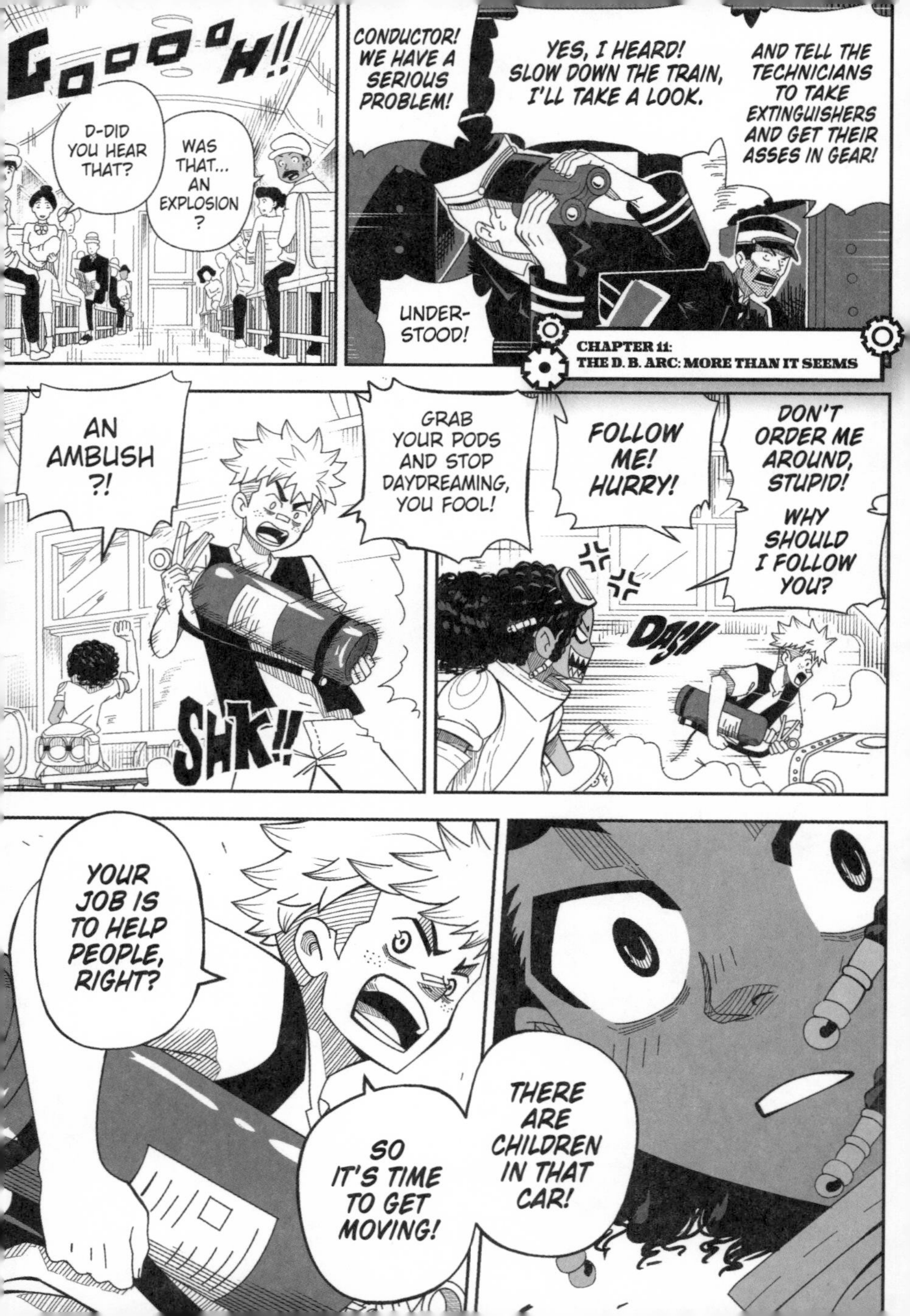
GOOOOOH!!
D-DID YOU HEAR THAT?
WAS THAT... AN EXPLOSION?
CONDUCTOR! WE HAVE A SERIOUS PROBLEM!
YES, I HEARD! SLOW DOWN THE TRAIN, I'LL TAKE A LOOK.
AND TELL THE TECHNICIANS TO TAKE EXTINGUISHERS AND GET THEIR ASSES IN GEAR!
UNDER-STOOD!
CHAPTER 11:
THE D. B. ARC: MORE THAN IT SEEMS
AN AMBUSH?!
SHK!!
GRAB YOUR PODS AND STOP DAYDREAMING, YOU FOOL!
FOLLOW ME! HURRY!
DON'T ORDER ME AROUND, STUPID!
WHY SHOULD I FOLLOW YOU?
DASH
YOUR JOB IS TO HELP PEOPLE, RIGHT?
SO IT'S TIME TO GET MOVING!
THERE ARE CHILDREN IN THAT CAR!

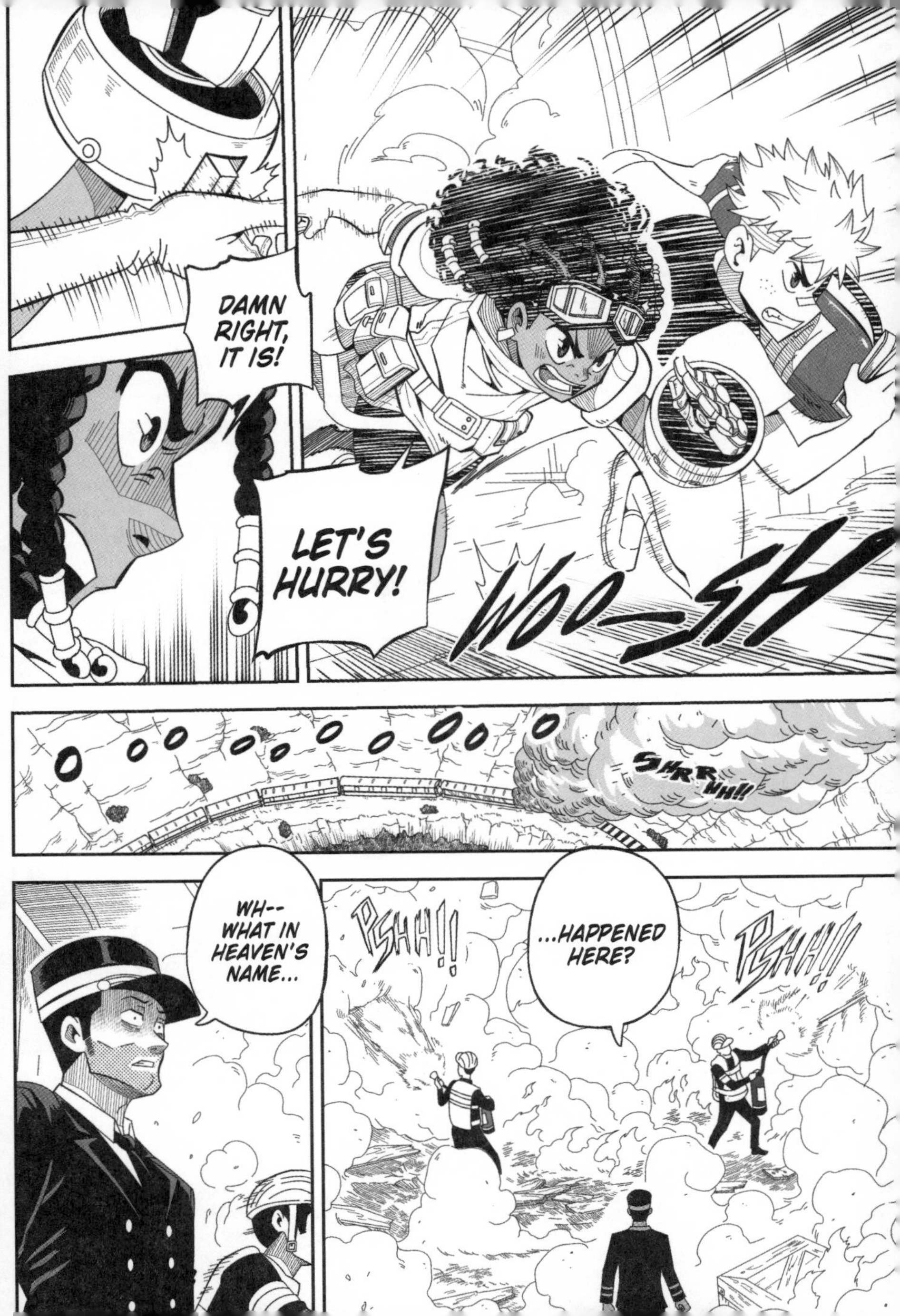
DAMN RIGHT, IT IS!
LET'S HURRY!
WOO--SH
SHRRUHH!!
WH-- WHAT IN HEAVEN'S NAME...
PSHH!!
...HAPPENED HERE?
PSHH!!

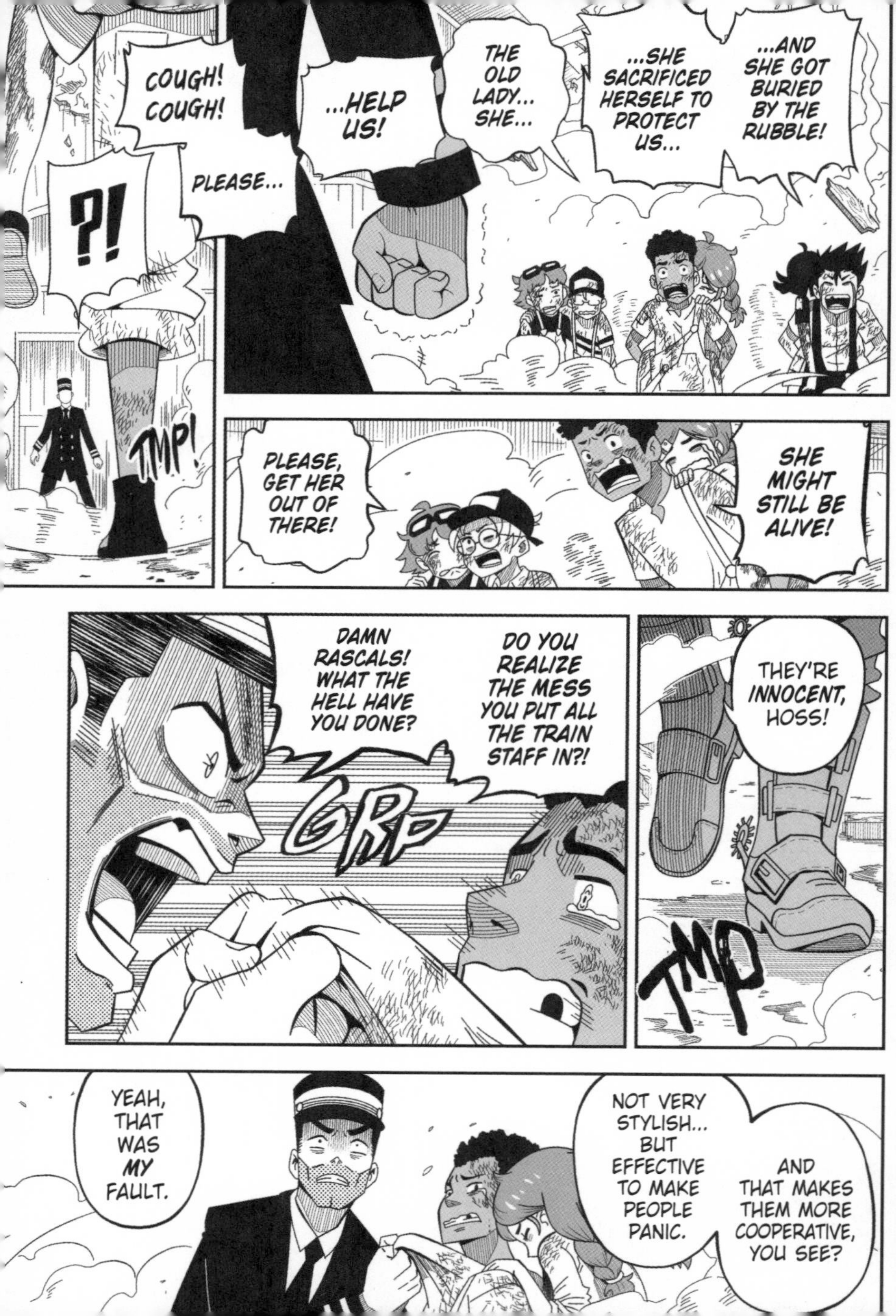
COUGH! COUGH!
?!
PLEASE...
TMP!
...HELP US!
THE OLD LADY... SHE...
...SHE SACRIFICED HERSELF TO PROTECT US...
...AND SHE GOT BURIED BY THE RUBBLE!
PLEASE, GET HER OUT OF THERE!
SHE MIGHT STILL BE ALIVE!
DAMN RASCALS! WHAT THE HELL HAVE YOU DONE?
DO YOU REALIZE THE MESS YOU PUT ALL THE TRAIN STAFF IN?!
GRP
THEY'RE INNOCENT, HOSS!
TMP
YEAH, THAT WAS MY FAULT.
NOT VERY STYLISH... BUT EFFECTIVE TO MAKE PEOPLE PANIC.
AND THAT MAKES THEM MORE COOPERATIVE, YOU SEE?

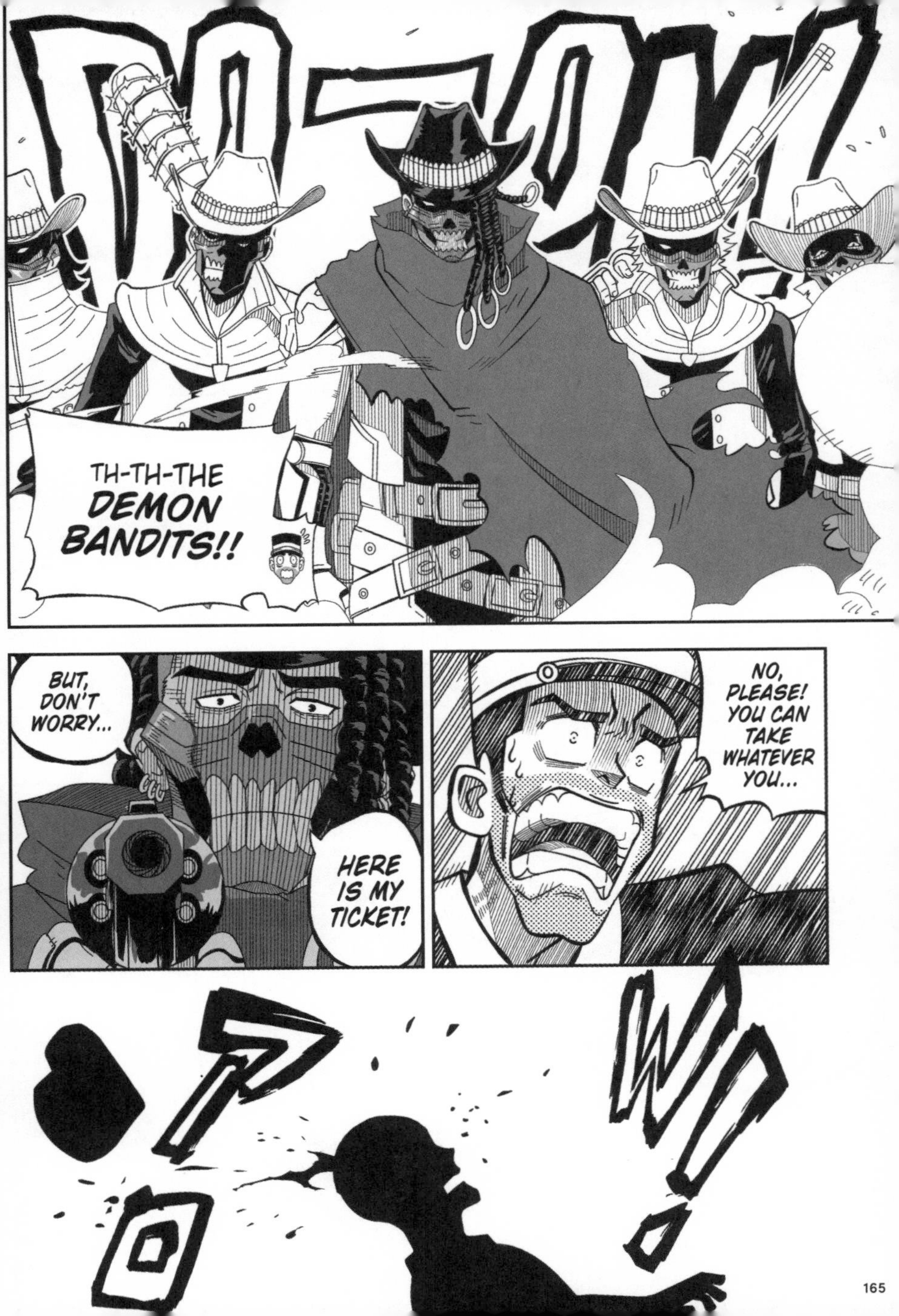
TH-TH-THE DEMON BANDITS!!
BUT, DON'T WORRY...
HERE IS MY TICKET!
NO, PLEASE! YOU CAN TAKE WHATEVER YOU...

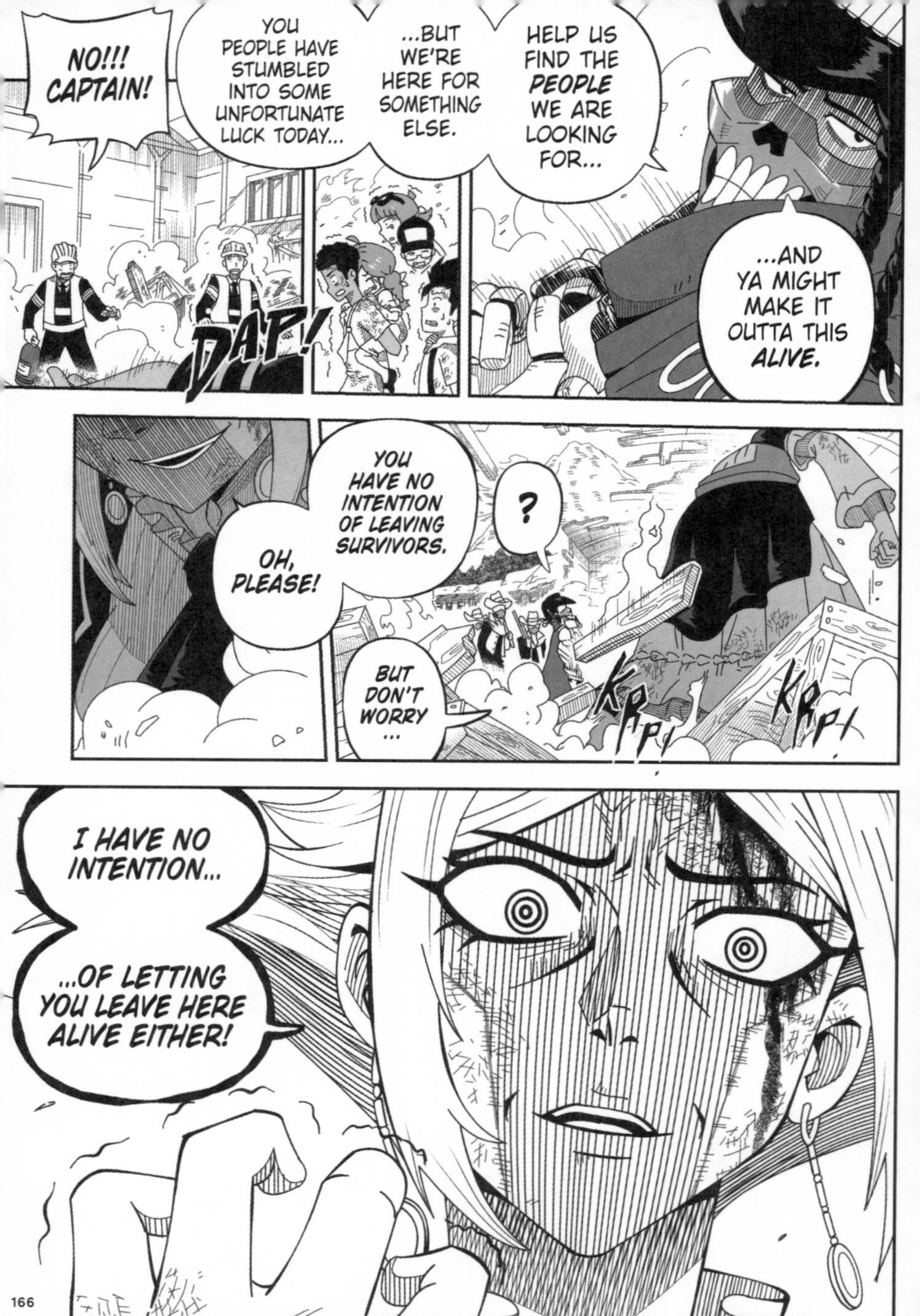
NO!!! CAPTAIN!
YOU PEOPLE HAVE STUMBLED INTO SOME UNFORTUNATE LUCK TODAY...
...BUT WE'RE HERE FOR SOMETHING ELSE.
HELP US FIND THE PEOPLE WE ARE LOOKING FOR...
DAP!
...AND YA MIGHT MAKE IT OUTTA THIS ALIVE.
YOU HAVE NO INTENTION OF LEAVING SURVIVORS.
OH, PLEASE!
?
BUT DON'T WORRY ...
KRP!
KRP!
I HAVE NO INTENTION...
...OF LETTING YOU LEAVE HERE ALIVE EITHER!

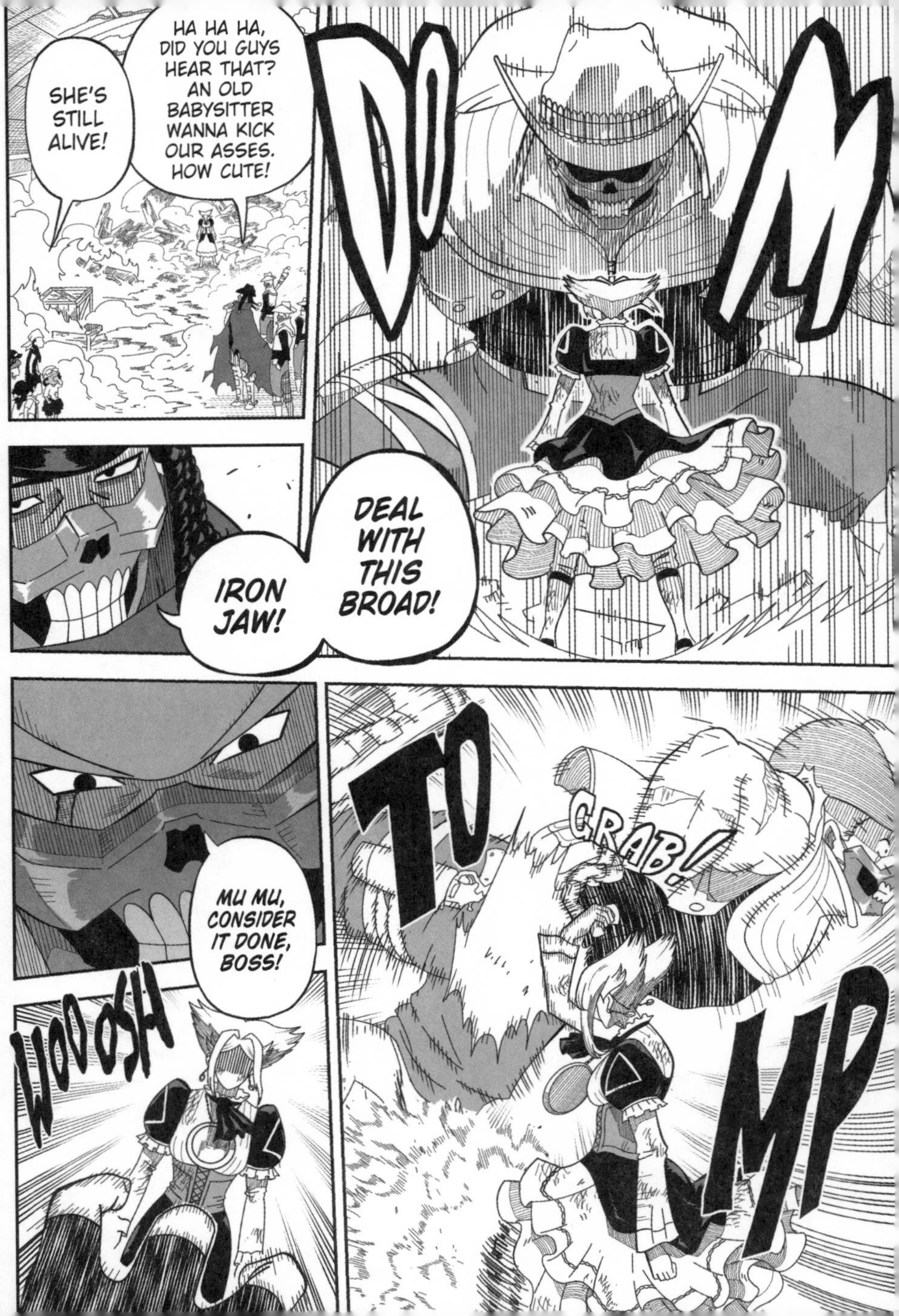
SHE'S STILL ALIVE!
HA HA HA, DID YOU GUYS HEAR THAT? AN OLD BABYSITTER WANNA KICK OUR ASSES. HOW CUTE!
IRON JAW!
DEAL WITH THIS BROAD!
DO
M
MU MU, CONSIDER IT DONE, BOSS!
WOOOSH
TO
GRAB!
MP

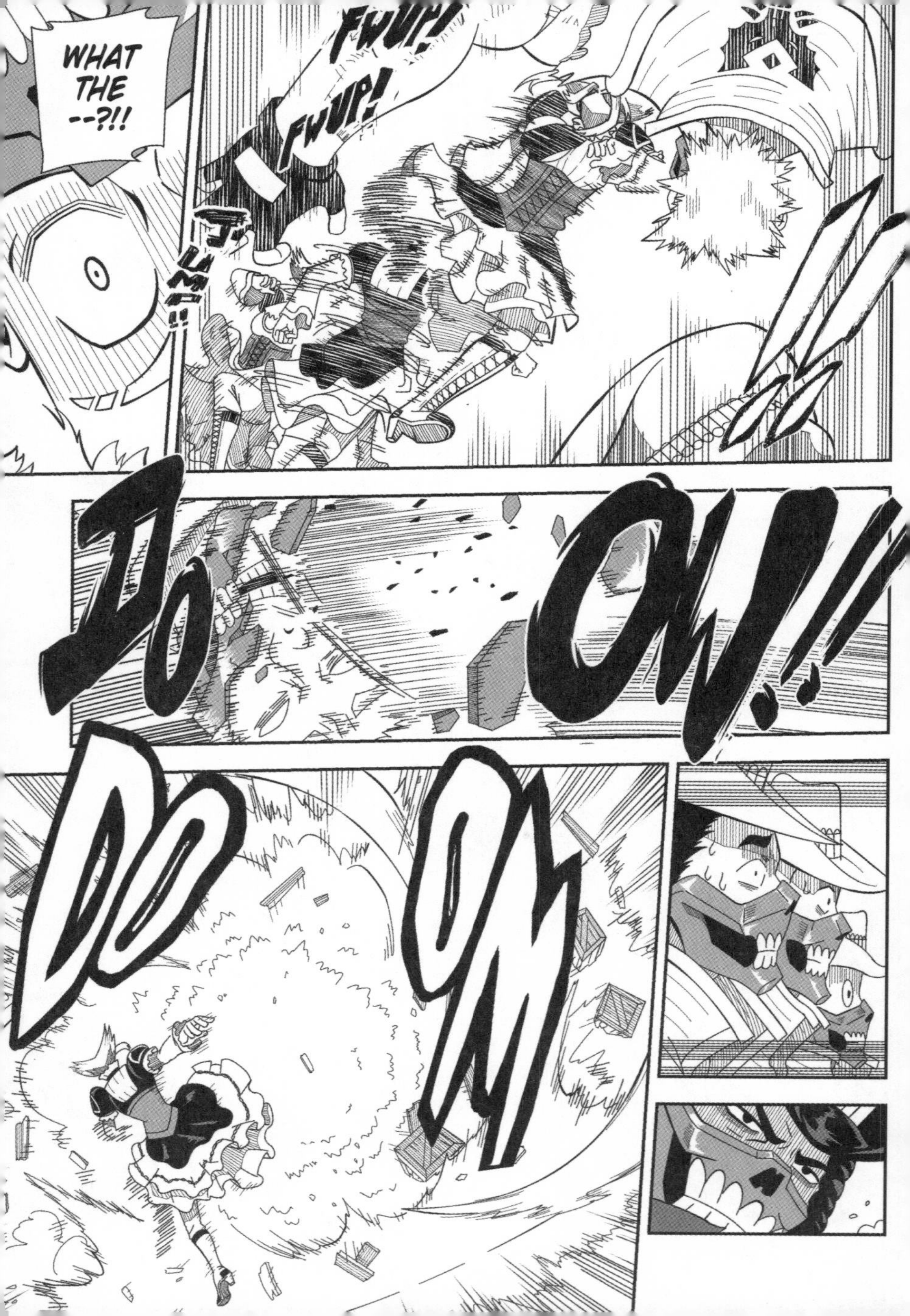
WHAT THE --?!!
FWUP!
FWUP!
FLAMP!!
DOOM!!
BOOM

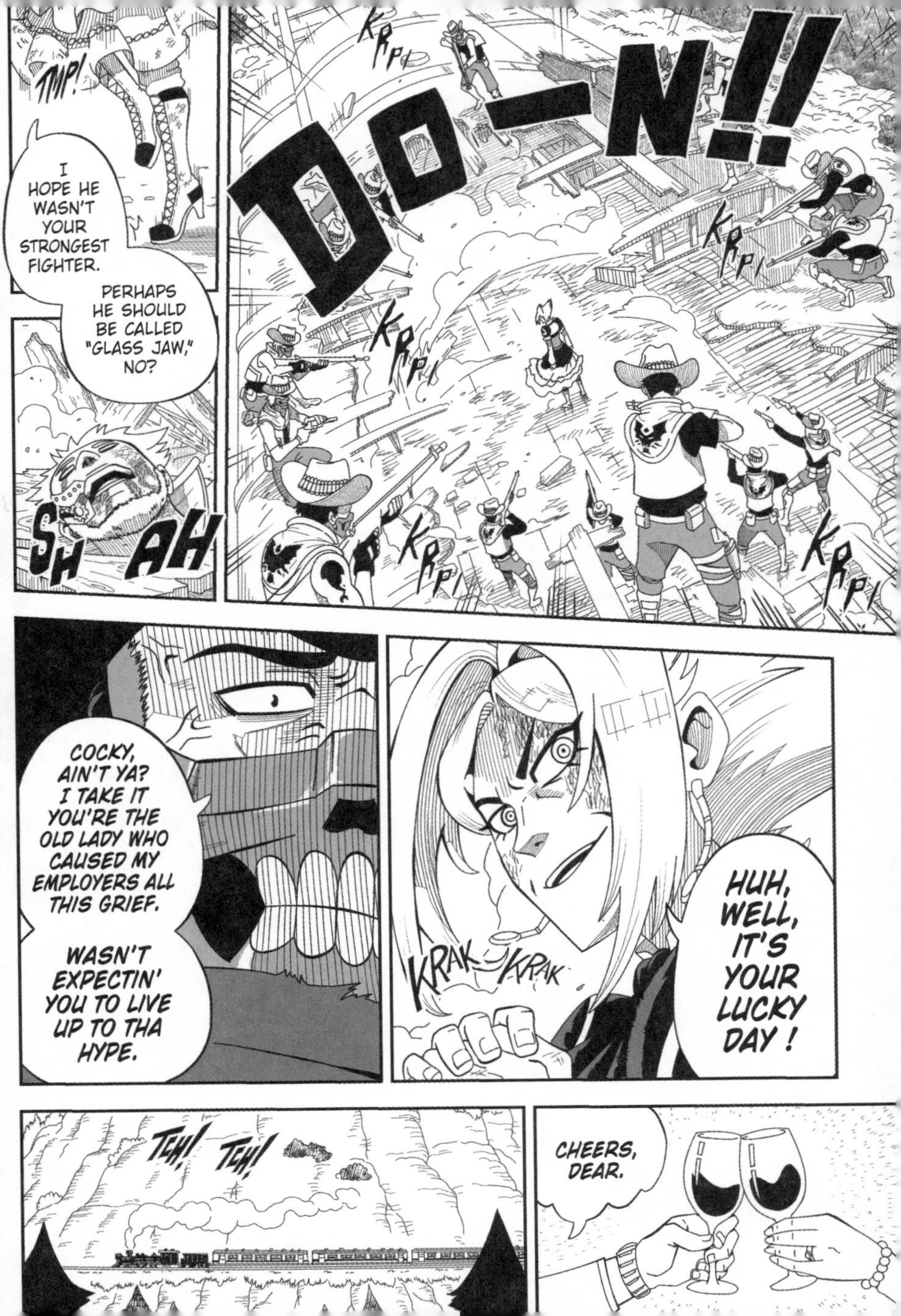
TMP!
I HOPE HE WASN'T YOUR STRONGEST FIGHTER.
PERHAPS HE SHOULD BE CALLED "GLASS JAW," NO?
SHAH
KRPI
DO—N!!
KRPI
KRPI
KRPI
KRPI
COCKY, AIN'T YA? I TAKE IT YOU'RE THE OLD LADY WHO CAUSED MY EMPLOYERS ALL THIS GRIEF.
WASN'T EXPECTIN' YOU TO LIVE UP TO THA HYPE.
KRAK KRAK
HUH, WELL, IT'S YOUR LUCKY DAY !
TCH! TCH!
CHEERS, DEAR.

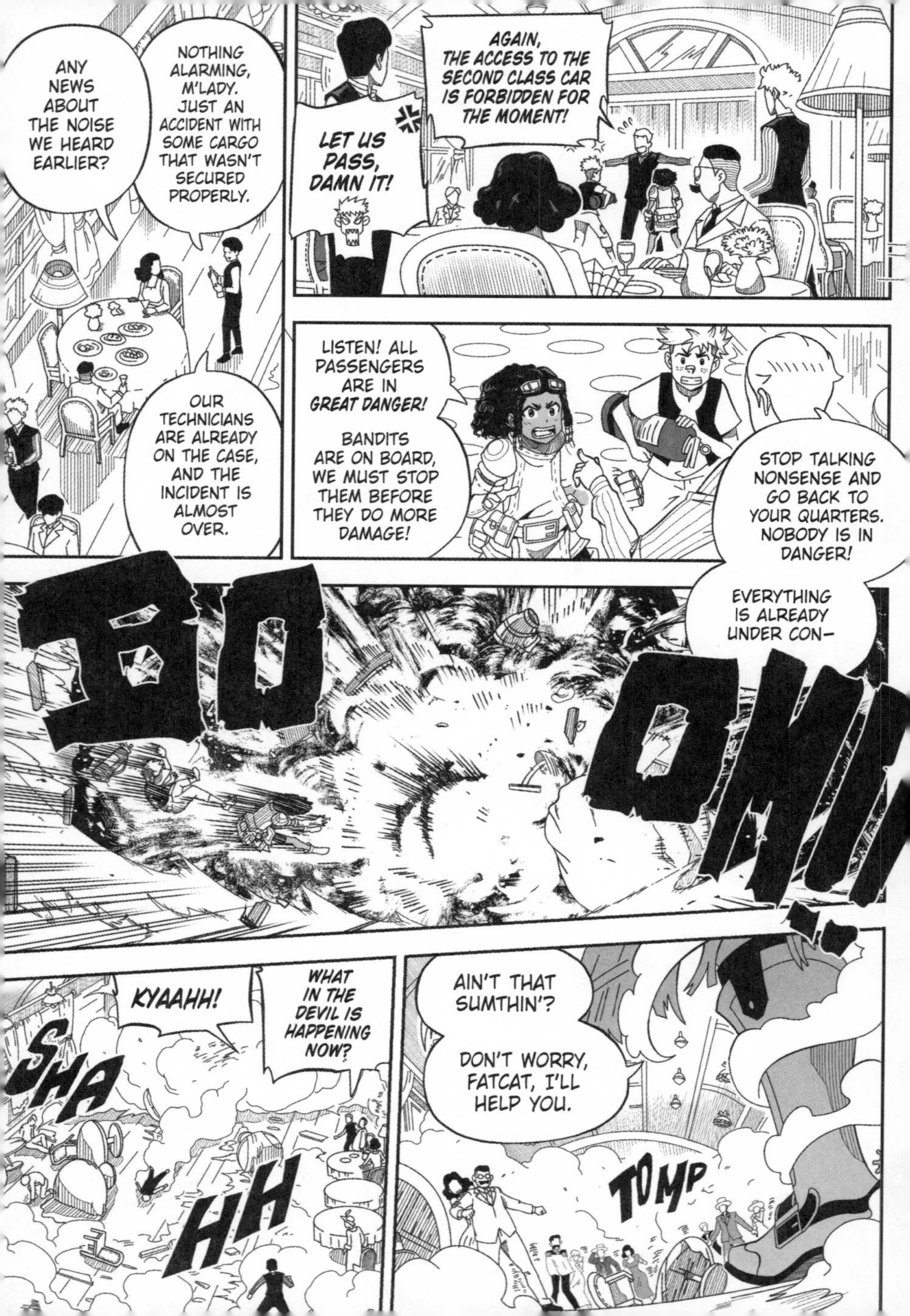
ANY NEWS ABOUT THE NOISE WE HEARD EARLIER?
NOTHING ALARMING, M'LADY. JUST AN ACCIDENT WITH SOME CARGO THAT WASN'T SECURED PROPERLY.
OUR TECHNICIANS ARE ALREADY ON THE CASE, AND THE INCIDENT IS ALMOST OVER.
LET US PASS, DAMN IT!
AGAIN, THE ACCESS TO THE SECOND CLASS CAR IS FORBIDDEN FOR THE MOMENT!
LISTEN! ALL PASSENGERS ARE IN GREAT DANGER!
BANDITS ARE ON BOARD, WE MUST STOP THEM BEFORE THEY DO MORE DAMAGE!
STOP TALKING NONSENSE AND GO BACK TO YOUR QUARTERS. NOBODY IS IN DANGER!
EVERYTHING IS ALREADY UNDER CON—
BOOM!!
KYAAHH!
SHAHH
WHAT IN THE DEVIL IS HAPPENING NOW?
AIN'T THAT SUMTHIN'?
DON'T WORRY, FATCAT, I'LL HELP YOU.
TOMP

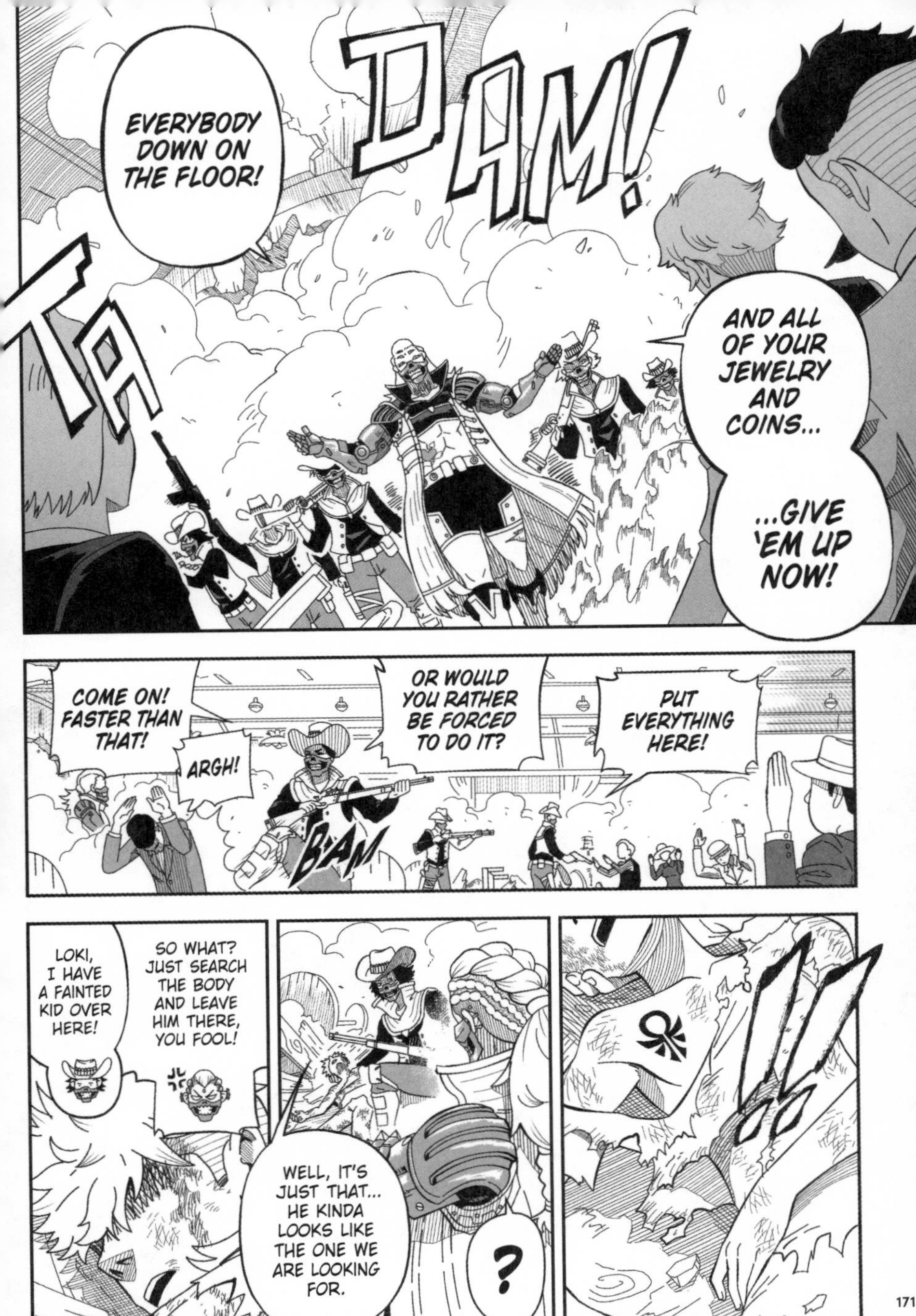
EVERYBODY DOWN ON THE FLOOR!
DAM!
TA
AND ALL OF YOUR JEWELRY AND COINS...
...GIVE 'EM UP NOW!
COME ON! FASTER THAN THAT!
ARGH!
OR WOULD YOU RATHER BE FORCED TO DO IT?
PUT EVERYTHING HERE!
BAM
LOKI, I HAVE A FAINTED KID OVER HERE!
SO WHAT? JUST SEARCH THE BODY AND LEAVE HIM THERE, YOU FOOL!
WELL, IT'S JUST THAT... HE KINDA LOOKS LIKE THE ONE WE ARE LOOKING FOR.
?
!!

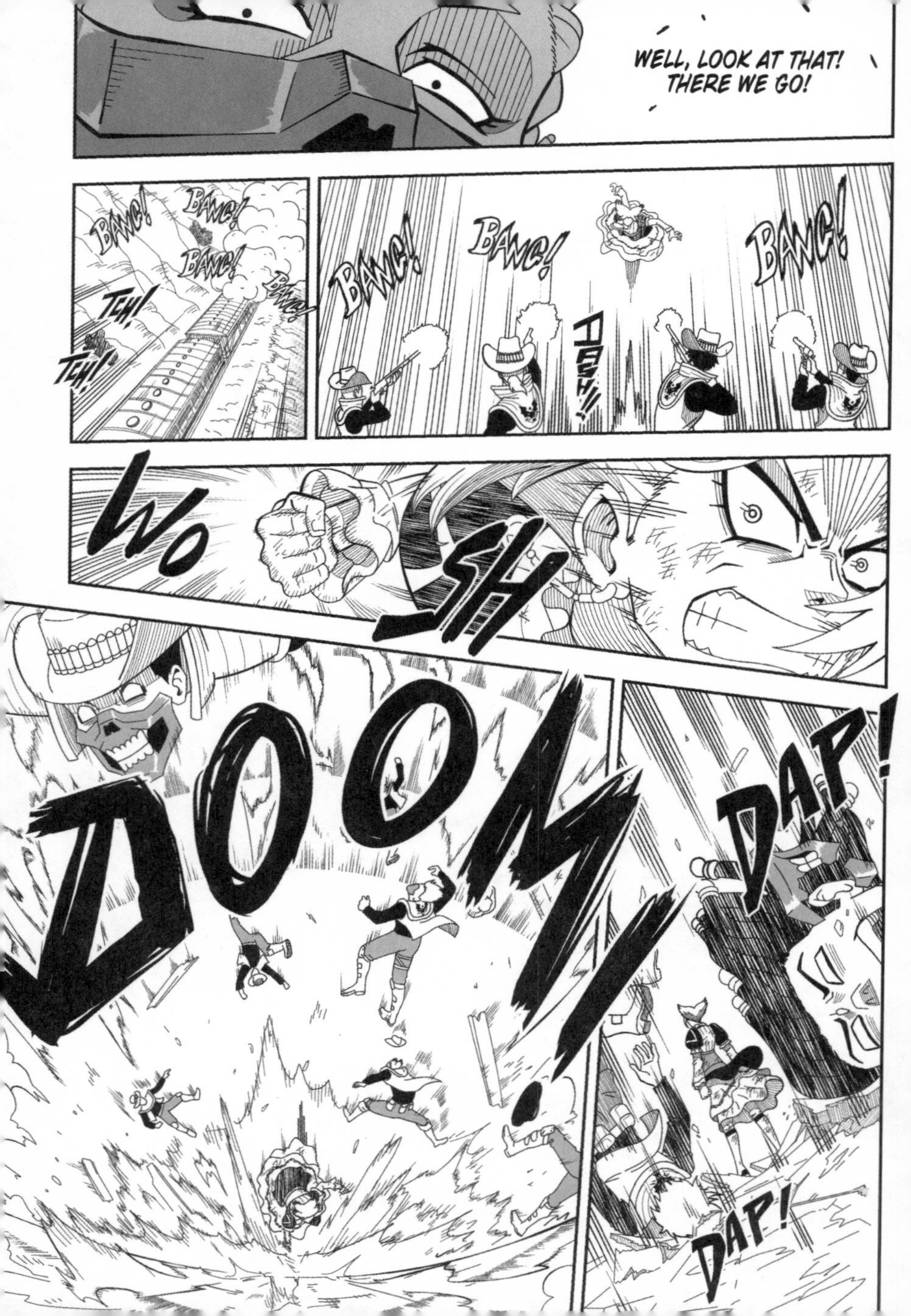
WELL, LOOK AT THAT! THERE WE GO!
BANG!
BANG!
BANG!
BANG!
TCH!
TCH!
BANG!
BANG!
TESH!!
BANG!
WOOSH
ZOOM!
DAP!
DAP!

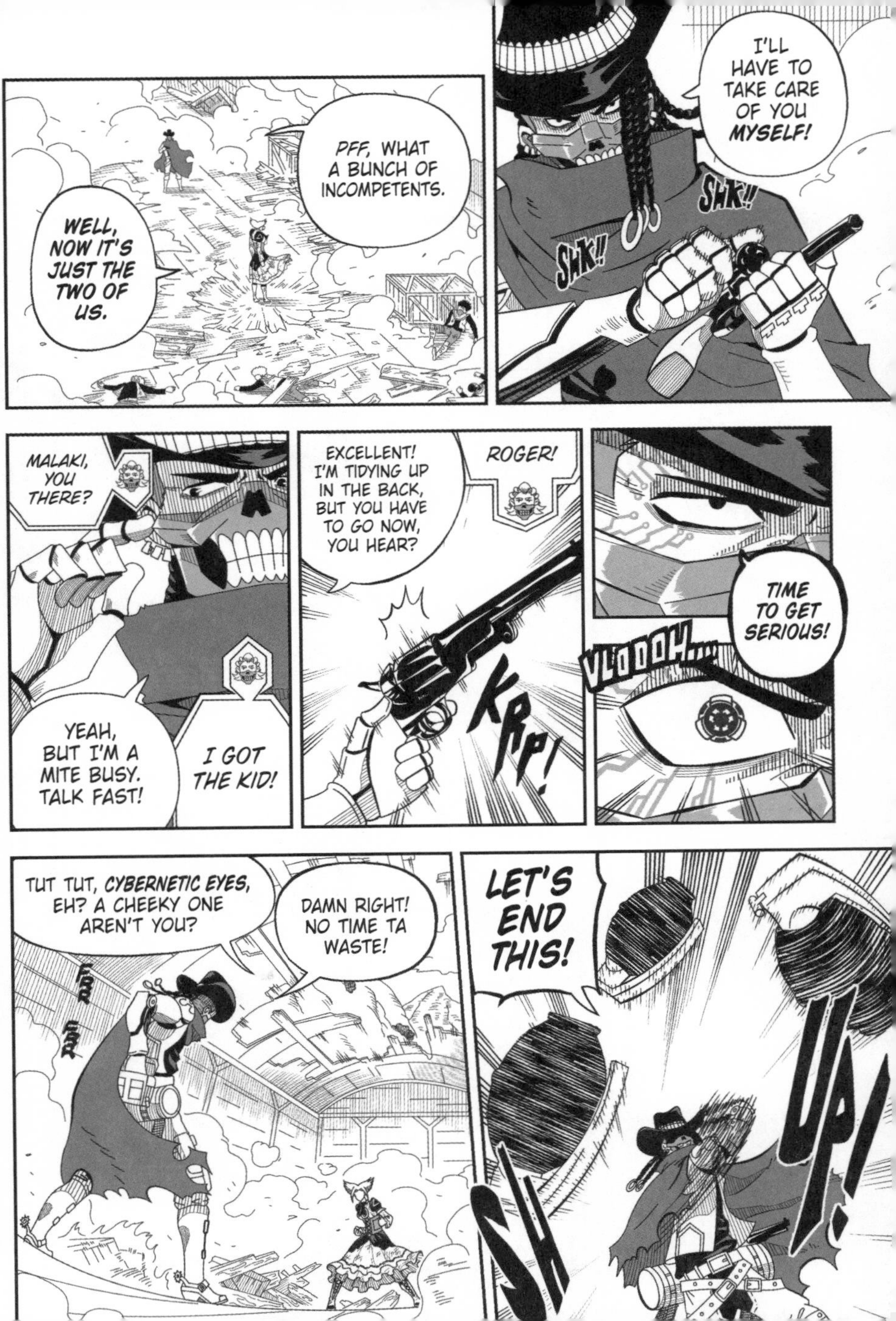
PFF, WHAT A BUNCH OF INCOMPETENTS.
WELL, NOW IT'S JUST THE TWO OF US.
I'LL HAVE TO TAKE CARE OF YOU MYSELF!
SHK!!
SHK!!
MALAKI, YOU THERE?
YEAH, BUT I'M A MITE BUSY. TALK FAST!
I GOT THE KID!
EXCELLENT! I'M TIDYING UP IN THE BACK, BUT YOU HAVE TO GO NOW, YOU HEAR?
ROGER!
KRP!
TIME TO GET SERIOUS!
VLOOOH...
TUT TUT, CYBERNETIC EYES, EH? A CHEEKY ONE AREN'T YOU?
DAMN RIGHT! NO TIME TA WASTE!
LET'S END THIS!
SHUP!

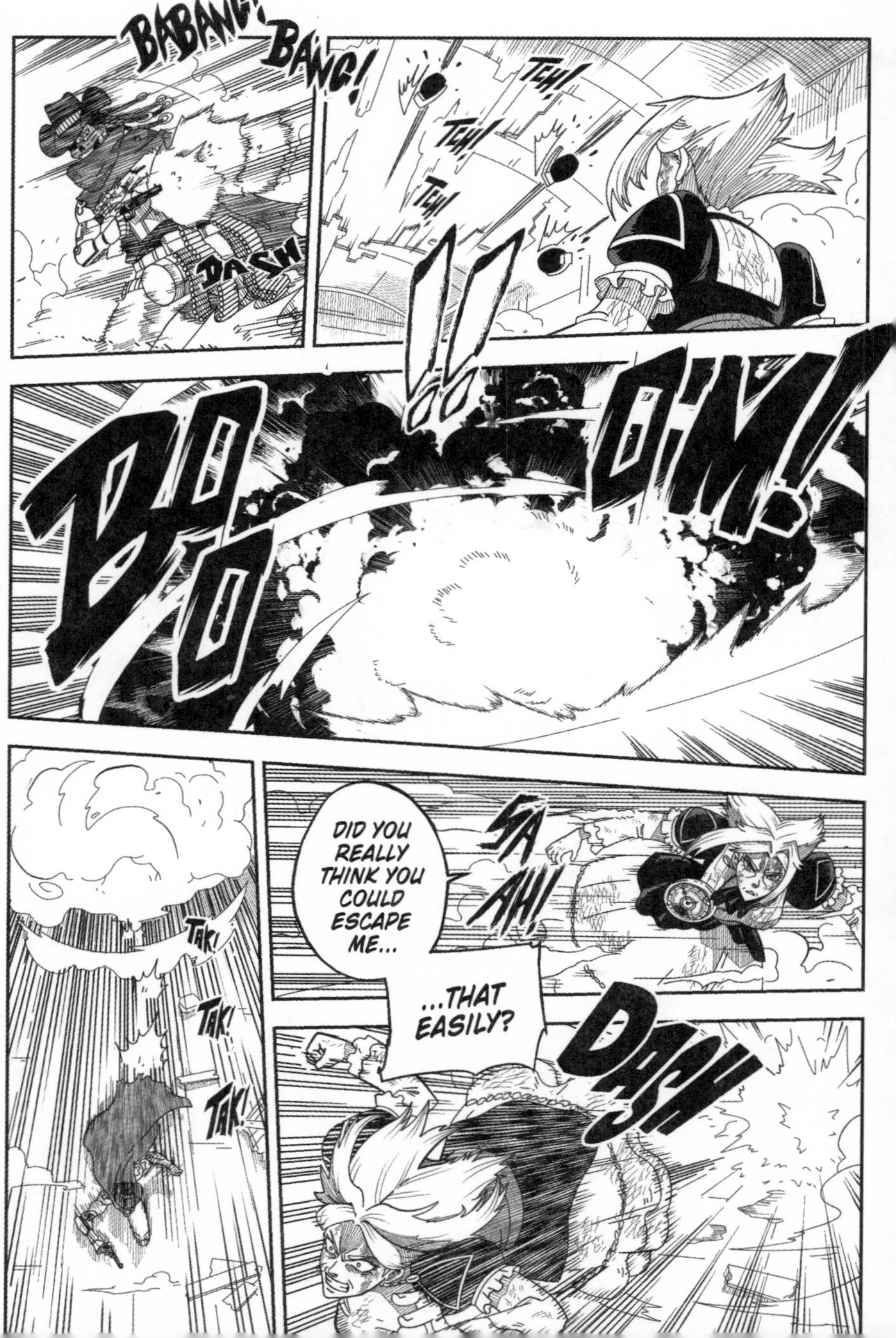
BABANG! BANG!
DASH
TCH!
TCH!
TCH!
!!
BOOOOM!
TAK!
TAK!
TAK!
SHA AH!
DID YOU REALLY THINK YOU COULD ESCAPE ME...
...THAT EASILY?
DASH

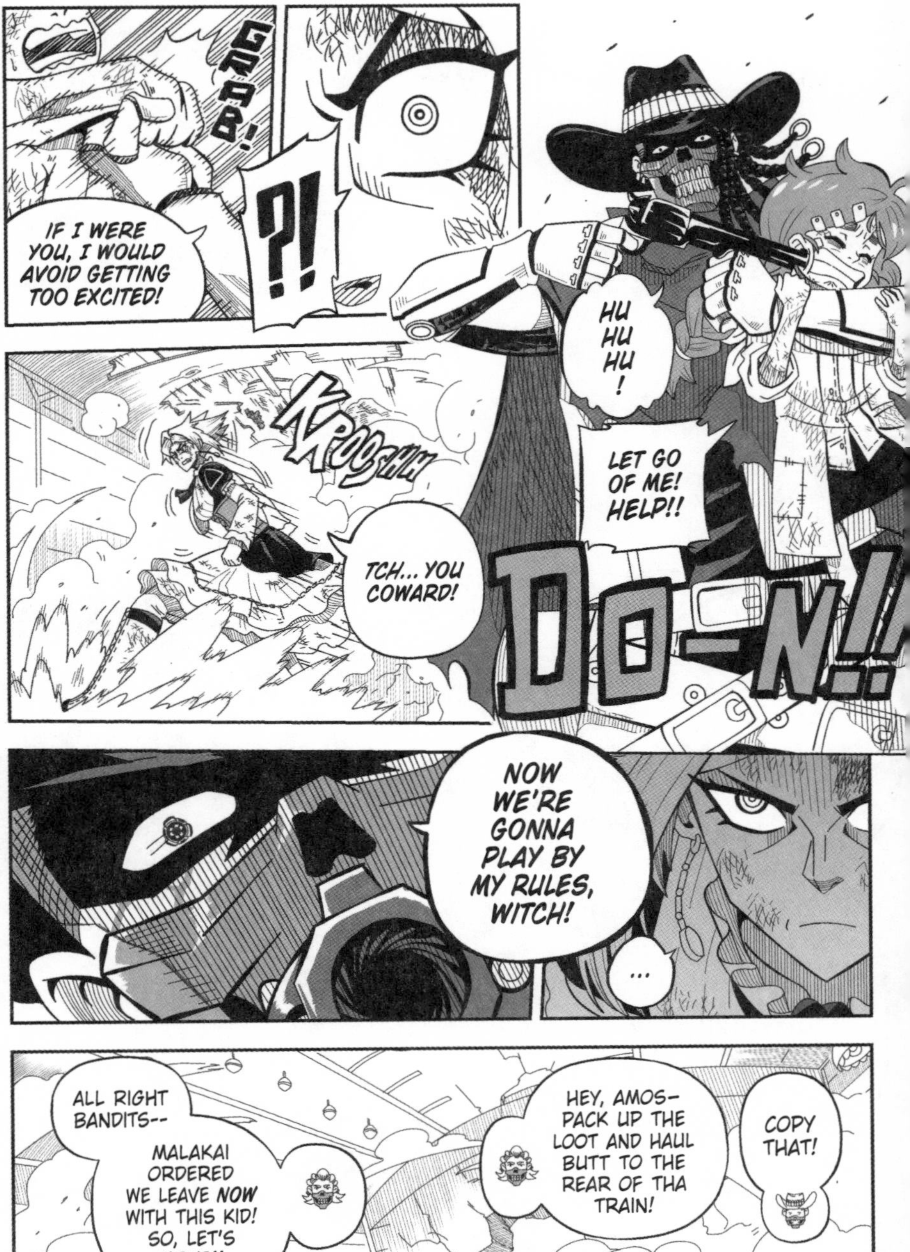
GRAB!
IF I WERE YOU, I WOULD AVOID GETTING TOO EXCITED!
?!
KRCCSHH
TCH... YOU COWARD!
HU HU HU!
LET GO OF ME! HELP!!
DO-N!!
NOW WE'RE GONNA PLAY BY MY RULES, WITCH!
...
ALL RIGHT BANDITS--
MALAKAI ORDERED WE LEAVE NOW WITH THIS KID! SO, LET'S MOVE!!
HEY, AMOS– PACK UP THE LOOT AND HAUL BUTT TO THE REAR OF THA TRAIN!
COPY THAT!

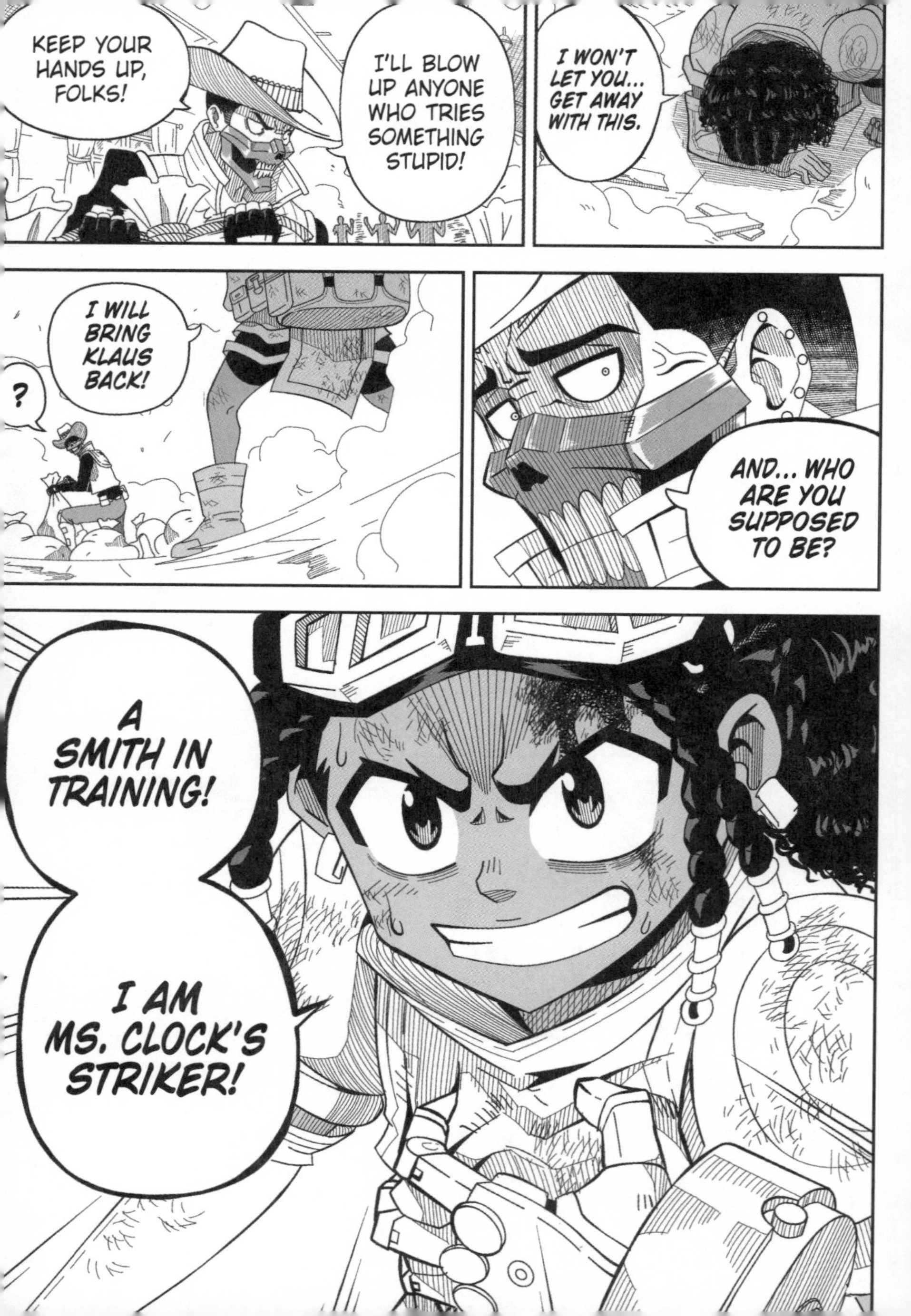
KEEP YOUR HANDS UP, FOLKS!
I'LL BLOW UP ANYONE WHO TRIES SOMETHING STUPID!
I WON'T LET YOU... GET AWAY WITH THIS.
I WILL BRING KLAUS BACK!
?
AND... WHO ARE YOU SUPPOSED TO BE?
A SMITH IN TRAINING!
I AM MS. CLOCK'S STRIKER!

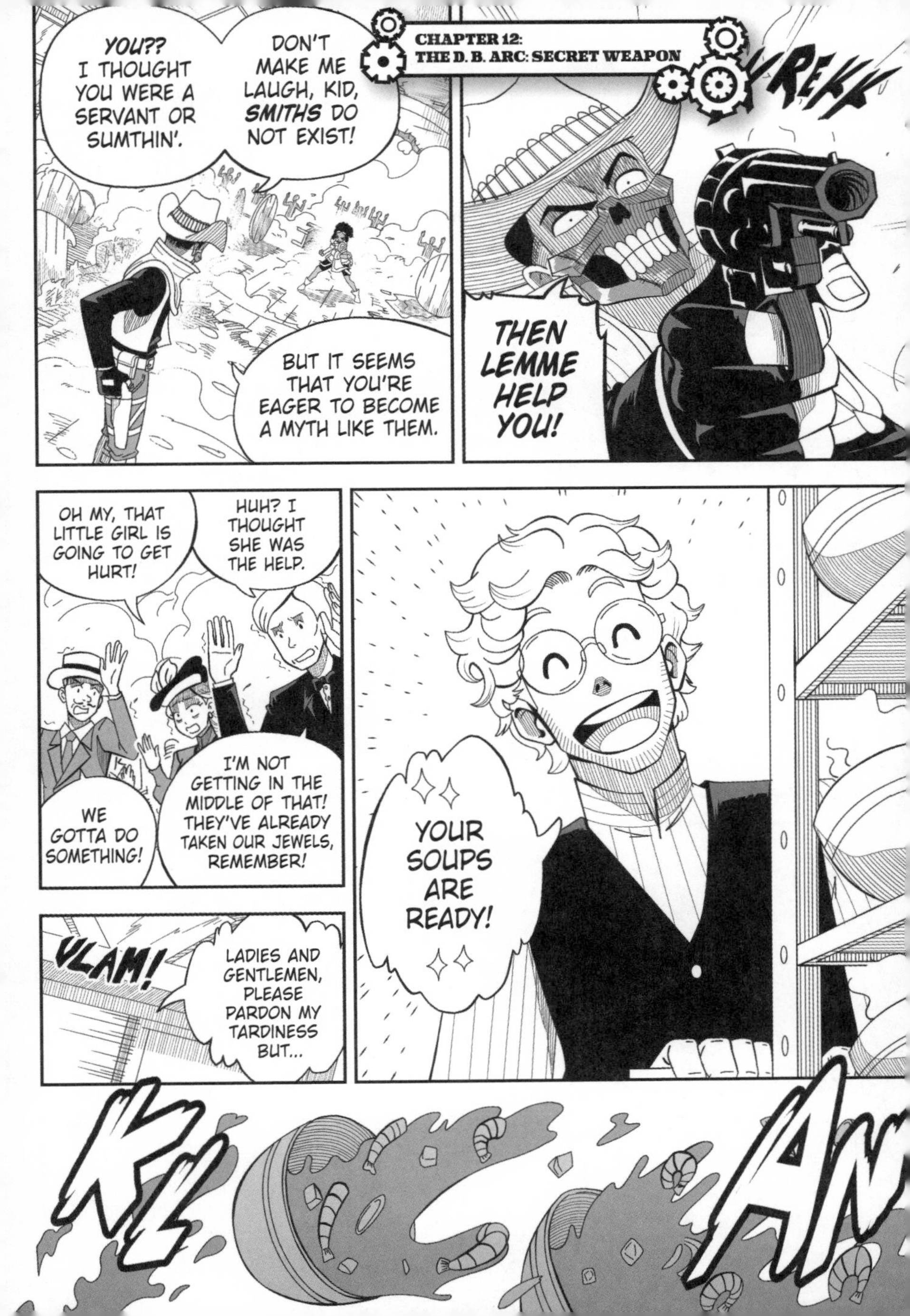
CHAPTER 12:
THE D. B. ARC: SECRET WEAPON
YOU?? I THOUGHT YOU WERE A SERVANT OR SUMTHIN'.
DON'T MAKE ME LAUGH, KID, SMITHS DO NOT EXIST!
BUT IT SEEMS THAT YOU'RE EAGER TO BECOME A MYTH LIKE THEM.
VREKK
THEN LEMME HELP YOU!
OH MY, THAT LITTLE GIRL IS GOING TO GET HURT!
HUH? I THOUGHT SHE WAS THE HELP.
WE GOTTA DO SOMETHING!
I'M NOT GETTING IN THE MIDDLE OF THAT! THEY'VE ALREADY TAKEN OUR JEWELS, REMEMBER!
VLAM!
LADIES AND GENTLEMEN, PLEASE PARDON MY TARDINESS BUT...
YOUR SOUPS ARE READY!
KLAN

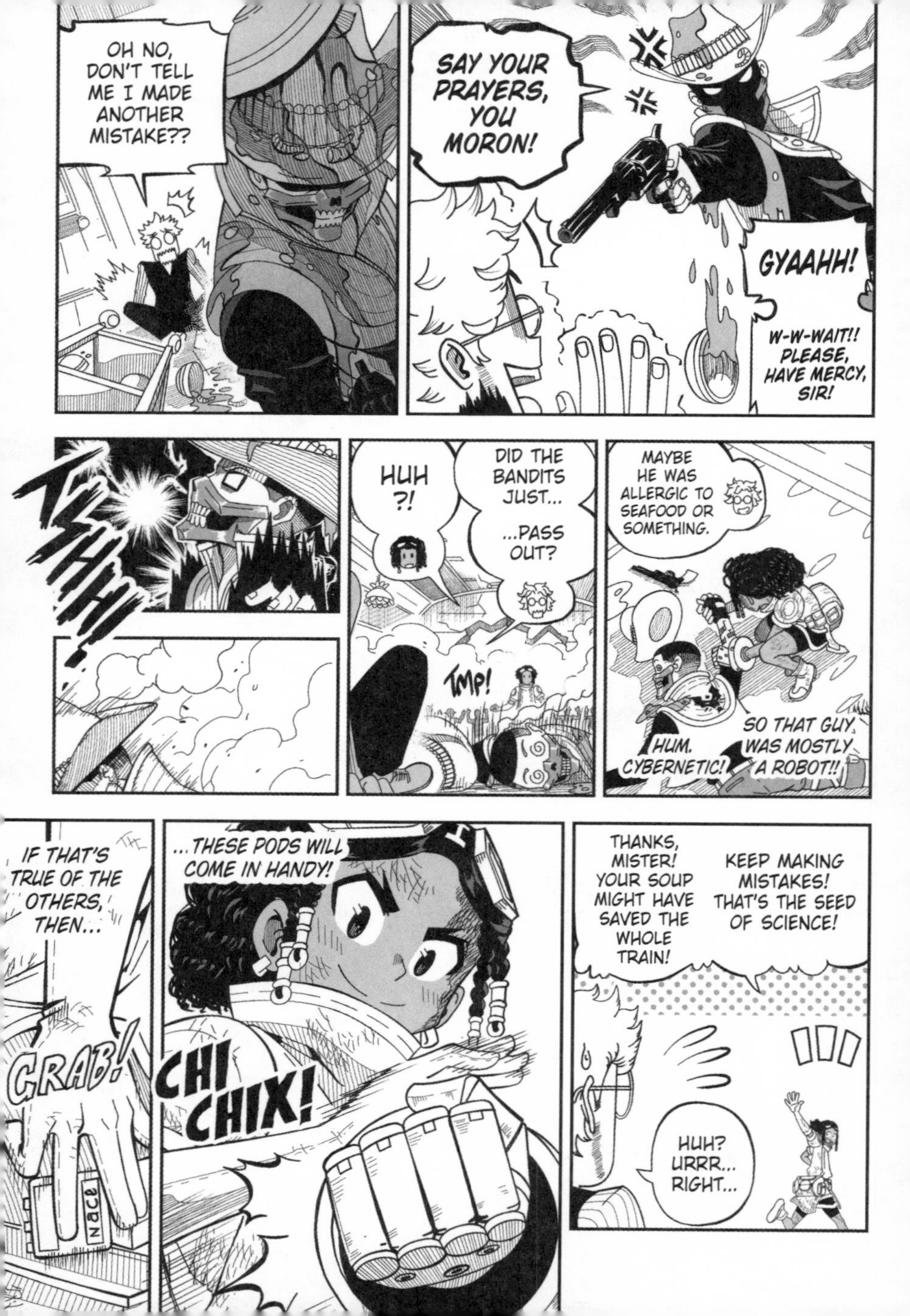
OH NO, DON'T TELL ME I MADE ANOTHER MISTAKE??
SAY YOUR PRAYERS, YOU MORON!
GYAAHH!
W-W-WAIT!! PLEASE, HAVE MERCY, SIR!
HUH ?!
DID THE BANDITS JUST...
...PASS OUT?
TMP!
MAYBE HE WAS ALLERGIC TO SEAFOOD OR SOMETHING.
HUM. CYBERNETIC!
SO THAT GUY WAS MOSTLY A ROBOT!!
IF THAT'S TRUE OF THE OTHERS, THEN...
GRAB!
...THESE PODS WILL COME IN HANDY!
CHI CHIX!
THANKS, MISTER! YOUR SOUP MIGHT HAVE SAVED THE WHOLE TRAIN!
KEEP MAKING MISTAKES! THAT'S THE SEED OF SCIENCE!
HUH? URRR... RIGHT...

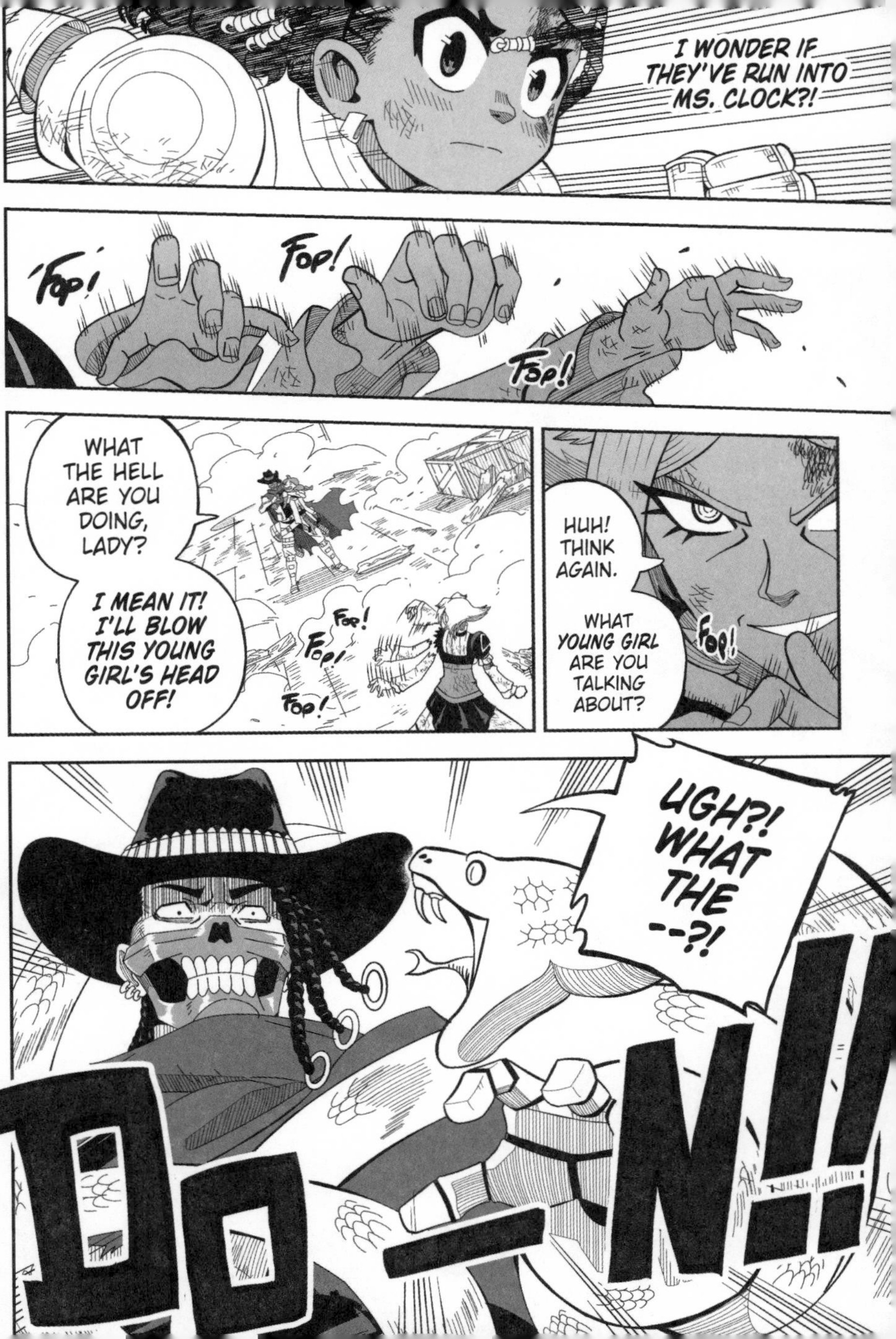
I WONDER IF THEY'VE RUN INTO MS. CLOCK?!
FOP!
FOP!
FOP!
WHAT THE HELL ARE YOU DOING, LADY?
I MEAN IT! I'LL BLOW THIS YOUNG GIRL'S HEAD OFF!
FOP!
FOP!
FOP!
HUH! THINK AGAIN.
WHAT YOUNG GIRL ARE YOU TALKING ABOUT?
FOP!
UGH?! WHAT THE --?!
DO-N!!

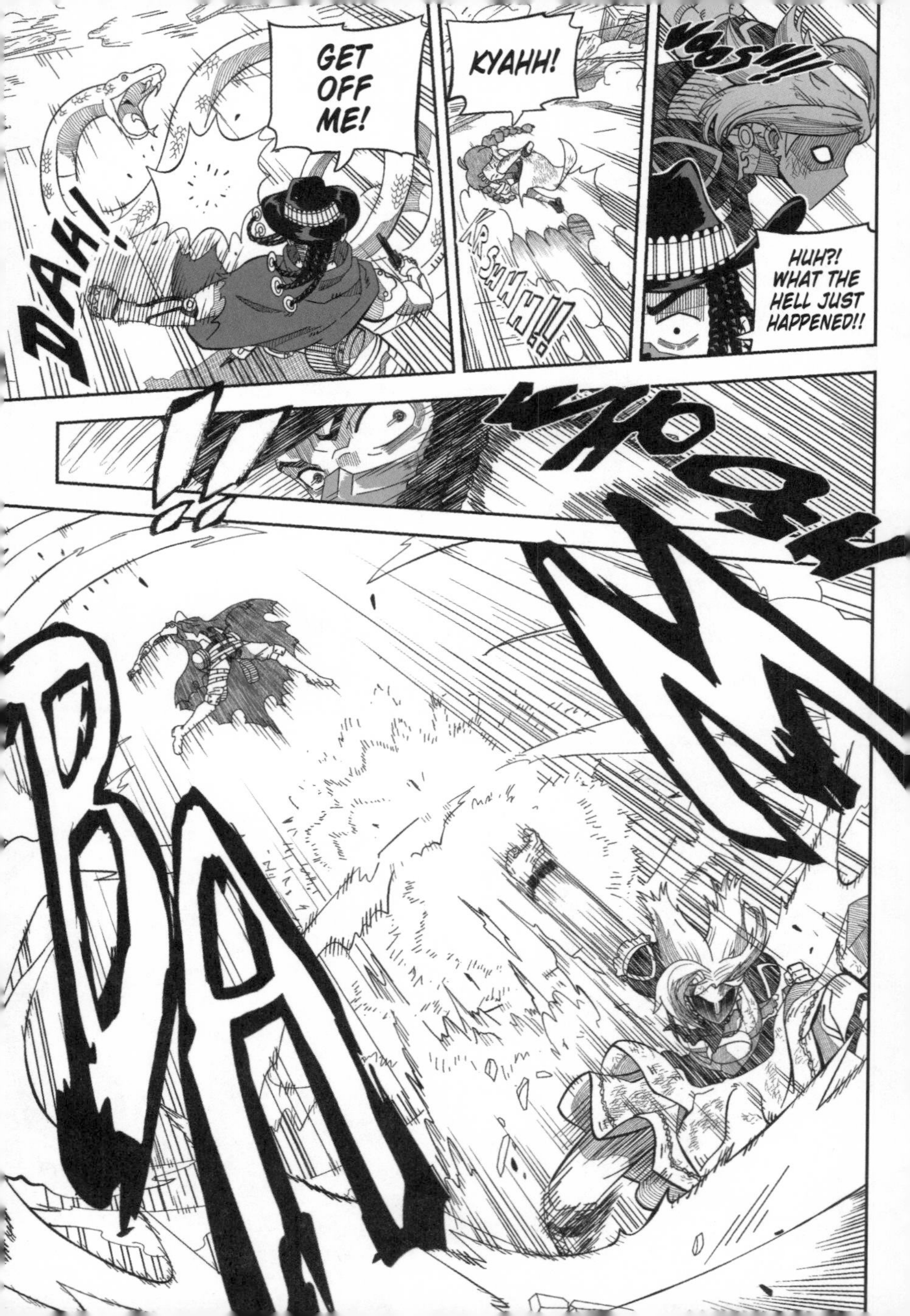
DAH!
GET OFF ME!
KYAHH!
KRSHHH!!
VOOSH!!!
HUH?! WHAT THE HELL JUST HAPPENED!!
!!
WHOOSH
BAMM

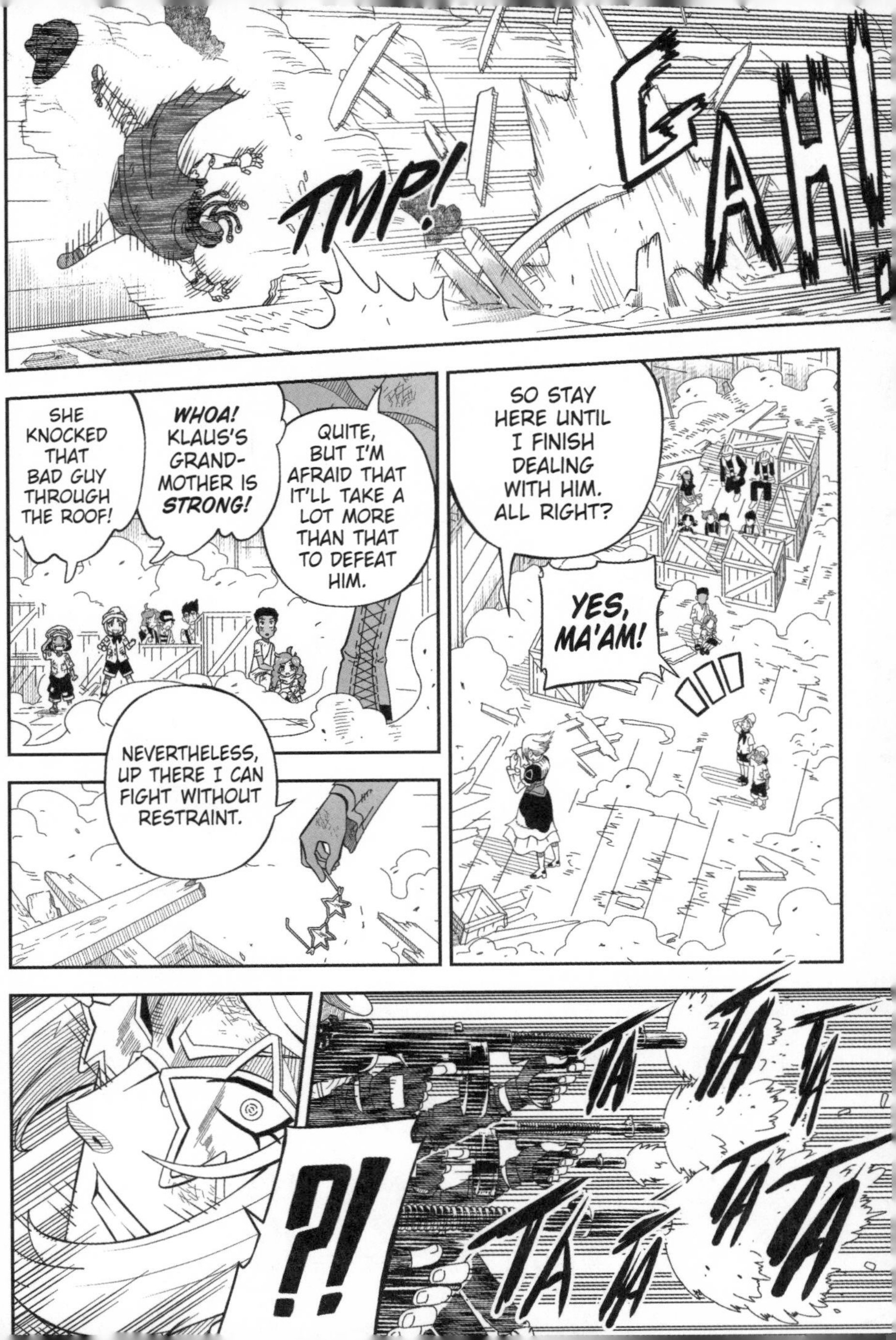
TMP!
GAH!
SHE KNOCKED THAT BAD GUY THROUGH THE ROOF!
WHOA! KLAUS'S GRANDMOTHER IS STRONG!
QUITE, BUT I'M AFRAID THAT IT'LL TAKE A LOT MORE THAN THAT TO DEFEAT HIM.
NEVERTHELESS, UP THERE I CAN FIGHT WITHOUT RESTRAINT.
SO STAY HERE UNTIL I FINISH DEALING WITH HIM. ALL RIGHT?
YES, MA'AM!
?!
TA-TA-TA
TA-TA-TA
TA-TA-TA

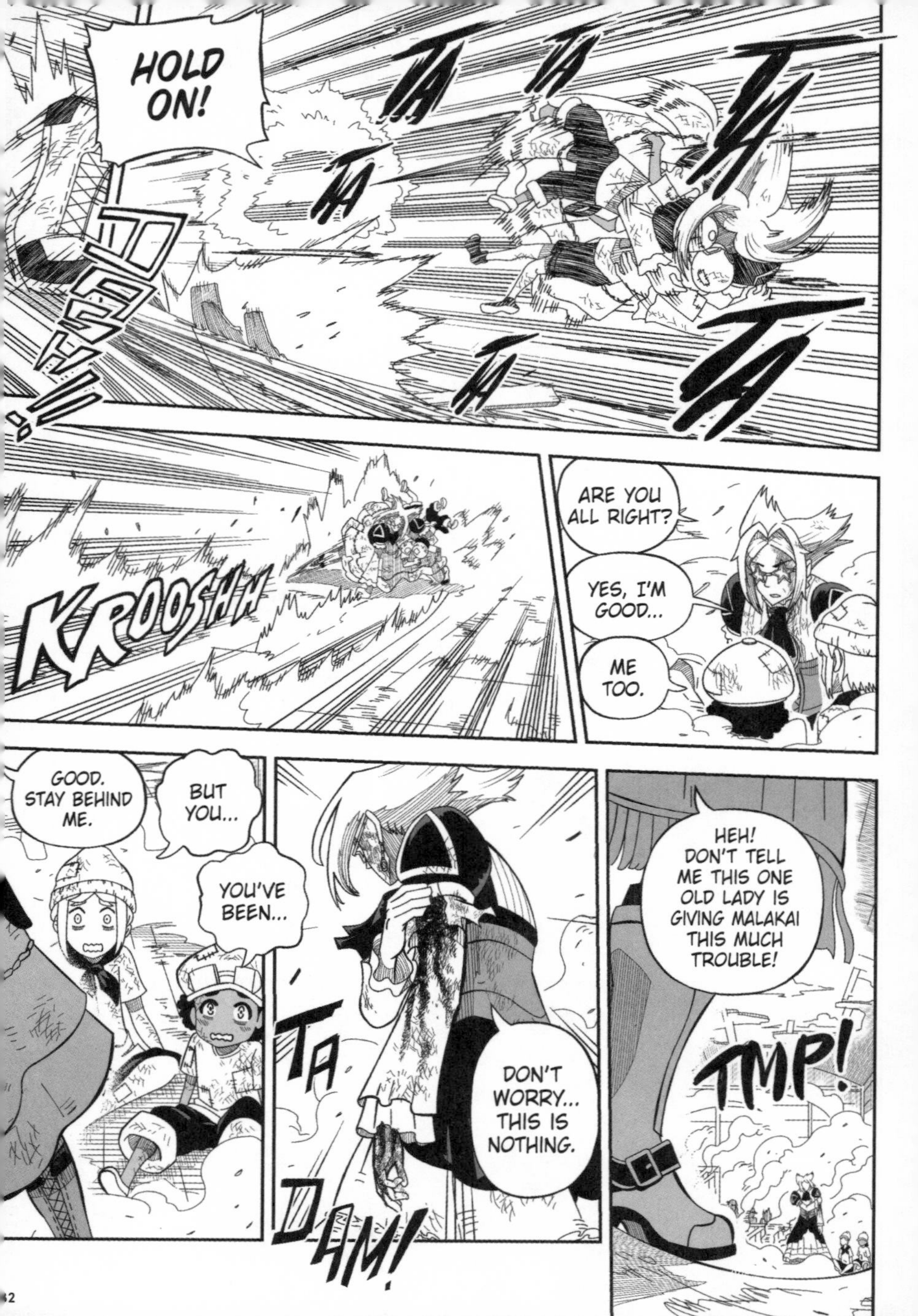
HOLD ON!
TA
TA
TA
TA
KROOSHH
ARE YOU ALL RIGHT?
YES, I'M GOOD...
ME TOO.
GOOD. STAY BEHIND ME.
BUT YOU...
YOU'VE BEEN...
TA
DON'T WORRY... THIS IS NOTHING.
DAM!
HEH! DON'T TELL ME THIS ONE OLD LADY IS GIVING MALAKAI THIS MUCH TROUBLE!
TMP!

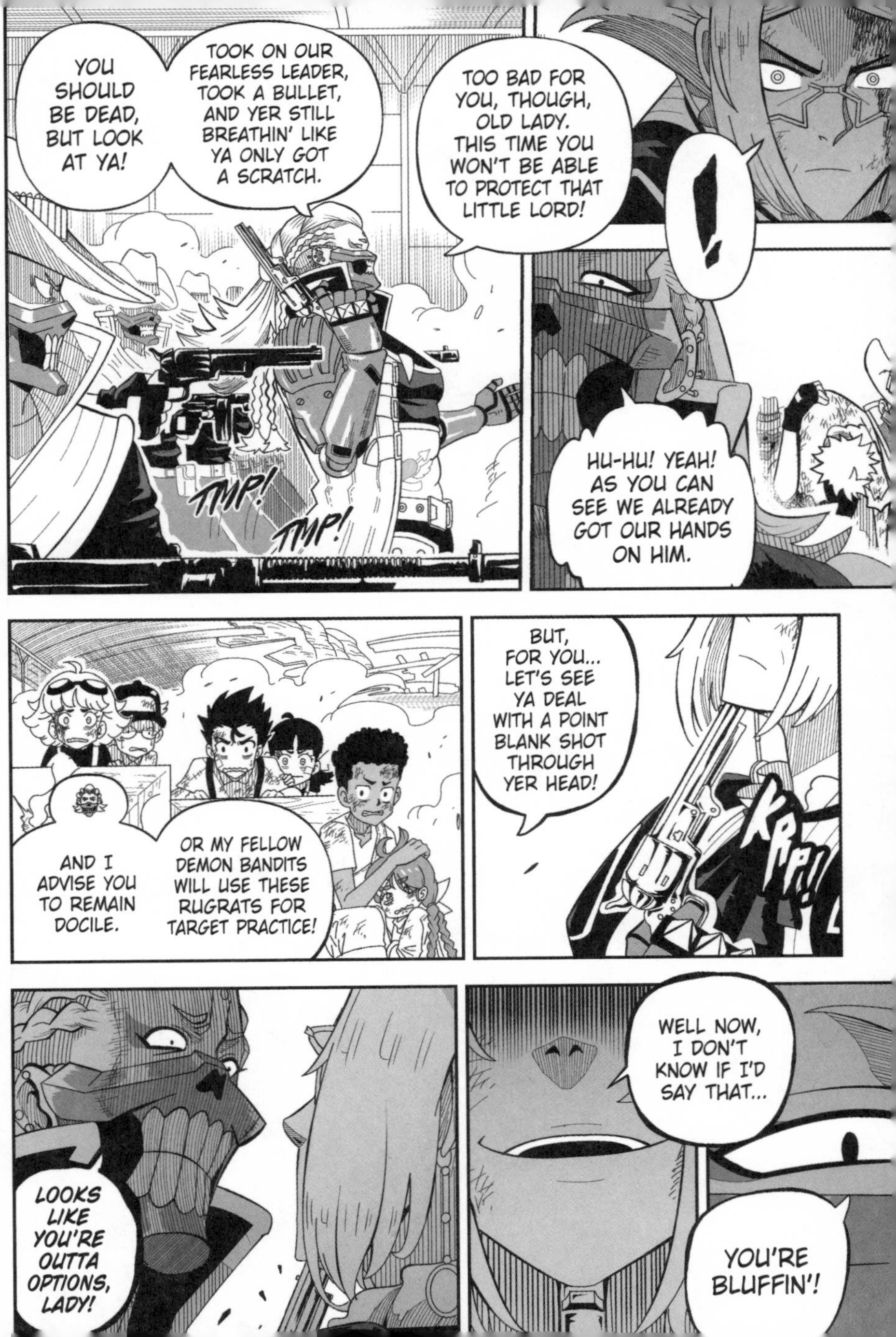
YOU SHOULD BE DEAD, BUT LOOK AT YA!
TOOK ON OUR FEARLESS LEADER, TOOK A BULLET, AND YER STILL BREATHIN' LIKE YA ONLY GOT A SCRATCH.
TOO BAD FOR YOU, THOUGH, OLD LADY. THIS TIME YOU WON'T BE ABLE TO PROTECT THAT LITTLE LORD!
TMP!
TMP!
!
HU-HU! YEAH! AS YOU CAN SEE WE ALREADY GOT OUR HANDS ON HIM.
AND I ADVISE YOU TO REMAIN DOCILE.
OR MY FELLOW DEMON BANDITS WILL USE THESE RUGRATS FOR TARGET PRACTICE!
BUT, FOR YOU... LET'S SEE YA DEAL WITH A POINT BLANK SHOT THROUGH YER HEAD!
KRRP!
LOOKS LIKE YOU'RE OUTTA OPTIONS, LADY!
WELL NOW, I DON'T KNOW IF I'D SAY THAT...
YOU'RE BLUFFIN'!

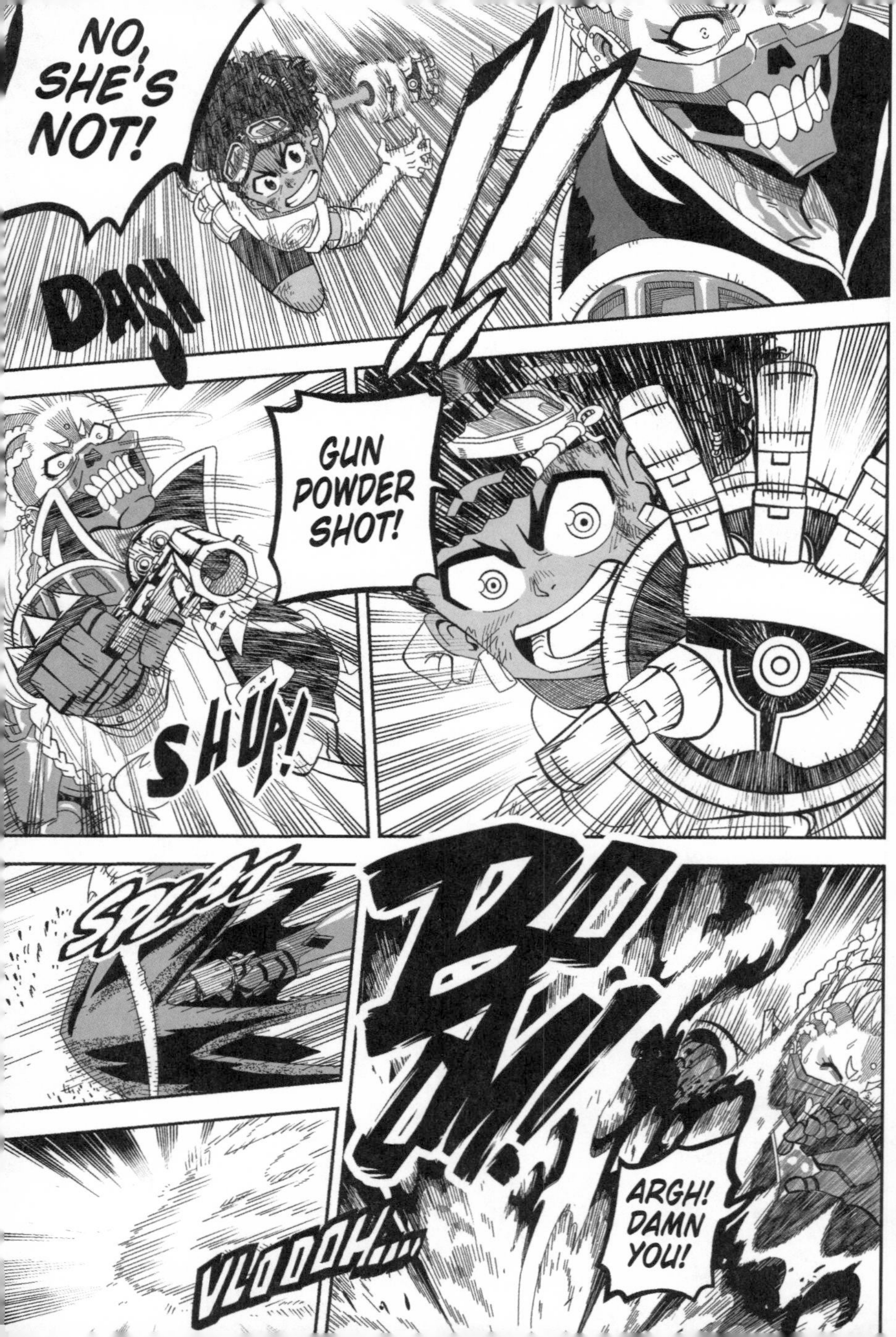
NO, SHE'S NOT!
DASH
SHUP!
GUN POWDER SHOT!
SPLASH
VLOOOH...
ARGH! DAMN YOU!

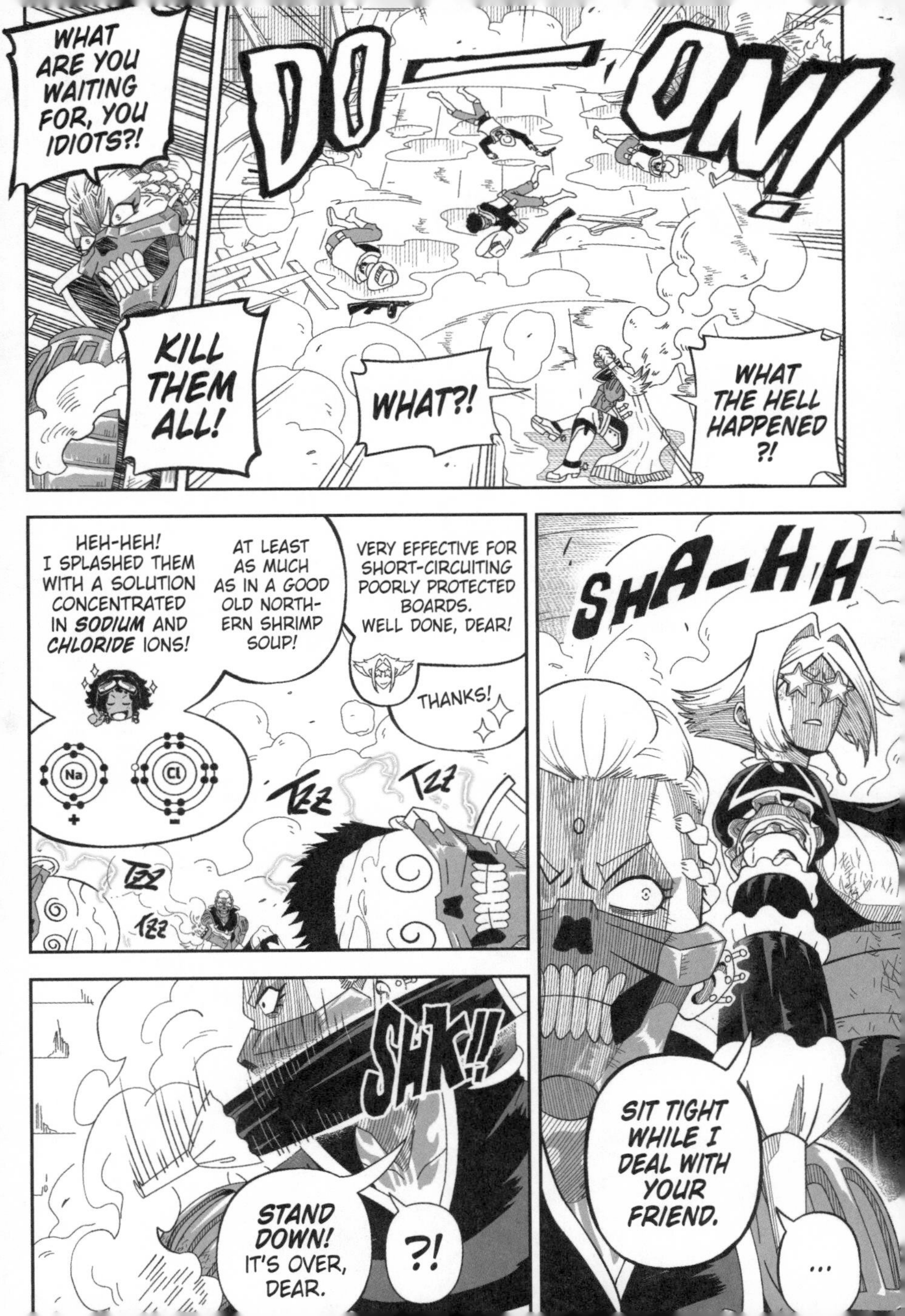
WHAT ARE YOU WAITING FOR, YOU IDIOTS?!
DO—OM!
KILL THEM ALL!
WHAT?!
WHAT THE HELL HAPPENED?!
HEH-HEH! I SPLASHED THEM WITH A SOLUTION CONCENTRATED IN SODIUM AND CHLORIDE IONS!
AT LEAST AS MUCH AS IN A GOOD OLD NORTHERN SHRIMP SOUP!
VERY EFFECTIVE FOR SHORT-CIRCUITING POORLY PROTECTED BOARDS. WELL DONE, DEAR!
THANKS!
Na
+
Cl
-
TZZ
TZZ
TZZ
TZZ
SHA-HH
SHK!!
STAND DOWN! IT'S OVER, DEAR.
?!
SIT TIGHT WHILE I DEAL WITH YOUR FRIEND.
...

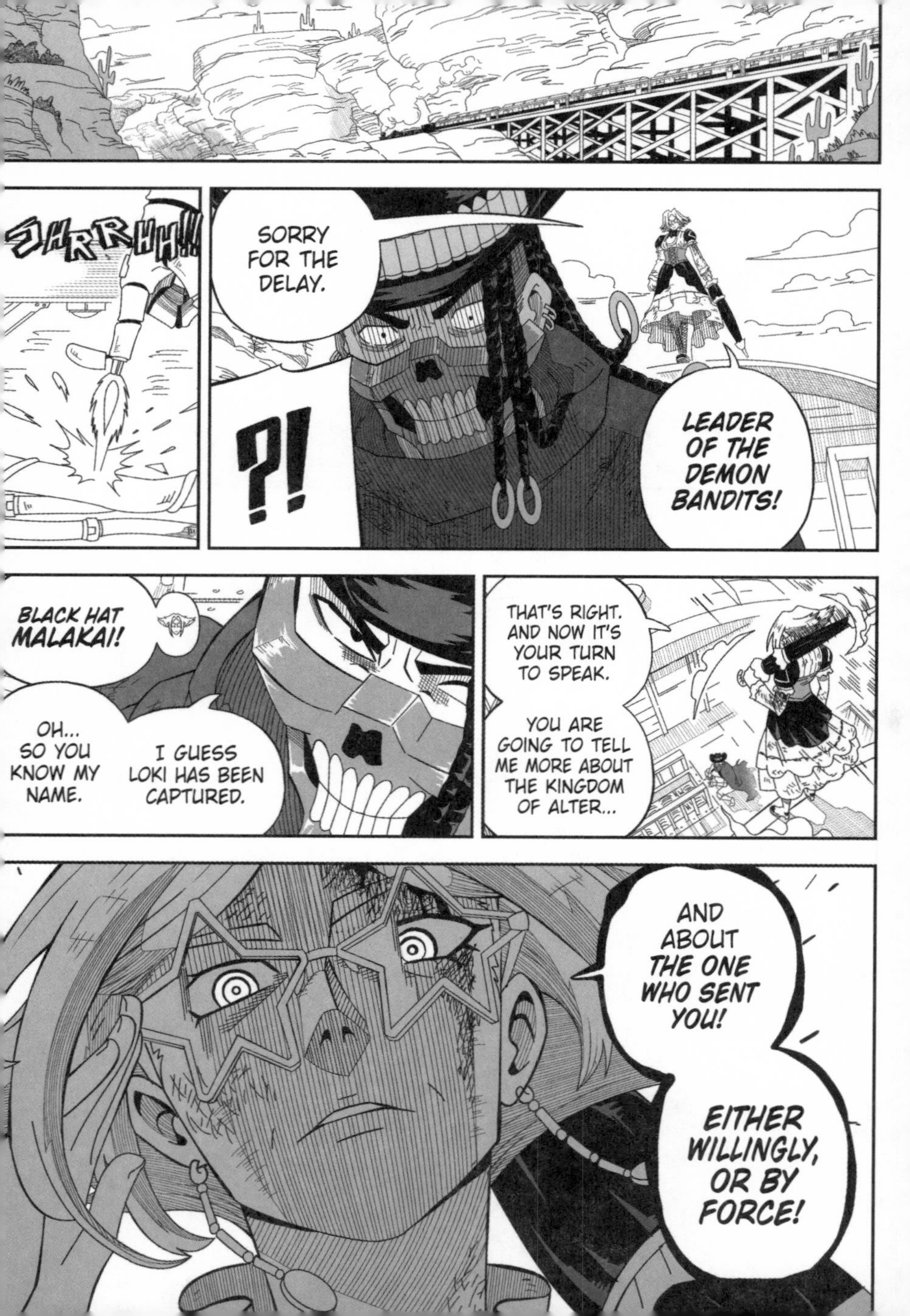
SHRRHH!!!
SORRY FOR THE DELAY.
?!
LEADER OF THE DEMON BANDITS!
BLACK HAT MALAKAI!
OH... SO YOU KNOW MY NAME.
I GUESS LOKI HAS BEEN CAPTURED.
THAT'S RIGHT. AND NOW IT'S YOUR TURN TO SPEAK.
YOU ARE GOING TO TELL ME MORE ABOUT THE KINGDOM OF ALTER...
AND ABOUT THE ONE WHO SENT YOU!
EITHER WILLINGLY, OR BY FORCE!

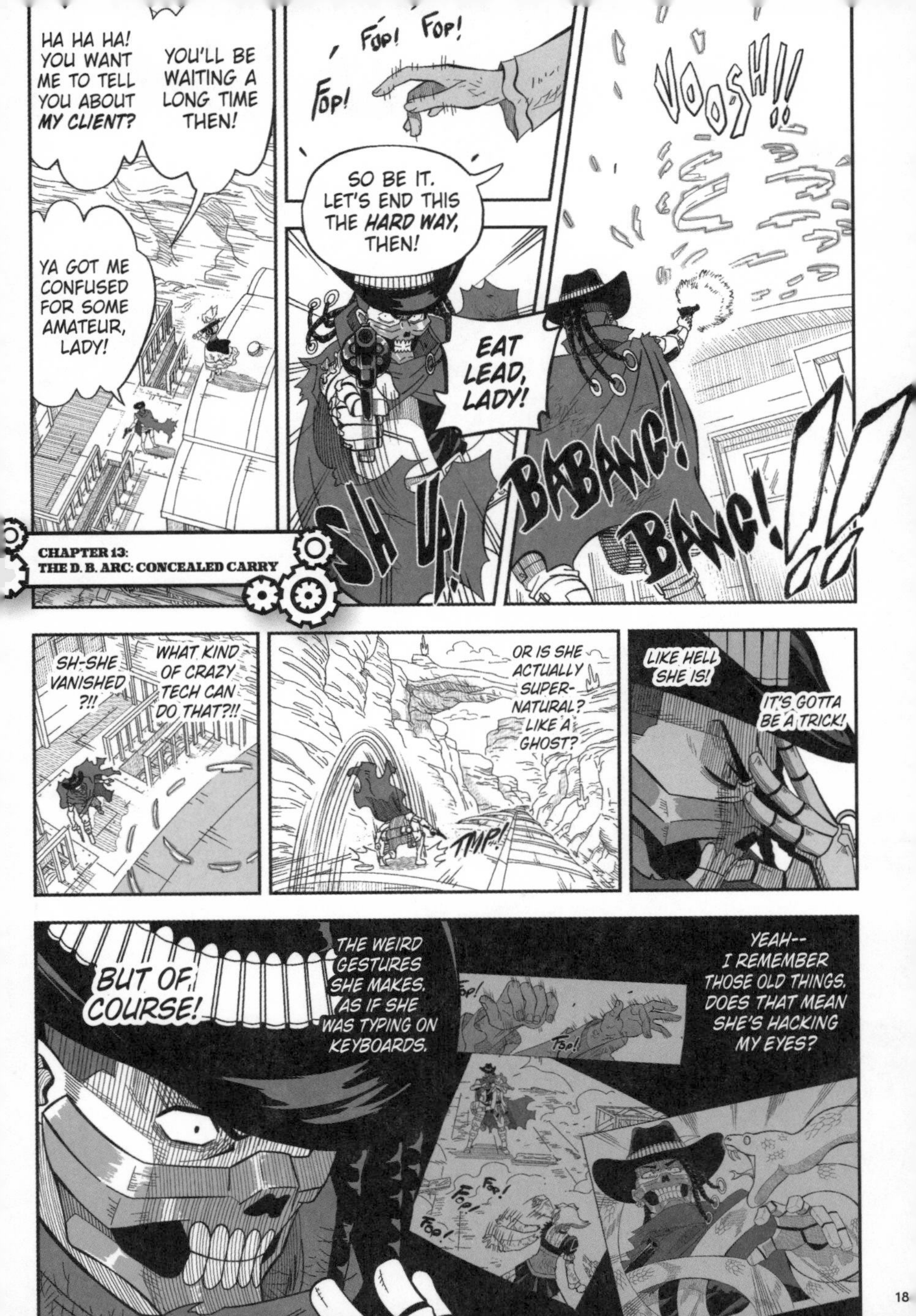
HA HA HA! YOU WANT ME TO TELL YOU ABOUT MY CLIENT?
YOU'LL BE WAITING A LONG TIME THEN!
YA GOT ME CONFUSED FOR SOME AMATEUR, LADY!
FOP! FOP!
FOP!
SO BE IT. LET'S END THIS THE HARD WAY, THEN!
VOOSH!!
EAT LEAD, LADY!
SH UP!
BABANG!
BANG!!
CHAPTER 13:
THE D. B. ARC: CONCEALED CARRY
SH-SHE VANISHED?!!
WHAT KIND OF CRAZY TECH CAN DO THAT?!!
OR IS SHE ACTUALLY SUPER-NATURAL? LIKE A GHOST?
TMP!
LIKE HELL SHE IS!
IT'S GOTTA BE A TRICK!
BUT OF COURSE!
THE WEIRD GESTURES SHE MAKES. AS IF SHE WAS TYPING ON KEYBOARDS.
FOP!
TSP!
YEAH-- I REMEMBER THOSE OLD THINGS. DOES THAT MEAN SHE'S HACKING MY EYES?
FOP!
FOP!
FOP!

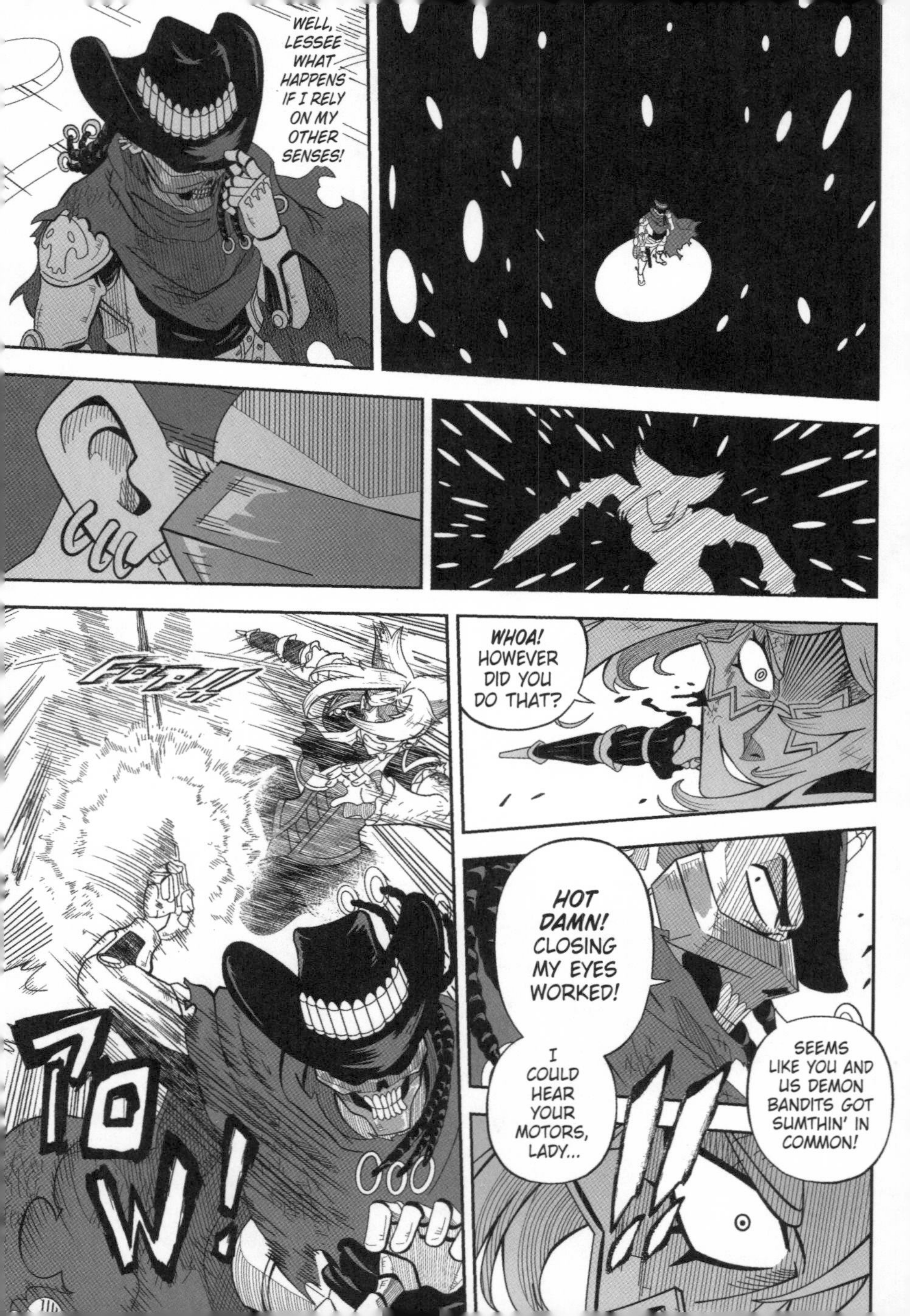
WELL, LESSEE WHAT HAPPENS IF I RELY ON MY OTHER SENSES!
FOP!!
POW!
WHOA! HOWEVER DID YOU DO THAT?
HOT DAMN! CLOSING MY EYES WORKED!
I COULD HEAR YOUR MOTORS, LADY...
SEEMS LIKE YOU AND US DEMON BANDITS GOT SUMTHIN' IN COMMON!

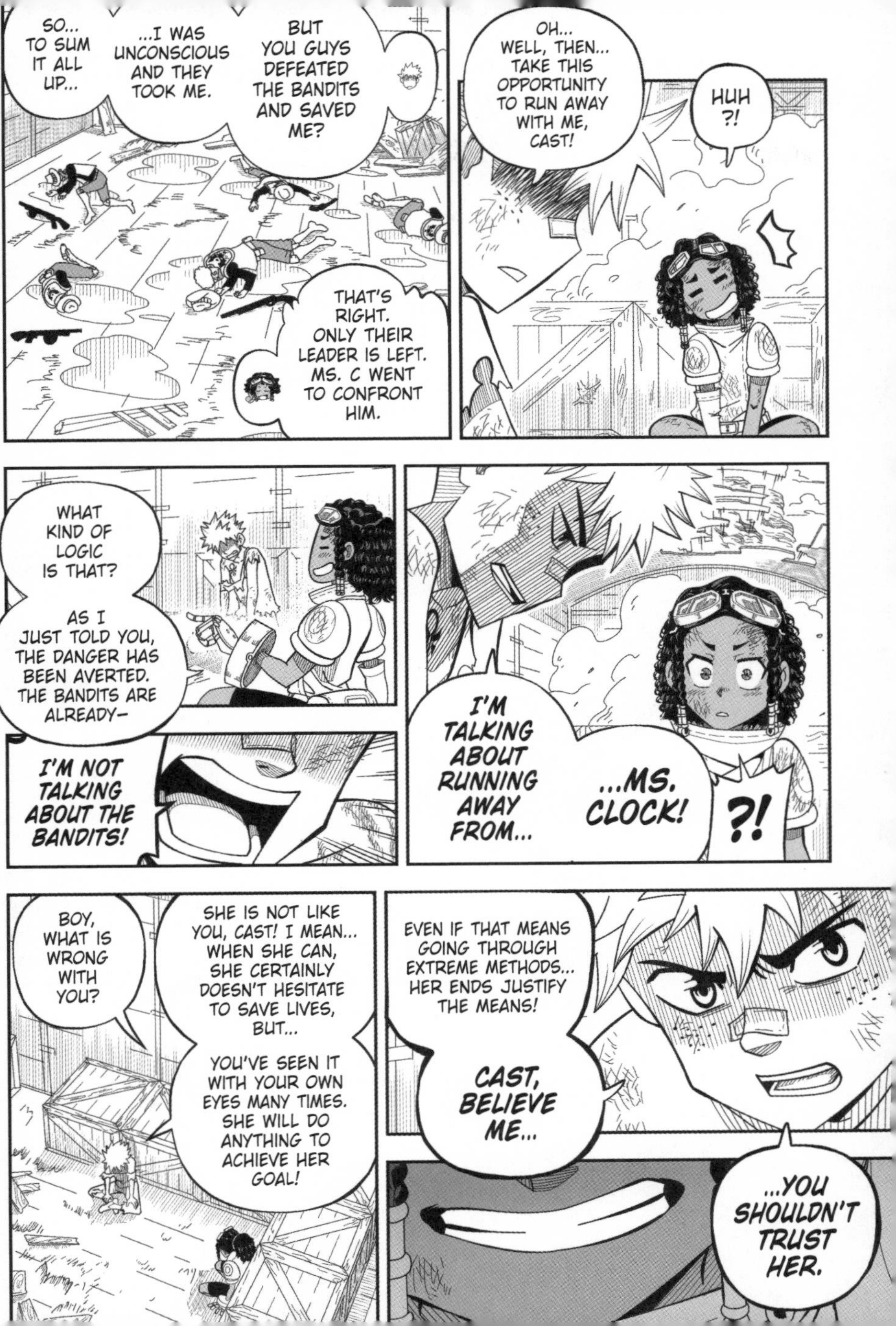
SO... TO SUM IT ALL UP...
...I WAS UNCONSCIOUS AND THEY TOOK ME.
BUT YOU GUYS DEFEATED THE BANDITS AND SAVED ME?
THAT'S RIGHT. ONLY THEIR LEADER IS LEFT. MS. C WENT TO CONFRONT HIM.
OH... WELL, THEN... TAKE THIS OPPORTUNITY TO RUN AWAY WITH ME, CAST!
HUH ?!
WHAT KIND OF LOGIC IS THAT?
AS I JUST TOLD YOU, THE DANGER HAS BEEN AVERTED. THE BANDITS ARE ALREADY—
I'M NOT TALKING ABOUT THE BANDITS!
I'M TALKING ABOUT RUNNING AWAY FROM...
...MS. CLOCK!
?!
BOY, WHAT IS WRONG WITH YOU?
SHE IS NOT LIKE YOU, CAST! I MEAN... WHEN SHE CAN, SHE CERTAINLY DOESN'T HESITATE TO SAVE LIVES, BUT...
YOU'VE SEEN IT WITH YOUR OWN EYES MANY TIMES. SHE WILL DO ANYTHING TO ACHIEVE HER GOAL!
EVEN IF THAT MEANS GOING THROUGH EXTREME METHODS... HER ENDS JUSTIFY THE MEANS!
CAST, BELIEVE ME...
...YOU SHOULDN'T TRUST HER.

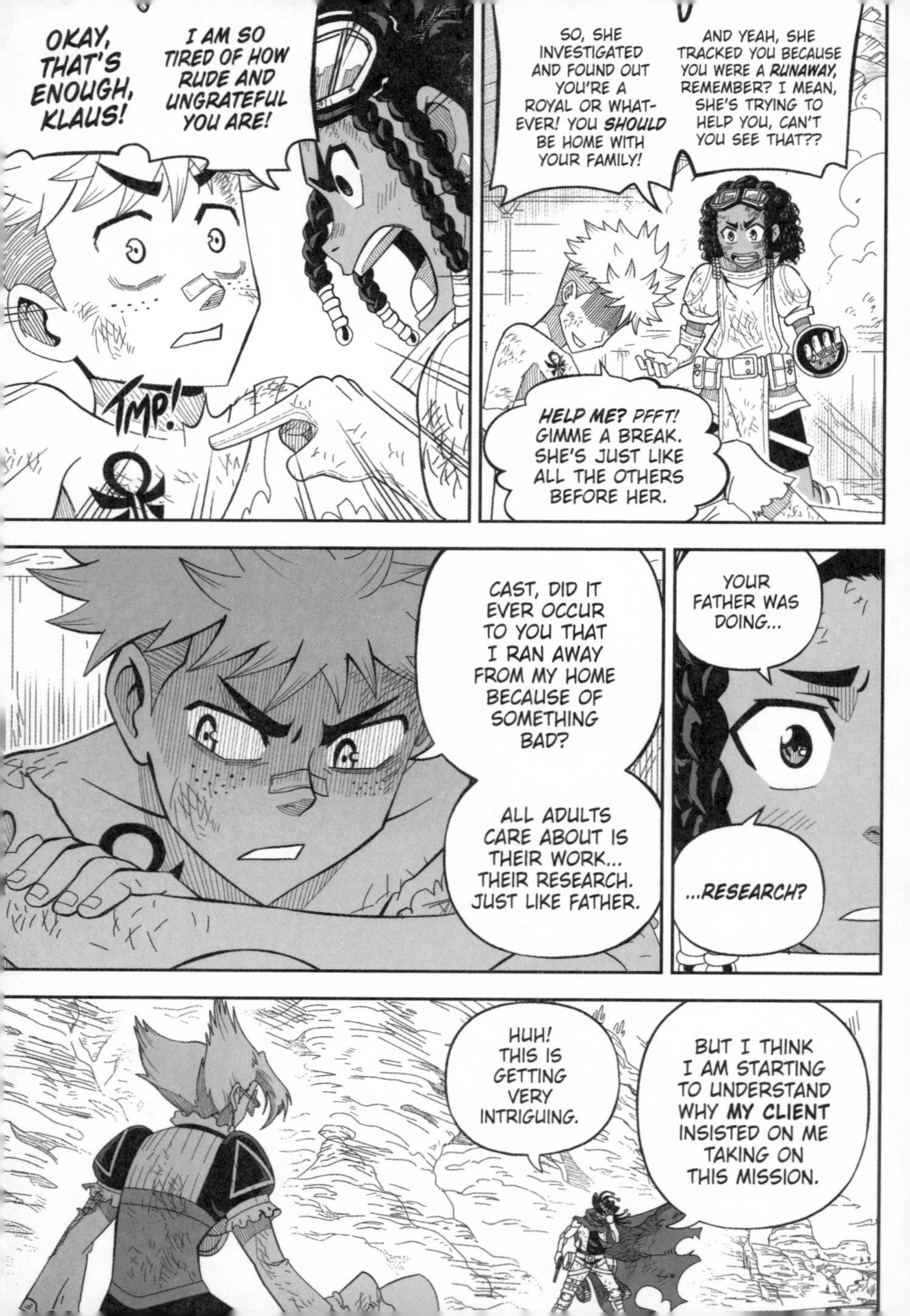
OKAY, THAT'S ENOUGH, KLAUS!
I AM SO TIRED OF HOW RUDE AND UNGRATEFUL YOU ARE!
TMP!
SO, SHE INVESTIGATED AND FOUND OUT YOU'RE A ROYAL OR WHAT-EVER! YOU SHOULD BE HOME WITH YOUR FAMILY!
AND YEAH, SHE TRACKED YOU BECAUSE YOU WERE A RUNAWAY, REMEMBER? I MEAN, SHE'S TRYING TO HELP YOU, CAN'T YOU SEE THAT??
HELP ME? PFFT! GIMME A BREAK. SHE'S JUST LIKE ALL THE OTHERS BEFORE HER.
CAST, DID IT EVER OCCUR TO YOU THAT I RAN AWAY FROM MY HOME BECAUSE OF SOMETHING BAD?
ALL ADULTS CARE ABOUT IS THEIR WORK... THEIR RESEARCH. JUST LIKE FATHER.
YOUR FATHER WAS DOING...
...RESEARCH?
HUH! THIS IS GETTING VERY INTRIGUING.
BUT I THINK I AM STARTING TO UNDERSTAND WHY MY CLIENT INSISTED ON ME TAKING ON THIS MISSION.

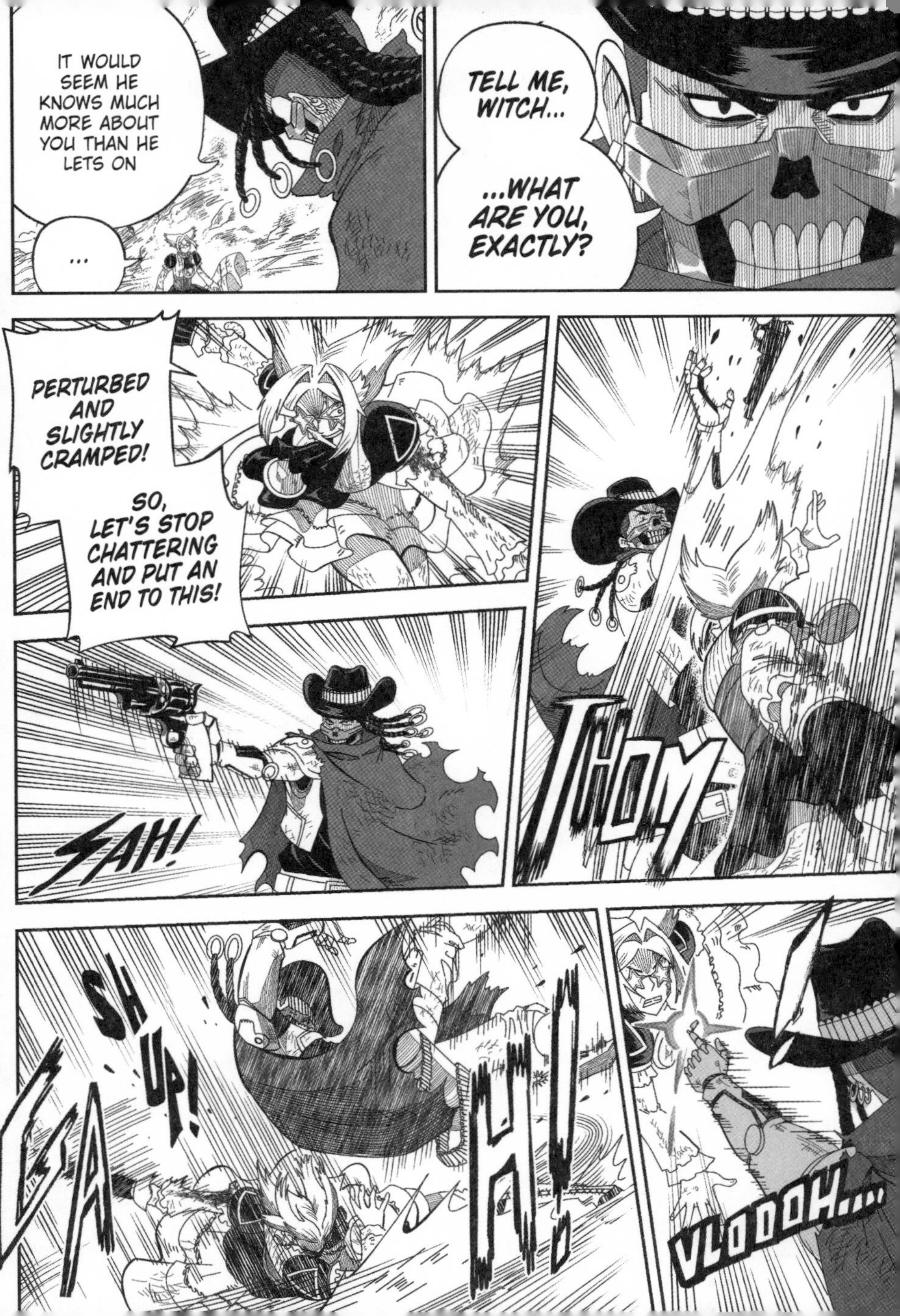
IT WOULD SEEM HE KNOWS MUCH MORE ABOUT YOU THAN HE LETS ON
...
TELL ME, WITCH...
...WHAT ARE YOU, EXACTLY?
PERTURBED AND SLIGHTLY CRAMPED!
SO, LET'S STOP CHATTERING AND PUT AN END TO THIS!
SAH!
THOM
SH UP!
GA
H!
VLOOOH...

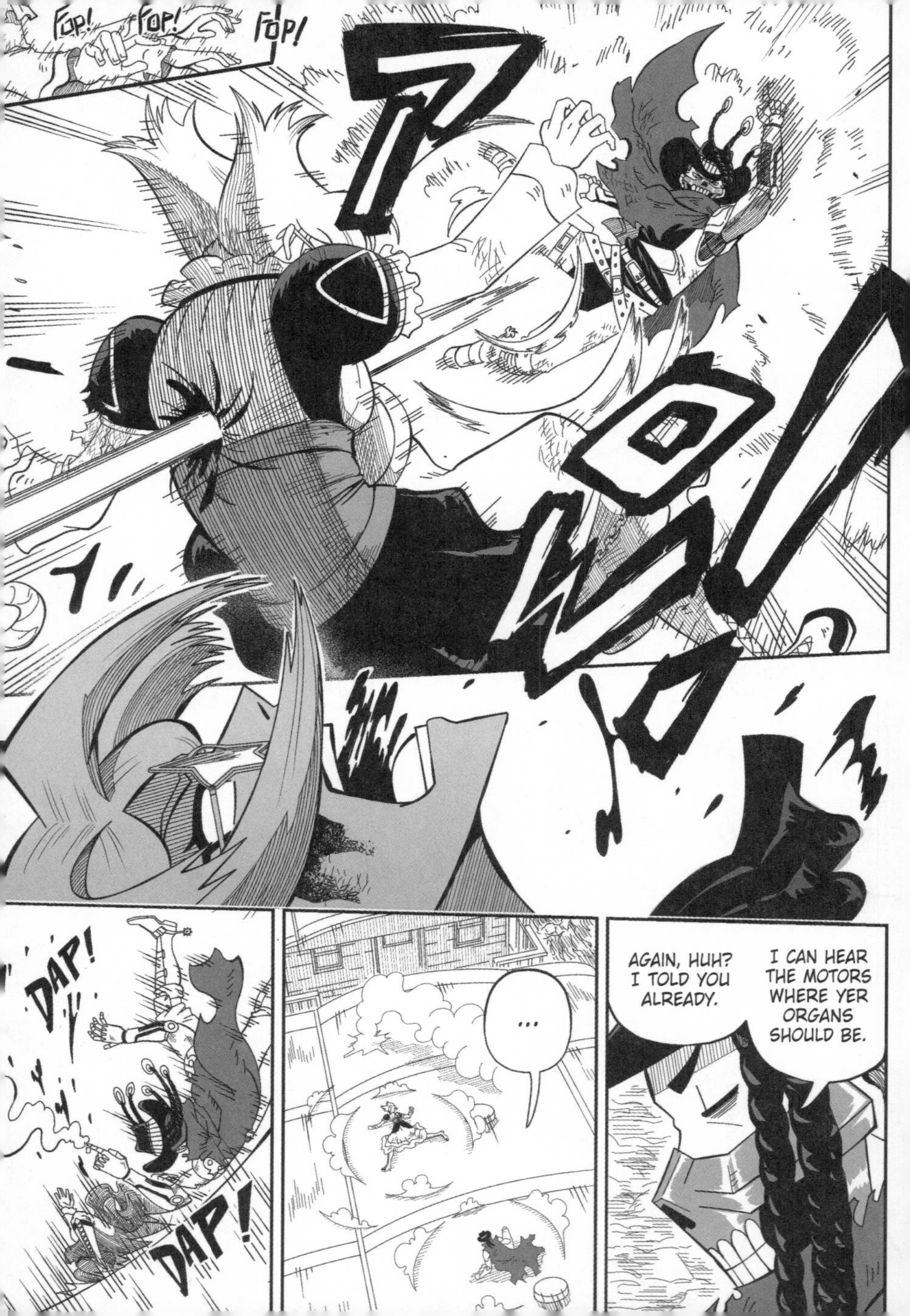
FOP!
FOP!
FOP!
DAP!
DAP!
...
AGAIN, HUH? I TOLD YOU ALREADY.
I CAN HEAR THE MOTORS WHERE YER ORGANS SHOULD BE.

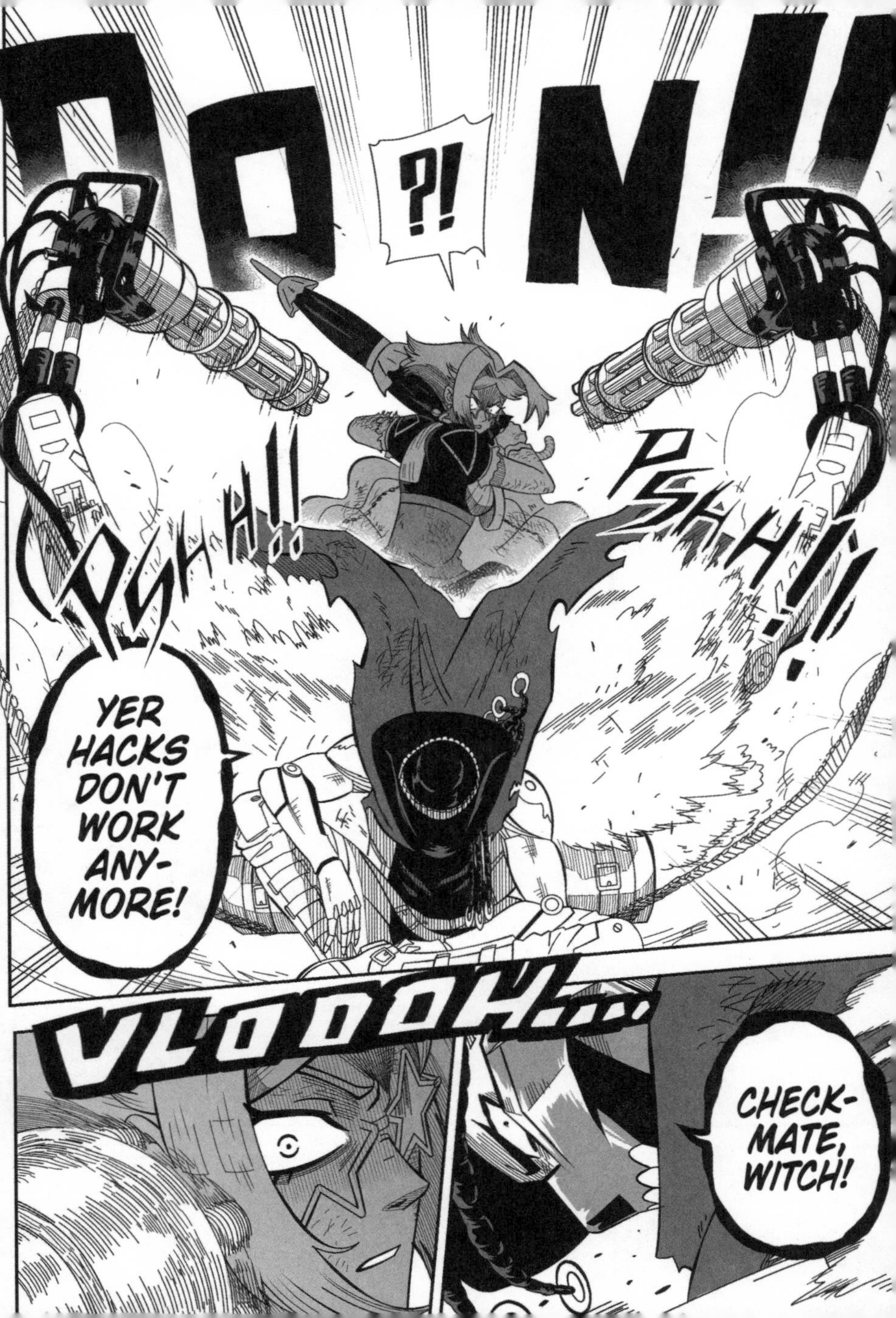
DOON!!
?!
PSHH!!
PSHH!!
YER HACKS DON'T WORK ANY-MORE!
VLOOOH....
CHECK-MATE, WITCH!

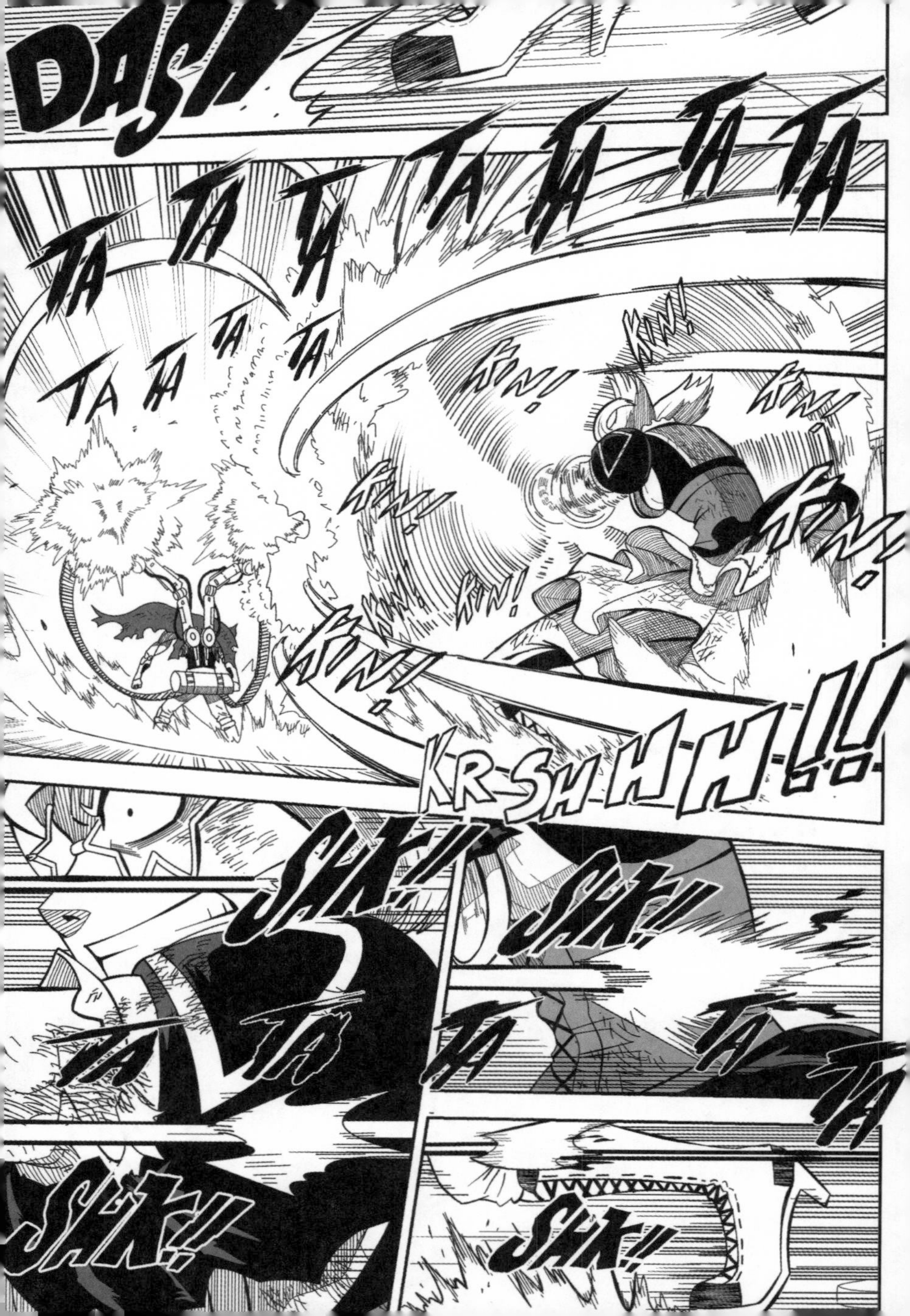
DASH
TA TA TA TA TA TA TA TA
TA TA TA TA
KIN! KIN! KIN! KIN! KIN! KIN! KIN! KIN!
KIN!
KR-SHHHH!!
SHK!!
SHK!!
TA TA TA
TA TA TA
SHK!!
SHK!!

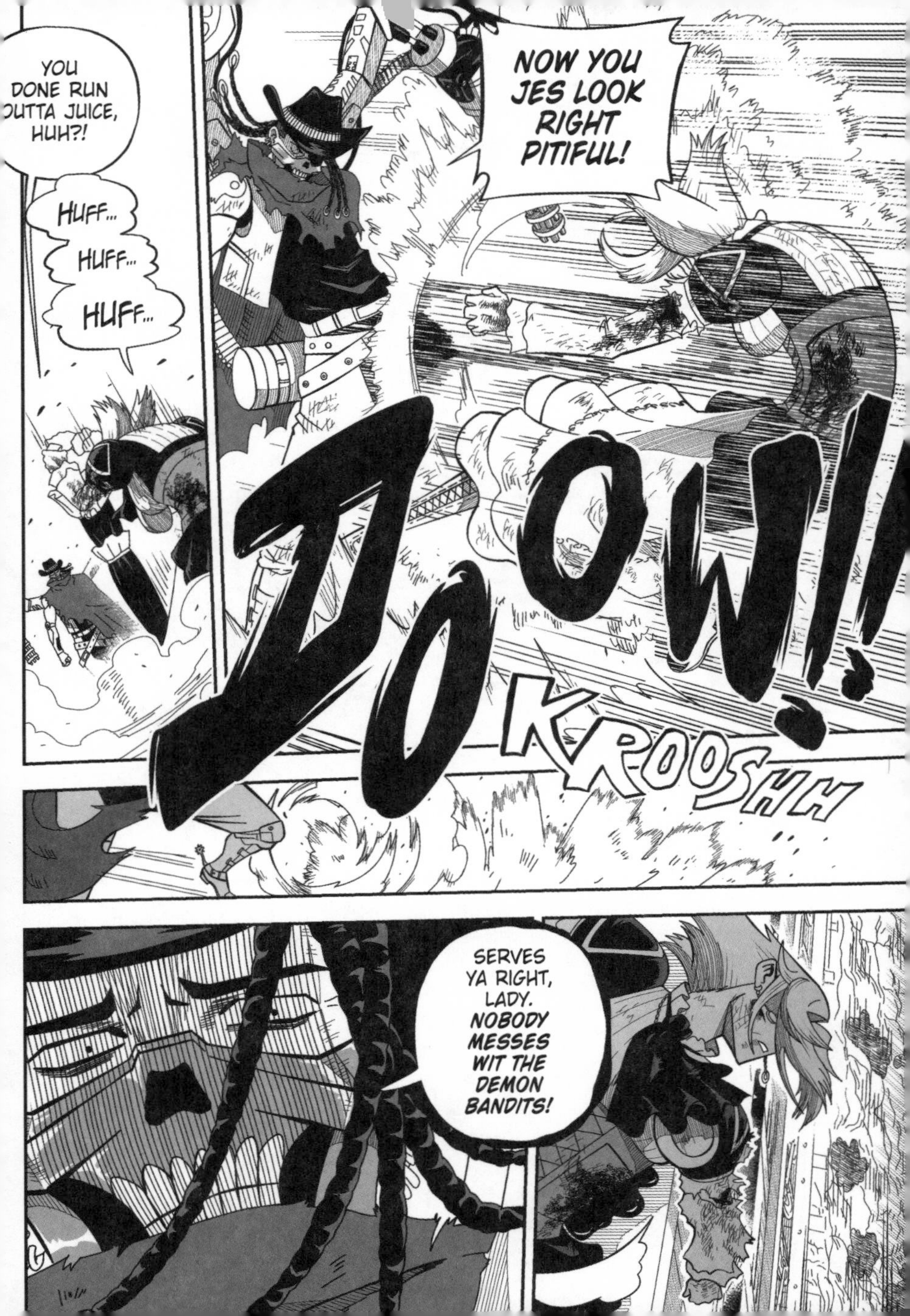
YOU DONE RUN OUTTA JUICE, HUH?!
HUFF... HUFF... HUFF...
NOW YOU JES LOOK RIGHT PITIFUL!
ZOOW!!
KROOSHH
SERVES YA RIGHT, LADY. NOBODY MESSES WIT THE DEMON BANDITS!

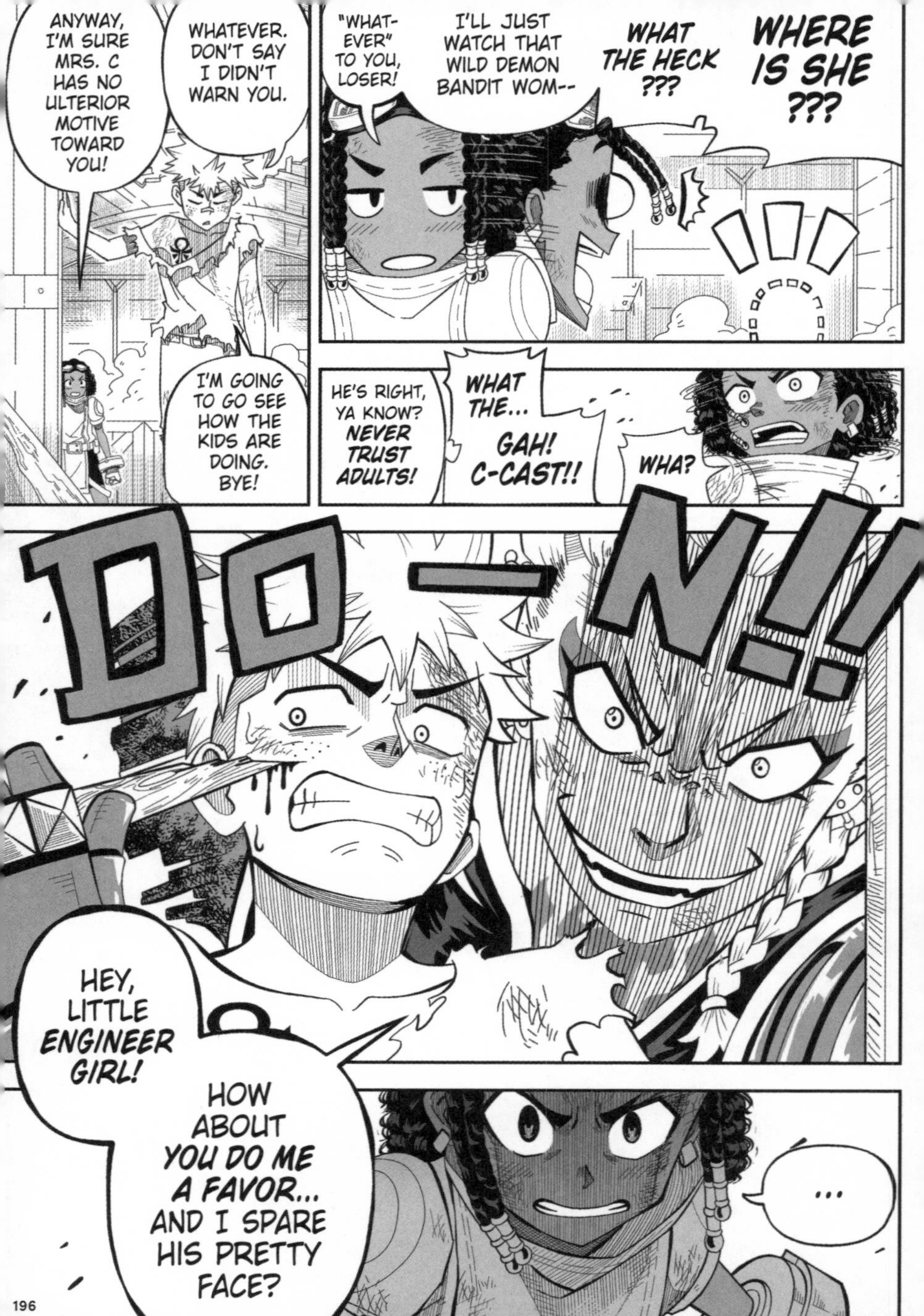
ANYWAY, I'M SURE MRS. C HAS NO ULTERIOR MOTIVE TOWARD YOU!
WHATEVER. DON'T SAY I DIDN'T WARN YOU.
I'M GOING TO GO SEE HOW THE KIDS ARE DOING. BYE!
"WHAT-EVER" TO YOU, LOSER!
I'LL JUST WATCH THAT WILD DEMON BANDIT WOM--
WHAT THE HECK ???
WHERE IS SHE ???
HE'S RIGHT, YA KNOW? NEVER TRUST ADULTS!
WHAT THE... GAH! C-CAST!!
WHA?
DO-N!!
HEY, LITTLE ENGINEER GIRL!
HOW ABOUT YOU DO ME A FAVOR... AND I SPARE HIS PRETTY FACE?
...

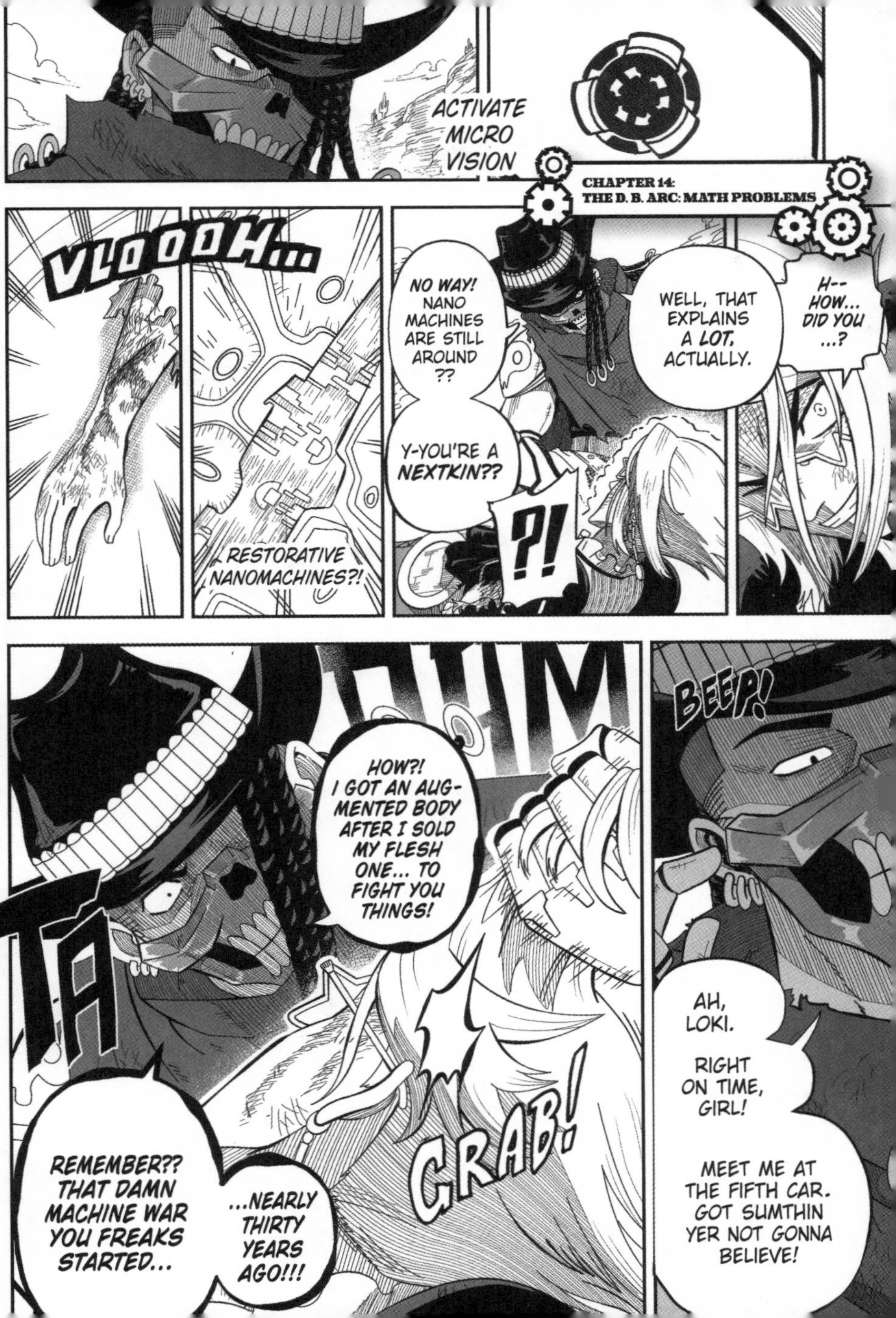
ACTIVATE MICRO VISION
CHAPTER 14: THE D. B. ARC: MATH PROBLEMS
VLOOOH...
RESTORATIVE NANOMACHINES?!
NO WAY! NANO MACHINES ARE STILL AROUND ??
Y-YOU'RE A NEXTKIN??
?!
WELL, THAT EXPLAINS A LOT, ACTUALLY.
H-- HOW... DID YOU ...?
TA
HOW?! I GOT AN AUG-MENTED BODY AFTER I SOLD MY FLESH ONE... TO FIGHT YOU THINGS!
REMEMBER?? THAT DAMN MACHINE WAR YOU FREAKS STARTED...
...NEARLY THIRTY YEARS AGO!!!
GRAB!
BEEP!
AH, LOKI.
RIGHT ON TIME, GIRL!
MEET ME AT THE FIFTH CAR. GOT SUMTHIN YER NOT GONNA BELIEVE!

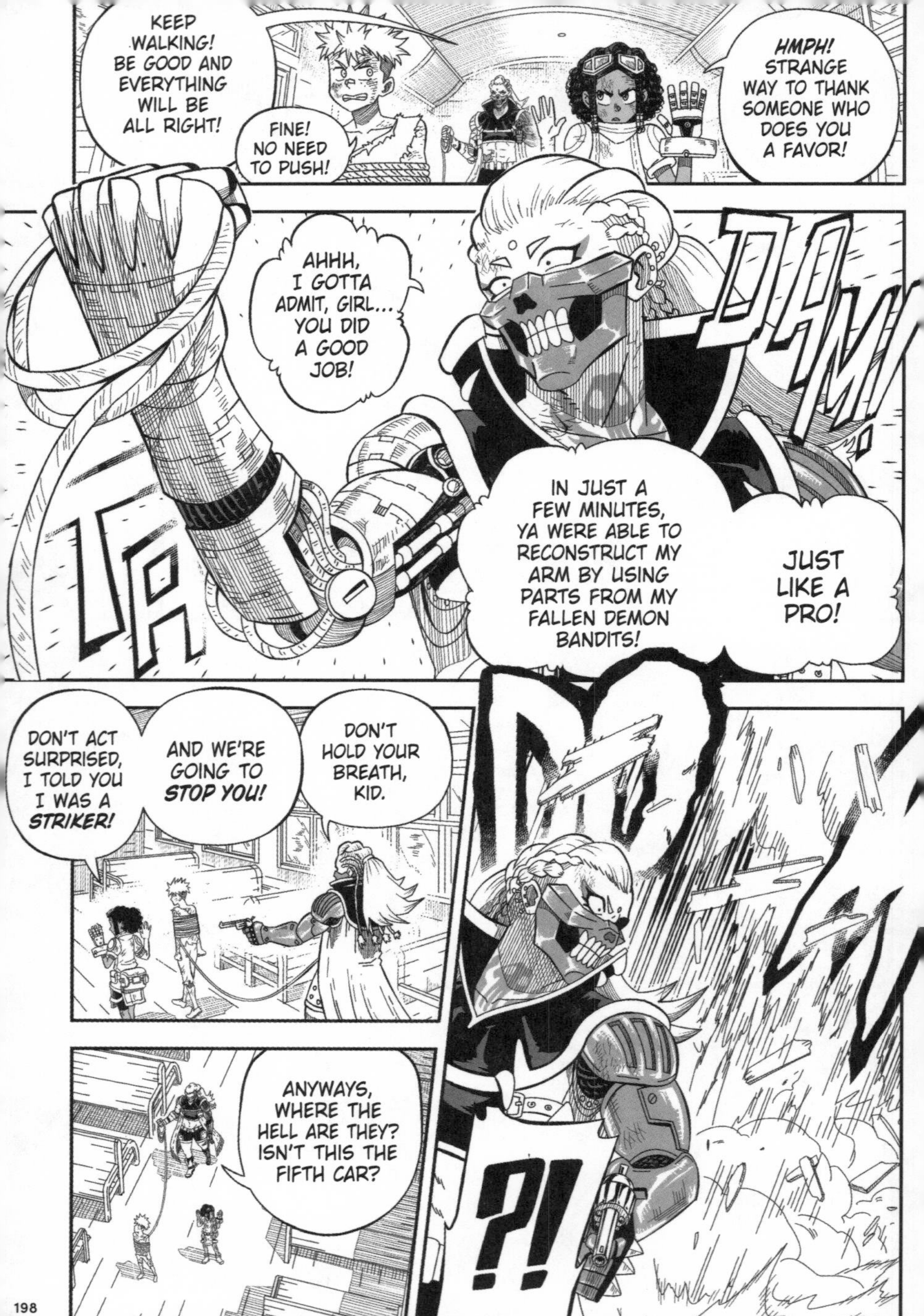
KEEP WALKING! BE GOOD AND EVERYTHING WILL BE ALL RIGHT!
FINE! NO NEED TO PUSH!
HMPH! STRANGE WAY TO THANK SOMEONE WHO DOES YOU A FAVOR!
AHHH, I GOTTA ADMIT, GIRL... YOU DID A GOOD JOB!
TA
DAM!
IN JUST A FEW MINUTES, YA WERE ABLE TO RECONSTRUCT MY ARM BY USING PARTS FROM MY FALLEN DEMON BANDITS!
JUST LIKE A PRO!
DON'T ACT SURPRISED, I TOLD YOU I WAS A STRIKER!
AND WE'RE GOING TO STOP YOU!
DON'T HOLD YOUR BREATH, KID.
ANYWAYS, WHERE THE HELL ARE THEY? ISN'T THIS THE FIFTH CAR?
?!

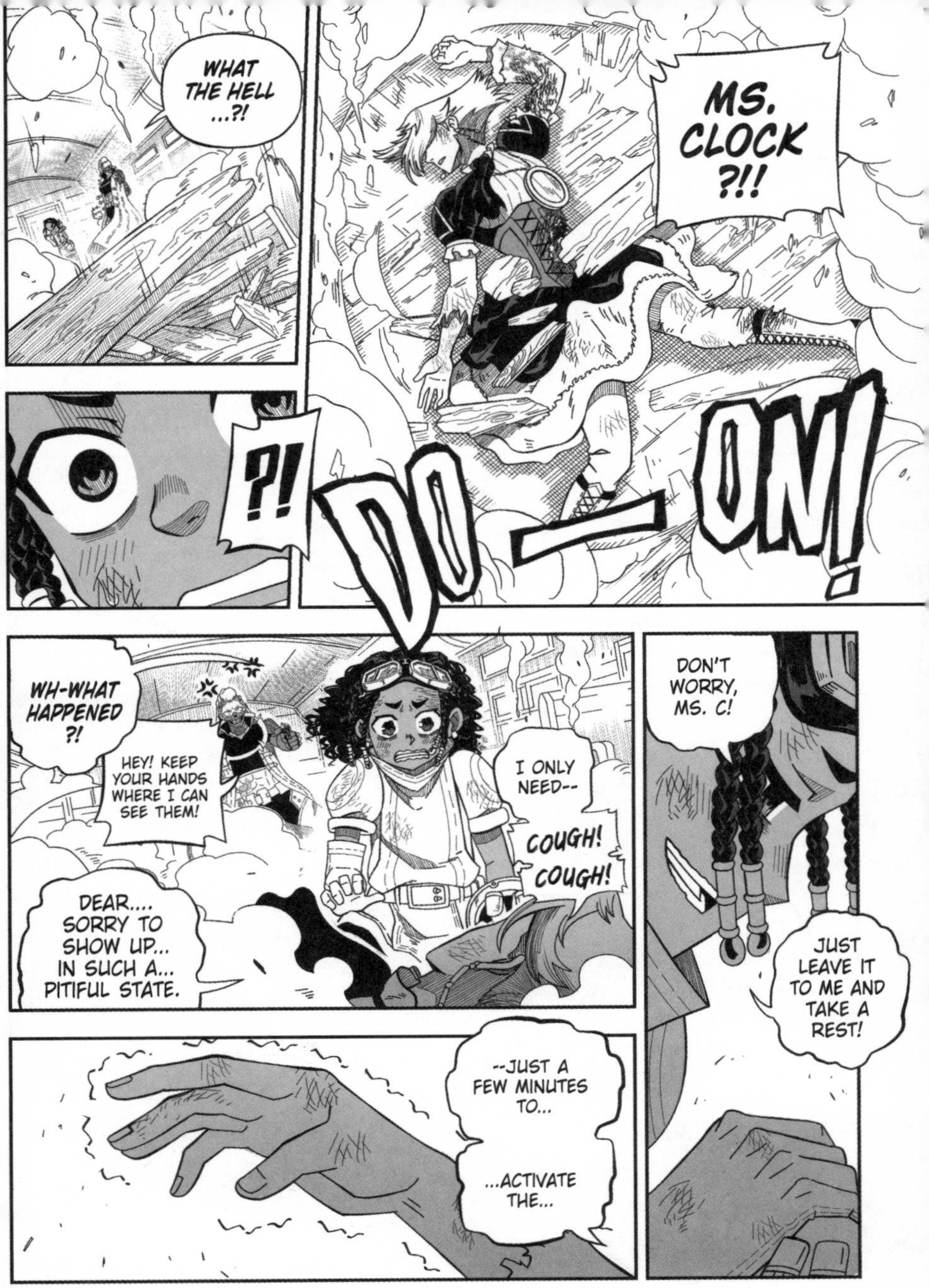

WHAT THE HELL ...?!
MS. CLOCK ?!!
?!
DO—ON!
WH-WHAT HAPPENED ?!
HEY! KEEP YOUR HANDS WHERE I CAN SEE THEM!
DEAR.... SORRY TO SHOW UP... IN SUCH A... PITIFUL STATE.
I ONLY NEED--
COUGH! COUGH!
DON'T WORRY, MS. C!
JUST LEAVE IT TO ME AND TAKE A REST!
--JUST A FEW MINUTES TO...
...ACTIVATE THE...

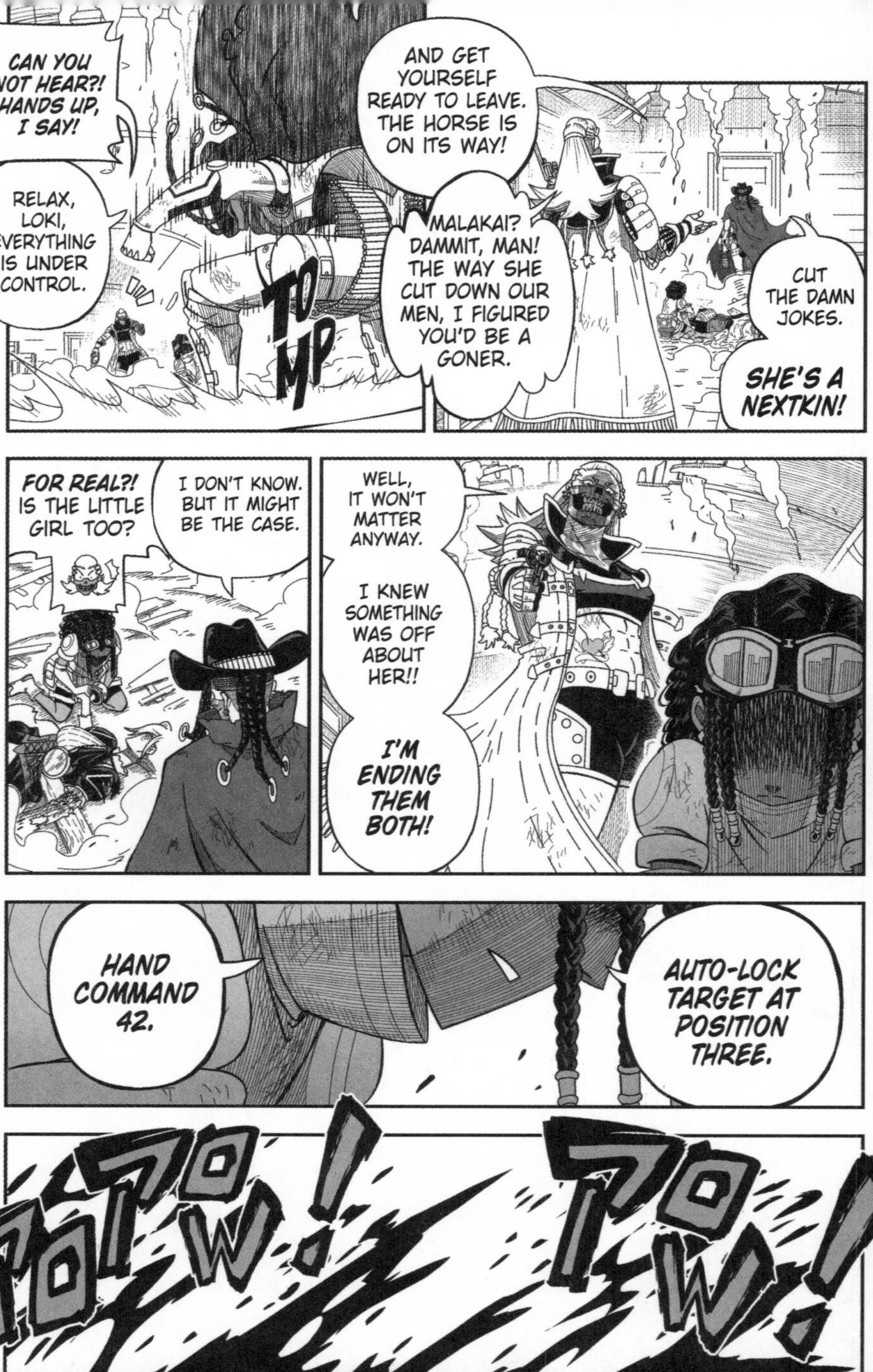
CAN YOU NOT HEAR?! HANDS UP, I SAY!
RELAX, LOKI, EVERYTHING IS UNDER CONTROL.
TOMP
AND GET YOURSELF READY TO LEAVE. THE HORSE IS ON ITS WAY!
MALAKAI? DAMMIT, MAN! THE WAY SHE CUT DOWN OUR MEN, I FIGURED YOU'D BE A GONER.
CUT THE DAMN JOKES.
SHE'S A NEXTKIN!
FOR REAL?! IS THE LITTLE GIRL TOO?
I DON'T KNOW. BUT IT MIGHT BE THE CASE.
WELL, IT WON'T MATTER ANYWAY.
I KNEW SOMETHING WAS OFF ABOUT HER!!
I'M ENDING THEM BOTH!
HAND COMMAND 42.
AUTO-LOCK TARGET AT POSITION THREE.
POW! POW! POW!

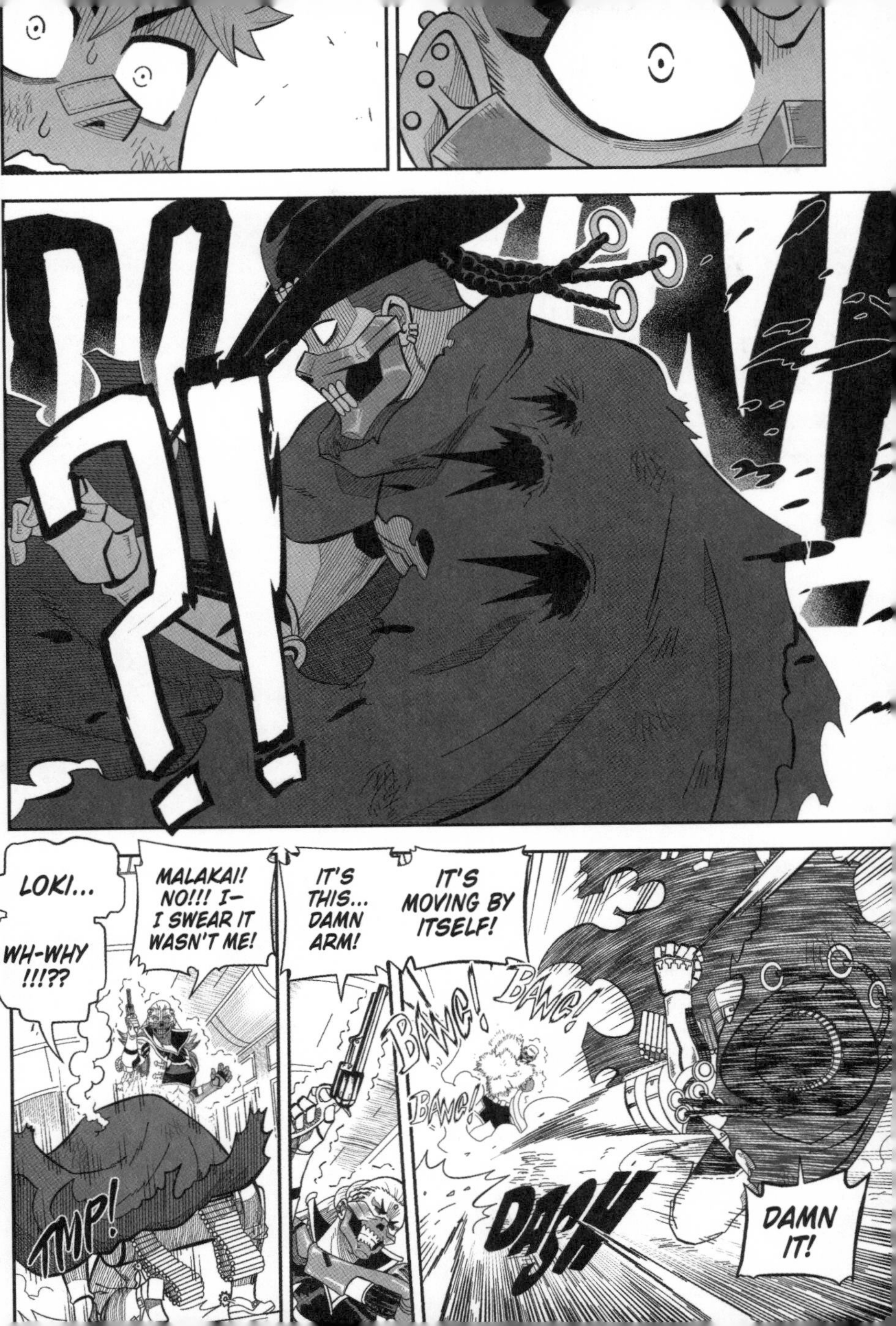
?!
LOKI...
WH-WHY !!!??
MALAKAI! NO!!! I— I SWEAR IT WASN'T ME!
TMP!
IT'S THIS... DAMN ARM!
IT'S MOVING BY ITSELF!
BANG!
BANG!
BANG!
BANG!
DASH
DAMN IT!

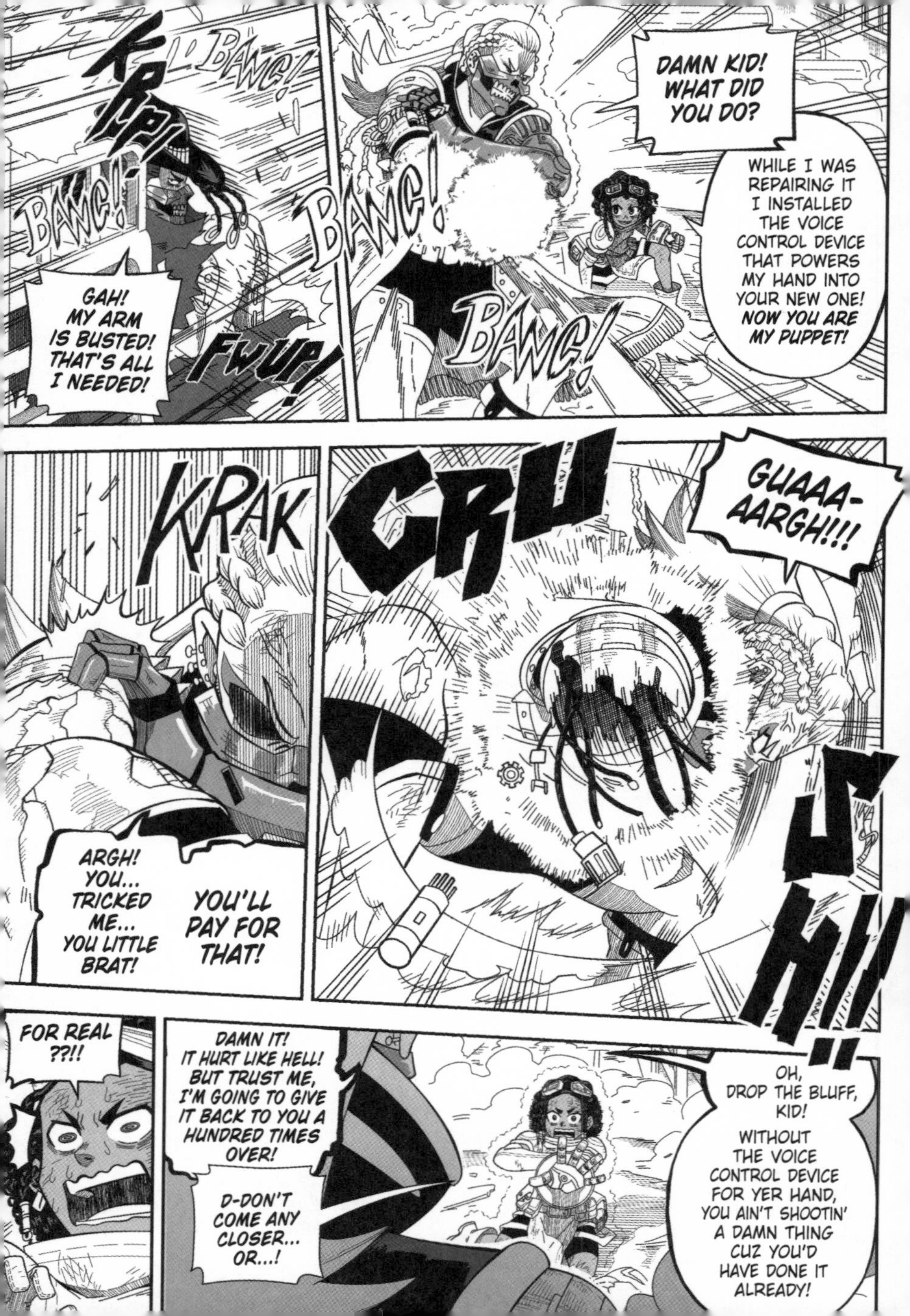
KRPL!
BANG!
BANG!
GAH! MY ARM IS BUSTED! THAT'S ALL I NEEDED!
FWUP!
BANG!
DAMN KID! WHAT DID YOU DO?
WHILE I WAS REPAIRING IT I INSTALLED THE VOICE CONTROL DEVICE THAT POWERS MY HAND INTO YOUR NEW ONE! NOW YOU ARE MY PUPPET!
BANG!
KRAK
CRU
GUAAAA-AARGH!!!
SH!!
ARGH! YOU... TRICKED ME... YOU LITTLE BRAT!
YOU'LL PAY FOR THAT!
FOR REAL ??!!
DAMN IT! IT HURT LIKE HELL! BUT TRUST ME, I'M GOING TO GIVE IT BACK TO YOU A HUNDRED TIMES OVER!
D-DON'T COME ANY CLOSER... OR...!
OH, DROP THE BLUFF, KID!
WITHOUT THE VOICE CONTROL DEVICE FOR YER HAND, YOU AIN'T SHOOTIN' A DAMN THING CUZ YOU'D HAVE DONE IT ALREADY!

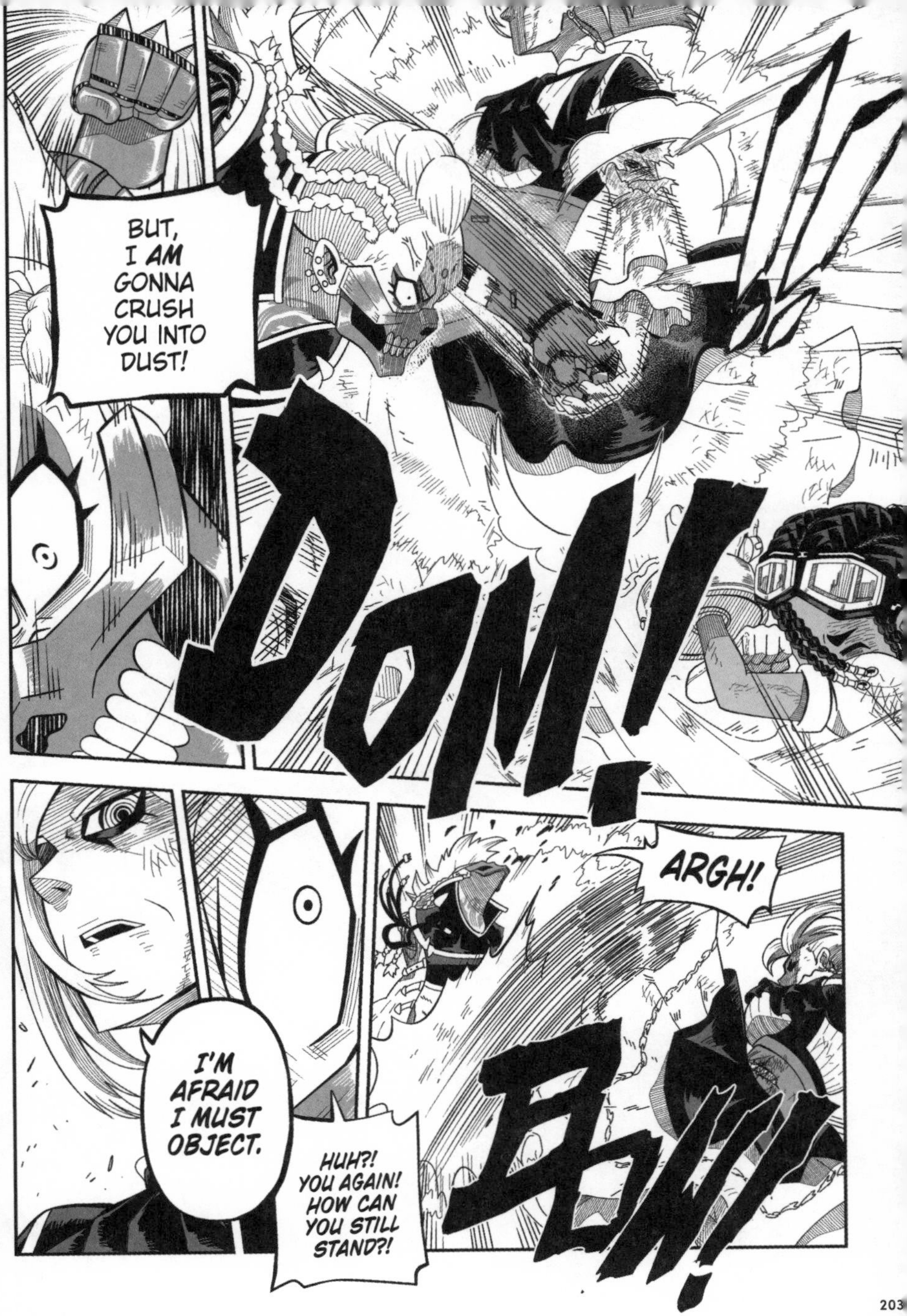
BUT, I AM GONNA CRUSH YOU INTO DUST!
DOM!
I'M AFRAID I MUST OBJECT.
ARGH!
HUH?! YOU AGAIN! HOW CAN YOU STILL STAND?!
BAM!!

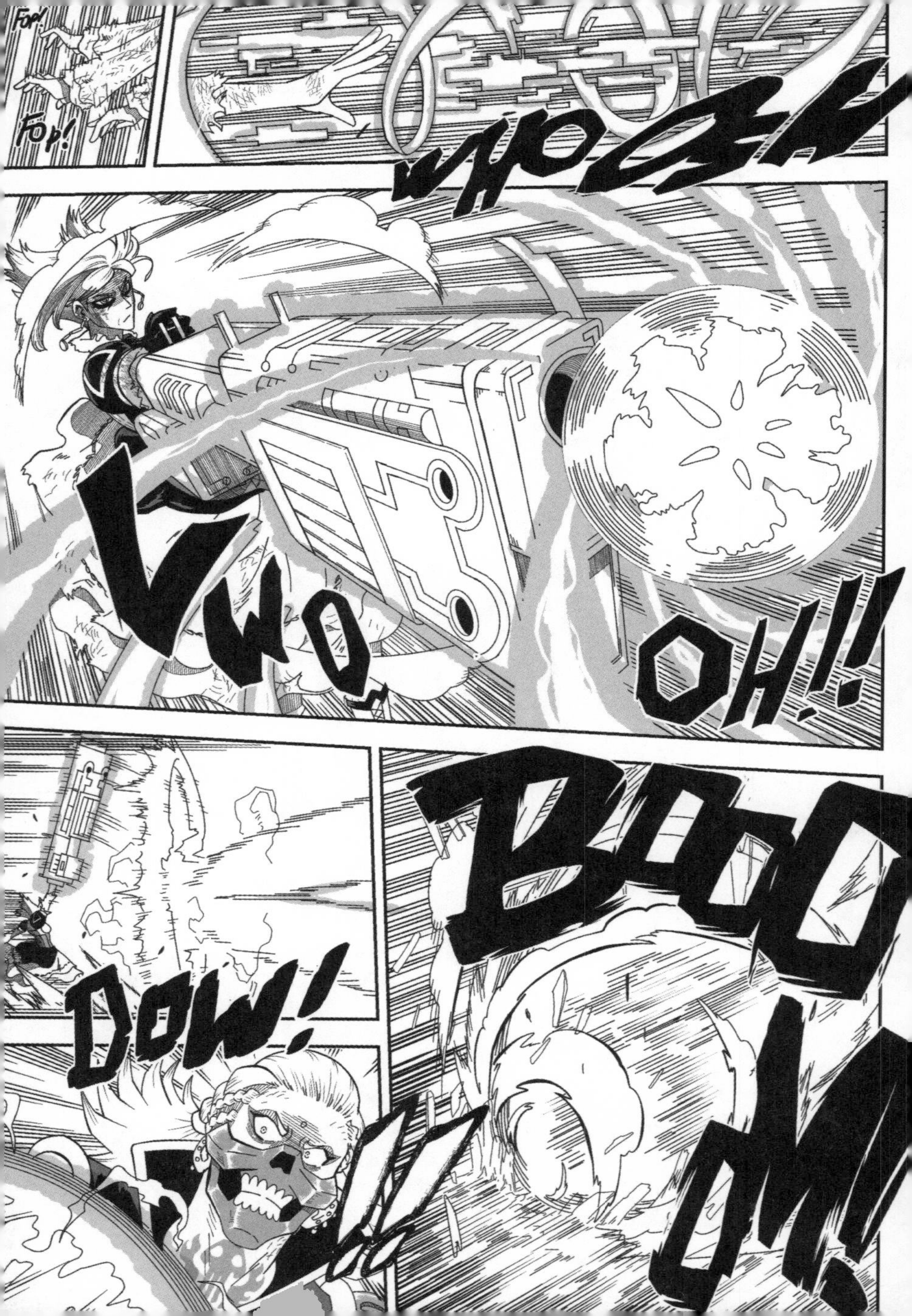

Fop!
Fop!
WHOOSH
VWOOH!!
DOW!
!!
BOOOM!!

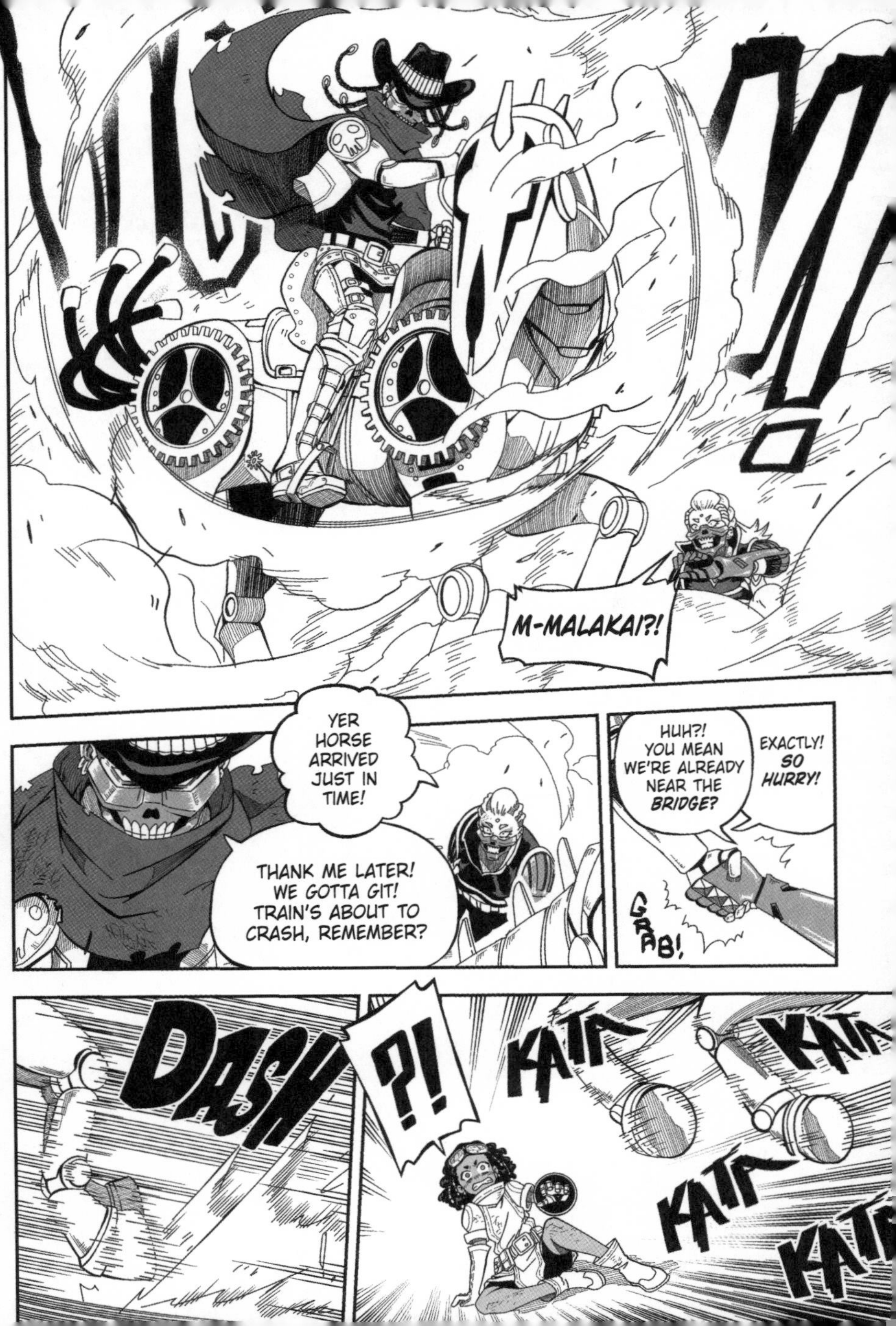
M-MALAKAI?!
YER HORSE ARRIVED JUST IN TIME!
THANK ME LATER! WE GOTTA GIT! TRAIN'S ABOUT TO CRASH, REMEMBER?
HUH?! YOU MEAN WE'RE ALREADY NEAR THE *BRIDGE?*
EXACTLY! ***SO HURRY!***
GRAB!
DASH
?!
KATA KATA KATA

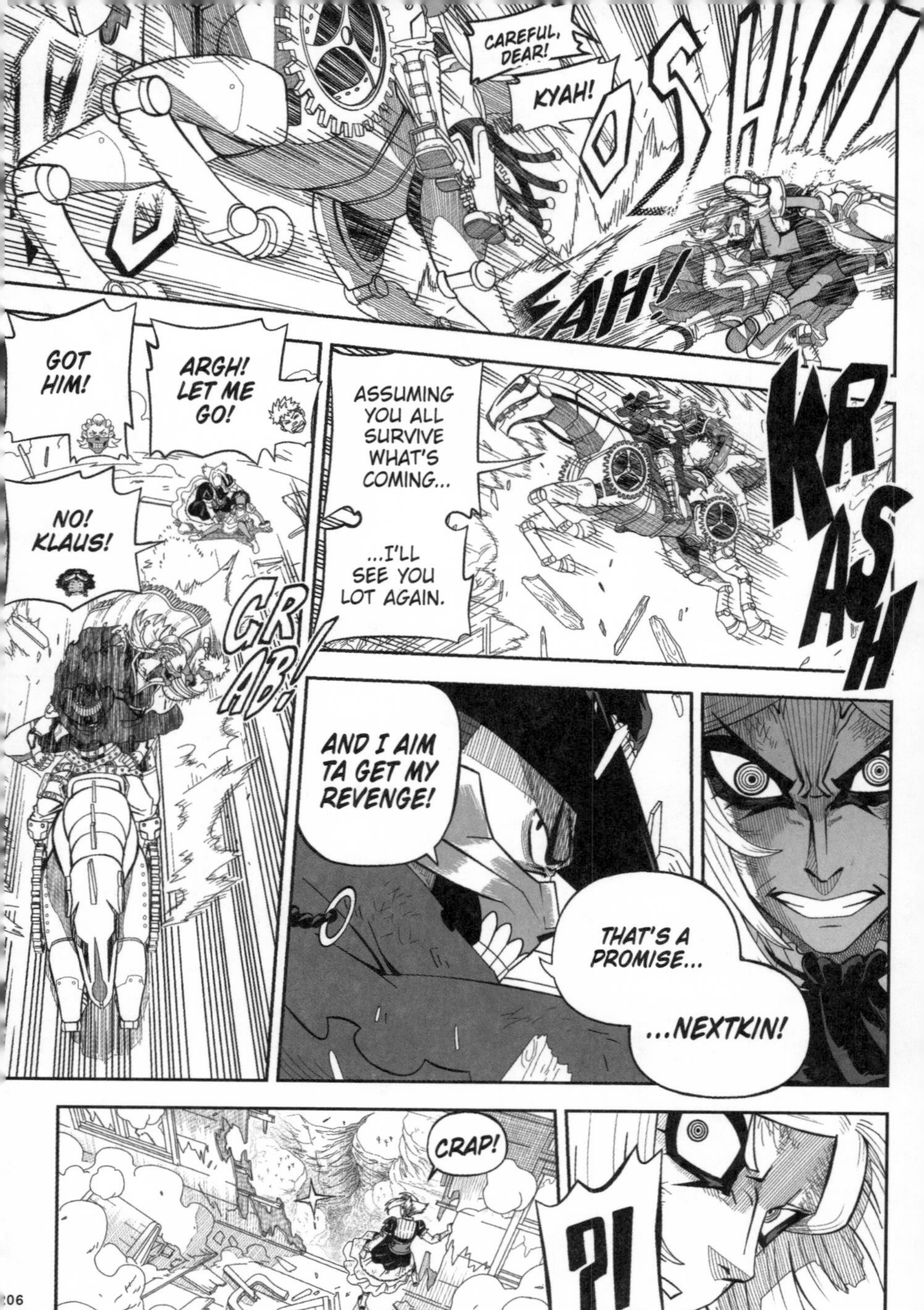
CAREFUL, DEAR!
KYAH!
GOT HIM!
ARGH! LET ME GO!
NO! KLAUS!
ASSUMING YOU ALL SURVIVE WHAT'S COMING...
...I'LL SEE YOU LOT AGAIN.
AND I AIM TA GET MY REVENGE!
THAT'S A PROMISE...
...NEXTKIN!
CRAP!
?!

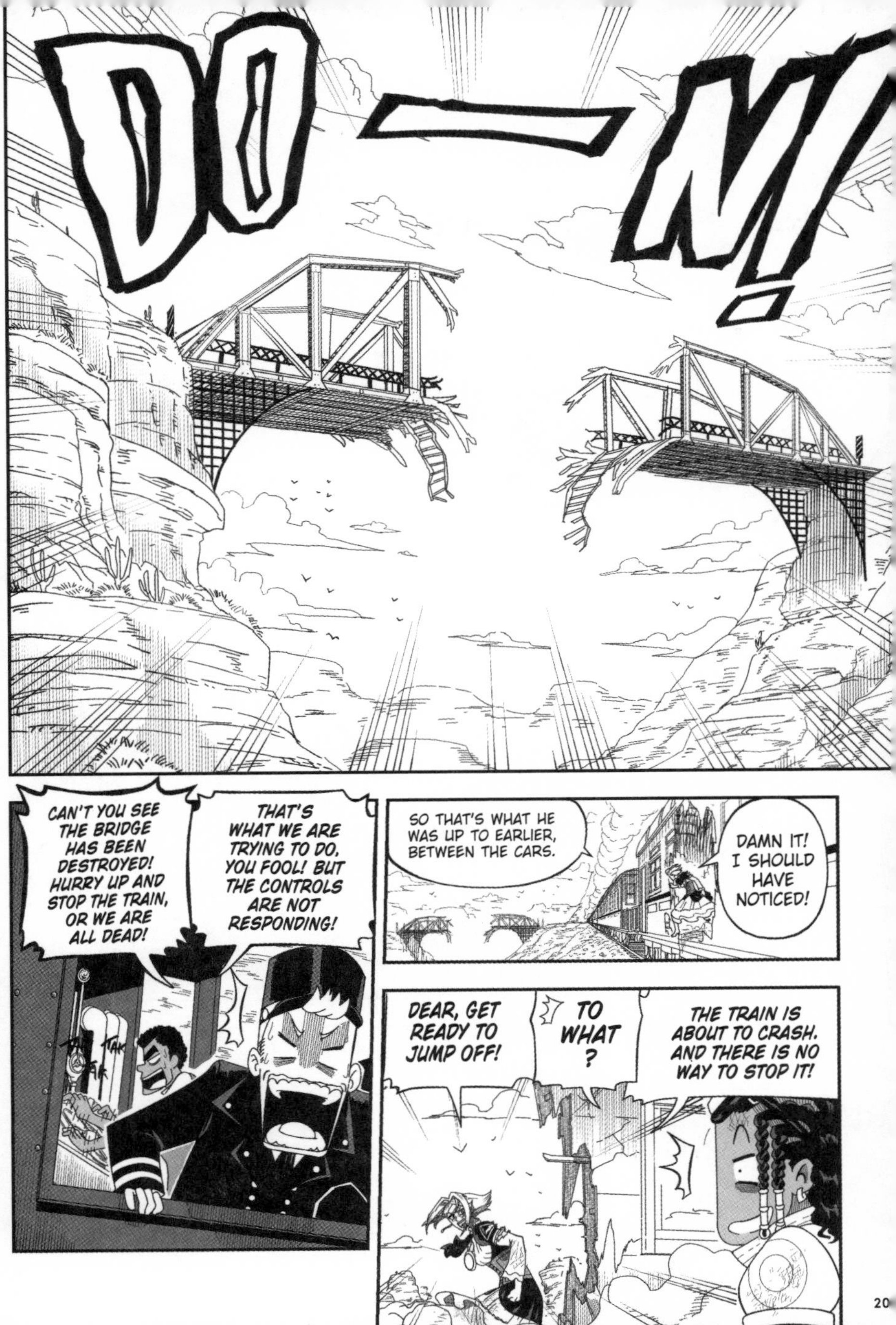
DO—M!
CAN'T YOU SEE THE BRIDGE HAS BEEN DESTROYED! HURRY UP AND STOP THE TRAIN, OR WE ARE ALL DEAD!
THAT'S WHAT WE ARE TRYING TO DO, YOU FOOL! BUT THE CONTROLS ARE NOT RESPONDING!
SO THAT'S WHAT HE WAS UP TO EARLIER, BETWEEN THE CARS.
DAMN IT! I SHOULD HAVE NOTICED!
DEAR, GET READY TO JUMP OFF!
TO WHAT?
THE TRAIN IS ABOUT TO CRASH. AND THERE IS NO WAY TO STOP IT!

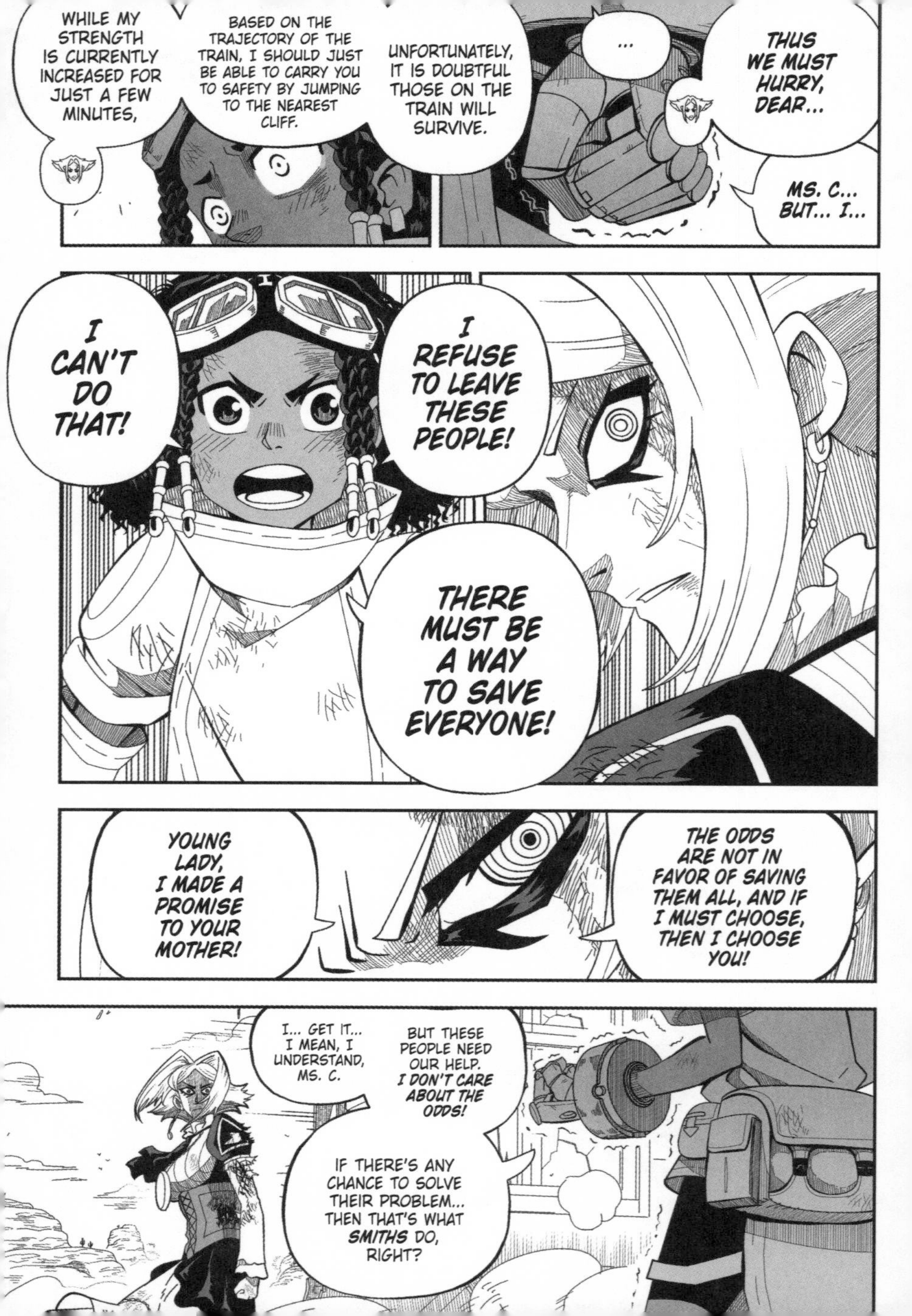
WHILE MY STRENGTH IS CURRENTLY INCREASED FOR JUST A FEW MINUTES,
BASED ON THE TRAJECTORY OF THE TRAIN, I SHOULD JUST BE ABLE TO CARRY YOU TO SAFETY BY JUMPING TO THE NEAREST CLIFF.
UNFORTUNATELY, IT IS DOUBTFUL THOSE ON THE TRAIN WILL SURVIVE.
...
THUS WE MUST HURRY, DEAR...
MS. C... BUT... I...
I CAN'T DO THAT!
I REFUSE TO LEAVE THESE PEOPLE!
THERE MUST BE A WAY TO SAVE EVERYONE!
YOUNG LADY, I MADE A PROMISE TO YOUR MOTHER!
THE ODDS ARE NOT IN FAVOR OF SAVING THEM ALL, AND IF I MUST CHOOSE, THEN I CHOOSE YOU!
I... GET IT... I MEAN, I UNDERSTAND, MS. C.
BUT THESE PEOPLE NEED OUR HELP. I DON'T CARE ABOUT THE ODDS!
IF THERE'S ANY CHANCE TO SOLVE THEIR PROBLEM... THEN THAT'S WHAT SMITHS DO, RIGHT?

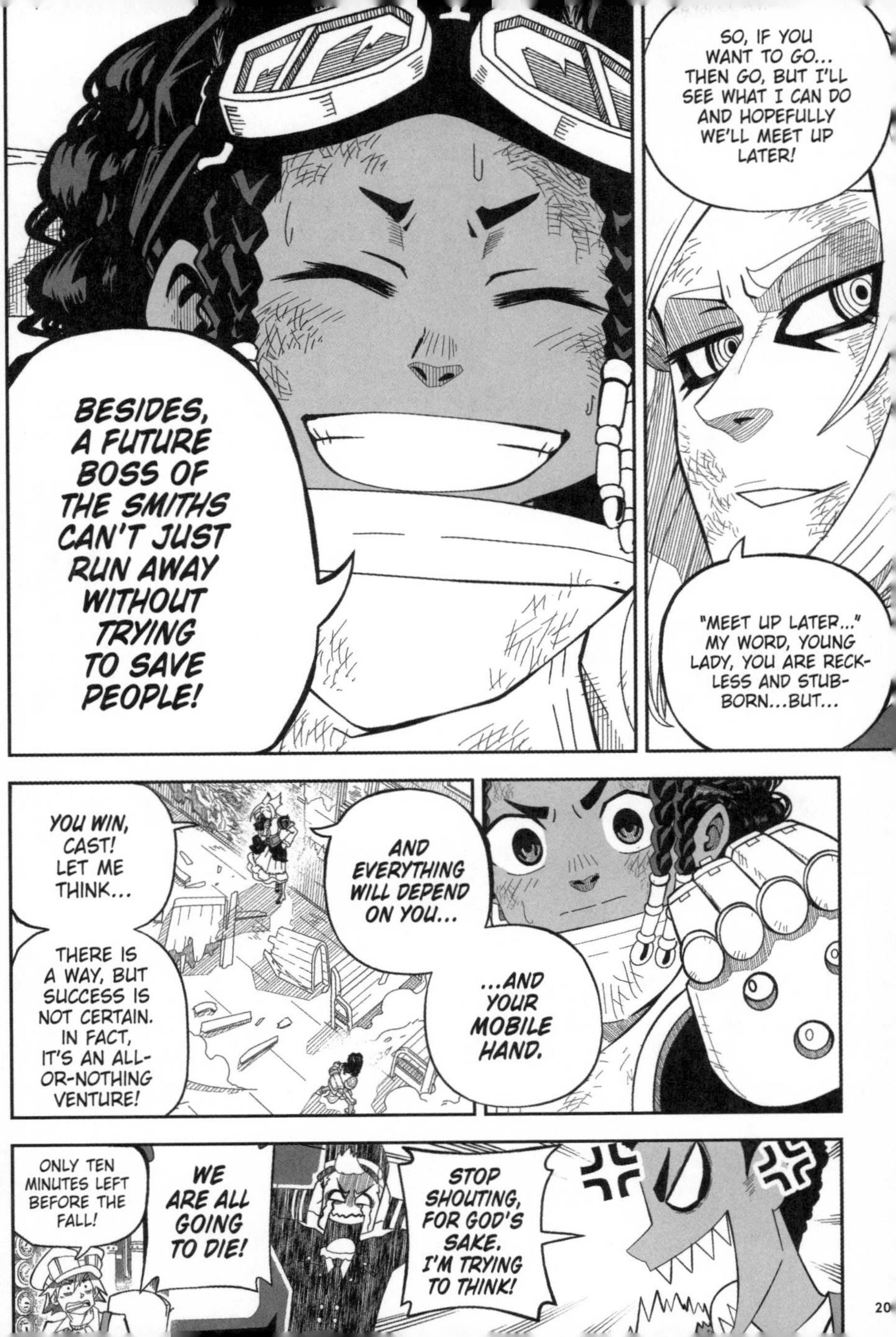
BESIDES, A FUTURE BOSS OF THE SMITHS CAN'T JUST RUN AWAY WITHOUT TRYING TO SAVE PEOPLE!
SO, IF YOU WANT TO GO... THEN GO, BUT I'LL SEE WHAT I CAN DO AND HOPEFULLY WE'LL MEET UP LATER!
"MEET UP LATER..." MY WORD, YOUNG LADY, YOU ARE RECK-LESS AND STUB-BORN...BUT...
YOU WIN, CAST! LET ME THINK...
THERE IS A WAY, BUT SUCCESS IS NOT CERTAIN. IN FACT, IT'S AN ALL-OR-NOTHING VENTURE!
AND EVERYTHING WILL DEPEND ON YOU...
...AND YOUR MOBILE HAND.
ONLY TEN MINUTES LEFT BEFORE THE FALL!
WE ARE ALL GOING TO DIE!
STOP SHOUTING, FOR GOD'S SAKE. I'M TRYING TO THINK!

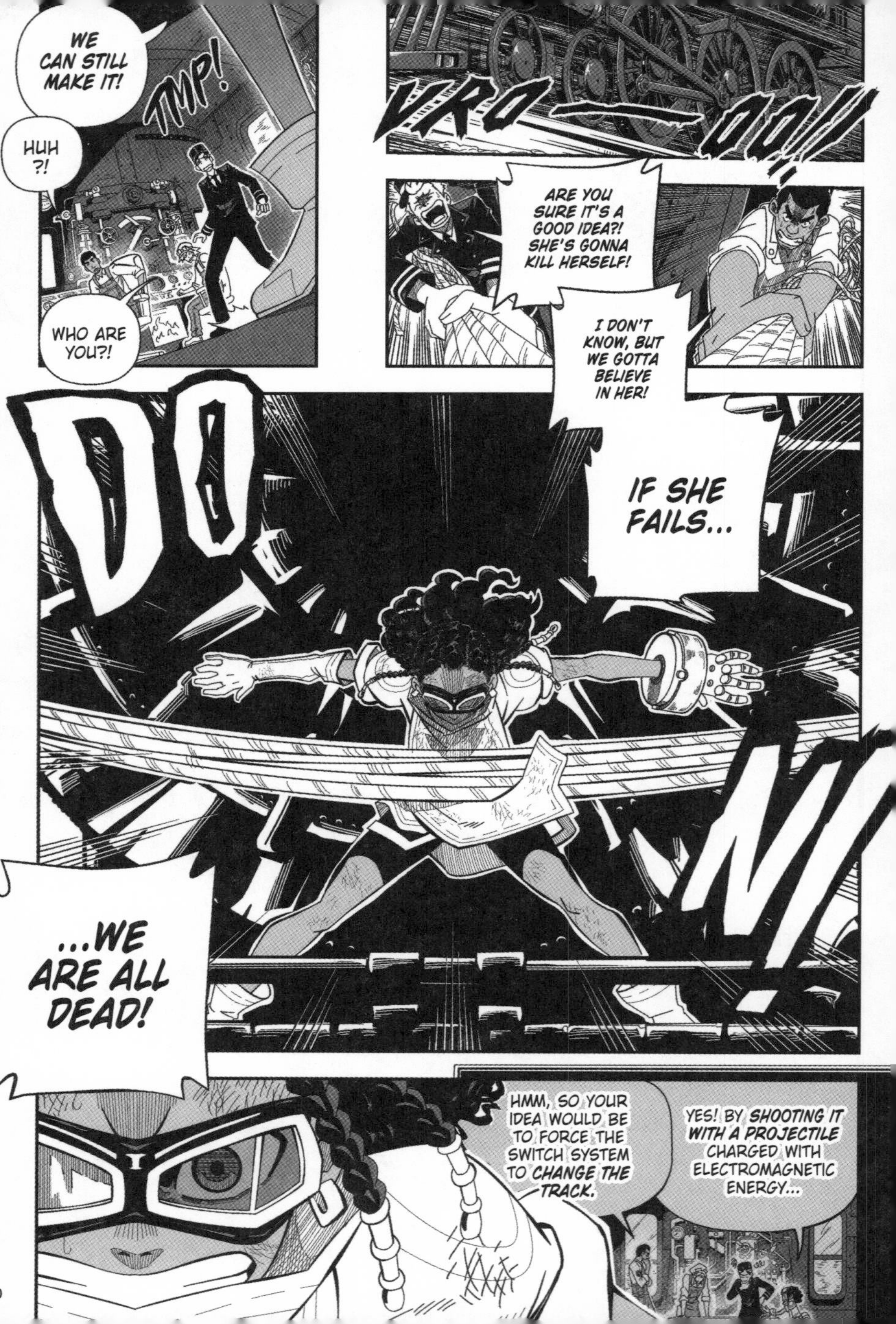
WE CAN STILL MAKE IT!
TMP!
HUH ?!
WHO ARE YOU?!
VRO——OO!!
ARE YOU SURE IT'S A GOOD IDEA?! SHE'S GONNA KILL HERSELF!
I DON'T KNOW, BUT WE GOTTA BELIEVE IN HER!
DO
IF SHE FAILS...
N!!
...WE ARE ALL DEAD!
HMM, SO YOUR IDEA WOULD BE TO FORCE THE SWITCH SYSTEM TO CHANGE THE TRACK.
YES! BY SHOOTING IT WITH A PROJECTILE CHARGED WITH ELECTROMAGNETIC ENERGY...

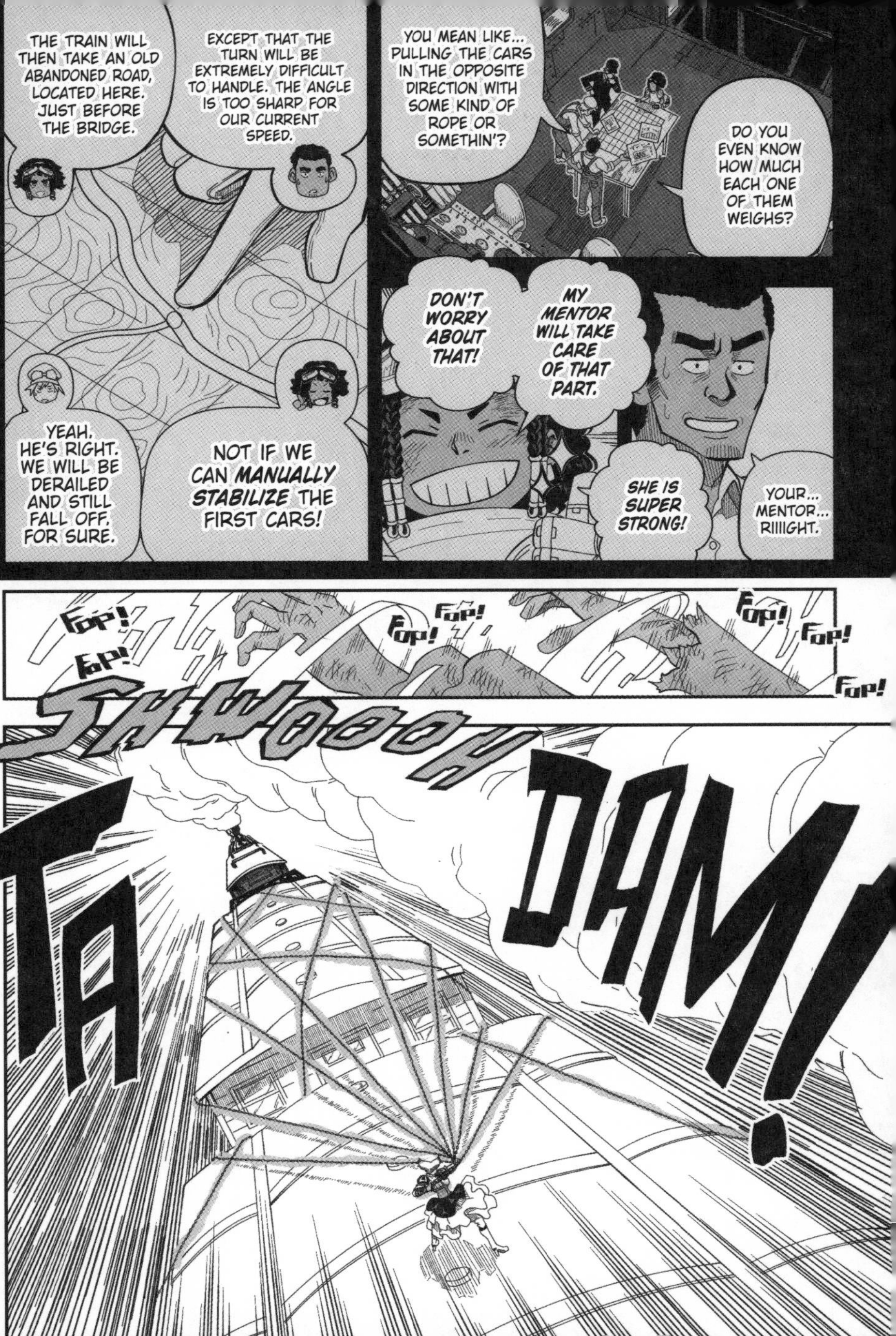
THE TRAIN WILL THEN TAKE AN OLD ABANDONED ROAD, LOCATED HERE. JUST BEFORE THE BRIDGE.
EXCEPT THAT THE TURN WILL BE EXTREMELY DIFFICULT TO HANDLE. THE ANGLE IS TOO SHARP FOR OUR CURRENT SPEED.
YEAH. HE'S RIGHT. WE WILL BE DERAILED AND STILL FALL OFF. FOR SURE.
NOT IF WE CAN MANUALLY STABILIZE THE FIRST CARS!
YOU MEAN LIKE... PULLING THE CARS IN THE OPPOSITE DIRECTION WITH SOME KIND OF ROPE OR SOMETHIN'?
DO YOU EVEN KNOW HOW MUCH EACH ONE OF THEM WEIGHS?
DON'T WORRY ABOUT THAT!
MY MENTOR WILL TAKE CARE OF THAT PART.
SHE IS SUPER STRONG!
YOUR... MENTOR... RIIIGHT.
Fop!
Fop!
Fop!
Fup!
Fop!
Fop!
Fup!
SHWOOOOH
TA
DAM!

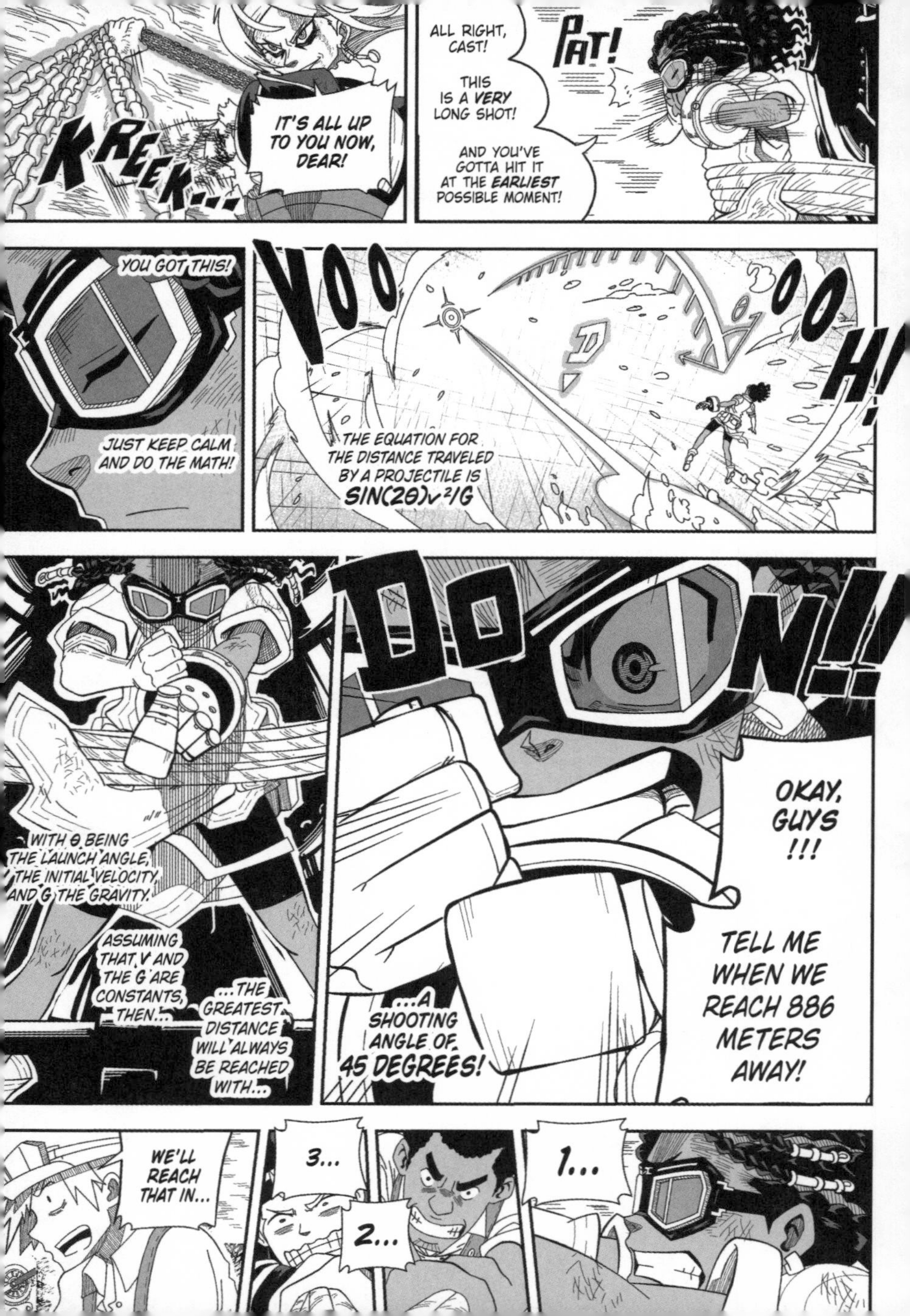
KREEK...
IT'S ALL UP TO YOU NOW, DEAR!
ALL RIGHT, CAST!
THIS IS A VERY LONG SHOT!
AND YOU'VE GOTTA HIT IT AT THE EARLIEST POSSIBLE MOMENT!
PAT!
YOU GOT THIS!
JUST KEEP CALM AND DO THE MATH!
VOOOOH!
THE EQUATION FOR THE DISTANCE TRAVELED BY A PROJECTILE IS
$SIN(2\theta)v^2/G$
WITH θ BEING THE LAUNCH ANGLE, THE INITIAL VELOCITY, AND G THE GRAVITY.
ASSUMING THAT V AND THE G ARE CONSTANTS, THEN...
...THE GREATEST DISTANCE WILL ALWAYS BE REACHED WITH...
DOON!!
...A SHOOTING ANGLE OF 45 DEGREES!
OKAY, GUYS !!!
TELL ME WHEN WE REACH 886 METERS AWAY!
WE'LL REACH THAT IN...
3...
2...
1...

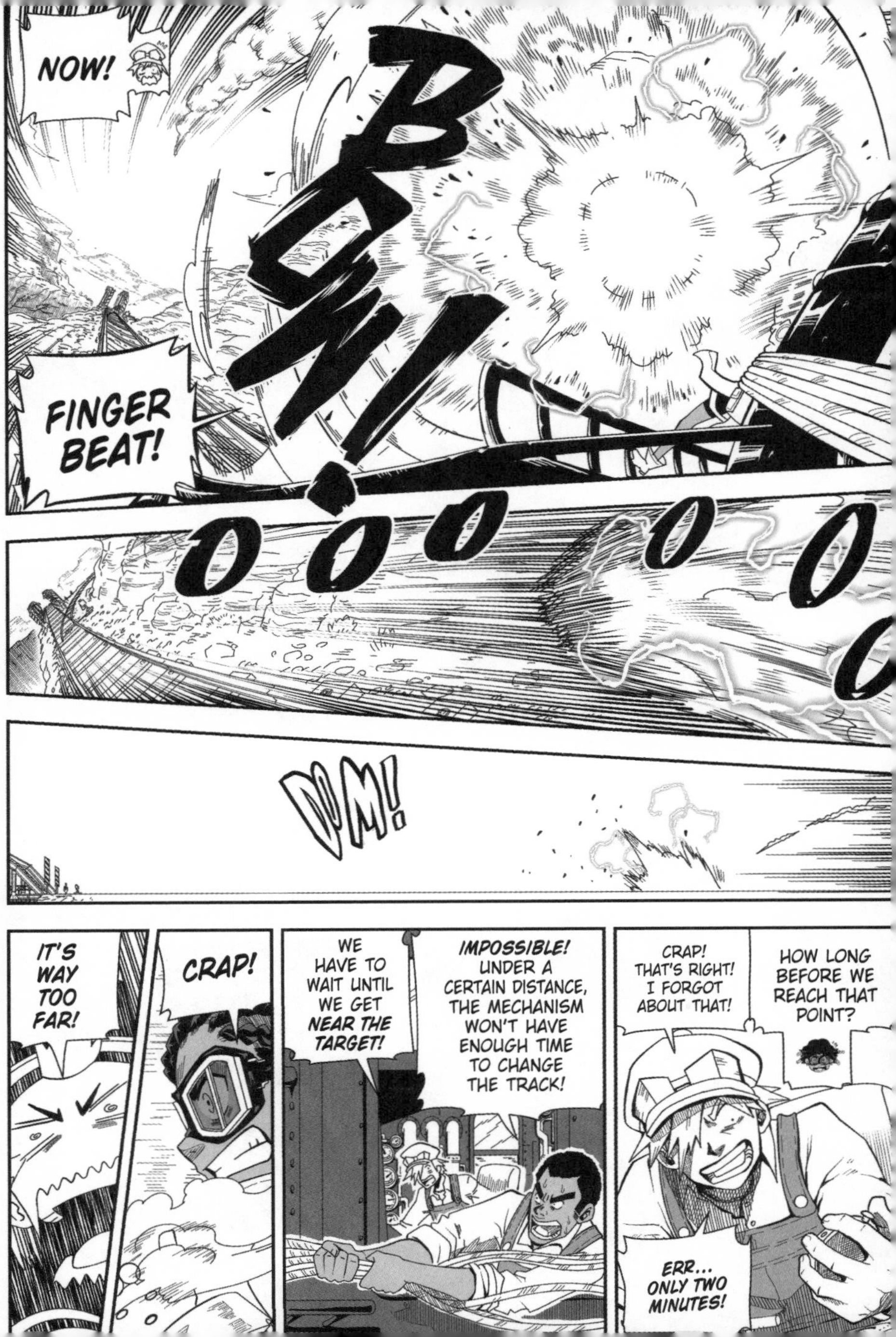
NOW!
FINGER BEAT!
BOOOOOOOO
OOM!
IT'S WAY TOO FAR!
CRAP!
WE HAVE TO WAIT UNTIL WE GET NEAR THE TARGET!
IMPOSSIBLE! UNDER A CERTAIN DISTANCE, THE MECHANISM WON'T HAVE ENOUGH TIME TO CHANGE THE TRACK!
CRAP! THAT'S RIGHT! I FORGOT ABOUT THAT!
HOW LONG BEFORE WE REACH THAT POINT?
ERR... ONLY TWO MINUTES!

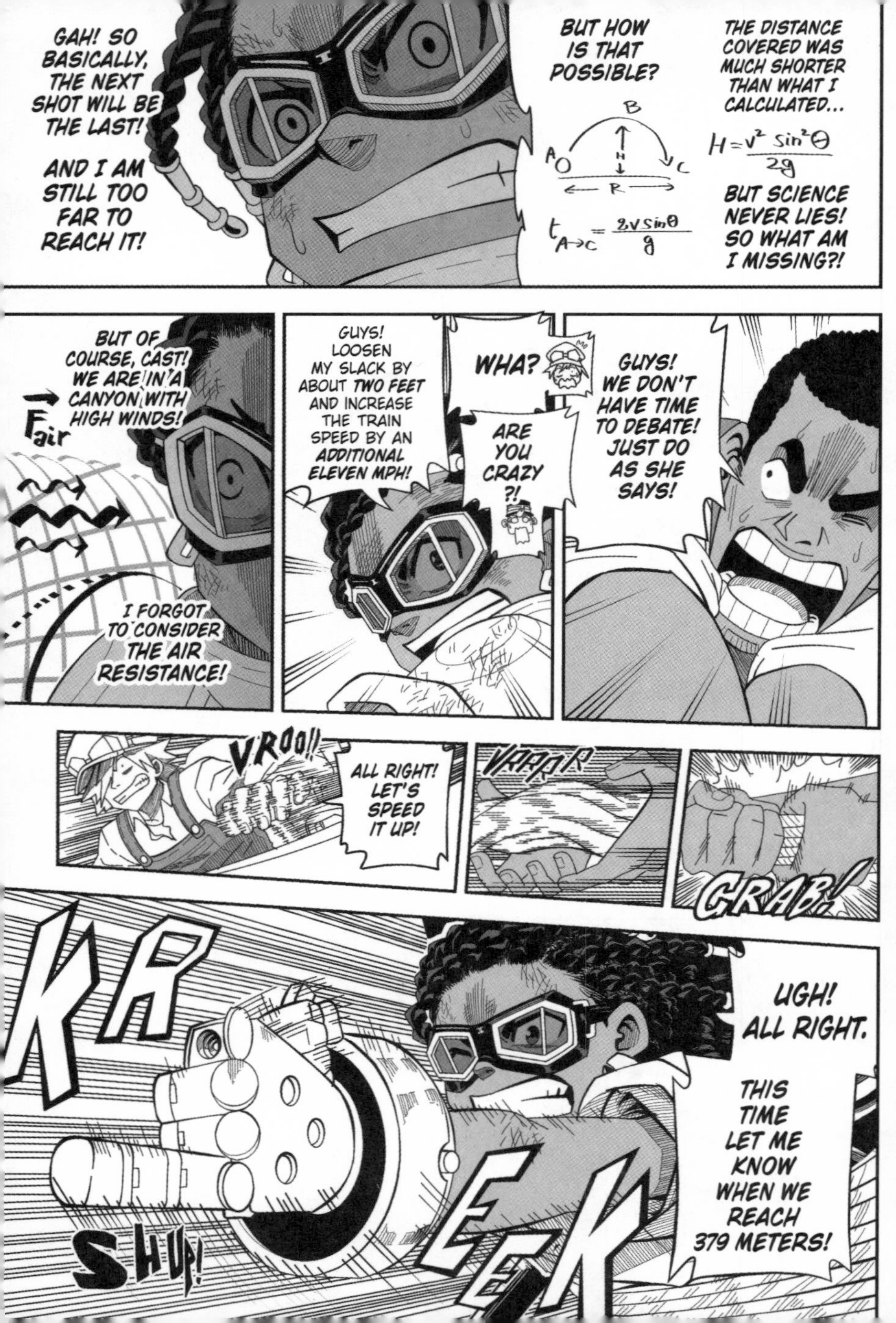
GAH! SO BASICALLY, THE NEXT SHOT WILL BE THE LAST!
AND I AM STILL TOO FAR TO REACH IT!
BUT HOW IS THAT POSSIBLE?
B
A
H
C
R
$t_{A \to C} = \frac{2v \sin\theta}{g}$
THE DISTANCE COVERED WAS MUCH SHORTER THAN WHAT I CALCULATED...
$H = \frac{v^2 \sin^2\theta}{2g}$
BUT SCIENCE NEVER LIES! SO WHAT AM I MISSING?!
BUT OF COURSE, CAST! WE ARE IN A CANYON WITH HIGH WINDS!
$\vec{F}_{air}$
I FORGOT TO CONSIDER THE AIR RESISTANCE!
GUYS! LOOSEN MY SLACK BY ABOUT TWO FEET AND INCREASE THE TRAIN SPEED BY AN ADDITIONAL ELEVEN MPH!
WHA?
ARE YOU CRAZY ?!
GUYS! WE DON'T HAVE TIME TO DEBATE! JUST DO AS SHE SAYS!
VROOM!
ALL RIGHT! LET'S SPEED IT UP!
VRRRR
GRAB!
KREEK
SHUP!
UGH! ALL RIGHT.
THIS TIME LET ME KNOW WHEN WE REACH 379 METERS!

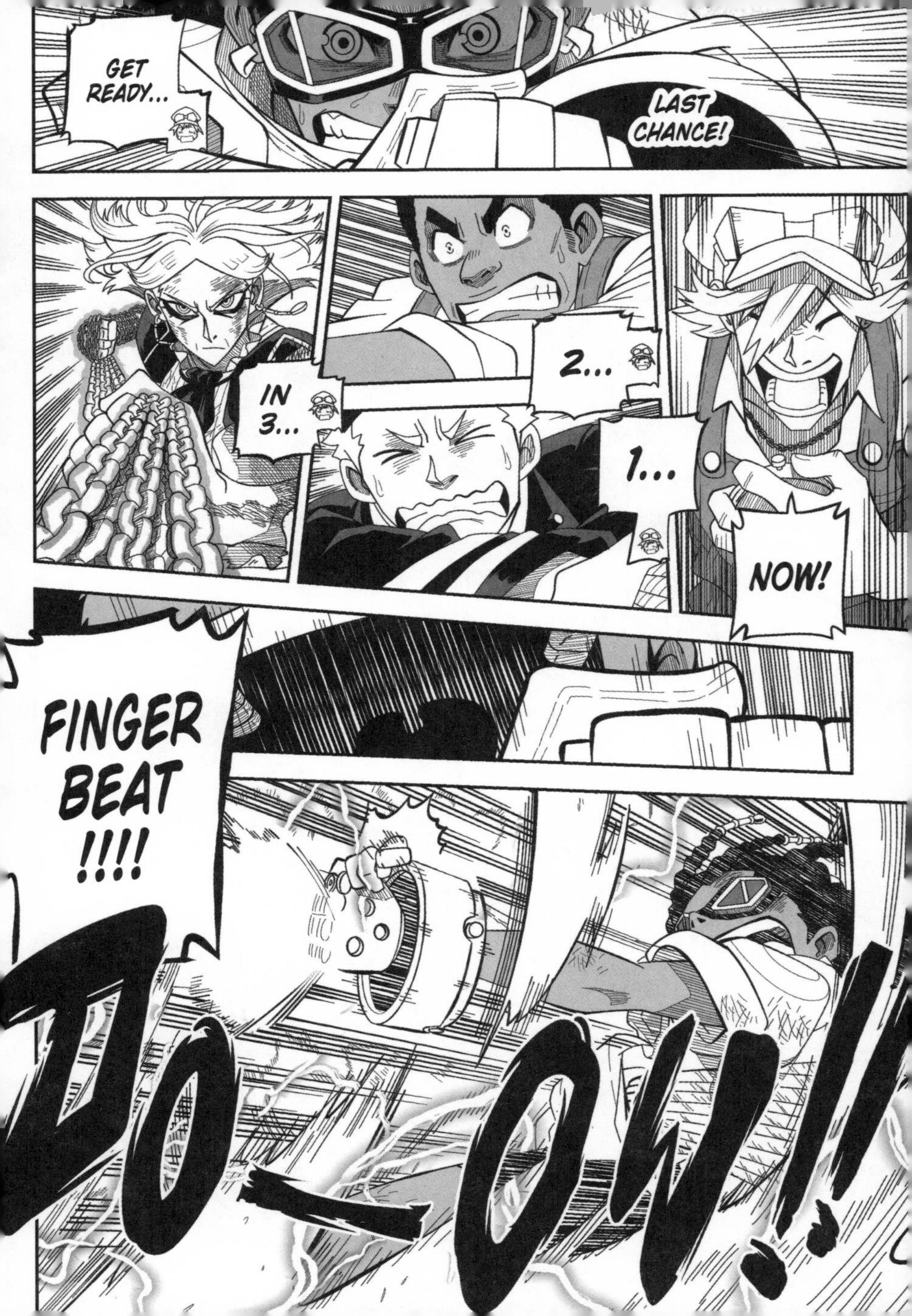
GET READY...
LAST CHANCE!
IN 3...
2...
1...
NOW!
FINGER BEAT !!!!
DO-ON!!

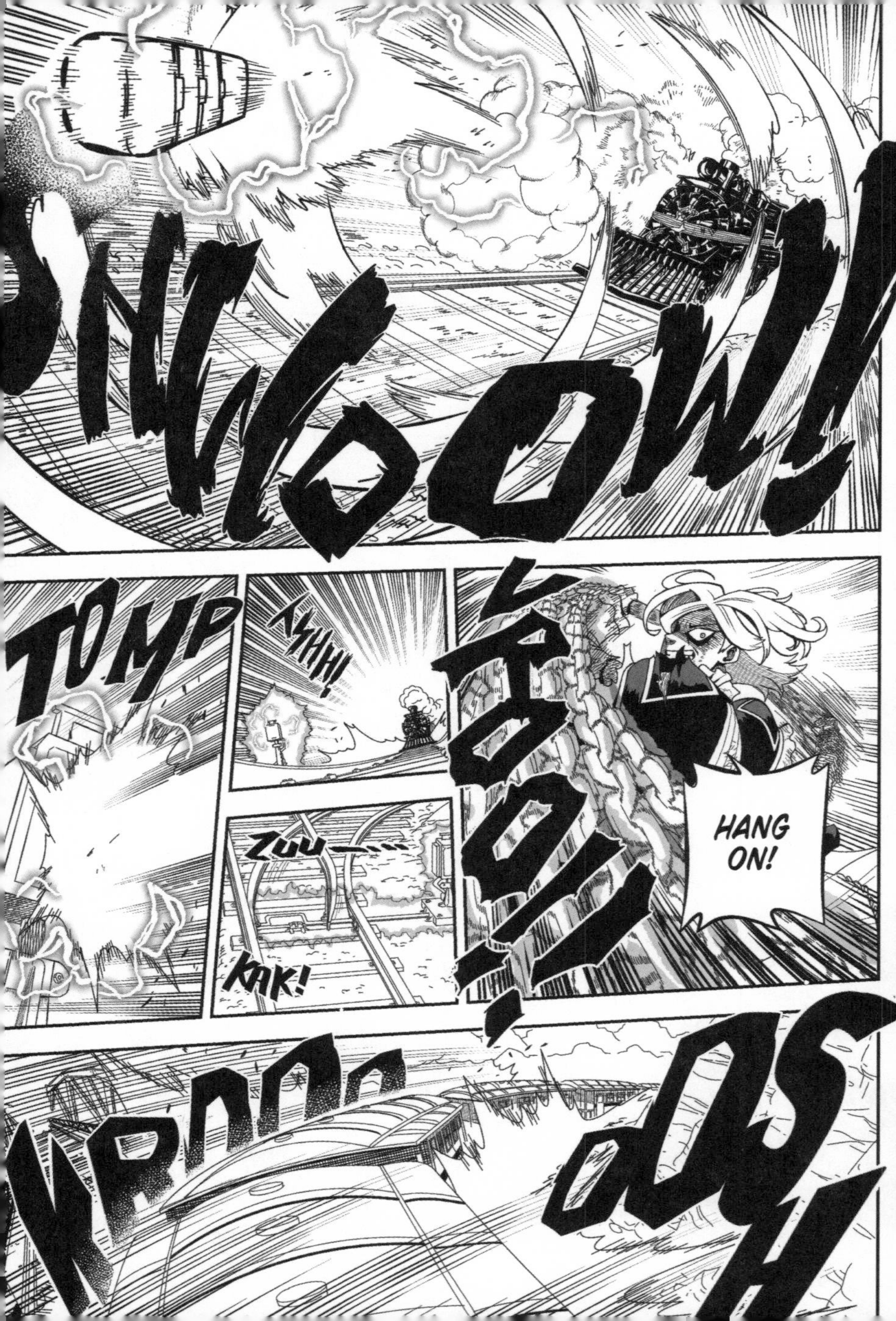
TOMP
ZUU——
KAK!
HANG ON!

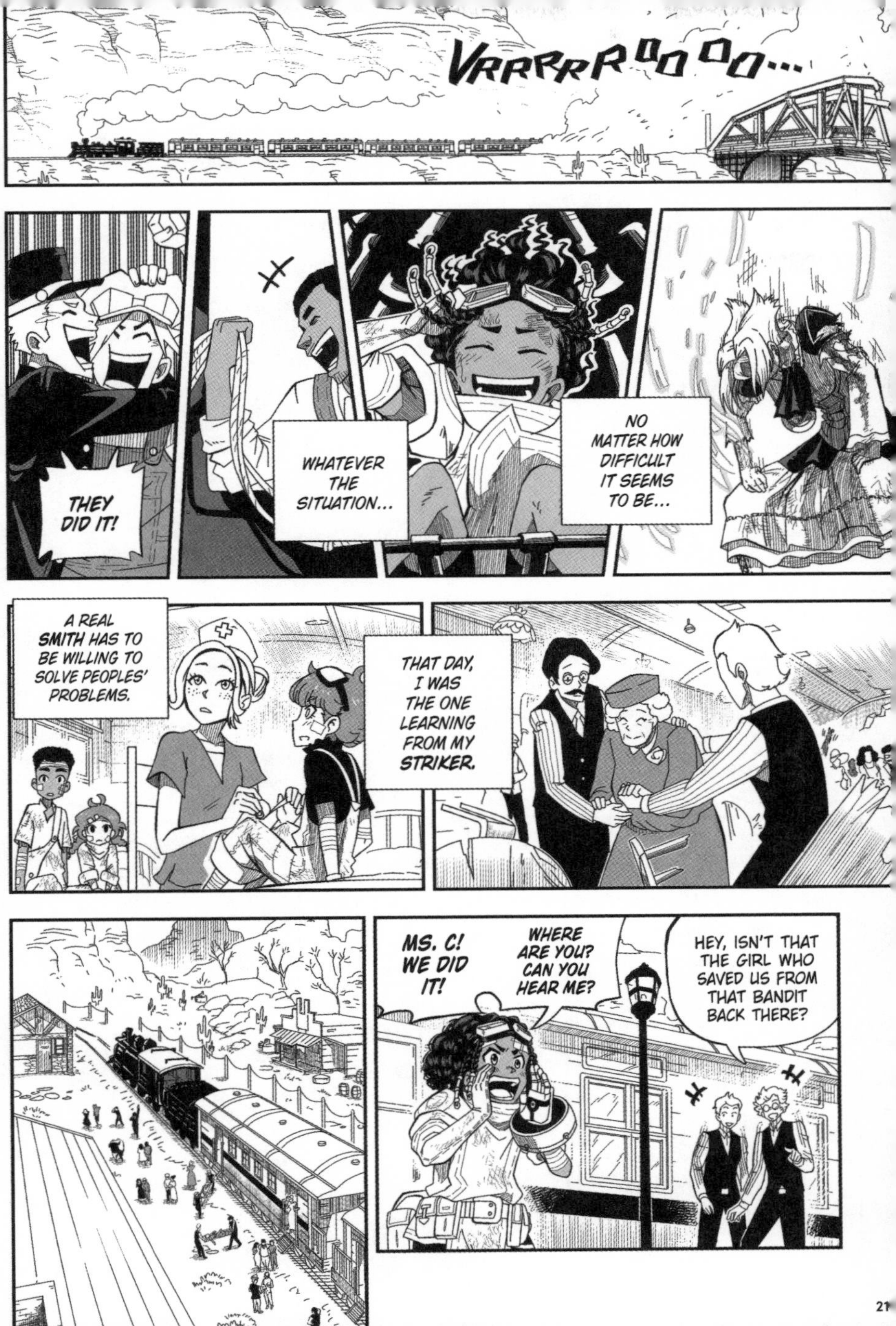
VRRRRRROOOOO...
THEY DID IT!
WHATEVER THE SITUATION...
NO MATTER HOW DIFFICULT IT SEEMS TO BE...
A REAL SMITH HAS TO BE WILLING TO SOLVE PEOPLES' PROBLEMS.
THAT DAY, I WAS THE ONE LEARNING FROM MY STRIKER.
MS. C! WE DID IT!
WHERE ARE YOU? CAN YOU HEAR ME?
HEY, ISN'T THAT THE GIRL WHO SAVED US FROM THAT BANDIT BACK THERE?

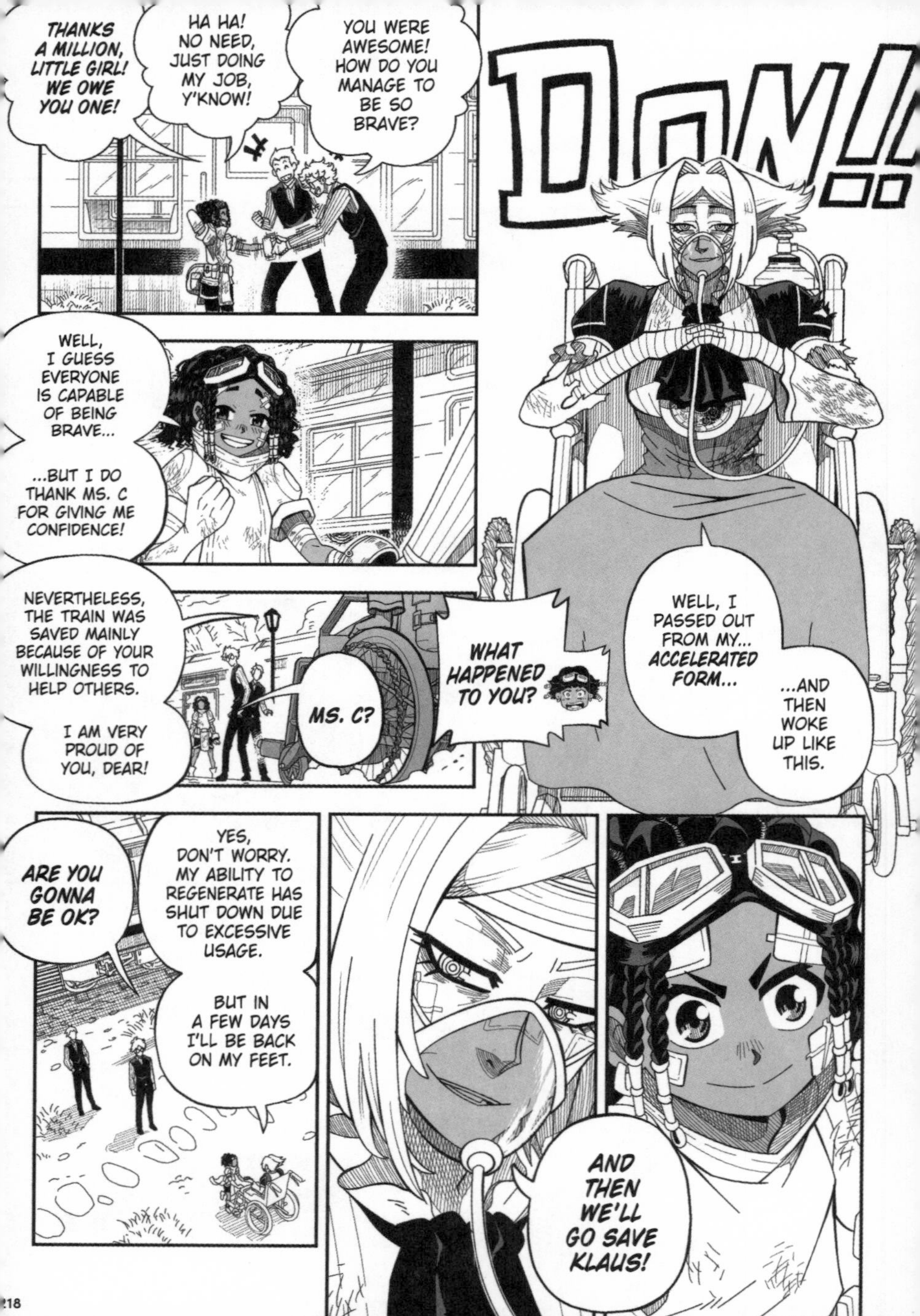
THANKS A MILLION, LITTLE GIRL! WE OWE YOU ONE!
HA HA! NO NEED, JUST DOING MY JOB, Y'KNOW!
YOU WERE AWESOME! HOW DO YOU MANAGE TO BE SO BRAVE?
WELL, I GUESS EVERYONE IS CAPABLE OF BEING BRAVE...
...BUT I DO THANK MS. C FOR GIVING ME CONFIDENCE!
NEVERTHELESS, THE TRAIN WAS SAVED MAINLY BECAUSE OF YOUR WILLINGNESS TO HELP OTHERS.
I AM VERY PROUD OF YOU, DEAR!
MS. C?
DON!!
WHAT HAPPENED TO YOU?
WELL, I PASSED OUT FROM MY... ACCELERATED FORM...
...AND THEN WOKE UP LIKE THIS.
ARE YOU GONNA BE OK?
YES, DON'T WORRY. MY ABILITY TO REGENERATE HAS SHUT DOWN DUE TO EXCESSIVE USAGE.
BUT IN A FEW DAYS I'LL BE BACK ON MY FEET.
AND THEN WE'LL GO SAVE KLAUS!

CLOCK STRIKER

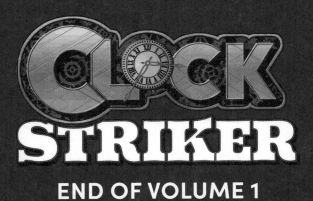

END OF VOLUME 1

ABOUT THE AUTHORS

ISSAKA GALADIMA

Issaka Galadima is from Niger Republic, where he lived until the end of high school, then went to France to study IT Engineering, until he graduated. He now lives there as a mobile application developer and freelance artist.

FREDERICK L. JONES

Frederick L. Jones graduated from the University of North Carolina at Chapel Hill with a BA in communication studies. After a decade as an executive in the video game industry, Frederick combined his experiences in product marketing, product development, and brand management with his lifelong love of anime to create the diverse manga brand Saturday AM in 2013.

ACKNOWLEDGMENTS

THANKS TO EVERYONE ON THE TEAM WHO HELPED ME SO MUCH. SPECIAL THANKS TO MY ASSISTANTS TALIANE, YVES, CASTANE, AND MY 3D DESIGNER OLIVIER. WITHOUT YOU GUYS, THE ART WOULDN'T BE SO DETAILED. ALSO, SPECIAL THANKS TO MY AWESOME WIFE, RAÏSSA, WHO SUPPORTED ME DAILY THROUGHOUT MAKING THIS BOOK. THANKS TO FREDERICK (WRITER AND CEO OF SATURDAY AM) FOR BEING OPEN TO MY IDEAS AND FOR THE FREEDOM HE GIVES ME ON THE PAGES. THANKS TO SATURDAY AM FOR ALLOWING ME TO BE A PART OF THIS ADVENTURE, AND SPECIAL THANKS TO ODUNZE (WHYT MANGA) FOR MAKING ME DISCOVER THE PROJECT. (IT ALL STARTED WITH HIM.) SPECIAL THANKS TO JD, PARLONS MANGA FRANÇAIS, ACTUMANGAFRANÇAIS, THE DNDPARIS FAMILY, AND ALL THE FRENCH COMMUNITY FOR YOUR SUPPORT. YOU GUYS ARE AWESOME! THANKS TO MY FAMILY, AND FINALLY, THANKS TO YOU FOR READING THIS BOOK. SEE YOU SOON WITH VOLUME 2!

—Issaka Galadima

I HONESTLY HAVEN'T HAD TIME TO PROCESS THIS BOOK'S RELEASE UNTIL NOW. I'M BEYOND PLEASED WITH CLOCK STRIKER VOLUME 1 AS IT REPRESENTS SO MUCH OF MY LIFE. WHEN I FIRST DISCOVERED ANIME AND MANGA IN THE LATE 70S AND EARLY 80S, THE IDEA THAT I COULD SEE A BLACK LEAD CHARACTER IN THEM WAS A DREAM. WHEN I STARTED SATURDAY AM, THE NOTION THAT I WOULD CREATE ONE OF OUR BIGGEST TITLES SEEMED LIKE A DREAM. AND WHEN THE CONCEPT FIRST DEBUTED, I HOPED I'D HAVE AN ARTIST CAPABLE OF DELIVERING AN AUTHENTIC BLACK GIRL WITH MANGA AESTHETICS BUT FEARED IT WOULD BE A PIPE DREAM. AND HERE WE ARE...A DREAM COME TRUE. I CREATED THE LEAD CHARACTER, CAST, BASED ON A VERY IMPORTANT PERSON IN MY LIFE. AND IMPORTANT PEOPLE ARE WHAT HAVE MADE THIS BOOK POSSIBLE. MY INCREDIBLE ARTIST, ISSAKA GALADIMA, IS ONE OF THE MOST COMPETENT AND TRUSTWORTHY PEOPLE I'VE EVER MET. OUR DESIGNERS, MITCH PROCTOR AND JOSHUA THOMAS, HAVE CRAFTED A BEAUTIFUL-LOOKING BOOK THAT CAN PROUDLY SIT ALONGSIDE TRADITIONAL JAPANESE MANGA. OBVIOUSLY, FAMILY, FRIENDS, AND FANS HAVE PLAYED MINOR ROLES OF SUPPORT THAT KEEP CREATORS LIKE ME SANE. FINALLY, OUR TEAMS AT SATURDAY AM AND QUARTO GROUP HAVE PROVIDED SUCH SWEET SUPPORT THAT I WAS ABLE TO DO THE MOST IMPORTANT THING—NOT JUST DREAM ABOUT THIS BOOK BUT MAKE THIS BOOK A REALITY.

I HOPE YOU ENJOY IT AND HELP MAKE CLOCK STRIKER SOMETHING THAT INSPIRES THE NEXT GREAT GROUP OF MANGA CREATORS.

—Frederick L. Jones
Founder, Saturday AM
Creator, CLOCK STRIKER

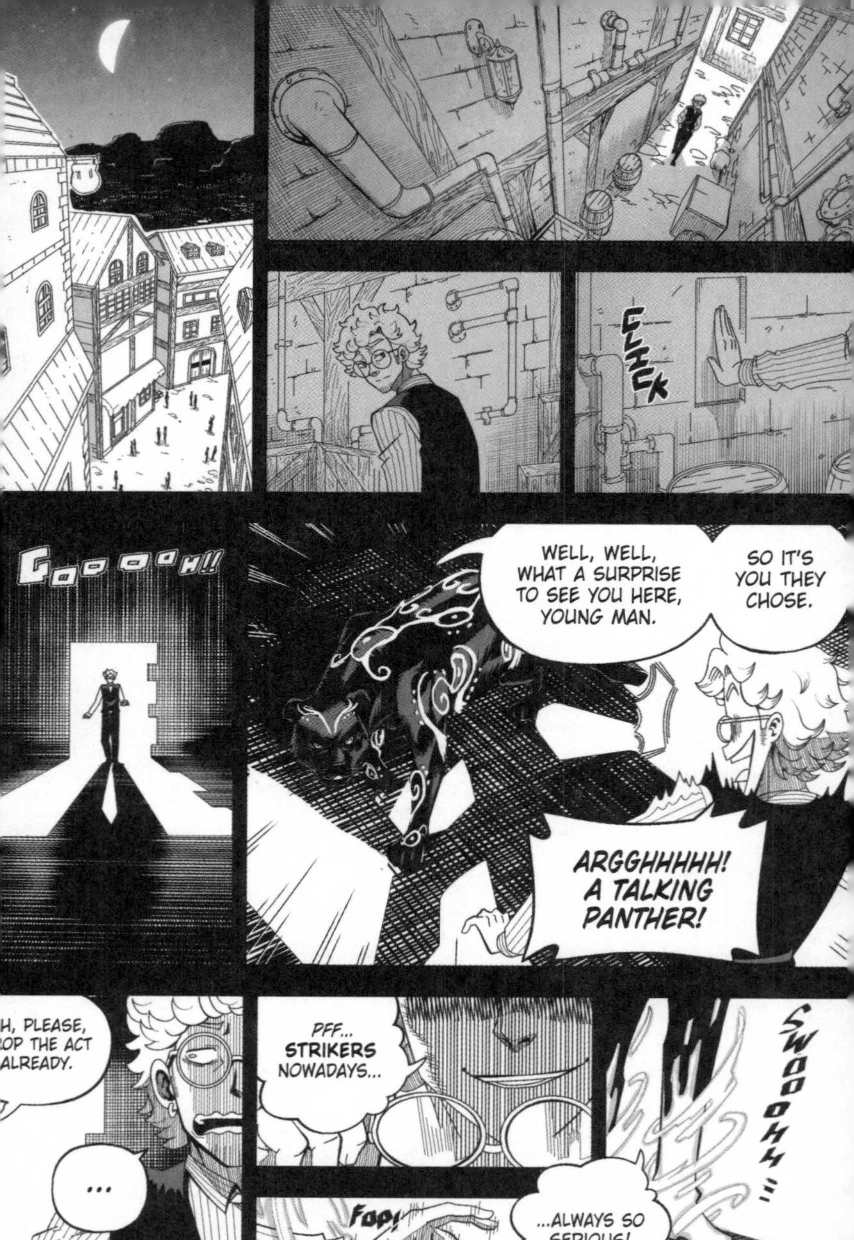
CLICK
GOOOOOH!!
WELL, WELL, WHAT A SURPRISE TO SEE YOU HERE, YOUNG MAN.
SO IT'S YOU THEY CHOSE.
ARGGHHHHH! A TALKING PANTHER!
H, PLEASE, ROP THE ACT ALREADY.
...
PFF... STRIKERS NOWADAYS...
SWOOOOHH!!
FOP!
FOP!
...ALWAYS SO SERIOUS!

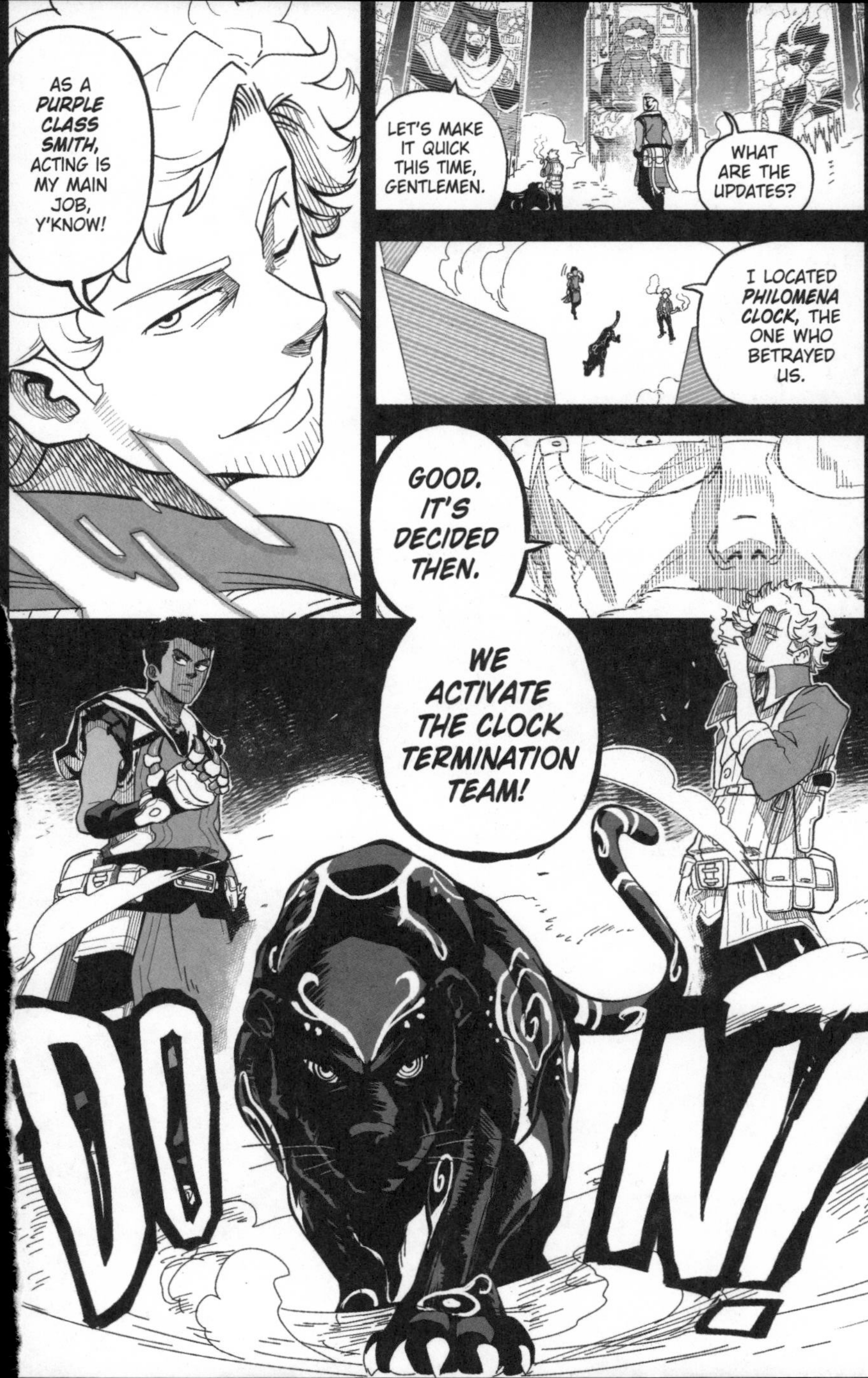

AS A PURPLE CLASS SMITH, ACTING IS MY MAIN JOB, Y'KNOW!
LET'S MAKE IT QUICK THIS TIME, GENTLEMEN.
WHAT ARE THE UPDATES?
I LOCATED PHILOMENA CLOCK, THE ONE WHO BETRAYED US.
GOOD. IT'S DECIDED THEN.
WE ACTIVATE THE CLOCK TERMINATION TEAM!
DOON!

Brimming with creative inspiration, how-to projects, and useful information to enrich your everyday life, quarto.com is a favorite destination for those pursuing their interests and passions.

First published in 2023 by Rockport Publishers, an imprint of The Quarto Group, 100 Cummings Center, Suite 265-D, Beverly, MA 01915, USA. T (978) 282-9590 F (978) 283-2742 Quarto.com

Rockport Publishers titles are also available at discount for retail, wholesale, promotional, and bulk purchase. For details, contact the Special Sales Manager by email at specialsales@quarto.com or by mail at The Quarto Group, Attn: Special Sales Manager, 100 Cummings Center, Suite 265-D, Beverly, MA 01915, USA.

10 9 8 7 6 5 4 3 2

ISBN: 978-0-7603-8157-1

Digital edition published in 2023
eISBN: 978-0-7603-8179-3

Library of Congress Cataloging-in-Publication Data is available.

Story and Art: Frederick L. Jones and Issaka Galadima
Assistants: Taliane POATY, Yves PAMBOU, Castane and Olivier ELÈGBÉDÉ
Design: Joshua Thomas and Mitch Proctor
Editors: Frederick L. Jones and Austin Harvey

Printed in USA

Clock Striker, Volume 1 is rated T for Teen (ages 13+). It contains action scenes and mild profanity.